Accountant's Guide to Fraud Detection and Control

Second Edition

Accountant's Guide to Fraud Detection and Control

Second Edition

Howard R. Davia
Patrick C. Coggins
John C. Wideman
Joseph T. Kastantin

JOHN WILEY & SONS, INC.
New York • Chichester • Weinheim • Brisbane • Singapore • Toronto

This book is printed on acid-free paper. ∞

Copyright © 2000 by John Wiley and Sons, Inc. All rights reserved.

Published simultaneously in Canada.

The first edition is titled *Management Accountant's Guide to Fraud Discovery and Control.*

This publication is designed to provide accurate and authoritative information in regard to the subject matter covered. It is sold with the understanding that the publisher is not engaged in rendering legal, accounting, or other professional services. If legal advice or other expert assistance is required, the services of a competent professional person should be sought.

Library of Congress Cataloging-in-Publication Data:

Accountant's guide to fraud detection and control / Howard R. Davia . . . [et al.].— 2nd ed.
    p. cm.
    Earlier ed. published under: Management accountant's guide to fraud discovery and control. 1992.
    Includes bibliographical references and index.
    ISBN 0-471-35378-7 (cloth: alk. paper)
    1. Auditing, Internal. 2. Managerial accounting. 3. Fraud. I. Davia, Howard R., 1947–
    HF5668.25.M36 2000
    657′.458—dc21   99-088273

Printed in the United States of America.

10 9 8 7 6 5 4 3 2 1

About The Authors

Howard R. Davia is a certified public accountant, with over 30 years of experience in government, industry, and public accounting. As an audit executive with both the U.S. General Accounting Office and the General Services Administration, and subsequently as a chief executive operating officer with the General Services Administration, he gained vast experience in the opportunities for fraud, as well as for its detection and deterrence. Mr. Davia was also president and cofounder of Executive Education Series, Inc., which provided training and consulting in fraud detection and control. As an adjunct professor of accountancy, Mr. Davia engaged in a joint venture with the College of Business Administration, University of Wisconsin-La Crosse, for the purpose of conducting nationally the Fraud Discovery and Control Workshop. He has also lectured on the subject of fraud detection and control to Institute of Management Accountant's members, CPA state society members, and corporate management groups. He was the principal author of the fraud training material presented in these workshops, upon which much of the *Accountant's Guide to Fraud Detection and Control* is based. Mr. Davia is the principal author of Part 1, *Proactive Fraud-Specific Examinations and Internal Control.*

John C. Wideman, Ph.D., has over 28 years of experience in the civil, criminal, and military intelligence fields as an investigator at the federal and state levels, and as a private practitioner. He is a graduate of the FBI National Academy, the Federal Law Enforcement Training Center, and the U.S. Army Intelligence Center and School. He has taught investigative courses for the U.S. government and several state agencies. Dr. Wideman is a practicing private investigator. He is the author of Part 2, *Investigating Fraud.*

Patrick C. Coggins is the Dupont Endowed Chair Professor at Stetson University and holds J.D. and Ph.D. degrees in Administration and Adult Development and Education. He has over 28 years of experience in the areas of governmental and public sector financial management, contract management, legal issues, organizational diagnosis, and income taxes. He has published books, articles, and papers nationally and has extensive lecturing and consulting experience. Professor Coggins is the author of Part 3, *Prosecuting Fraud.*

Joseph T. Kastantin is a consultant, author, and assistant professor of accountancy at the University of Wisconsin-La Crosse. Mr. Kastantin is a certified public accountant and a certified management accountant. He earned a master's degree in business administration from Butler University, Indianapolis, Indiana. He is the author of a book entitled *Professional Accounting Practice Management* (Quorum Books, 1988) and has authored and co-authored several articles on the topics of management, business control, and taxation. Mr. Kastantin contributed to Part 1.

Preface

For all accountants, including auditors, the possibility of fraud occurring in their parent organizations or among their clients is an ever-present nightmare. As *de facto* custodians of internal control, management generally considers accountants to be primarily responsible for the prevention of all fraud and auditors are normally held responsible for failures to detect all fraud whenever it surfaces. That these beliefs are largely without merit is academic once fraud is exposed. In most fraud discoveries, someone has to be at fault and it is convenient to blame the auditors. Once, when the authors had detected a major fraud case that was reported by the media, a critic rhetorically asked "Where were the auditors?" In actuality, it is often management itself who is to blame, through its complacency and resulting failure to allocate resources and emphasis to fraud-specific internal controls and to proactive fraud-specific examinations.

The *Accountant's Guide to Fraud Detection and Control*, Second Edition, revises the *Management Accountant's Guide to Fraud Discovery and Control* with the objective of arousing accountant and auditor interests and capabilities for proactively evaluating, devising, and installing effective fraud-specific internal controls, and for conducting fraud-specific examinations. This book provides comprehensive intermediate training for those purposes.

Although there are many books which deal with various aspects of fraud, their contents either (1) are heavily skewed to the needs of certified public accountants in public practice and of little value to operating accountants, (2) contain reference material rather than providing comprehensive instruction, and (3) are designed to be of interest primarily to the more fraud-experienced auditors rather than accountants. The *Accountant's Guide to Fraud Detection and Control* was written to meet the largely unfulfilled needs of operating accountants, as well as to serve the needs of the many auditors who do not have fraud-specific experience.

The *Accountants Guide to Fraud Detection and Control* is designed to be a stand-alone reference. It is comprehensive in its coverage of fraud-specific examinations to an intermediate level of difficulty, and lets the average accountant know how to deter fraud, how to detect fraud, and what to do when indicia of fraud are found. Also, although the text has been designed primarily for use by persons not normally familiar with fraud-specific internal controls and proactive examinations, auditors not trained or experienced in proactive fraud-specific examinations (auditing) will find it useful as well.

The authors recognize that fraud-specific examinations cannot be conducted effectively in an organization without the dedicated support of top management. Therefore, great care has been taken to avoid highly technical terms and details where possible, and to explain them when they are used. This has been done to encourage wider distribution of this guidebook and to include the interests of individuals in top management regardless of their prior experience. The authors feel that if top management has an overall understanding of the need and urgency in performing proactive fraud-specific examinations and its importance in protecting its organizations, it will more readily provide the resources and encourage its accountants and auditors to become involved.

This text is not only a guidance manual for accountants interested in fraud detection and control, it also attempts to provide compelling reasons Why every entity's accountants *must* develop a capacity for detecting and controlling fraud. Those reasons include the fact that fraud detection—other than fraudulently misstated financial statement balances—is a responsibility not assumed or undertaken by independent auditors. Entities wishing independent auditors to examine their activities for the presence of fraud would find their requests declined. The reason? There are no generally accepted standards to guide an auditor's examination activities into this largely uncharted area, efforts which would expose the auditor to significant liability were he or she to fail to detect all fraud. Liability insurance carriers are extremely reluctant to insure auditing firms that engage in fraud-specific auditing. However, a fraud auditing service, performed by independent auditors in accordance with generally accepted principles and standards is proposed in Chapter 3, Principles and Standards for Fraud-Specific Examinations.

In the interim, an entity's accountants and internal auditors are the most likely candidates to engage in fraud-specific auditing. They are on-site and have a firm grasp of the existing internal controls, their strengths, and their weaknesses. However, for these individuals to engage in proactive fraud-specific examinations, they desperately require suitable training and a clear line of authority and commitment from top management. Additionally, management must encourage them to act swiftly and visibly upon the discoveries and disclosures they make. In most cases, this should include a determination to prosecute the perpetrators for internal control effect.

There are two separate types of fraud that are addressed in this book. Fraudulent financial reporting, which is often also referred to as *Treadway* fraud, prompts the greatest investor and lender attention. The other type we have called *asset-theft* fraud, which is self-descriptive, for want of a better term. Specific acts of asset-theft fraud—which does not involve fraudulent financial reporting—are far more common and far more costly to victim entities than fraudulent financial reporting. Furthermore, the two types of fraud have different origins. Fraudulent financial reporting tends to be generated and practiced solely by top management and business owners, often in order to attract investor and lender capital. Middle management may also play the fraudulent reporting game by leading top management into believing that certain goals have been met or exceeded. Compensation tends to be tied to managerial performance. Therefore, middle management has a built-in incentive to make financial statements look as good as possible. Asset-theft fraud is likely to be practiced by literally anyone, including outsiders.

The *Accountant's Guide to Fraud Detection and Control* has been primarily devoted to asset-theft fraud, the specific fraudulent acts of individuals which result directly in the theft of an entity's assets. The essential difference between the two types of fraud is that in Treadway fraud, also called *financial statement balance fraud,* there is no direct loss of an entity's actual assets, whereas asset-theft fraud does result in loss. Generally, in Treadway fraud, assets or sales are inflated to give the impression of prosperity for various nefarious reasons. Although stockholders or creditors may be deceived as to the values of over-stated financial statement balances, there is no actual theft of the entity's assets or profits. To the contrary, where asset-theft fraud is involved, there has been an actual reduction of assets and profits—as a result of the fraud—but there is no distortion of reported financial balances.

The *Accountant's Guide to Fraud Detection and Control* is designed to serve as a detailed guide to persons interested in becoming competent in fraud-specific examinations into the intermediate level of proficiency.

Howard R. Davia
Patrick C. Coggins
John C. Wideman
Joseph T. Kastantin

Contents

PART 2   INVESTIGATING FRAUD
        by John C. Wideman, Ph.D.

PART 3   PROSECUTING FRAUD
         by Patrick C. Coggins, J.D., Ph.D.

Introduction

ABOUT THIS GUIDE

The authors, in structuring the *Accountant's Guide to Fraud Detection and Control,* have attempted to compose a text that is of particular interest to accountants and responds to their needs. Auditors should also find the contents useful, particularly if their training and experience does not include significant proactive fraud-specific auditing. As principal text objectives, the authors sought to provide:

- A sense of the enormity of the fraud menace, which the text estimates is significantly more threatening than is generally perceived
- Intermediate training in the proactive recognition and detection of fraud, as would be useful to accountants generally
- An appreciation of the nature of evidence required by the justice system to support allegations of fraud
- Guidance in fraud investigative techniques useful in gathering evidence needed to support allegations of fraud
- A methodology for the evaluation of internal control strengths and weaknesses, and internal control system design recommendations

In addition to the foregoing, Parts 2 and 3 are provided to assist the accountant in understanding the process involved in determining whether or not a suspected case of fraud is a candidate for prosecution. First, a trained investigator must determine whether or not the necessary evidence for prosecution exists and then he or she must assemble the evidence. Second, the evidence must be evaluated by a lawyer experienced in criminal prosecution to determine whether or not it meets the various legal criteria required for prosecution. Although accountants involved in fraud-specific examinations are not expected to be competent in the investigative and legal processes, their general knowledge of the entire process is essential.

Who Is Held Accountable for Fraud Occurrences and Fraud Detection?

Two questions are inevitably asked whenever fraud is discovered. The first question is often "Who was responsible for not preventing it?" The second question is "Where were the auditors?" The most common response to the first question is the accountants. Accountants have always had a custodial responsibility for maintaining the integrity of recorded transactions. After all, as it is often said, every fraud passes through the hands of an accountant. The answer to the second question is implied in the question itself—that the auditor somehow failed in the expectation that he or she was the ultimate defense against fraud.

The comments are usually not fair or appropriate. However, it is difficult for accountants and auditors to deny responsibility, because the charges are not wholly without merit. It is accountants who are considered the first line of defense against fraud in that it is they who are usually responsible for internal control processes, fraud deterrence, and safeguarding assets. The fact that they may have performed admirably in these tasks is often of little defense when a significant case of fraud surfaces. It is much the same—if not worse—for auditors. It has been the frustrating experience of one of the authors while serving as a fraud auditor that fraud disclosures brought about by aggressive auditing have served as the basis for outcries of "Where were the auditors?"

Regardless of the lack of merit in any criticism that may confront their culpability in preventing or detecting fraud, it is extremely difficult for accountants and auditors to ever shed responsibility for fraud that existed and/or was discovered on their watch. There is always a presumption of responsibility implying that they could have done more and that they somehow failed to perform satisfactorily. Accordingly, accountants and auditors who may not yet have been exposed to this frustrating experience are counseled that a good offense is the best defense. It is advisable for them to anticipate that their time in the barrel will someday come and to take defensive action before fraud is discovered, particularly before it is discovered accidentally. When the controversy is raging, it is often too late to be concerned with fraud-specific internal controls.

Although auditors are generally recognized as being responsible for the *detection* of fraud, once fraud has been discovered, management frequently looks to accountants for explanations as to how it could have happened. Accordingly, it is strongly advised that accountants assign appropriate priority to fraud-specific internal control, become more sensitive to the possibility of fraud in their domains, and devote time to periodically performing fraud-specific examinations. It is presumed that auditors are already well aware of their need to devote adequate attention to proactive fraud-specific auditing, which should include the regular evaluation of fraud-specific internal controls.

A Suitable Attitude

Once accountants have accepted a responsibility for fraud deterrence and detection and before learning the craft of fraud detection, they should adopt an attitude conducive to fraud deterrence and detection. Without an appropriate attitude, success in pursuing the craft will be relatively unsuccessful. What is meant by a proper attitude? Accountants tend to be nice people; they find it difficult to suspect that fellow employees may be guilty of fraud. This attitude often causes them to overlook indicia of fraud that a properly sensitized auditor would rarely overlook. As distasteful as it may be, to properly pursue evidence of fraud, the accountant must identify suspects and pursue the evidence bearing upon the person(s) chosen. It is people who commit fraud and when looking for evidence of fraud, one must examine and suspect human behavior. The authors found that when this was mentioned during lectures on fraud detection and control, many accountants found it offensive to suspect people who they associated with at work and often socially.

Preventing Fraud versus Detecting Fraud

It is frequently argued that it is more efficacious to concentrate on the prevention of fraud as opposed to its detection. This had led many entities to concentrate on fraud-specific internal controls in lieu of proactive fraud detection efforts. Strong internal controls are important but it is a mistake to think in terms of one versus the other. Proactive fraud-specific examinations can be very effective internal controls. Fraud is best deterred through a balanced program of well-thought-out internal controls, followed by fraud-specific examinations to reinforce them. The chapters on internal controls make their function very clear. An interesting analogy can be found in Japanese temple lore. Entrances to religious shrines are often adorned with two large stone dogs. The ones stationed on the left are intended to protect the temple. It can be said they serve an "internal control" purpose. They are menacing and snarling; their function is to deter evil spirits from entering the holy places. The dogs on the right are depicted as sleeping peacefully. It is said that the temple architects recognized that some evil spirits would not be deterred and would be able to sneak past the vicious dogs. To get them out of the temples, they were given an escape path past the sleeping dogs. Similarly, internal controls are not impregnable. Many are at most merely an inconvenience for fraud perpetrators. Their effectiveness is limited and entities at risk must employ supplementary measures designed to detect the fraud that slips by the "dog on the left." Text chapters on fraud-specific internal control and fraud-specific examinations embrace these tactics.

Prosecution or Restitution?

Entities which have been lucky enough to discover fraud and have enough evidence to consider prosecution, frequently make business-like decisions to prosecute the perpetrators or to accept some measure of restitution. They would rather recover their fraud losses than—as they see it—dispense justice to the perpetrator! Text chapters dealing with investigations (John C. Wideman, Ph.D.) and the law (Patrick C. Coggins, J.D., Ph.D.) discuss the problem of prosecution or restitution. You will hear that a surprising number of entities choose restitution over prosecution. However, it is the considered opinion of the authors that where prosecution is a viable option and not merely a pre-prosecution bluff where a successful prosecution is doubtful, it is a grave mistake for entities to elect restitution over prosecution. It sends the wrong message to all would-be perpetrators that clearly advertises:

> If you steal from us and we don't catch you, you get to keep the money. However, if we catch you and you return whatever it is that you stole from us, you need not fear prosecution.

General

Peter Lucas of the Boston *Herald American* once wrote that "fraud is still a growth industry." Some readers may be contemplating fraud, in which case the *Accountant's Guide to Fraud Detection and Control*, Second Edition, may provide a few new ideas. Nevertheless, all persons who aspire to be effective in finding fraud and controlling it must also know how to commit fraud. Succinctly but tritely put, "it takes one to know one." Throughout the *Accountant's Guide to Fraud Detection and Control*, Second Edition, we will show you situations that involve fraud and lead you to think about how fraud occurs. Through the presentation of discussion material and some case studies, we hope to teach you a few tricks. All of our case studies are taken from or inspired by actual cases of fraud.

All cases have been sanitized and simplified for illustration purposes. Regardless of how unlikely some of the case studies may appear, you can be sure that they describe incidents that have indeed happened to someone, somewhere. Facts, names, and places have been changed. Any identification with real persons, situations, or events is purely accidental and is not intended.

We do admit to at least one flaw in this material which is regrettably unavoidable. Since the most successful perpetrators have not yet been detected, we can't show you the best examples of fraud. However, case studies will be presented which provide excellent illustrations of clear signs of fraud (known as indicia), which often go unnoticed except by the sensitive eyes of the fraud examiner. Although apparent indicia of fraud do not necessarily mean that fraud is present, the failure to investigate such signs denies the entity involved the opportunity to discover fraud and may even leave potential perpetrators unable to resist the temptation to commit fraud in the future.

One of the current problems in fraud detection is that the professionals normally involved in combating fraud are not usually competent in the disciplines needed to successfully pursue detection through prosecution. Accountants and auditors are functionally illiterate in the area of proper investigative procedures and investigators generally are not sufficiently well-versed in accounting and auditing to deal with some of the complex issues which may surface in a fraud investigation. The result is that accountants, auditors, and investigators often fail to communicate their needs and the relevance of their findings to each other. Although our material is designed principally for accountants and auditors, it may also prove useful for investigators who wish to increase their competency in performing proactive fraud-specific examinations. Last but not least, there is the law. Many of the professionals who find themselves immersed in fraud-specific audits and investigations do not have a clear understanding of the preponderance of evidence required to prosecute a suspected perpetrator. As a result, perpetrators often escape punishment, leaving victims frustrated.

We do *not* plan to make readers expert on fraud detection. There is no such person except, perhaps, in the relative sense. This text will, however, provide the reader with a balanced view on what is important on this subject.

John C. Wideman is currently a practicing criminal investigator and the principal author of the text material relating to investigative procedures. The rules of evidence are so highly technical in nature that it is essential for accountants and auditors to be exposed to the fundamentals of the rules of evidence. The materials addressing this topic were written by

Patrick C. Coggins, a professor of law and ethics, who also has experience in auditing and accounting procedures.

Contacting the Authors

For those persons interested in more intensive training or lectures in any of the topics covered, please contact any of the authors at the address shown below. If sufficient interest is expressed, training lectures will be arranged, at convenient locations, for any experience level:

Author's name:	Patrick C. Coggins, *Law*
	Howard R. Davia, *Fraud-Specific Examinations*
	John C. Wideman, *Criminal Investigations*
Mailing address:	c/o Howard R. Davia, CPA
	347 Warren Court
	Warrenton, VA 20186
	USA

Incidentally, we recently saw an ad for fraud-detection software. For only $395, the ad claims to take the guesswork out of fraud detection. Fraud is a very personal crime. It often involves very talented individuals who perpetrate frauds in diverse and devious ways. Since software is rigid in its ability to handle data, and since decision software to date has not been able to emulate the human thought process, we are skeptical about claims such as those made in this ad. That is not to say that such software would not or could not be useful to accountants or auditors; but the software itself is only a tool that contains a series of audit procedures much like those found in any internal control manual. The reason we bring this up now is that fraud is just beginning to be recognized as a true menace. Those who wish to defend their companies against fraud are advised to become competent in proactive fraud examinations, rather than rely totally on the skills and tools of others to protect them.

Although there are many people who will protest, given the right circumstances—which includes the right opportunity to commit fraud— literally anyone will commit fraud. Luckily for some businesses, those right circumstances never arise. However, driven by need, greed, boredom, or whatever else motivates them, there are many who will find and seize opportunities to commit fraud. Quite often, they are the nicest people. Let us relate to you an interesting case involving the nicest man, or so everyone thought.

The story is true. Charlie Brown (not his real name) was an extremely personable middle-aged man, well-liked by everyone, and employed as an accounting clerk. One day, Charlie announced to his many friends that a dear old, rich aunt had died and left him her sizable fortune. Soon after the announcement, it became obvious that Charlie was enjoying his new-found wealth. He took many of his office friends out to lunch, always with cocktails, and always picked up the check. He joined a prestigious and expensive athletic club, where he also maintained a sleeping room. He bought luxury cars and an expensive condo in a luxury condominium.

It was probably about two years after Charlie's aunt died that two old friends were talking during a coffee break. One was an accounting supervisor, the other a manager from a nearby city. The accountant was teasing his old friend because just a month earlier the manager had been complaining that he did not have enough money in his financial plan for essential preventive maintenance. The accountant teased his friend about the fact that, after complaining about his tight budget, he was now spending large sums on low-priority discretionary projects, such as cleaning venetian blinds and carpets.

The manager looked at his friend strangely and said, "I don't know what you are talking about!" He insisted that he had made no such spending. Further investigation disclosed that large expenditures had in fact been made for non-essential services; however, all transactions questioned had the apparent approval of the protesting manager. The manager claimed that the signatures authorizing the expenditures were forgeries.

It was then discovered that many similarly questionable payments had been made, involving other managers as well. Although different vendor names were involved in the different building services provided, all mailing addresses on the questionable invoices bore the same post office box address. Investigation disclosed that the subject post office box was rented to Charlie Brown.

In his job as accounting clerk, Charlie had access to budgetary records for all departments and would regularly scan the budgetary accounts, noting particularly those that appeared to have excess funds. He would then prepare a phony purchase order, requesting various services—such as venetian blind or rug cleaning—and forge the manager's signature. Using computer access numbers he had gotten through trickery, the phony purchase orders would then be put into the entity's computer system as duly authorized purchase orders. Charlie would then submit phony invoices and receiving reports attesting to the receipt of the services ordered. About a week or so later, he would receive a check in his post office box. When his schemes were revealed, no one could believe that "good old Charlie" was a crook.

Easily identified through his post office box, Charlie pleaded guilty. He was subsequently indicted for stealing $300,000, although audit compilations showed that the amount of the theft was closer to $900,000. Charlie Brown's personal property was seized as a small partial recovery payment of the amount stolen; however, most of the money was never traced or recovered. Charlie was prosecuted in a federal district court and found guilty. He was sentenced to a one-year prison term—with a work-release provision—much of which was satisfied by Charlie's pretrial confinement. This story seems to contradict the adage that "crime doesn't pay."

Part 1

Fraud-Specific Examinations and Internal Control

Howard R. Davia, CPA

with contributions by Joseph T. Kastantin, CPA, CMA

Chapter 1

Audit Responsibility for Fraud Detection After Cohen and Treadway

THE COMMISSION ON AUDITOR'S RESPONSIBILITIES

Also known as the Cohen Commission after its distinguished chairman Manuel F. Cohen, this body was an independent commission appointed by the American Institute of Certified Public Accountants (AICPA) in November 1974. Appointed during a time of intense scrutiny by the U.S. Congress, its purpose was to:

> . . . *develop conclusions and recommendations regarding the appropriate responsibilities of independent auditors. It should consider whether a gap may exist between what the public expects or needs and what auditors can and should reasonably expect to accomplish. If such a gap does exist, it needs to be explored to determine how the disparity can be resolved.*

> —The Commission on Auditors' Responsibilities: Report, Conclusions, and Recommendations, 1978, *Introduction,* pp xi.

THE NATIONAL COMMISSION ON FRAUDULENT FINANCIAL REPORTING

In June 1985, this commission, also known as the Treadway Commission after its distinguished chairman James C. Treadway, Jr., was jointly sponsored by the AICPA, American Accounting Association (AAA), the Institute of Management Accountants (IMA), and the Financial Executives Institute (FEI) to determine

> what factors contribute to fraudulent financial reporting and to develop practical, constructive recommendations for reducing the incidence of this problem.

THE COHEN COMMISSION'S REPORT, CONCLUSIONS, AND RECOMMENDATIONS

This report was published in early 1978. It culminated a most commendable and informative piece of work, with the committee reporting on the following important issues:

- The Independent Auditor's Role in Society
- Forming an Opinion on Financial Presentations
- Reporting on Significant Uncertainties in Financial Presentations
- Clarifying Responsibility for the Detection of Fraud
- Corporate Responsibility and the Law
- The Auditor's Communication with Users
- The Education, Training, and Development of Auditors
- Maintaining the Independence of Auditors
- The Process of Establishing Audit Standards
- Regulating the Profession to Maintain the Quality of Audit Practice

The Commission's report is recommended reading for all accountants. In a most notable observation the Committee reported that

> a gap does exist between the performance of auditors and the expectations of the users of financial statements.

Continuing, the Commission reported that

> principal responsibility (for the gap) does not appear to lie with the users of financial statements. . . . Many users appear to misunderstand the role of the auditor and the nature of the service he offers.

Section 4 of the Commission's report dealt with "Clarifying Responsibility for the Detection of Fraud." As excellent as the work of the Cohen

Commission was, we believe that they failed—as the AICPA has failed, before and after their study—to clarify the auditor's responsibility.

There is little doubt that there was (and still is) a communication gap between the expectations of the users of financial statements and independent auditors, with regard to the auditors' responsibility to discover fraud. The AICPA, in numerous attempts to clarify auditors' responsibility for discovering fraud, has formulated and published practice guidelines, with little success in closing the gap. The problem, we believe, results from the AICPA's attempt to clarify what independent auditors are responsible for, while remaining silent in declaring what they are not responsible for. In this respect, we submit that they would be more successful, if, like housekeepers who clearly proclaim "We don't do windows!", they would directly state what fraud they *are not* responsible for detecting, and do not make a significant effort to detect!

Interestingly, the essence of this problem is substantially one of semantics. Speaking specifically of fraud detection, there is no doubt that the AICPA has been making a sincere attempt over the last five decades to clarify the gap between what users expect from auditors, and what the AICPA thinks users expect.

Incredible as it may appear, much of the expectation gap—or perhaps we can call it the "semantics gap"—can be traced to the careless usage of two words: *users* (of financial statements) and *fraud.*

Consider, for example, that there are at least two principal categories of users of financial statements:

1. The investing public and creditors
2. Entity management and owners

With regard to fraud detection, the audit expectations of each group are not alike. The first group of users, the investing public and creditors, should be reasonably satisfied with the work of independent auditors. The audits are conducted in accordance with the practice guidelines set forth by the AICPA, which are responsive to the first group's requirements as well as those of the Securities and Exchange Commission (SEC).

However, the second group—entity management and owners—has good reason to be dissatisfied with independent audit results, as do the auditors themselves. Their audits are limited by the AICPA practice guidelines, which generally do not provide or permit audit procedures designed to meet the expectations of the second group. This exclusion was clearly articulated by the AICPA in 1939 in Statement on Auditing Procedure

No. 1, which was only slightly modified in their Codification of Statements on Auditing Procedure issued in 1951

> ... The ordinary examination incident to the issuance of an opinion respecting financial statements is not designed *and cannot be relied upon* to disclose defalcations and other similar irregularities. ... If an auditor were to attempt to discover [them] he would have to extend his work to a point where its cost would be prohibitive ...

As a result of the foregoing limitation, which remains to the present day, the independent auditor does not institute audit procedures designed to discover fraud, other than that which may distort financial statement balances. Entity management and owners, as well as the courts, have generally not been content with this exclusion of responsibility. This occurs primarily because independent auditors have not made their exclusion of this category of fraud clear in their various statements that "they are responsible for discovering fraud," that is, in financial statement balances. To avoid criticism, they should also clearly state "We are not responsible for discovering fraud which does not distort financial statement balances." In other words, "We do not do windows!"

FINDINGS AND RECOMMENDATIONS OF THE TREADWAY COMMISSION

The Treadway Commission sought to determine the factors that contributed to fraudulent financial reporting, and to develop practical, constructive recommendations for reducing the incidence of this problem. Understandably, however, simple solutions were elusive and the Committee placed ultimate responsibility for financial statement accuracy upon entity management, and its need to set a tone of personal and professional ethics within the company. In addition to several other recommendations, the Committee stressed the need for enhancing internal controls.

As a direct result of the Treadway recommendations, the Treadway sponsoring organizations cooperated in a comprehensive study culminating in a series of recommendations on issues related to internal control over the preparation of an entity's published financial statements. Their report *Internal Control—Integrated Framework,* was issued in September 1992.

Although the Treadway Commission's work appears to be better recognized among many government regulators and accountants, in our judgment it was the lesser known Cohen Commission which made the greater contribution to clarifying auditor responsibilities for fraud detection.

TWO TYPES OF FRAUD: FINANCIAL STATEMENT BALANCE FRAUD AND ASSET-THEFT FRAUD

These two categories must be clarified when speaking of the Treadway Commission's activities and interests. What we choose to call asset-theft fraud differs from financial statement fraud in that financial statement fraud does not involve the theft of assets. At first blush, the topic of this chapter sounds like one that should simply recount the activities of the accounting profession and the business and regulatory agencies since the Treadway Commission. The chapter title, however, contains some ambiguities that must first be resolved. In order to have a case of fraudulent financial reporting, it is assumed that either someone within the reporting company or its independent auditors, or both in collusion, have issued a financial report containing false or misleading information concerning the company's financial condition or results of operations. From a legal viewpoint, in order to prove that fraud has taken place, it is necessary that the perpetrator or perpetrators intended to defraud a third party, perhaps a creditor or potential investor.

As its title (The National Commission on Fraudulent Financial Reporting) clearly states, fraudulent financial reporting is what the Treadway Commission Report was all about. When fraud is discussed these days, the conversation eventually leads to the role that the Treadway Commission has played in rooting out fraud. Yet there is considerably more to fraud than fraudulent financial reporting. The question is, shall we discuss fraudulent financial reporting? Or shall we discuss the auditor's responsibility for fraud detection? This is a much larger question.

To complicate the matter further, when we talk about auditors shall we refer to internal auditors or external auditors? Each group of auditors plays a different role in fraud detection, and each group serves a different master. The result is that these groups have varying interests in fraud and auditor responsibility for detecting it.

Fraud detection in general seems to refer to detecting fraud that has been committed within the company, but not necessarily by the company. The fraud referred to here, when discussing the focus of the Treadway Commission, is fraudulent financial reporting. The topic of fraud detection can vary widely, however, depending on whether one's audience consists principally of accountants, internal auditors, external auditors, or other financial professionals. The *Accountant's Guide to Fraud Detection and Control,* Second Edition, was written for the accounting profession. However, since fraud means different things to different groups, we will discuss both categories of fraud to make this chapter as orderly and yet as effective as possible. We will explain the differences between the two categories and then explain the roles that internal and external auditors should play in dealing with both categories of fraud. The accounting profession should also take careful note of the priorities and interests of other groups, in as much as they significantly impact on the interests of management accountants.

Fraudulent Financial Reporting

The Treadway Commission addresses most of its efforts to fraudulent financial reporting. The Commission defines fraudulent financial reporting as "intentional or reckless conduct, whether act or omission, that results in materially misleading financial statements." The Commission focuses on public companies.

The causes of fraudulent financial reporting include:

• Incentives such as the desire to drive up the price of the company's stock, to satisfy investors' expectations, to postpone dealing with existing financial difficulties, or for a variety of personal gain schemes such as compensation and promotion

• Pressures such as sudden declines in market share or sales, unrealistic budgets, or short-term economic performance objectives

• Opportunities too tempting to ignore, such as an inattentive board of directors, weaknesses in the internal control system or internal control staff, complex transactions, or accounting estimates

The primary perpetrators of fraudulent financial reporting, not necessarily in order of frequency or importance, are sales personnel, accountants, decision-making middle managers, and top management. Either these persons are drawn into their schemes by a soft ethical climate or, as individuals, foster a soft ethical climate that leads others into temptations that are too great, or too easy, to pass up.

Since the October 1987 Treadway Commission Final Report was issued, several significant events have taken place within the accounting profession and in the business world in general. Some of what has taken place has been very positive and some has not. For example, during 1988, the Auditing Standards Board issued its *Statement on Auditing Standards,* numbers 53 through 61, all of which address the independent auditor's responsibility for conducting the audit and discovering fraud. (These are covered in detail later in this chapter). Before the ink was completely dry on SAS 53-61, the GAO issued its report to the Chairman of the Committee on Banking, Finance and Urban Affairs, House of Representatives, titled *CPA Audit Quality*. The diatribe was printed in the March 1989 issue of the *Journal of Accountancy* without comment, with the exception of the following 78-word preface:

> Following is the complete text of the General Accounting Office's report on its review of the quality of CPA audits of 11 savings and loan associations that failed in the Dallas area. The report is reprinted here to respond to the GAO's recommendation that the American Institute of CPAs communicate its contents to all AICPA members. The Institute urges all members to read this report carefully and consider whether its criticisms and recommendations are applicable to their practices.

The tone of this preface speaks for itself. In addition to other blistering criticism of the accounting profession, the report demanded that the AICPA rewrite its 10-year-old *Audit and Accounting Guide for Savings and Loan Associations* to respond to the vast changes in the savings and loan industry during that 10-year-period.

Just to make sure no one got the idea that the savings and loan industry contained the only examples of fraudulent financial reporting, the previously nearly unblemished credit union industry discovered its largest fraud-related disaster on November 4, 1988, when the Franklin Federal Credit Union of Omaha, Nebraska, failed. Subsequent examination revealed that the president of Franklin had misappropriated in excess of $39 million in deposits over his 13-year career as leader of the organization. His motto was "A hand up, not a hand out." One congressman, on reflection, asked, "Or was it a hold up?"

What makes the failure of a federal or state chartered financial institution even more difficult to deal with is that many of these organizations are subject to three different levels of audit:

1. The internal auditor, armed with the industry's internal audit manual
2. The independent external auditor, armed with audit programs and appropriate AICPA industry audit guides
3. The regulatory agency auditor, armed with the agency's audit guide and programs

Is it any wonder congress and the general public scratch their heads and wonder, often out loud or in print, if the auditing profession ought to be federally regulated?

Asset-Theft Fraud

The Treadway Commission has provided a framework for effectively dealing with the fradulent financial reporting problem. It is clear that the public accounting profession has accepted responsibility for detecting material occurrences of such fraudulent reporting. The Treadway Commission, however, has failed to address the other category of fraud, which we will refer to here—for want of a better term—as *asset-theft fraud.* The focus of the Treadway Commission's concern centered on fraudulently misstated financial statement balances, which usually means "inflated asset balances." Here, although assets are not stolen the results are inflated determinations of shareholder equity. In asset-theft fraud, financial statement balances are usually not misstated, but assets are stolen. Consider, for example, that asset-theft fraud can be significant and yet financial statement balances will be correctly stated. Reported profit may be lower as a result of an undisclosed asset-theft fraud, but any calculation of stockholder equity as a result of using the reported balances are likely to be correct, and there is no deception of creditors using the financial statements. Asset-theft fraud does not distort financial statement balances *per se,* but reduces an entity's profit. The public accounting profession steadfastly declines responsibility for detecting asset-theft fraud. This creates a serious perception problem. It is generally understood that Treadway deals with all fraud, and the public accounting profession declares that it accepts responsibility for detecting all fraud, not just fraudulent financial reporting.

Pity the independent auditors, for there is no easy solution to the problem. They are literally caught between a rock and a hard place. To begin with, independent auditors are obliged to perform their audits in accordance with generally accepted auditing standards (GAAS), that is, auditing standards determined and published by the AICPA. Those standards do not permit auditors to perform audit procedures designed to detect asset-theft fraud. Were they to do so without the sanction of AICPA auditing standards, the auditors would expose themselves to potentially disastrous charges of negligence by clients using their services. Second, were independent auditors so audaciously inclined as to provide a client asset-theft fraud audit service without the benefit of AICPA auditing standards, they would face a second obstacle of convincing the client that a separate fee was required. The two audits, that is (1) a financial statement audit and (2) an asset-theft fraud audit, require totally different audit techniques and hence separate efforts which must be reimbursed. In brief, whereas a financial statement audit is designed to verify the accuracy of financial statement (balance sheet) balances, an asset-theft fraud audit is most likely to delve into the accuracy of operating accounts. The audit procedures and techniques are quite unlike each other.

The fraud auditor's training and job experience also include the accumulation of mental templates for the myriad variations of asset-theft fraud. These templates are invaluable in detecting the often scant evidence of fraud that is normally encountered. Of course, when it comes to fraud that does not involve a client's accounting entries, the ordinary audit stands little or no chance of discovering it.

RESPONSES TO TREADWAY RECOMMENDATIONS

In an article in *Management Accounting* magazine (Sweeney, Robert, "Executive Summary: The Report of the National Commission on Fraudulent Financial Reporting," March 1989), the author prepared an executive summary of the Treadway Commission Report. Recommendations were directed at four audiences:

1. Public companies
2. Independent Certified Public Accountants
3. The Securities and Exchange Commission and other regulatory and law-making bodies
4. Education

Public Companies

The recommendations directed to the top management of public companies called for top management education on the causes of fraudulent financial reporting and the development of codes of corporate conduct.

According to the March 1989 article in *Management Accounting,* a survey of some 8,500 companies revealed that 42 percent had already adopted written corporate codes of conduct. The article did not say how many of these were adopted as a result of the Treadway Commission. As heartening as this fact is, an almost equal number of respondents did not have a written corporate code of conduct and had no plans to adopt one in the near future.

One might note that, as with many of the recommendations made by Treadway, some are objectively measurable and others are not. Of course, one could ask what difference it makes whether the recommendations are objective. We believe it does make a difference for the following four reasons:

1. The Treadway Commission was not intended to be a smokescreen defense against federal regulation of the accounting profession. It was, however, a necessary precedent in demonstrating to congress that the accounting profession intends to spearhead an effort to clean up financial reporting problems.
2. As such, the recommendations had to be clearly written and had to address the heart of the issue of fraudulent financial reporting.
3. In addition to having substance, the recommendations must *appear* to have substance, even to the eyes of a casual lay observer. It is, after all, the casual lay observer who votes for the members of congress who oversee appointments of certain regulatory officials. It is also the casual lay observer who watches the evening news and reads the newspapers and news magazines for juicy tidbits about the latest fraud scandal.
4. If the recommendations are to be proven useful in retrospect, the measure of their usefulness will likely be in terms of whether they precipitated a reduction in the occurrence of fraudulent financial reporting. For this to work, there must be a measurable cause-and-effect relationship between the implementation of the recommendations and the anticipated outcome. The objectivity of the recommendations, in effect, will determine the worth of the Treadway Commission's efforts.

The recommendations concerning internal controls were fairly predictable and, to a certain extent, were not objective. The recommendations addressed such issues as effectiveness of the internal control staff and their internal control activities, the objectivity of the internal audit function, consideration of nonfinancial audit findings on the company's financial statements, and coordination of internal audit activities with the independent public accounting audit function. Although these recommendations are laudable, they are not new.

Incidentally, the same *Management Accounting* article mentioned earlier reported that 46 percent of the companies responding to the survey indicated that they did not have a separate internal auditing staff. Presumably, this means that the accounting department or the controller takes care of the internal audit function in smaller companies.

There are six recommendations directed to independent audit committees that are relevant, innovative, and objective. Herein lies the heart of the Treadway Commission Report:

1. The board of directors of all public companies should be required by SEC rule to establish audit committees composed solely of independent directors.

2. Audit committees should be informed, vigilant, and effective overseers of the financial reporting process and the company's internal controls.

3. All public companies should develop a written charter setting forth the duties and responsibilities of the audit committee. The board of directors should approve the charter, review it periodically, and modify it as necessary.

4. Audit committees should have adequate resources and authority to discharge their responsibilities.

5. The audit committee should review management's evaluation of factors related to the independence of the company's public accountant. Both the audit committee and management should assist the public accountant in preserving his or her independence.

6. Before the beginning of each year, the audit committee should review management's plans for engaging the company's independent public accountant to perform management advisory services during the coming year, considering both the types of services that may be rendered and the projected fees.

The *Management Accounting* survey revealed that 79 percent of the responding companies had independent audit committees, although only about half of the smaller companies even had audit committees.

The first, third, fourth, and sixth recommendations are objective. The first, third, and fourth recommendations taken together will create the best line of defense against fraud in general and against fraudulent financial reporting specifically. Board members are nominated for their positions for reasons other than managerial competence or technical knowledge more often than not. A strong, knowledgeable, independent audit committee becomes the third party to the audit process. The other two parties are the company's management and the independent auditor. The second and fifth recommendations are well-intentioned and sound good, but are probably not objectively measurable; hence their effectiveness after the fact will be difficult to correlate to the results of the adoption of the recommendations.

According to an article in the *Journal of Accountancy* (Bull, Ivan, and Sharp, Florence Cowan, "Advising Clients on Treadway Audit Committee Recommendations," Feb. 1989), a significant number of CEOs and audit committee heads shared two concerns:

1. They believe that both the time demand and the legal liability exposure of audit committee members will likely be increased as a result of the Treadway Report. One chairman referred to the liability exposure as enormous and said he is resigning from all directorships of public companies. If this concern proves to be well-founded, competent people who are willing to serve on audit committees may become harder to find.

2. They are concerned that recommendations for informed, vigilant, and effective oversight of the reporting process and internal controls, and of the quarterly reporting process, may encourage what one CEO terms "micro-management" by the board of directors.

In a *Financial Executive* magazine article (author not named, "The Treadway Commission—What Happens Next?" June 1988), six auditing experts were interviewed concerning the Treadway Commission Report. One panel member said, "One of the criticisms of the Treadway Commission Report is that it wanders rather widely from fraudulent financial reporting. It addresses much larger issues. My own personal concern is that you get very quickly into morality and religious belief when you start talking about ethical behavior. . . . If the audit committee thinks its role is to get down into the bowels of management, to interview lower-level employees about the code of business conduct or anything else, then I think the audit committee is moving into a management function and I submit that that is a mission impossible."

The *Journal of Accountancy* article mentioned earlier cited several qualities needed for audit committee service:

- Financial statement literacy, including an understanding of how business activities are reflected in the financial statements
- An ability to recognize potential problems through analyses and discussions
- An understanding of the auditing process—internal and external
- The disposition to ask probing questions and get answers to them
- Skill in communicating with managers, statement preparers, and auditors
- Natural curiosity

Although the SEC Practice Section specifically prohibits CPA firms from recruiting board members for audit clients, CPAs can help identify reports useful to the audit committee, such as:

- Quantified plans and budgets
- Monthly financial reports, with explanations for budget variations
- Details of unusual transactions and adjustments
- Internal audit reports
- CPA audit reports and letters

Two additional recommendations concerning the annual financial report to stockholders are ways of implementing the previous recommendations:

1. All public companies should be required by SEC rule to include management reports signed by the chief executive officer and the chief accounting officer and/or the chief financial officer in their annual reports to stockholders. The management report should acknowledge management's responsibilities and how these responsibilities were fulfilled, and provide management's assessment of the effectiveness of the company's internal controls.
2. All public companies should be required by SEC rule to include a letter signed by the chairman of the audit committee in their annual reports to stockholders, describing the committee's responsibilities and activities during the year. Other recommendations in this area seem to be either intuitively obvious or a rehash of already existing practices.

Independent Certified Public Accountants and Revised Statements on Auditing Standards

In the independent public accountant's area of responsibility there were several critical recommendations. After all, no matter how vehemently the public accounting profession protests to the contrary, the general public looks to the independent auditor to find fraud and protect the investing public from charlatans. The recommendations admonished the Auditing Standards Board (ASB) to revise standards of responsibility to detect fraudulent financial reporting, including the provision of guidance to CPAs for assessing risk and pursuing detection when risks are identified. Without question, the actions of the ASB subsequent to the issuance of the Treadway Report are among the most visible. As mentioned earlier, the ASB has issued a number of new Statements on Auditing Standards (SAS), addressing most of the Treadway's recommendations. Recall, however, that it was the Cohen Commission that first confirmed that there was an expectation gap. The new standards issued in 1988 and 1989 were written to address the expectation gap. They came to be known as "the expectation gap standards," and are as follows:

- The SAS No. 53, Auditor's Responsibility to Detect and Report Errors and Irregularities
- SAS No. 54, Illegal Acts by Clients
- SAS No. 55, Consideration of the Internal Control Structure in Financial Statement Audit
- SAS No. 56, Analytical Procedures
- SAS No. 57, Auditing Estimates
- SAS No. 58, Reports on Audited Financial Statements
- SAS No. 59, The Auditor's Consideration of an Entity's Ability to Continue as a Going Concern
- SAS No. 60, Communication of Internal Control Structure Related Matters Noted in an Audit
- SAS No. 61, Communication with Audit Committees
- SAS No. 62, Special Reports
- SAS No. 63, Compliance Auditing Applicable to Governmental Entities and Other Recipients of Governmental Financial Assistance
- SAS No. 64, Omnibus
- SAS No. 65, The Auditor's Consideration of the Internal Audit Function in an Audit of Financial Statements

Nine years after it was issued in April 1988, SAS No. 53, *The Auditor's Responsibility to Detect and Report Errors and Irregularities,* was superceded by SAS No. 82, *Consideration of Fraud in a Financial Statement Audit.* SAS No. 82 was touted as being "the most highly publicized statement on auditing standards in year," providing " . . . expanded operational guidance on the auditor's consideration of material fraud in conducting a financial statement audit" (*Journal of Accountancy,* April 1997).

SAS No. 82 came to be written after the Public Oversight Board (POB) of the AICPA SEC Practice Section, in their March 1993 report *In the Public Interest,* noted that:

> Attacks on the accounting profession from a variety of sources suggested a significant public concern over the profession's performance. Of particular moment is the widespread belief that auditors have a responsibility for detecting management fraud which they are not now meeting.

With specific regard to what was accomplished by SAS No. 82, the following amendment to "Responsibilities and Functions of the Independent Auditor" (SAS No. 1) speaks for itself:

> ... The auditor has no responsibility to plan and perform the audit to obtain reasonable assurance that misstatements, whether caused by errors or fraud, that are not material to financial statements are detected. (February 1997)

In an additional amendment, to SAS No. 47, SAS No. 82 provided the following clear statement on auditor responsibility for detecting fraud:

> Although fraud is a broad legal concept, the auditor's interest specifically relates to fraudulent acts that cause a misstatement of financial statements. Two types of misstatements are relevant to the auditor's consideration in a financial statement audit—misstatements arising from fraudulent financial reporting and misstatements arising from misappropriation of assets. ...

In our opinion, the issuance of the expectation gap Statements on Auditing Standards did nothing to clarify the expectation gap. We cannot explain why, except to speculate that the AICPA Auditing Standards Board did not clearly understand the nature of the expectation gap.

All things considered, however, the expectation gap standards are a substantial improvement over those they replaced. In some cases, the pronouncement topics have been promoted to the status of separate publications. Given the litigation-oriented society in which we operate, the attitudes of investors concerning risk-shifting and the malpractice liability insurance industry, the new statements should be quite effective. They are most assuredly a visible response to Cohen and Treadway recommendations.

Two recommendations directed to the auditor's report are worthy of discussion and of perhaps a little criticism.

1. The ASB should revise the auditor's standard report to state that the audit provides reasonable but not absolute assurance that the audited financial statements are free from material misstatements as a result of fraud or error.

2. The ASB should revise the auditor's standard report to describe the extent of internal accounting control. The ASB should also provide explicit guidance to address the situation where, as a result of his or her knowledge of the company's internal accounting controls, the

independent public accountant disagrees with management's assessment stated in the proposed management report.

With regard to the first recommendation, the ASB has issued a new standard auditor's report. The report is considerably different from its predecessor; however, it is still silent in regard to fraud, irregularities, and illegal acts. Granted, these are addressed in the new SAS, but the fact remains that Treadway's intent was explicitly to communicate the auditor's level of responsibility for detecting fraud. This still has not been done, and perhaps with good reason.

The second recommendation all but puts the independent auditor in an adversarial role *vis à vis* the client. This is a new and different way for CPAs to deal with clients who do not agree with their assessment of internal controls. Of course, the disagreement may result in the auditor's being fired and replaced with a new firm. Presumably, the purpose of the replacement is to secure a report that is not critical of management's internal control system. This seems to be a problem-ridden recommendation. SAS 60 responds to this recommendation.

Interestingly, in the *Financial Executive* panel discussion article mentioned earlier, one panel member said he felt that external auditors should decrease compliance testing on internal controls. "The external auditor needs to stop thrashing around the bowels of our client's accounting systems and move to the areas where he or she has real expertise. For it's also in those areas where the unreliable financial reporting occurs. Even crooks need good data."

Securities and Exchange Commission and Other Regulatory Agencies

Many of Treadway's recommendations deal with enforcement issues. Among others are the following:

- The SEC should seek explicit statutory authority to bar or suspend corporate officers and directors involved in fraudulent financial reporting from future service in that capacity in a public company. (Although the intention of this recommendation is clear, it is not certain that it is workable within our permissive society.)
- Criminal prosecution of fraudulent financial reporting cases should become a higher priority.

- The SEC must be given adequate resources to perform existing and additional functions that help to prevent, detect, and deter fraudulent financial reporting.

It seems that the message conveyed by these recommendations is two-fold. First, if we are going to get excited about controlling fraudulent financial reporting, we have to have enforceable and meaningful sanctions that can be imposed against perpetrators. Second, the SEC must be able to do its job efficiently and effectively. SEC registrants and their independent CPAs must have confidence that the reporting and disclosures required of them are necessary and that they will be acted upon in a swift and unbiased manner. Furthermore, registrants must feel confident that their reports are being processed in an objective manner, without suffering any unwarranted harassment or intimidation.

Having to do directly with CPA firms that serve SEC clients, the Commission recommended that CPA firms which audit public companies be required to undergo a peer review and an independent oversight function approved by the SEC, such as the SEC Practice Section of the AICPA's Division for CPA Firms. The recommendations also include enforcement action when a public accounting firm fails to remedy deficiencies cited in the public accounting profession's quality assurance program.

Without regard to action on the part of the SEC, the AICPA now requires any firm that performs so much as one audit must subject itself to peer review. According to Joe Sperstad, former Executive Director of the Wisconsin Institute of Certified Public Accountants, this requirement seeks to find and eliminate "One Audit Charlie" (a practicing CPA who only conducts one audit per year and thus is assumed to lack competence in auditing). The cost of the review is about $1,000. The additional requirement that the CPA firm become a member of the SECPS is already in force.

Several of Treadway's recommendations seem to be more political pleas or statements than serious recommendations.

- Parties charged with responding to various tort reform initiatives should consider the implications that the perceived liability crisis holds for long-term audit quality and the independent public accountant's detection of fraudulent financial reporting.
- The SEC should reconsider its long-standing position; insofar as it applies to independent directors, that the corporate indemnification of officers and directors for liabilities that arise under the Securities Act of 1933 is against public policy and therefore unenforceable.

EDUCATION

Overall, the Treadway recommendations had to be and appear to be two-dimensional. They had to address immediate problems with immediate solutions. The outcry from the general public and its echoes, the congress and news media demand swift and sure remedies to fraudulent financial reporting. Of course, no matter how diligent the accounting profession becomes, it will be difficult if not impossible to cure all the fraudulent reporting problems that exist and will surface during the coming years.

One of the misconceptions held by the general public concerning disclosures of fraud is that the disclosures themselves are signs of flaws in the system. Quite the contrary is true, depending on how the fraud is discovered and disclosed. If the discovery is made and documented in the course of an audit and its disclosure is made through the proper channels, this is a sign that the system is working the way it is supposed to. In other words, fraud is out there waiting to be discovered. If those who are responsible for finding it are indeed finding and disclosing it, then congress and the general public should be pleased, not outraged.

The second dimension to the Treadway Report looks into the future. During the past 30 years or so, the education system has concentrated on producing technically competent businesspeople, including accountants. In earlier times, students were educated in arts, letters, and sciences. Those who demonstrated managerial competency were promoted into management. Therefore, managers had to be both skilled in the industry in which they were employed and able to demonstrate competence in managing resources.

Now we train managers in college. These bright-eyed wonders exit academia armed with management skills taught by professors who generally have little or no management experience outside the classroom. These graduates have high expectations of wealth, fame, and mobility. They also have two very negative characteristics. First, for the most part they have not achieved a level of maturity consistent with their expectations or the responsibilities with which they will be charged by their employers, who have equally high expectations of their expensive recruits.

Second, many of these graduates have little or no interest in what they have been trained to do. They are interested in megabucks. Many of our graduates today look at two factors in choosing a major. First is the latest starting-salary survey. If they can find a profession that is even remotely interesting to them, they will probably pursue it if it is high enough on the salary list. Second is the amount of resistance anticipated on the path to that profession. The more difficult the program, the less likely candidates are to pursue it.

With regard to education, the accounting profession has a few advantages over other business-related professions. If an accounting graduate wants to optimize his or her career opportunities, then a professional designation is a must. The best known is the Certified Public Accountant (CPA), followed by Certified Management Accountant (CMA) and Certified Internal Auditor (CIA). There are a whole host of designations that have recently surfaced in addition to these.

Now that the word is out that specialization is necessary because of the complexity of the business environment, we can expect to see certificates in many business professions in the future. For now at least, the accounting profession can serve as a quality-control mechanism for accounting education. If an accounting graduate gets through an accounting program and cannot pass the appropriate examination, or for some reason elects not to take one, then the graduate is doomed to an inferior status and salary within the accounting profession. Of course, this is not to say that the person will not become a resounding success in some field other than accounting.

Furthermore, even if the graduate passes the CPA examination, he or she still has to satisfy the state accountancy board's experience requirement. After certification and licensing, the CPA has to maintain continuing education requirements or risk losing the license to practice.

The Treadway Commission rose to meet the education challenge. The Commission also addressed the problem of ethics in education. The jury is still out on whether we can successfully teach good ethics in college which will produce graduates who practice good ethics in the workplace. In fact, it will be many years before we have a legitimate verdict on this matter. In the meantime, there are several recommendations that focus on this long-term aspect of fraudulent financial reporting. The Commission has asked educators and licensing accountants to put out the word that fraudulent financial reporting is a no-no. The business education community has been charged with increasing students' analytical, problem-solving, and judgment skills as well as to emphasize ethical values, all in an effort to curb fraudulent financial reporting. The Commission has even gone so far as to ask business schools to overhaul their faculty rewards system to encourage faculty to develop their own personal competence in skills that would help to prevent, detect, and deter fraudulent financial reporting.

Realizing the short-term nature of legislated solutions to the fraudulent financial reporting problem, Treadway had enough foresight to address one of the long-term solutions, which has already been mentioned: education, certification, and licensing. In its simplest form, this solution conveys the message to the entering accountant that what is right and what is wrong is a matter of fact, rather than opinion which depends upon personal value systems to provide appropriate guidance. Then accountants must be tested before they are certified. The test presumably will become evidence that the participant, at least at the time of examination, was aware of what constituted acceptable behavior. With licensing, we can ensure that only those who have been tested, who comply with continuing education requirements, and who do not violate the certifier's code of ethics will behave in an acceptable manner. Another March 1989 *Management Accounting* article coauthored by Alfred King, then Managing Director of the Institute of Management Accountants, suggested that anyone who issues financial reports be certified by a professional society that maintains a code of ethics. The article proposed that the CMA certification might be appropriate for such persons. The authors' intent in the article was not to usurp authority from either the CPA or the Certified Internal Auditor (CIA) designations, but rather to call attention to their opinion that in most instances of fraudulent financial reporting, one or more chief accounting or financial officers were not doing their jobs. Certification would at least ensure that the responsible party was completely informed as to the level of responsibility being assumed in the issuance of the company's financial statements.

SUMMARY

The significance of the foregoing account of the independent auditor's responsibility for detecting fraud might not be fully understood by casual readers. Accordingly, at the risk of over simplification, we offer the following summarization.

First of all, there is no question that there has been an expectation gap between what independent auditors have promised in the way of fraud detection, and the more comprehensive detection service that their clients expected. This was confirmed by the Cohen Commission. The AICPA, in response to Cohen Commission and Treadway Commission recommendations, took action to revise its auditing standards to "close" the expectation gap, with the result that revised expectation gap auditing standards were issued in 1988, and again in February 1997 (*Consideration of Fraud in a Financial Statement Audit*, SAS No. 82). However, despite the best efforts by the AICPA the expectation gap continued to exist! Why? Because they failed to address the true nature of the expectation gap in revising auditing standards.

The expectation gap results because there is not a clear understanding—between independent auditors and the entities which use the services of independent auditors—as to specifically what fraud detection services are performed and what fraud detection responsibilities are assumed. We believe this misunderstanding results because the AICPA's proprietary definition of the word fraud, in stating the independent auditor's responsibilities differs significantly from the common understanding of what fraud is, which their clients have come to know. Specifically, the AICPA does not adequately clarify—when proclaiming that *"independent auditors are responsible for detecting fraud"*—that they do not mean ALL fraud, but only fraud that may be distorting financial statement balances. As a result, although an independent auditor may satisfactorily discharge his or her responsibility to disclose financial statement balance fraud, he or she has not satisfactorily fulfilled the client's expectation of an opinion on *all* fraud, particularly asset-theft fraud, which may have materially impacted on the client's bottom line.

The expectation gap began to evolve around 1910, when auditors began to depart from their primary mission of detecting all fraud to a primary mission involving the verification of financial statement balances. Eventually, with the emergence of generally accepted auditing standards, the departure from fraud auditing became institutionalized and the expectation gap was firmly entrenched.

At this point, it is appropriate to mention that although it appears that the expectation gap controversy involves a dispute between independent auditors on the one hand, and their clients on the other, this requires a further explanation. Many individual independent auditors are equally unhappy with the expectation gap. The problem lies in the fact that independent auditors must abide by auditing standards published by the AICPA, which essentially limit an auditor's fraud search activities to financial statement balances. Many independent auditors are desirous of extending their fraud auditing services to clients, but are unwilling to do so without the sanction of generally accepted auditing standards. It is interesting to note that although the AICPA is theoretically an organization of independent auditors and theoretically its auditing standards are "generally accepted" by the membership, many of its independent auditor members—particularly the smaller practitioners—are not happy with the AICPA's closure of or failure to address the true expectation gap. Although the

AICPA has made many attempts to close the expectation gap and has revised the auditing standards on many occasions—most recently in 1997—they have not been successful. Why?

The AICPA has long been devoted to writing auditing standards for independent auditors to produce audit products of interest to parties external to the audited entity. These parties include the SEC, the investing public, lenders, and the like. Their primary objectives lie in the accurate reporting of an entity's equity. Obviously, fraudulently inflated asset balances would distort any equity determination.

Entity management and owners, however, have interests considerably beyond those of external parties. They are primarily interested in an entity's profitability and knowing what fraud may be depleting an entity's profits enters into profitability. Auditing standards do not provide independent auditors an opportunity to develop this information, and hence, they cannot report it to management. This is the essence of the expectation gap. It will never be closed until independent auditors institute proactive audit procedures designed to detect fraud which reduces profits but does not inflate financial statement equity account balances.

Chapter 2

New Perspectives on Fraud

THE FRAUD UNIVERSE

No one will ever be able to describe the makeup of the fraud universe with certainty because most of it will always be hidden from public view. However, by using information we know to be true, and deductive reasoning, it is possible for reasonable men and women to hypothesize as to its vital characteristics. Begin the hypothesis with an incontestable conclusion that the fraud universe is made up of three main categories of fraud:

1. Fraud that has been prosecuted
2. Fraud that has been discovered, but which has not been prosecuted
3. Fraud which has not been discovered

Of the three categories the public can only know the composition of the first category with reasonable certainty. As case details are presented to the court during prosecution, we gain the opportunity to examine them and to develop knowledge as to the makeup of fraud in this category. However, no such opportunity for observation exists to study the cases in the second and third categories. Unless the laws governing slander and libel change drastically, the particulars of Category 2 fraud cases will be kept secret forever by the millions of victims throughout the world. The public will never be able to learn the details of more than the relatively few cases that are inadvertently disclosed. Also remaining forever secret is the fraud that makes up Category 3, the fraud which has not been detected. Accordingly, unless we speculate, using deductive reasoning to fathom the sizes of the unseen categories of the fraud universe, we will never have the answer to the questions:

- "How much of the fraud universe has been discovered?"
- "How much of the fraud universe has been discovered and not prosecuted?"
- "How much of the fraud universe has not been discovered?"

More important are answers to the questions:

- "Is the fraud that constitutes Category 2 and Category 3 similar to Category 1, or is it more ominous?"
- "Should we be intensifying our fraud protection and detection efforts?"

The pages that follow describe the bases for estimating the relative sizes of all three types of fraud, as well as the alarming danger it presents to business and public entities at risk. Our findings are sufficiently accurate to elevate significantly the concerns of all world entities at risk and cause them to reconsider the adequacy of their protective measures.

Having considered various facts and circumstances available for forecasting, our personal experience with the first two types of fraud, the auditing and investigative resources and practices applied to the pro-active detection of fraud, and the respected opinions of more than a thousand accountants, auditors and investigators, we conclude that the relative sizes of the main components of the fraud universe are about:

- Category 1: Fraud that has been prosecuted—20 percent
- Category 2: Fraud that has been discovered, but which has not been prosecuted—40 percent
- Category 3: Fraud which has not been discovered—40 percent

If these statistics are reasonably realistic, there is considerable reason for public and private entities to be concerned. The statistics basically indicate that the average entity, to a significant extent

- Has no suspicion that it has been victimized by any of the fraud that has occurred in the third category, which is twice what is being prosecuted, or 40 percent of all cases
- Is not motivated or otherwise inclined to take the necessary steps to stem their losses without these suspicions
- Has no hope of recovering any losses suffered without knowledge that fraud has occurred

In the second category—the 40 percent of fraud that is discovered but not prosecuted—it is extremely important to reconsider just what fraud discovery means here. It is a popular misconception that many entities that discover fraud choose not to prosecute for various reasons, such as the unfavorable publicity that might result. There are undoubtedly some instances where that may be true. However, we believe that in most instances there is simply not enough evidence to support prosecution!

It is also important to bear in mind that the first evidence of fraud a victim usually discovers often only serves to create a suspicion of fraud, and may or not be followed by the discovery of additional evidence. In fact, as initial fraud evidence begins to surface, many victims either fail to recognize the discovered evidence as indicia of fraud, or are far from certain as to what they have found. Accordingly, decisions to prosecute fraud often depend upon how much evidence the victim has discovered, rather than being a simple matter left to a victim's discretion. If the fraud in the second category could be visualized, you would see cases near the bottom of the category for which only the very minimum of evidence existed to induce a suspicion of fraud. As you proceeded upward in the category, you would see cases for which there would be gradually more and more evidence, until your vision reached the line between the first and second categories, at which time you would see cases for which sufficient evidence had been accumulated to support prosecution. It is only these cases, near the top of the second category, that prosecutors would be likely to consider for prosecution. See Exhibit 2.1 for an illustration of the three categories of fraud.

In only 20 percent of all fraud—category 1—are the victims ever absolutely certain they have been victims, have at least partially determined their losses, and have a chance to recover these losses. However, even when a perpetrator is identified and sufficient evidence exists to prosecute, they are never likely to recover all their losses. Often, only enough of the *strongest* evidence is normally chosen for trial to assure conviction. To illustrate, in a government fraud that occurred in Chicago in the late 1970s, the perpetrator was discovered (accidentally) and prosecuted. At trial, the U.S. Attorney prosecuting the case charged and proved to the court that the defendant embezzled about $300,000. In reality, the auditors had determined that the defendant had stolen over $900,000 when they stopped counting. Very little of the amount stolen was recovered. The convicted perpetrator had been ordered to make restitution; however, the monthly restitution payments ordered were so very low, had he paid them, they would have been insufficient to cover the interest cost on the money

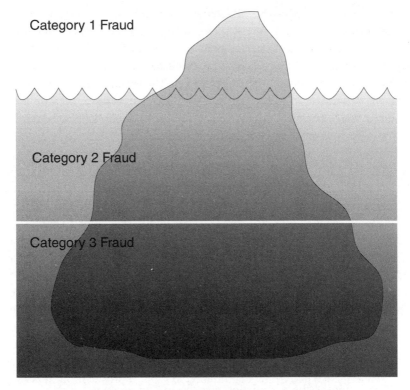

Category 1 Fraud

Category 2 Fraud

Category 3 Fraud

Exhibit 2.1.   The Three Categories of Fraud

stolen. We learned later that he had defaulted on the restitution payments. Incidentally, he was convicted and was given a one-year prison sentence with a work release during the day. Of his one-year sentence, much of it had been satisfied by his pre-trial confinement.

Most fraud losses are never fully assessed—usually a very difficult task—and victims rarely recover, for example through insurance, more than a portion of their actual losses.

How the Proportion of Fraud in Each Category Was Estimated

Although it is not possible to add up the fraud in each group and to calculate arithmetically the relative proportion of fraud in each one, there are certain existing facts and conditions which make reasonable speculation possible.

Estimating the Percentage of Fraud in Category 1. We began the estimating process by considering the actual characteristics of the fraud that is in category 1 because it is the only group on which we have any factual knowledge.

We know a great deal about category 1 perpetrators, based on the many category 1 cases that scholars and practitioners have observed and/or examined many times over many years. With few exceptions, their conclusions on the nature of category 1 fraud have been sufficiently similar to corroborate what has become a generally accepted view on the nature of fraud perpetrators:

> Fraud is largely perpetrated by inept and often careless perpetrators, who—
> if not at the outset—ultimately become careless and/or greedy, and who
> make fatal mistakes that lead to the accidental discovery of their fraud.

The results of one study[1] by a very reputable researcher found that auditors discover only 20 percent of all fraud. The rest, about 80 percent, was discovered accidentally (including that resulting from co-worker complaints). However, we suspect that the percentage of fraud discovered accidentally, per his study, may be even higher than he expressed in that he did not classify fraud discovered by auditors as accidental. Many auditor discoveries of fraud occur accidentally in the course of doing other work.

As alarming as these statistics may be to entities, many are likely to be even more alarmed to discover why so much of the fraud that is discovered is discovered accidentally. They should be uncomfortable with the explanation that many fraud scholars seem to favor: most cases are discovered accidentally because the perpetrators ultimately get careless and greedy and make mistakes that result in their accidental discovery. Although this is undoubtedly true of some perpetrators, it conflicts with out experience with fraud perpetrators over the years. Most perpetrators are relatively intelligent people, not prone to be inept or careless. After due consideration, we concluded that, contrary to popular opinion, most of the discovered fraud is discovered accidentally because:

> No one is effectively, proactively searching for evidence of fraud.
> As a direct result, primarily, only the work of inept and careless
> perpetrators is revealed, and fraud by clever and careful perpetrators
> is not being revealed.

It logically follows that if a perpetrator is careless and makes mistakes, he or she is likely to be discovered. It also follows that if a fraud perpetrator is not inept, careless, or greedy, he or she is not likely to be discovered, unless of course, someone is skillfully and proactively searching for him or her. Further, it is reasonable to assume that if auditors were effectively and proactively searching for fraud, a great deal more than 20 percent of the cases would be discovered by auditors, and fewer by accident. This is true if the cases in the fraud universe as a whole—as in category 1— were perpetrated by inept, careless, and/or greedy perpetrators.

There is little doubt that entities are generally not adequately proactively examining themselves—or having themselves proactively examined—to detect the existence of fraud. Public accountants have chosen not to accept responsibility for detecting fraud, except for fraud in financial statement balances, for over 50 years[2]. In lieu of auditing, they recommend that entities rely upon good internal control, surety bonds, and systems of accounting for fraud protection[3]. Based upon our many discussions with internal auditors, as well as our own experience in internal auditing, internal auditors have been influenced by public accounting pronouncements and have not been effective and/or active in searching for pre-emergent fraud.

One can draw two conclusions as to the competencies of the different fraud perpetrators:

1. The less competent fraud perpetrators are being discovered. They largely populate the category 1 group.
2. The more competent perpetrators are not being discovered! They largely populate the second and third categories. Of the perpetrators in these two groups, it may be generally assumed that the more competent populate category 3, and the less competent fall into category 2.

The question to ask is, "In a world where discovery can mean embarrassment and severe punishment, including loss of employment, what percentage of fraud perpetrators in the entire fraud universe are likely to be so inept as to take the sort of risks that result in up to 80 percent of their numbers being accidentally discovered when no one is looking for them?"

Our experience with fraud perpetrators over the years has generally shown them to be relatively intelligent people, not prone to take extraordinary risks which would jeopardize their lives. Accordingly, we chose as our answer 20 percent of all perpetrators in the fraud universe. We actually think it is less than 20 percent, but are comfortable with 20 percent.

Incidentally, we would appreciate hearing if readers agree or disagree on this point. If you disagree, we would sincerely like to hear what you believe the percentage should be, and why. Please include your personal experience if your answer is based upon it. Please see Introduction— Contacting The Authors for a mailing address.

Estimating the Percentages of Fraud in the Second and Third Categories. If the size of category 1 fraud is 20 percent, by subtraction we derive 80 percent as the size of second and third category fraud. The question which presents itself here is how to make a reasonable separation of the 80 percent between the second category and the third. In the absence of a better basis, we divided the 80 percent into two equal sub-universes of 40 percent each. There is actually a good basis for it.

If it were somehow possible to rank *all* fraud in descending order, from fraud with the most evidence to fraud with the least evidence, the top 20 percent would be the category 1 fraud that was prosecuted. Prosecutors were satisfied that the evidence assembled was sufficient to justify prosecution. In the bottom 40 percent of the listing would be fraud that literally produced no discernable evidence. At the 80 percent level, considerable evidence of fraud was assembled, but prosecution was declined for want of sufficient evidence to dispel reasonable doubt.

The question here is, "going up the scale" from zero percent evidence to 80 percent evidence, at what point does the average victim begin to suspect fraud? Of course, no one can possibly know for sure, but somewhere along the line a victim becomes suspicious that they have encountered fraud. It is at that point that the victim responds by initiating a reactive examination to confirm that he or she has or has not been defrauded, and to collect the necessary evidence to quiet suspicions or to think prosecution. Percentage-wise, it is fair to set that point at about halfway to the 80 percent, or at the 40 percent mark. Accordingly, the amount of fraud in the second category may be around 40 percent and the amount in the third category may be about 40 percent. More precise figures here are not as relevant as knowing that there is a vast amount of fraud that is not even suspected by victims.

Incidentally, the 40 percent amount in the third category is all the more believable when it is recalled that entities are generally not proactively searching for fraud, and accordingly are not trained or sensitive to indicia of fraud when they encounter it! In fact, most people tend to be very naive when it comes to having to choose between suspecting fraud or suspecting human error.

To illustrate, a 1998 case was reported in a Northern Virginia newspaper which involved a town clerk's discovery that a vendor had "accidentally" overcharged the town. The clerk was lauded for her alert discovery of the overcharge, which saved the town thousands of dollars. The vendor was most appreciative of the clerk's calling the "error" to their attention and promptly refunded the over-payment. Few people are likely to have considered the possibility that the overcharge was not accidental, but a deliberate attempt to defraud the town. If so, there was very likely a conspirator working for the town who had initially approved the vendor's payment and who did not rejoice in the clerk's discovery of the "error."

WHAT IS FRAUD?

There are many definitions for fraud, depending on who provides the definition. However, most tend to embellish the following basic definition taken from *The American Heritage Dictionary, Second College Edition,* which defines fraud as *a deception deliberately practiced in order to secure unfair or unlawful gain.* For the management accountant, auditor, or investigator, who may be considering what may be necessary to fully articulate a case of fraud, he or she must normally identify:

- a victim
- details of the deceptive act thought to be fraudulent
- the victim's loss
- a perpetrator (i.e., a suspect)
- evidence that the perpetrator acted with intent
- evidence that the perpetrator profited by the act(s)

TIP: There is one bit of advice that we offer here to all management accountants, which may very well be one of the most important lessons learned in this entire text. If an act appears to meet the definition of fraud, it probably is fraud. As they say, "if it walks like a duck, has feathers, and talks like a duck, it must be a duck!" However, no matter how fully the definition is met, and no matter how preponderant the evidence is, don't ever openly declare the finding to be *fraud!* Fraud can only be decided in a court of law. To ignore this caution risks defamation litigation. Further, be very careful in terminating an employee suspected (or known) to be guilty of fraud. If you fire him or her because you suspect they were involved in fraud without prosecuting and without a guilty verdict, you may be liable for wrongful termination and subject to damages for defamation. If you do fire an employee for this reason, you must never acknowledge the fact to a prospective employer seeking references. In fact, even if you maintain absolute secrecy, informing only the employee that they are being fired for fraud, without a court determination, you may subsequently be sued for slander if the terminated employee tells a prospective employer why he or she was fired. This is known in some states as "compelled self-publication", and may trigger a lawsuit on the basis of compulsory defamation.

Fraud always involves one or more persons who, with intent, act secretly to deprive another of something of value, for their own enrichment. If any element of this definition is missing, the act may not be fraud. For example, if a victim is simply robbed of a sum of money, perhaps from an open safe, and the theft is not done secretly so as to deceive the victim that he has lost something of value, the act is more likely to be defined as burglary or larceny. Of course, all are criminal acts. However, for the management accountant the difference lies more in the proof required to prosecute and convict a suspect. Proving that a suspect is guilty of fraud is often considerably more difficult than ordinary larceny.

Whenever attempting to determine whether or not a fraudulent act has occurred, gather evidence that will allow prosecution of a fraudulent act, or judge whether or not a suspect may be guilty of fraud, it is essential that all elements of the definition be considered.

PROVING THAT A SUSPECTED PERPETRATOR *INTENDED* TO COMMIT FRAUD

This is perhaps one of the most important and most difficult aspects of a fraud investigation and prosecution. Many lay people seem not to fully comprehend the difficulty involved in proving in a court of law that fraud has occurred and proving that the suspect intended to commit fraud. If you find one instance where you think an individual may have committed fraud, no matter how strong the evidentiary support is, chances are the case will never be prosecuted.

To get some appreciation of just how difficult this is, consider the following:

Assume that an entity contracted to have the roof of a warehouse redone, specifying that an expensive rubberized sheeting be used. The job is advertised and contractor A submits the lowest bid. After the job is completed, the entity discovers that the roof leaks. Further investigation discloses that a much cheaper roofing material was installed, inferior to the quality of product that was specified in the contract. The cost difference between the two grades of roof sheeting was $10,000, and it will cost $5,000 to repair the leak.

Question: What course of action should the entity follow? Should it seek to prosecute the contractor for "defective delivery fraud", or should it seek civil remedies to recover its losses? Why?

The entity will probably be advised to seek civil remedies. Its claim for damages will probably be successful if it can prove the misrepresentation. The example given, however, is a frequent ideal fraud for a perpetrator. The perpetrator profits by (1) winning the contract by bidding a bit lower than what would be a fair price, never intending to conform to contract specifications, and (2) gaining $10,000 by substituting cheaper materials, thereby profiting. He or she is hoping that the cheaper materials are never discovered, at least not immediately. The longer the intervening time, the better the chances of never being questioned. Chances are the fraud won't be discovered at all. If discovered, however, the perpetrator simply apologizes profusely, makes restitution claiming human error, and indicates that there was no intent to defraud the contracting entity. This fraud involves making a large profit by risking a small loss. It may even involve a small bribe to the entity's inspector to pass the cheaper materials.

What is the risk of being charged with fraud? Not likely in today's world where entities are not inclined to have experienced fraud-specific audit resources at their disposal. Why would the contractor not be charged with fraud? Because one example, possibly a mistake, does not prove beyond a reasonable doubt that there was intent to defraud the entity! How would an experienced fraud-specific auditor make a difference? The auditor would know that reputable contractors don't make this sort of mistake often, and will gather the necessary evidence to demonstrate intent. To do this, other transactions involving this contractor will be examined to determine if this contractor had worked this same fraud before. A dishonest perpetrator probably has. If so, the auditor will develop additional examples, the more the better to prove intent. Two or more clear examples of the same practice presented to a court will tend to erase any reasonable doubt as to intentions and very likely evoke a guilty finding. It will also increase the likelihood of the entity recovering its losses.

It should be mentioned here that the victim entity will probably not wish to prosecute the contractor, feeling that it would be more trouble than it is worth. However, we believe it is always a mistake not to prosecute. It sets a dangerous precedent with regard to deterring other would-be perpetrators. A victim's failure to prosecute takes the risk out of perpetration, eliminates a powerful internal control, and may very well be the deciding reason why the perpetrator in this case chose to risk the fraud attempt. Entities should resolve to prosecute all who perpetrate fraud and make this policy known for its deterrent value. The risk of prosecution can and will deter fraud.

WHAT SORT OF PERSON COMMITS FRAUD?

We would like to be able to tell you that the average perpetrator is probably a male, of shifty appearance, in need of a shave and a haircut, wearing a black shirt with a white tie, exhibiting a periodic muscular spasm which causes him to jerk his head as though his collar were too tight, and sneering a lot. But we cannot. If anything, we might suggest that you look elsewhere when you spot such a person. Fraud perpetrators tend to be the least suspected. This characteristic provides excellent cover for the cautious perpetrator.

Do Only Men Commit Fraud?

No. Federal Bureau of Investigation figures show that between 1976 and 1985 the number of women arrested for embezzlement increased 55 percent, compared with a 1 percent decrease for men. Fraud arrests among women shot up 84 percent in the same period, nearly twice the rise among men. A May 29, 1987 *Wall Street Journal* article, "Broken Barrier: More Women Join Ranks of White Collar Criminals," reported:

As white-collar crime among women has increased, some telling contrasts between male and female offenders have become apparent. A recent Yale University study found, for example, that white-collar men who steal typically take far more money than women—an average of 10 times more.

The study also found that female white-collar criminals, who are largely clerical workers, tend to get involved in simpler fraud, and usually act alone and out of concern for their families. Many of their male counterparts, by contrast, tend to be conspiring managers. And while men tend to use stolen funds for luxury items rich as sports cars, women embezzlers may be motivated more from a need to make ends meet. However, . . . a former female insurance broker in St. Petersburg, Florida, who owned several companies and a 24 percent stake in a Florida bank, began a three-year prison sentence in 1985 after embezzling more than $1.8 million from escrow accounts she managed for a Philadelphia insurance company.

Do Offenders Look Any Different from Non-Offenders?

No. In fact, many offenders are the nicest people. The government worker in Chicago, for example, who stole $900,000, was extremely well liked by his coworkers. After "his rich aunt died" and left him a sizable inheritance, he was known to take them out frequently for expensive lunches. He was friendly and very nice-looking. He was not known to wear black shirts or white ties and he shaved every day.

If Not Personal Appearance, What Then Do You Look For?   Ordinarily, there are few if any clues in a person's countenance that would indicate he or she is a white-collar criminal. If we were to recommend looking for anything, it would be a person's lifestyle. Many white-collar criminals cannot resist spending their ill-gotten gains, and few in our experience save their money. Although some spend conservatively, many others spend extravagantly. It's as if they are thinking "Now that I've taken the risks to successfully steal, I'm going to enjoy it!" The government worker in Chicago, for example, who stole over $900,000 suddenly became quite extravagant, attributing his good fortune to an inheritance. His sudden generosity to his fellow employees, investments in cars, condominiums, and athletic club memberships should have made people suspicious. However, it did not. People tend, perhaps subconsciously, to prefer to accept explanations such as inheritances or Las Vegas winnings. Many of those who stole fortunes in the savings and loan scandal were known to have spent fortunes on private yachts, jet aircraft, vacation homes, and the like.

The management accountant or auditor, however, cannot afford to be deluded by explanations of sudden good fortune to explain unusual spending patterns. A few years ago, an offender who embezzled $10 million was discovered only when an investigator visited his home—in connection with a government security clearance investigation—and immediately was suspicious of the man's ability to afford the home on his salary. There are many examples of instances in which perpetrators were suspected when they were observed wearing expensive suits and enjoying expensive nights out that it was known they could not afford on their salaries.

Are White-Collar Criminals Content To Steal Just Once?

No, not usually. This is perhaps the most useful knowledge that the fraud auditor or investigator can possess. If a management accountant or auditor can depend on any one characteristic of the white-collar criminal, it is that he or she is, or will be, a repeat offender. Many who have been caught have been found to have perpetrated their crimes over and over again. Accordingly, when any indicia of fraud are discovered, (1) the person (or persons) identified with those indicia should be determined, and (2) any further examination, audit or investigation should be extended to examine all facets of that person's (or persons') activities for an extended period of time. If more evidence of fraud is discovered, it will confirm the auditor's original findings and more than likely provide the evidence of multiple offenses needed to prove intent. If no additional evidence is discovered, the original findings of fraud indicia should be reexamined.

By the same token, evidence of additional crimes perpetrated by the same person can improve the case for the prosecution. Prosecutors are frequently concerned with the difficulty of convincing the court of a defendant's guilt when evidence is scant or when there is evidence of only one crime. Successful prosecution of a fraud case requires that the prosecutor clearly show the defendant's intent to commit fraud. Scant evidence often fails to do that. In addition, one instance of reasonably documented fraud is often not sufficient to convince a benevolent jury to convict a defendant with a reasonably clean record. Rather than due to a lack of desire, the lack of sufficient evidence is perhaps most frequently the reason that so many business victims of fraud choose not to prosecute, and that many judges tend to be lenient. Of course, prosecution of perpetrators is one of the best internal controls a business can employ and is always recommended, especially where fraud is material.

To illustrate exactly how important this is, we once had a case where a freight carrier had been "short" delivering stock to government agencies in the Chicago area, who he apparently knew to be lax in checking incoming freight. By short delivering, we mean if 20 items were to be delivered, he would only deliver 18, and the recipient would carelessly sign as having received 20. One night he loaded his truck with a large quantity of the stolen merchandise he had accumulated. While en route somewhere with it, he got stuck in a snowstorm and abandoned the truck. The Chicago police towed the truck away to clear the roadway and discovered the government merchandise. A government investigation disclosed the carrier's fraud and he was prosecuted in federal court. The carrier's guilt was never in doubt and he was found guilty and sentenced to a one year prison term. However, the federal district court judge who heard the case was very disturbed with the U.S. attorney's office for indicting and prosecuting the man for the one "apparent" violation. Although we can't be sure, it apparently entered into the light sentence that was given.

We have a simple theory about persons who would perpetrate fraud that will well serve the accountant wishing to write an examination program. It is "Only thieves commit fraud; and a thief is a thief is a thief." Simply said, it means that when evidence of a fraud is discovered, it is very likely that—if a suspect is truly guilty—there are more frauds and more evidence to be found. The accountant discovering the first evidence of fraud should immediately speculate upon a suspect and assume (being *extremely* discrete about it) that the suspect may be guilty of more than one fraud. Subsequent examinations should be focused in the suspect's area of responsibility. For example, if the man or woman has responsibility for leasing space (a fertile fraud area), that area should be examined in depth. All previous activities the suspect has been involved in, for a reasonable period of time, should be examined. If a suspect is in fact innocently involved, the accountant's failure to disclose additional evidence may clear him or her, and at least lessen the suspicions. If, however, additional evidence of fraud is disclosed, the perpetrator can be appropriately dealt with.

Many accountants have difficulty in focusing their reviews on real people, as we have recommended here. They like to keep anything involving criminal acts impersonal. For them we can only say "Have someone else do the work!" They will have difficulty bringing a suspected fraud case to conclusion. We made this recommendation in a lecture given to Sony Corporation middle managers one time, and when we recommended that once a suspect is identified, it is necessary to concentrate further review on him or her to either corroborate suspicions with additional evidence, or possibly clear the suspect when no additional evidence can be found. A very nice man in the audience said later "I would find it very difficult to suspect an *innocent* person, and target him or her to prove that they were perhaps guilty. I don't think I could do that!" He was not unusual. Many accountants, even auditors, enjoy their work when it involves impersonal number-crunching, but find it difficult to select individuals as the targets for evidentiary searches.

Regardless of who may be suspected as a fraud perpetrator, or how many perpetrators there are, the accountant is reminded that investigating fraud is a very personal thing. People commit fraud! It's always one or more persons acting with a criminal intent to covertly take possession of the property of another. Accordingly, in seeking evidence of fraud, unlike traditional auditing, it is essential to bear in mind that a person is always the object of any fraud-specific search. A favorite tactic of some fraud-specific auditors, without any specific leads to pursue, is to examine the transactions of persons who have opportunities for committing fraud, for the purpose of detecting indicia of fraud. If any indicia of fraud is detected, the auditor intensifies the examination, concentrating on transactions involving that person. The personal aspect of fraud auditing is most distasteful to many traditional auditors. Insufficient attention to the personal aspect of a discovered fraud is often the prime reason that white-collar thieves are not prosecuted, or not successfully prosecuted. The auditor or investigator simply does not make a sufficiently strong case against the perpetrator to enable successful prosecution. Without clear evidence of "who did what," there is often no case.

There is a short poem by Rudyard Kipling which should serve all management accountants well in attempting to collect evidence of a suspected fraud. It is worth memorizing.

> *I keep six honest serving men*
> *(They taught me all I knew);*
> *Their names are What and Why and When*
> *And How and Where and Who.*

Obviously, any proactive audit or investigative work which involves specific individuals should be conducted with the utmost discretion. The accountants or auditors involved should be careful to cover their work by giving the pretense of undertaking other work to mask their more limited objectives, and to preclude embarrassment to and slander of the innocent persons who are suspect, and to themselves.

ROLES IN FRAUD DETECTION

The management accountant, the independent auditor, the fraud-specific auditor, and the criminal investigator all have roles in fraud detection. All four groups have a responsibility in combating fraud. The role of the criminal investigator is easiest to describe. He or she generally functions in a reactive manner. Once there is reasonable evidence that fraud has occurred, the criminal investigator enters the scene and collects the evidence necessary to prove that fraud has occurred, and enables prosecution. A good investigator is, in many respects, a paralegal who is trained in criminology, in interviewing witnesses and suspects, and taking sworn testimony. Wherever their services are available, they should be brought into a fraud investigation when accountants and auditors are reasonably confident that they have discovered evidence of fraud.

Management accountants, independent public accountants, and internal auditors are in most respects similarly trained in basic accounting skills, differing primarily in experience acquired in the pursuit of the accounting specialty chosen by each—the management accountant concentrating in accounting and the internal auditors and independent public accountants in auditing. All have considerable skills to offer in combating fraud.

The management accountant's role in combating fraud normally entails the responsibility for internal control—the first line of defense against fraud. The management accountant also has the somewhat awesome responsibility of keeping the accounting system, and is the conduit for all accounting transactions—including those involving fraud. As the keeper, he or she has the opportunity for detecting fraudulent or suspicious transactions as they occur. Their responsibilities are particularly awesome in smaller entities where internal auditors are not employed.

There are at least three audit specialties which have responsibilities in combating fraud. There are public accountants (CPAs in public practice), internal auditors, and fraud-specific auditors. The CPAs in public practice limit their responsibilities for discovering fraud to financial statement balances which may be fraudulently distorted. They decline responsibility for detecting fraud that does not result in a misrepresentation of financial statement balances. Normally, internal auditors are considered to have the responsibility for discovering fraud, and do detect some fraud. However, they have been relatively ineffective. Most fraud that has been discovered has been found accidentally. With adequate fraud-specific training and sufficient audit resources devoted to proactive fraud-specific auditing, they could become significant factors in fraud control. The third category of auditors—fraud-specific auditors—are generally employed by a relatively few entities, are few in number, and as yet do not constitute a major threat to fraud. However, this group will undoubtedly grow in number, training and experience, and are the future's best hope for having a significant impact on fraud.

The Fraud-Specific Auditor

The fraud auditor is a sort of hybrid who is fundamentally a traditional auditor by education and experience, but who has been cross-trained in rules of evidence and investigative skills and sensitized to more readily recognizable fraud indicia. Using these combined skills, fraud auditors are uniquely equipped to function in a proactive mode, to search out and find fraud. It is always advisable that persons trained and experienced in fraud auditing be dedicated to, or substantially employed in fraud auditing, in order that they may continually sharpen their fraud-finding skills and enhance their sensitivity to the indicia of fraud.

Chapter 3

Principles and Standards for Fraud-Specific Examinations

THE PROBLEM

Entities wishing to be proactively examined for evidence of fraud, or wishing to establish the deterrent effect that such regular examinations convey, will find it impossible to engage a licensed firm—such as a certified public accounting company—to provide the service[4]. The basic reason is not because existing firms do not have the capability or inclination to provide such a professional service, but because there are no generally accepted principles and standards to guide their performance. Put differently, if they were to accept such engagements without examination standards, they would also be accepting an undefined liability for detecting fraud and risking subsequent litigation charging them with negligence for any failures to detect fraud. This situation is not new and has existed for well over 50 years.

The alternative for all entities has been, and still is, to either develop an in-house capability for proactive fraud-specific examinations, using accountants or internal auditors, or to do without the protection an independent examination would provide. Many entities believed that there was a third alternative—audits by independent public accountants—in the expectation that their audits provided adequate fraud protection. There was considerable justification for this belief. Independent public accountants have long proclaimed that they accepted responsibility to detect significant fraud, without articulating any limitations. Many entities took comfort in this assurance. They did not realize, however, that there were significant limitations. Although public accountants clearly stated that they accepted responsibility for detecting fraud, the fraud they were referring to applied only to the intentional misstatement of financial statement (i.e. balance sheet) balances. Whereas the public was thinking that the proclamations applied to all fraud, as declared, the public accountants were intending only part of all fraud. A clear case of miscommunication existed. As a result, if an entity happened to be the victim of a fraud which did not involve the intentional distortion of a reported financial statement balance—for example, as the result of an embezzlement—the entity involved would receive absolutely no fraud detection service as a result of an audit by an independent public accountant. Public accountants do not deny this, and have long maintained that:

> Reliance for the prevention of fraud should be placed principally upon an adequate accounting system with appropriate internal controls. ... If an object of an independent auditor's examination were the discovery of all fraud, he would have to extend his work to a point where its cost would be prohibitive. Even then he could not give assurances that all types of fraud had been detected, or that none existed, because items such as unrecorded transactions, forgeries, and collusive fraud would not necessarily be uncovered. Accordingly, it is generally recognized that good internal control and fidelity bonds provide protection more economically and effectively. ...
> —Codification of Auditing Standards and Procedures, Statement on Auditing Standards No. 1, the American Institute of Certified Public Accountants, November 1972.
>
> The ordinary examination incident to the issuance of an opinion respecting financial statements is not designed *and cannot be relied upon* to disclose defalcations and other similar irregularities. ... If an auditor were to attempt to discover defalcations and other similar irregularities, he would have to extend his work to a point where its cost would be prohibitive.
> —The American Institute of [Certified Public] Accountants, Statement on Auditing Procedure No. 1, *Extensions of Auditing Procedure,* 1939, as slightly modified in a codification of auditing pronouncements issued in 1951.

Note that the foregoing AI[CP]A quotations (which continue to remain AICPA policy) appear to conflict with other AICPA pronouncements that declare that public accountants are responsible for discovering fraud. Nevertheless, they are very clear in communicating that independent public accountants could not assure the discovery of all fraud—to do so would require prohibitive audit cost—and that there were more economical and effective alternatives. This clearly implies that public accountants would not search for asset-theft fraud at all.

We believe that this was a most regrettable decision. Although their statement is correct—they could never assure the detection of *all* fraud—

it is inconsistent with their standard audit policy regarding the examination of financial statement balances. Public accountants do not assure that financial statement balances are wholly correct, only that they are *materially* correct! Were they to perform fraud-specific examinations, in accordance with generally accepted fraud-specific auditing standards, it would be possible to detect all material fraud as well. Not all fraud, but all material fraud. By not searching for fraud, not only are many clients unaware that they have not received a fraud-specific examination, the clients have lost a powerful fraud deterrent. New fraud-specific auditing standards, which are put forward below, suggest including a caveat that a fraud-specific examination does not guarantee the discovery of all fraud.

Incidentally, the AICPA policy statements are quite correct in mentioning the cost of a fraud-specific examination. Any fraud-specific examination procedures which would be required would be totally in addition to the procedures required for an ordinary financial statement audit. For the most part, there would be little benefit derived from a traditional financial statement audit that would be useful to a fraud-specific examination, or vice-versa.

Many entities today are in extreme jeopardy from fraud because they do not have the in-house capability to perform fraud-specific proactive examinations, and they are unable to acquire the service elsewhere. Without a proactive examination service, they are deprived of a valuable internal control, known to deter fraud. Without it, fraud perpetrators have little to fear that they cannot foresee. The entities are literally deprived of an opportunity to defend themselves. Without the positive deterrent that "if you steal from me someone competent is going to come looking for you," there is an increased likelihood that entities so deprived will become fraud victims.

THE SOLUTION

The solution is not that difficult in theory, although it may be considerably more difficult in execution. What must be done is to write principles and standards for a fraud-specific examination practice which literally doesn't exist, but for which a need does exist. Further, without a professional community of professionals from which fraud-specific expertise can be drawn to (1) guide the development of the new practice, (2) draft the principles and standards for the practice of fraud-specific examinations, and (3) administer the practice. The problem is further complicated by the inability to determine who is competent to perform fraud-specific examinations and to draft standards, and who is not. The fact that there are many self-professed experts in fraud detection is not reassuring, and brings to mind the anecdote of the 13-year-old who thought his father was stupid. At 19 years of age, the child was amazed at how intelligent his father had become in the intervening six years. Fraud is very interesting in that the more you learn about it, the more you realize how little you know about it, or ever knew about it. Experience is very humbling.

If there is to be progress in conquering fraud, there is a need for a large organization with sufficient human resources, suitable experience to respond to issues, the conservatism to not rush to judgment, and a vested interest in getting the job done. We see that exact organization in the American Institute of Certified Public Accountants (AICPA).

The AICPA is ideally constituted to take on the additional responsibility:

- Over 110 years young, it is an organization of 330,000 members, all of whom have demonstrated a required level of technical excellence in accounting matters. The people making up their membership are ideally suited to become fraud-specific auditors, particularly if Elbert Hubbard's description is correct in observing that:

    "The typical auditor is a man just past middle age, spare, wrinkled, intelligent, cold, passive, noncommital, with eyes like a codfish, polite in contact, but at the same time unresponsive, calm, and damnably composed as a concrete post or a plaster of paris cast; a human petrification with a heart of feldspar and without the charm of a friendly germ, minus bowels, passion, or a sense of humor. Happily, they never reproduce and all of them finally go to Hell."

- The AICPA has the experience and knowledge to administer the development and publication of fraud-specific auditing principles and standards.

- AICPA Member firms would undoubtedly be major beneficiaries of a solution, and by many accountants are ready, willing, and able to engage in proactive fraud-specific examinations—offering a lucrative and comprehensive service that past audits lacked.

- It can be said that public accountants have a vested interest and a clear responsibility to provide what their clients already expect they are receiving, and to clearly advise their clients, in explicit language, the extent to which they are at risk from fraud, and the shortcomings in the service provided under existing audit standards.

- In our lecture experience, which has included many CPAs, we found many of them totally in agreement with the contents of this chapter, very concerned with their legal liability for not performing proactive fraud-specific examinations, and ready and willing to welcome change.

INCEPTION OF AUDITING STANDARDS FOR
INDEPENDENT PUBLIC ACCOUNTANTS

From the time an auditor (CPA) issued his first certification of a client's financial position in 1903, through 1938, there was little in the way of audit standards to guide the auditor's practice. An auditor simply provided his best judgment. What began the process of audit standard setting, at a relatively rapid pace, was the discovery of a massive fraud involving a non-existent inventory that had apparently existed for years before being discovered. The auditor, in certifying the correctness of certain assets, had failed to verify them. In so doing, he had failed to discover that $10 million of inventory and $9 million of receivables were fictitious. The case was the infamous McKesson & Robbins case, and it occurred in 1937. At the time, existing auditing standards suggested that confirmation of receivables and inventories was "desirable" but was not "required." Not long after that, the American Institute of (Certified Public) Accountants responded by preparing and publishing Statement on Auditing Procedure (SAP) No. 1, requiring that receivables will be "confirmed" and inventories will be "observed".

In 1947, the Institute issued nine Statements of Auditing Standards (SAS), supplemented by another a short time later. These statements, supplemented many times to provide further guidance, continue to the present, and serve to guide many thousands of independent public accountants as to what constitutes generally accepted procedure. Although all are useful guides to independent accountants in the performance of their reviews, a most important purpose the standards serve is that the auditor operating "in accordance with published standards" is following procedures that are generally accepted by his peers. Accordingly, for the most part, any criticism that an auditor was negligent, must articulate how the auditor failed to abide by the published standards. It is this sort of audit standards that must be conceived and published to guide the firms that will engage in proactive fraud-specific examinations of client entities.

PRINCIPLES AND STANDARDS TO GUIDE THE PRACTICE OF
PROACTIVE FRAUD-SPECIFIC EXAMINATIONS

Given the immensity and "boot-strings" nature of the task of starting a fraud-specific auditing practice, the effort to design acceptable principles and standards will ultimately involve a lengthy process, which will continue as long as fraud-specific examinations are practiced—which can be expected to be a long, long time. There will always be plenty of perpetrators to go around. Conceivably, however, an initial package of principles and standards should be possible, which would enable the practice to go forward and to be supplemented from time-to-time on the basis of experience.

The logical place to begin is with the principles which will guide the subsequent design of standards. Accordingly, practitioners must consider what they hope to accomplish in establishing examination standards. At the very least, it would appear that the following concerns must be addressed:

- *Practitioners will provide NO assurances that they will discover fraud.* Practitioners must advise clients that there are no guarantees that material fraud will be discovered. However, clients may specify the magnitude of the search effort, and the chances of detecting fraud are directly relative to the time expended.

- *Practitioners will assure clients that their examinations will be conducted in accordance with "generally accepted principles and standards, copies of which will be provided to prospective clients."*

- *Fees will be based upon the magnitude of the search effort that the client specifies.* Independent public accountants normally set fees roughly based upon the number of hours of examination required to certify the condition of the client's financial statements. Since no certification can be considered in a fraud-specific audit, fees should be based roughly upon how much work an entity wishes to have a practitioner do to expertly comb the operations for the purpose of detecting indicia of fraud. A client may be informed as to the level of review intensity that will result from different fees, together with the probabilities of detecting fraud in each. An entity may choose to spend a stipulated amount of money, $10,000, $50,000, $100,000, or more "worth" of expert work performed. In return the entity is assured that whatever is spent, the sum will be invested in obtaining the most search value for the amount selected. Regardless, the fraud examiner's presence would definitely be observed and would represent a clear risk for would-be perpetrators in the organization.

  Entities considering how much to spend on proactive fraud-specific examinations must realize that fraud can easily take one to two percent of an entity's revenues without being noticed and occasionally much more. For an entity to spend .5 percent of their gross revenues on fraud-specific examinations should be the minimum amount considered.

- *Practitioners will agree to extend their service beyond the proactive review stage when their work has discovered bona fide evidence of fraud—at additional fees, to be negotiated.*

- *Practitioners will avoid any conflicts of interest or apparent conflicts of interest.*
- *Practitioners will maintain absolute confidentiality over all proactive fraud-specific audit activities.*
- *Practitioners employ or engage audit personnel specially trained and experienced in fraud-specific examinations and possessing experience compatible with the client's operating specialties.*
- *Practitioners will agree to remain available to participate in client prosecution of suspected perpetrators.*

ONE READER'S COMMENT

In response to a request for reader comments included in our original book, of which this text is a substantial revision, one reader's response in 1992 was particularly noteworthy and portions are excerpted below. Be advised that we hold all reader comments to be confidential, particularly where they may be potentially embarrassing to the writer. Accordingly, the writer's name and organization are not disclosed, other than to say that the writer is a partner in a 1999 Big 5 public accounting firm:

> ". . . I found your book interesting and hold many of your perceptions of external auditors. I would like to think that as a profession, the CPA could be compared to a cockroach, but time has proven that we aren't nearly so adaptable. Instead, we are about to become the dinosaurs of the 90s and we have no one to blame but ourselves. . . . I couldn't agree more that public accountants should formally accept a broader role in detecting fraud. Our colleges and universities should require accounting majors to take courses in criminology and investigation. . . .
>
> Many of our clients do not take fraud seriously. Management doesn't like fraud but it is not willing to pay the price to look for it. The cost of finding it outweighs the benefits derived from stopping it or preventing it. Even when management sets up an organizational structure for controlling fraud, more often than not there is a problem within that organization as to who has the responsibility of detecting it—security or internal audit. Each thinks it is the other's responsibility. Therefore it doesn't get done. A classic example of communication problems."

This person's comments are very typical of those offered by the many practicing CPAs we have spoken with throughout the United States during our lectures on fraud protection. They reveal a significant discontent by CPAs—this one a Big 5 firm partner—with the limitations imposed by the AICPA on their efforts to detect fraud. We generally agree with this person's comments. However, if you read the comments closely, the philosophy that limits CPA participation in fraud detection becomes very apparent.

The CPA tends to look at any practice of fraud detection as a failure if it does not detect all material fraud. In fact, any attempt to detect all material fraud would be foolhardy, and extremely expensive. It is understandable that management would not wish to pay the cost of finding it. However, this does not mean that a fraud-specific proactive audit by a CPA would have to be either expensive or detect all fraud. Rather, a nominal expenditure for a CPA examination, performed in accordance with generally accepted examination standards, would produce benefits to management far exceeding the alternative of not proactively examining their organizations at all. Management must be cultivated to understand that spending money for fraud-specific proactive auditing is much like buying fire insurance. The measure of whether or not fire insurance is worthwhile is not found in whether or not there is a fire. The CPA's examination would be likely to detect fraud if it were there. Regardless, the fraud-specific CPAs audit would establish a powerful deterrent to fraud that is not there now!

Chapter 4

Classifying Fraud for Improved Detection

THE IMPORTANCE OF CLASSIFYING FRAUD FOR DETECTION

To proactively search for fraud is to search for symptoms of fraud. Fraud rarely, if indeed ever, is discovered with all of its details intact, neatly wrapped in a package ready for prosecution. Rather, it is usually found in bits and pieces of evidence, which constitute a case of fraud when assembled. Usually, the most difficult aspect of fraud detection is discovering that bit or piece of evidence sufficient to generate the suspicion that this may be fraud. Once that is done, further case development—if it develops at all—is usually a matter of forensic auditing. With the lead provided by the proactive examination, it is a matter of unearthing and assembling whatever additional evidence may be needed to prove and prosecute the case discovered.

The following pages are devoted to a listing and explanation of some of the more common varieties of fraud which should be included in the accountant's agenda for periodic proactive fraud examinations. For each, we have attempted to provide expanded definitions, illustrations, and detection tips that accountants can readily apply. Readers should understand that the material presented herein is only a beginning to the art of detecting fraud conditions that are so pervasive, immeasurable, and multifaceted that there are no masters of the art. Regardless, the fundamentals advocated here will be applicable in the most difficult of fraud cases.

Training in detecting more advanced fraud is not as easily accomplished given the limitations of this text. It requires considerably more preparation, verbal instruction, and involvement in lengthy case studies which can more realistically simulate a real world environment. Even then, however, it is difficult to simulate real-world difficulty with a case study, if for no

other reason than that the student expects a case study to involve fraud
and looks for evidence of fraud the moment he or she begins to read it.
Real-world simulation would require many cases that don't involve fraud
which the student would have to pour through to learn which cases were
less likely to involve fraud and to utilize their time to maximum advantage.
This training is best accomplished in fraud workshops and through on-
the-job training.

The later part of this text will be devoted to case studies drawn from
real-world experiences that are within the context of the classifications
presented in the following pages. The names given to the fraud classifications that appear in the pages which follow were chosen for reference
purposes because we are not aware that anyone has previously classified
fraud in this manner—or named the classifications. Hence, the names may
or may not be generally recognized.

FRAUD DETECTION AND THE ART OF FISHING

It is useful to compare the art of fraud detection to the art of fishing
because the fundamental concepts are very similar. For example, expert
fishermen never simply go fishing for fish. Rather, they first decide what
type of fish they have a taste for. Next, they decide the how, with what
equipment, and where they will expertly search for that type of fish and
that type alone. If they have a taste for brook trout, they will specifically
fish for brook trout. They will require special gear, must look in a place
likely to have brook trout in it, and must fish at only certain times of the
day when the fish are likely to be feeding. Everything the trout fisherman
does is done to expertly fine tune the chances of catching this very elusive
fish—and even then he or she frequently does not catch any, even though
it is certain they lurk below the surface of the stream!

Accordingly, when a fraud auditor decides to search for fraud without
having a specific game plan in mind, he or she is not likely to be very
successful. Like the fisherman whose hook may be dangling inches away
from his quarry's mouth, the fish won't even nibble on it if it doesn't like
what's on the hook. Similarly, the accountant may actually have evidence
of fraud in his hands and never recognize that it is indicia of fraud, unless
he or she is looking for that exact type of evidence. The accountant's
"fish," when searching for fraud are the fraud classifications, particularly
the common types of fraud described in the later part of this chapter. As
the fisherman chooses to fish for a specific type of fish, the accountant
must select a type of fraud to search for—perhaps defective deliveries—

applying the techniques necessary to detect the type of fraud chosen as the subject of the search. If he or she doesn't, the fraud-finding effectiveness will be minimal.

WHAT DOES FRAUD LOOK LIKE WHEN FIRST DETECTED?

This is probably as good a place as any to talk about exactly what most fraud looks like before the auditors, investigators, and prosecutors have had an opportunity to assemble and refine the evidence. The fraud cases that are prosecuted, and therefore visible to most people, are usually neatly packaged and easily recognized as a case of fraud. The components are all in place—a suspect is identified, the many relevant details of the crime are articulately described, and sometimes the suspect has confessed—and a prosecutor may be spilling out the carefully rehearsed details to a jury. For the rookie, this is what they tend to look for when they search for evidence of fraud—the completed case.

This is, however, rarely the way a proactively discovered fraud case presents itself. Rather, most cases begin with the discovery of a few shreds of evidence that bear little if any resemblance to the cases which reach the courtrooms. In a way, finding and developing a case of fraud is much like working a jigsaw puzzle—except it is more difficult. If you were to find a piece of a jigsaw puzzle laying on a rug, you would know immediately that it is from a jigsaw puzzle and you would know there are more pieces somewhere to be found. An additional advantage in working a jigsaw puzzle is that a picture is usually provided of what the assembled puzzle will look like.

When finding a piece of evidence from a case of fraud, particularly when you may not be looking for fraud, you are not very likely to immediately recognize it as indicia of fraud! You may be processing an accounts payable invoice for supplies that were recently purchased and it may momentarily impress you that the unit prices on the invoice appear high, which may in fact be indicia of a kickback. However, you are likely to put it out of your mind and continue processing the accounts payable since you are not looking for evidence of kickbacks.

Assuming that the higher unit prices that attracted your attention were evidence of a kickback, this is how a kickback fraud case first appears to a trained and sensitized auditor. If the auditor is looking for kickbacks, he or she will note the evidence and continue to collect and assemble more evidence, like the jigsaw puzzle, until a clear picture emerges. In proactively searching for fraud, the auditor must imagine the picture, based upon the type of fraud he or she is looking for, then go looking for the pieces—which may not exist to be discovered. Of course, the advantage in working a case of fraud is that you don't have to put together all the pieces, only enough to convince a jury of the suspected perpetrator's guilt.

CLASSIFICATIONS OF FRAUD

There are undoubtedly many ways in which fraud can be grouped or regrouped, all of which are useful in pursuing proactive detection efforts. Here are just a few which will be discussed in the following paragraphs:

- Fraud involving multiple payments to the same payee
- Fraud involving multiple payees for the same product or service
- Fraud involving shell payments
- Fraud involving defective delivery
- Fraud involving rigged advertised contracts
- Fraud involving defective pricing
- Fraud involving conspiracy
- Fraud involving pseudo-conspiracy
- Fraud involving kickbacks
- Fraud involving unbalanced contracts or purchase orders
- Non-repeating fraud
- Repeating fraud
- Fraud on the books involving an entire transaction
- Fraud on the books obscured by a legitimate transaction
- Fraud which is not on the books

Fraud Involving Multiple Payments to the Same Payee

This is probably one of the oldest and simplest fraud types. It is easily accomplished and is practiced by many perpetrators having little capability or opportunity for anything else. Accountants must be alert to the possibility of its occurrence. Basically, it involves paying a vendor's legitimate invoice two or more times. The additional payments are recovered by the perpetrator(s) and cashed. Usually the payment amounts are relatively small and the payer never notices the duplicate payments. Small businesses often find it difficult to understand how the payment of an invoice can be paid more than once. However, where the business is large enough that transaction processing is conducted on a relatively impersonal basis, multiple payments can occur very easily. In fact, most accountants can recall the inadvertent payment of the same invoice more than once, which were discovered only when honest vendors returned the extra payment checks.

In its simplest form, the perpetrator simply submits the same vendor's invoice for payment more than once. In past years, the perpetrator may have notified the vendors that their invoices had been lost and requested a new copy. However, with modern color printers, it is a simple matter to reproduce copies of all necessary documentation needed to effect payment and submit them into the payment process. The fraud usually involves collusion within the victim's office and may involve collusion with someone in the payee's office. It may not require collusion at all, depending upon the victim's internal control system and the perpetrator's opportunities for generating the fraud. The extra payments are intercepted and cashed. Such fraud is frequently missed by auditors who do not design search procedures specifically suited to the detection of multiple payments.

If an accountant performs a traditional test of transactions during a conventional examination and happens to select one of the multiple transactions (it is highly unlikely he would be so fortunate as to select two or more of them at random), he or she will be likely to examine all the underlying documents (requisitions, purchase orders, receiving reports), and find that they are all in order, they are all originals, all bear the required signatures, and so forth. After examining receiving reports that attest to the actual receipt of the product or service that has been paid for, the accountant is likely to pass the transaction, because he or she is not testing to see if there are two or more identical invoices. If he or she happens to select any one of the multiple payments, the examination will disclose that everything is okay. Relatively speaking, the difficulty of discovering multiple payment fraud is ranked 1 on a scale of 1 to 10, 1 being easy and 10 being difficult. Each individual act of this fraud is distinct and on the books just sitting there waiting to be found.

Detection. This is likely if the searcher is looking for two or more identical payments to the same vendor. Accordingly, when searching for duplicate payments, it is useful to make a larger selection of payments to the same vendor and to review payments to the same vendor looking for identical amounts. A computer-assisted review of all payments to all vendors searching for identical amounts is also very useful and is an automatic internal control feature that can be incorporated into every payment processing system, which will continuously review all new payments for the identical characteristic amount. Identical payments are not necessarily fraudulent, but are worth a second look.

Fraud Involving Multiple Payees for the Same Product or Service

This type of fraud is related to duplicate payment fraud. There is, however, a sophistication that makes the detection process more difficult. In multiple payee fraud, only one of the payees is entitled to payment. The others are bogus. The contractor or vendor who legitimately performs a service or delivers a product to a customer, is properly paid. Subsequently, a different contractor, vendor, or a fictitious contractor or vendor, is paid for the identical project or product delivery. The subsequent payment(s) is fraudulent.

For example, $9,000 is paid to the Bates Company for remodeling a portion of Building A. There is no fraud involved at this point. Subsequently, the perpetrator initiates the necessary paperwork for the "Acme Company" to be paid $8,900 for the identical remodeling project. Acme has done no work to earn the payment.

A customary audit would not be likely to discover this fraud. An examination of all documentation would find it to be impeccable. Even a visit to the project site or an examination of the property records would confirm that the project or product was delivered as claimed. What is there to question?

Detection. Detecting this type of fraud is best effected by applying search procedures designed to detect multiple payee fraud. The accountant looking for multiple payee fraud should be sensitive to the name of. the firm paid to deliver the work being examined. For example, should the examination begin with the selection of a payment to the Acme company to remodel Building A, the auditor should focus upon proving that it was Acme who did the work. A visit to the site of the remodeling is often productive. The examiner should visit the site independently of anyone involved in the acquisition process who might possibly be involved in the fraud. When at the site, he or she asks entity employees who work in the area relevant details about the work. Who did it? When was it done? Had they worked there before?, and similar questions eliciting as many details as possible. If the interrogation is done properly and the Acme company did not do the work, there will be discrepancies in the answers. Even though the details are indicated on the transaction paperwork, the examiner should attempt to independently determine information such as, for example, the name of the contractor, the names of key contractor employees, the date of completion, and the entity's site supervisor. Don't be overly concerned with any failures to get full disclosure. Proactive fraud-specific examinations are a very imprecise business requiring conversation, intuition, and creativity, rather than bean counting.

Determine the extent of the entity's information systems. If property records are maintained, a review of the work records for the buildings may reveal clues. If the item being reviewed is a product, the storage site for the product should be visited. Actually examine the cartons containing the material to determine the shipper. Shipping vendors' names and addresses are often clearly labeled on the carton or other packing.

Incidentally, a multiple payee fraud is also an example of a distinct on the books fraud, a one-time fraud, and one which usually involves collusion. The Acme Company, if it is not fictitious, is likely to involve a conspirator at the entity.

Fraud Involving Shell Payments

Shell payment fraud involves a completely documented purchase for a fictitious product, service, or project. All the documentation is phony. The project simply does not exist; however, verification may be difficult if the perpetrator is clever.

Shell fraud may involve, for example, a $4,985 payment to the Brown Company for installing a dedicated 220 volt electric service line to the paint shop. However, the new electric line was never installed! Just as for legitimate payments, all the paperwork appears impeccable. Prescribed requisitions and purchase orders are complete and appear to be properly authorized. Signed receiving reports document that the item(s) ordered were received and invoices appear to be properly approved.

Detection. When examining payment transactions for shell fraud, the accountant or auditor must seek to determine if the item being purchased was actually delivered. Ordinarily, this is an easy task. If it involves a renovation or physical alteration to real property, the work site is visited and the work confirmed by sight inspection. If it involves the purchase of personal property, the examiner must locate the property and assure that it was purchased by the payment being examined. However, verification is not usually that easy. A perpetrator engaging in shell fraud will not want to make inspection easy and will tend to select a project that is not easily verified. Perhaps he will select a consumable product that is not likely to exist for verification too long after delivery. Or he or she may select a remodeling project which is not easily inspected.

The question that the accountant or auditor examining a transaction must ask to determine if shell fraud has occurred is, "Is it worth the trouble and expense I would have to go through to verify that the item purchased was actually delivered? How much destructive testing, if necessary, is it worth to verify a delivery? The accountant or auditor must always bear in mind that his or her examination at this stage involves a randomly selected transaction. There is no reason to suspect fraud. Statistically speaking, fraud is probably not involved. If it means having a plastered wall opened—and later repaired—to observe that new electric wires were actually installed, what is the answer? This is not as easily answered. A yes or no answer here would probably have to depend upon the nature of any mitigating circumstances. Conversation may be an acceptable substitute here for visual inspection. For the new electric line service discussed in the foregoing example, it is probably worth investing extra time looking into the need for the new electric line before considering breaking into the walls. Speak with paint shop employees, for example, to determine if the new line was really needed. Ask who requested the new line. Ask if the new line solved their problems. If all the answers are positive, the examiner can safely assume that a new line was installed without actually physically inspecting it. Obviously, if an examiner thoroughly checked everything out, he or she would not get much done and still would probably not find any fraud. The proactive fraud examiner can only use his or her judgment in performing a variety of procedures in the hope of getting lucky. Regardless of the examiner's findings, his or her examination and line of questioning will not go unnoticed by the undiscovered perpetrator. Very likely, any examination will be regarded as a risk by a perpetrator and produce a deterrent effect on future frauds.

One fraud auditor once told us about a $400,000 payment that he suspected may have involved shell fraud. It involved alterations to a medical building that was subsequently demolished to make way for a new building. He pointed out that he had no way of physically verifying that the work had been done. We discussed alternative verification methods, including interviewing the contractors that did the work as well as others who may have been involved. This sort of circumstance arises from time to time in the life of a fraud examiner and when it does, all sorts of bells go off at once. The obvious question it raises is "Why would anyone invest $400,000 in renovations to a building that was to be demolished to make way for a new building?" We never learned what ever happened as a result of his observation.

In another case, previously discussed, an office supply broker participated in a shell fraud with office supply store managers. He would "sell" ball-point pens to the store managers which were never

Continues

> *Continued*
>
> intended to be delivered, but send an invoice for their costs. The store managers would formally order the pens, and certify that they were delivered, creating all the documentation needed to satisfy internal control requirements and assure payment. These were shell payment frauds. As with many frauds, discovery frequently depends on the auditor's satisfactory determination that the goods or services were in fact delivered.

Fraud Involving Defective Delivery

Defective delivery fraud is very commonly practiced and all accountants are advised to watch for it. It usually involves the undisclosed delivery to the victim of fewer products or services or less quality of product than was ordered and paid for. The defective delivery can involve literally anything. Defective delivery fraud almost always involves conspiracy between a perpetrator, such as a supplier or contractor, and an employee of the victim who is able to certify that the delivery is in accordance with purchase order or contractual requirements, when it is not.

For example, the victim may order 5,000 widgets and only receive 4,500. The person checking the receipt of the widgets signs for the receipt of 5,000 widgets, knowing that only 4,500 were delivered. Of course, there is the possibility that the employee is merely negligent. The motor carrier, in a case such as this, is probably the co-conspirator, who drops off 500 of the widgets before arriving at the victim's plant, where only 4,500 are delivered. Most likely, the freight carrier and the victim's receiving employee have conspired to steal widgets. The victim's perpetual inventory records are updated to reflect that 5,000 widgets were received. No shortage is discovered until a physical inventory count is made, perhaps months later. When disclosed, attention will normally focus upon the question, "How did the merchandise get out of the warehouse?" In fact, it was never in the warehouse.

Another example that happens even more frequently is the delivery of substandard materials. A paving contractor agrees to pave a parking area with four inches of paving material, but only delivers three inches of material. A roofing contractor agrees to seal a warehouse roof with a premium rubberized roof sheeting, but installs a cheaper substitute instead. A painting contractor agrees to use a premium grade of paint but uses a cheaper grade, or agrees to apply two coats of paint but applies only one coat. A consultant agrees to provide 1,000 hours of senior engineer time at the going rate for senior engineers, but only provides intermediate engineers without reducing the billing.

The intentional delivery of any services or supplies of a lower number than those ordered or otherwise contracted for, or that are inferior in any way, without disclosing that fact to the buyer and offering an appropriately reduced price, is fraud.

Detection. Defective delivery fraud requires that the examiner inspect the product or service delivered to determine whether it is the exact material ordered and whether it has been delivered exactly as ordered. An accountant or auditor examiner may make the initial observations of materials delivered if he or she has sufficient experience to make an initial determination. This may require taking samples of materials used. However, if the examiner has suspicions that defective materials or other delivery is involved, he or she *must* consider having them tested by a qualified laboratory to obtain the expert testimony needed to properly support subsequent litigated claims that may be levied against the contractor delivering the inferior materials, or any possible prosecution for fraud.

Many defective deliveries are not possible to verify when a contract is completed. Contractual agreements, for example, which call for time to be spent by computer experts, architects, engineers, or lawyers, are difficult or impossible to verify. However, fraud does occur frequently in such contracts. The government once prosecuted a large computer software company for billing hours worked by various senior, intermediate, and junior programmers. Although a contract had been written agreeing to specified hourly rates for each experience level of programmer, the contractor cheated by billing time spent by juniors as intermediate time, and intermediate time as senior time. If this were to happen to a private entity, there is little they could do to verify the correctness of the billing. However, the government reserves the right to audit the records of all contractors it does business with. A very handy advantage. In this instance, an audit was performed and disclosed the fraud. In instances where verification would be difficult, or impossible, we would recommend that entities—in need of services or other deliveries impossible to verify—do not expose themselves to fraudulent defective deliveries. Entities should recognize that this sort of situation is likely to occur and avoid "time and material" type reimbursable contracts. Rather, attempt to negotiate, or advertise for, a fixed price contract, with verifiable completion objectives. Many contractors are reluctant to contract on this basis, where their expenditures for time and materials are uncertain, and may estimate high to cover unexpected contingencies. Accordingly, estimated contract amounts may be a bit pricey. However, it often is a choice of this, or the entity putting itself at the mercy of a contractor.

Fraud Involving Rigged Advertised Contracts

The universal practice of advertising large contracts is done in the expectation that competition will provide the best price, value, and protection for items acquired. Considering that the opportunity to bid on a contract is open to many vendors and contractors and that the price is fixed, advocates of advertised competitive contracts tend to ask "What could possibly go wrong?" In this climate, a rather cavalier attitude prevails which holds that there is no need to be concerned with fraud when using this contracting mechanism. Competitively advertised contracts are almost universally recommended as active internal controls against fraud. Most entities, large and small, use them. We believe, however, that the concept of advertising contracts was surely conceived in a world we don't live in. One in which everyone is naive, honest, and believes in the Easter Bunny.

Advertising contract awards does not necessarily result automatically in good procurement, nor is it a effective fraud-specific internal control. We recommend that advertised contracts be used with discretion, and only in *selected* circumstances. The competitive process tends to supplant the best judgement of management, substituting instead, the cunning of the fraud perpetrator.

The better course of action—one which actually reduces exposure to fraud—is for an entity to simply *trust* its management to select a reputable contractor and to negotiate contract terms. Contrary to popular belief, little if anything is gained by advertising. Even though an entity may feel it has no assurance of receiving the best price when sole sourcing is used, it is likely to provide a better price vs. value ratio than advertised competitive contracting. Who hasn't heard the anecdote about the two astronauts blasting off into outer space? One leans over and says to the other, "Does it comfort you to know that all the parts manufactured for this space vehicle were low bidders?"

For the many readers who will undoubtedly be surprised by our recommendation, let us emphasize that we are not saying that allowing management to sole source large contracts is a good idea but the alternative of competitively advertising contracts is worse. We might add that we speak with the advantage of having had top management experience. We also recommend that internal auditors perform fraud-specific examinations of all negotiated contracts.

Although many entities also believe that competitively advertised contracts protect them from fraud, the reverse is probably true. To dwell on this notion for a few moments, consider that—for the purposes of these comments—there are two categories of management, the honest and the dishonest. We believe that most managers are in the honest category. For them, an entity that requires contracts to be advertised in effect deprives the entity of the experienced judgement of these talented managers in the procurement process. For those managers who are not honest, the competitive process does little or anything to suppress their criminal inclinations—only to shield them.

For those who would say that advertising contracts also obtains the best price, we can only say that we respectively disagree, adding that it is usually true that "you get what you pay for." What an entity often gets when they advertise is a contractor who is shaving his or her cost margins and profits razor thin, jeopardizing his or her own longevity in the process, and forcing him or herself to cut corners everywhere. When forced, this contractor will cheat. It may surprise many people that there are more ways to cheat involving advertised contracts than there are in sole source contracts. For example, advertised contracts tend to be scrutinized less intensively than sole source contracts. Also, in many instances, you do not deal with the most reputable contractors. When advertising, the entity is usually compelled to select the lowest qualified bidder. This bidder may not be the entity's most reputable choice. For example, there are many instances where the government has been compelled to contract with firms that either had been convicted of defrauding them in the past, or were strongly suspected of fraud.

How They Are Rigged.   There are many ways to rig a contract to defeat the competitive process and commit fraud. Common to most rigged contracts are these features:

- Most are large contracts involving large sums of money. Hence, they tend to be advertised to allow the competitive process identify who the successful contractor shall be and the lowest possible price.
- The contracts are awarded to the low bidders, supposedly assuring the entity that there is no fraud or favoritism in the contracts. The low price submitted determines the winning contractor—nothing else!
- The low bidders, nevertheless, are crooks. In competing, they do whatever is necessary to offer the lowest initial bid—usually to the extent of submitting a loss price, if that's what it takes—to be awarded the contract. Offering the lowest bid is not a problem for them because

the crook does not need to include a profit in the price proposed. He will steal his profit later. The only objective is to get the contract award!

- The rigged contract is always changed at least once subsequent to the award, allowing the contractor the opportunity to recover any profits lost in the bidding process—and usually much more.

It is not possible to describe the many ways that a contract can be rigged. One will be described below, however, to illustrate how it can be done. Be advised, however, that anytime a contract is changed, for whatever reason, the change provides the contractor the opportunity to get the contract's price changed and to recover handsome profits sacrificed in the bidding process.

For those readers who may be thinking "But what if the contract is not changed? Does the contractor lose the opportunity to recover lost profits?" Good question! Be assured that the contract will be changed and the contractor will get the opportunity. A rigged contract always has a conspirator of one kind or another in the "woodpile" who assures that the contract will be changed. The conspirator either engineers the pre-contract circumstances which will require a post-award change, or is sufficiently influential that he or she can cause a change after the award. We cannot stress strongly enough that contract changes are the key to a rigged contract.

Accordingly, to entities wishing to avoid contract rigging fraud we recommend: Don't change your contracts. After signing, adopt a "no changes" policy. Some entities, fearful of contract rigging fraud, follow this policy religiously. However, even then, they will find that changes arise which are absolutely necessary. We recall one instance where a major building was advertised and a contractor selected. After the contract had been awarded, it was discovered that significant electrical system requirements had been inadvertently omitted from the bid specification packages mailed to bidding contractors.

Entities considering the adoption of a strict "no-changes" policy for the construction of real property must state this provision in their invitations for bid. It warns architects and builders that they will be responsible for correcting any flaws or omissions in the building specifications or contract. The contract, once signed, will require something to the effect that the entity will not be involved again until it is handed the keys to the front door of a satisfactorily completed building. Be warned, however, that although this policy protects a contracting entity from unexpected design changes, it also comes at an increased price to the entity. Any architect or builder assuming this risk can be expected to increase the price he or she proposes.

Detection Tip: Difficult!   For most of the classifications of fraud discussed in this text we offer tips for fraud-specific audits or examinations. None will be offered for contract rigging fraud because there is no way to detect and prosecute it. It is easy to discover instances where the fraud is suspected, and you may be convinced that the contract has been rigged. However, proof is very difficult to come by. The contracts involved will usually have been properly advertised, and the contractors properly selected. If the contracting entity did not change the contracts, the contractors would be legally required to perform at whatever low price he or she had bid, regardless of the profit. Accordingly, it is really an entity's responsibility when they choose to change a contract, not the contractor's, even though they may have been tricked into doing so. To prove fraud, it must be proven that an insider and the contractor had conspired to change the contract before it was awarded. This is very difficult to do.

The primary defense against rigged contracts is to stop them from happening in the first place! Don't allow changes, or be extremely careful in allowing—and particularly in pricing—changes. This is about the only practical protection we can advise. In the event contract rigging fraud is suspected, take care to identify those individuals who may have been instrumental in allowing it to happen. This information may be useful in preventing a recurrence.

The Rigged Contract.   A rigged contract is quite simple and almost always includes a conspirator on the inside. It could very well happen in this manner:

Company A decides to build a warehouse, estimated to cost around $1,000,000. An architect is engaged to design a suitable warehouse to meet Company A's needs. The architect's specifications are mailed to all interested contractors and cost proposals are requested. When the bids are received, Contractor Zee is the low bidder and is awarded the contract to construct the building. After construction is substantially under way, it is discovered that the entrances are not wide or high enough to admit the new forklifts that Company A has ordered. The architect's specifications are changed to reflect the new larger entrances required, and Contract Change Order Number 1 is issued to require that Contractor Zee comply. It also provides that he or she will be entitled to recover all costs occasioned by Change Order Number 1.

Continues

Continued

When the warehouse is completed the contractor submits the statement shown in Exhibit 4.1.

Exhibit 4.1 Sample Contractor Statement

CONTRACTOR ZEE

Contract Bid Price:	$1,000,000
Contract Change Order No. 1	
Cost of removal of doors and walls required by original contract	45,000
Cost of new doors and new materials	115,000
Cost of installation of doors and new materials	75,000
Overhead and profit on work required by Change Order No. 1	32,000
TOTAL	$1,267,000

A proactive examination of the case illustrated would raise the suspicions of an experienced fraud-specific auditor; however, it would not be likely to disclose any evidence of fraud. Please note that the original contract was advertised and Contractor Zee submitted the low bid to win the contract award. Both actions are above reproach. Although it is a bit suspicious that the entity or architect would have erred in designing the warehouse entrances, the designs were adequate to accommodate Company A's existing equipment. Errors do happen!

This a hypothetical illustration, designed to portray a very simple case of contract rigging fraud. The fraud was planned prior to the time the architect designed the warehouse. The architect was not told of the new forklifts required to use the building and designed the entrances to standard sizes. The plant superintendent, Able Goodfellow, however, was aware of the specifications of the new forklifts, but remained silent when the need for the new warehouse was being discussed. Goodfellow conspired with Contractor Zee. Informed as to the certainty that the entrance sizes would be changed, Zee submitted a bid of $1,000,000 for the warehouse, even though he knew he could not build it to award specifications for that price.

Once awarded the contract, Zee proceeded with construction anticipating that Change Order No. 1 would be issued. That is, he proceeded to construct the building in such a manner as to minimize the materials purchased and the work that would be required to effect the change.

However, when presenting his statement of costs at contract end, he will maximize the scrap costs and the rework that had to be done to tear out the walls and doors (that were never installed) and install the new wall and doors required by Change Order No. 1.

Although this illustration has been perhaps over-simplified for illustration purposes, the basic formula involved in all contract rigging is similar.

Federal, state, and local governments, most corporations, and public entities of all sorts are frequent victims of contract rigging fraud. Few of the perpetrators ever get caught and even fewer are ever prosecuted because of the difficulty in proving the fraud.

Fraud Involving Defective Pricing

Defective pricing fraud is widely practiced. In fact, many retail consumers are victims of the practice. The fraud basically involves falsely portraying the value—or criteria of value—of something, so as to delude the buyer on the appropriateness of the selling price. A classic example is "land flipping," a practice that occurred during the scandalous activity which followed deregulation of the nation's savings and loan industry in 1982.

"Land flipping," for those unfamiliar with the term, is a fraudulent practice wherein real property is sold and re-sold, usually over a short period of time, at ever increased prices. The object of the sales is to increase the apparent market value of a property, in anticipation that when the property is sold at a future date, the buyer will be comforted the asking price is in line with past sales prices. In one instance alone, investors purchased a piece of property for about $66,000, flipped it several times to increase its market value and then took out a loan on it for $487,000. They subsequently defaulted and the financing institution was left with a property worth far less. The financing institution was reimbursed by the government.

On a far lower scale, everyone who has ever responded to an apparent discount sale has been and usually is a victim of defective pricing fraud. Consider, for example, the buyer of a new automobile. A window sticker price shows it to be worth $30,000. However, few people ever pay the window price. It is intended to excite the buyer's interest that they can get a $30,000 car for perhaps $28,000. Is this fraud? It all depends upon what the dealer's intention was when he or she posted a $30,000 price on the window. If the intention was to get $30,000, then it was not fraud. If he or she intended to take something less, it may be considered to be defective pricing fraud. There is an old story about two merchants who competed in the sale of widgets on the same street. One day, one of them posed a sign that advertised "WIDGETS $25 EACH." The other merchant soon came by and asked "How can you sell Widgets for such a low price? That's below my cost." The first merchant replied, "Because I'm sold out!" The first merchant replied, "Oh, when I'm sold out, I sell them for $20 each."

Defective pricing takes various forms when practiced upon business and public entities. They are a very practical fraud for the perpetrator, usually an outside contractor or vendor, should their fraud be discovered. They will usually plead plausible error, and not have the error suspected as fraud by most entities who may discover it. Consider, for example, the following case that was missed by the auditor who found it.

An internal auditor selected a transaction involving approximately $8,900 at random for examination. It involved payment for "cleaning venetian blinds" in an office building. The auditor examined the documentation supporting the disbursement and found everything in order. An official of the entity ordering the cleaning service had reviewed and initialed the invoice for payment. The unit prices charged for the cleaning service were compared to the cleaner's latest price bulletin and were found to be in agreement with them. Everything appeared to be in order. However, before clearing the transaction, the auditor decided to go one step further. Noting that the cleaning contractor had performed under the provisions of an annual open-end contract, he decided to review the contract. It was there he learned that there were pricing provisions that were quite different than those charged in the invoice. In the contract, the contractor had agreed to clean venetian blinds at the price listed in the contractor's most current price bulletin, less a 35% discount. The contractor's invoice had failed to include the 35% discount agreed to in the contract. The entity's manager had approved the amount without the discount.

The auditor discovering the oversight reacted in a somewhat typical fashion for internal auditors not accustomed to fraud auditing and recommended that the entity seek a refund of the 35 percent discount it was entitled to, in the amount of $3,115.82. It was done, and the cleaning contractor quickly refunded the amount claimed. End of story.

The illustration raises interesting questions, however. Was the contractor's failure to apply the discount accidental? Or was it fraud? Was the entity manager who approved the invoice aware of the contract's discount pricing provision? Was he or she simply negligent, as was assumed? or was he or she a conspirator of the contractor? Should the auditor have considered the overcharge as indicia of fraud?

We'll never know the answers to the first five questions because the auditor did not recognize the finding as indicia of fraud. The answer to the sixth question, however, is yes! He or she should have considered the overcharge to be indicia of fraud! Note that we said indicia of fraud, not fraud. The fact that the overcharge happened once, is not evidence of fraud. If he or she found that it happened twice, it could be considered evidence of fraud, depending upon the circumstances. If he or she found that it happened three times, it should be considered intentional fraud. The entity should consider punitive actions such as contract cancellation, placing him or her on an ineligible list for future contracts, blacklisting, and possibly prosecution.

To prove fraud, the auditor must prove there was intent on the part of the contractor to defraud. To do that—for the illustration given—he or she must prove that the fraud happened multiple times. With each additional example, the auditor demonstrates the increased probability that the contractor intended to commit fraud, or at least was grossly negligent in billing for his or her services.

When the auditor discovered the first example of the overcharge, he or she should have kept the discovery confidential and proceeded to look for more examples. Since the cleaning contractor in this case was operating under a contract, it is likely that he or she performed under the contract for a number of times. If the contractor is truly a crook, a review of past invoices will show a similar pattern of overcharges. Depending upon the nature of them, prosecution can be considered. Prosecution of the contractor, of course, will not be the victim's only objective. He or she will wish to discover which employees participated to make the fraud possible and take appropriate action against them.

Fraud-specific examiners engaged in reviewing payment transactions are always advised to determine the pricing provisions of the contracts or purchase orders being involved.

Fraud Involving Conspiracy

Conspiracy involves "an agreement between two or more people to commit an act prohibited by law or to commit a lawful act by means prohibited by law" (Merriam-Webster's Dictionary of Law, 1996). Normally, cooperation is required to circumvent internal controls or to provide opportunities that either person acting alone would not have. Conspiracy may include cooperation between two or more of an entity's employees, or between an entity's employee and an outsider.

The term collusion is often used synonymously with conspiracy. Historically, for a time, many people believed that collusion referred to crimes perpetrated by women. It appears that many accountants prefer the term "collusion." Dictionaries make little real distinction. According to the *American Heritage Dictionary* (Second College Edition, 1985), conspiracy is described as "an agreement to perform an illegal, treacherous, or evil act," and collusion is described as "a secret agreement between two or more persons for a deceitful or fraudulent purpose." These terms will be used synonymously in this text; however, we prefer to use conspiracy because of its specific meaning in criminal law. Fraud examinations, whether proactive or reactive, must always be pursued with an expectation that prosecution and the courts will become involved.

Conspiracy in fraud schemes has become very common. At one time, it was widely thought that internal controls which provided for protective procedures, such as the separation of duties, made fraud a remote possibility. Conventional wisdom held that whereas one person might contemplate fraud, it was extremely unlikely that two or more persons would dare conspire to commit a fraudulent act. It was believed that would-be perpetrators would be extremely reluctant to expose their criminal intent to another person, or to trust another person with knowledge that could convict them of a crime. It would be pointless to attempt to discover if that conventional wisdom was ever valid because current experience discloses that most fraud involves conspiracy of one type or another (note: pseudo-conspiracy will be discussed in the next segment). Contrary to a popular belief of several decades ago that persons contemplating fraud would be reluctant to discuss their plans with others, especially relative strangers, they appear to be becoming particularly brazen.

In one fraud in our experience, an office supply broker would visit office supply store managers—with whom it is not likely he was intimately acquainted, or at least did not know very well—and successfully interest them in a fraud scheme in which they would both participate. Several store managers accepted his proposals and a conspiracy to defraud the parent entity worked very efficiently. As a broker of office supplies, he would visit the various stores and propose to the store managers that they issue purchase orders to him ordering wholesale quantities of various office supplies, such as ball-point

Continues

Continued

pens. Subsequent to the issuance of the purchase orders, the broker would provide the managers with shipping documents that indicated the items had been shipped to the store. Of course, nothing was ever shipped. The store manager certified that the items had been received and processed the necessary documents needed to effect payment. The broker would receive payment for the items never shipped and share the proceeds with the store managers involved. Although at least several office supply stores were involved, it is most interesting that no one ever reported the "friendly" broker or his criminal proposals. The entire scheme, after working very well for more than a year, came to an end one day when a jilted female companion of one of the store managers wrote a note to the parent entity saying that "something funny was going on" in the store her former boyfriend managed. A subsequent investigation revealed the particulars of the entire scheme, which involved stores in several U.S. cities.

This additional illustration provides an interesting variation of conspiracy. It occurred in the late 1970s and involved a U.S. Air Force "time and materials" contract with a contractor to repair or rebuild, and calibrate air base ground equipment, such as mobile starting generators, used on flight lines at various air bases. As the equipment required repair, the air bases would ship the units to the contractor. After repair, he would return them to the parent air base, charging an agreed upon sum for labor hours expended (including profit and overhead). During an audit of the contractor's records—a right retained by the government—it was discovered that a conspiracy existed between a sergeant at one large air base to ship perfectly good equipment to the contractor for "repair." The contractor would hold the equipment items for the time it would ordinarily take to repair them and then ship them back, billing the Air Force for fictitious repair costs. The sergeant was investigated by the Air Force and was probably court martialed. The contractor was prosecuted and convicted in a U.S. District Court. It was on this contract that fraud-specific auditors attempting to verify sub-contractors and material sources, discovered that the addresses given for suppliers and sub-contractors were often non-existent, or empty lots.

Conspiracy, including pseudo-conspiracy, is involved to some degree in most frauds, and is usually necessary to overcome existing internal controls that effectively deter fraud committed by perpetrators acting alone. Accordingly, fraud examinations must consider the high probability of conspiracy and perform examination testing as though there were conspiracy.

Fraud Involving Pseudo-Conspiracy

Pseudo-conspiracy is a term we coined to define a situation where two or more persons participate in a fraud scheme, similar to a regular conspiracy, but where one (or more) of the parties is an unsuspecting participant in the crime and has no criminal intention to defraud the victim. The pseudo-conspirator does not realize the significance of some action—or lack of action—on his or her part, which enables a perpetrator to execute a fraudulent act. Often his or her role involves an innocent failure to enforce an internal control due to some ruse put forth by the prime perpetrator. Or sometimes the pseudo-conspirator is just plain negligent. When a crime involving a pseudo-conspiracy is detected, the innocent "conspirator" can not be prosecuted.

The following actual case illustrates a pseudo-conspiracy.

A perpetrator who embezzled over $900,000 by submitting numerous fictitious invoices for building maintenance services was unable to accomplish his particular fraud scheme alone because active internal controls denied him entry to an automated financial payments system. Anyone using the system was required to affix a control number to all entries which identified him or her as an authorized user. Any transactions not bearing a unique unused document number would be rejected by the system. All series of numbers issued to authorized users were known to the processing system.

The issuance of control numbers, only to authorized users of the system, was the responsibility of an accounting clerk, an innocent, friendly young woman. The perpetrator was an employee in the accounting department, charismatic and well liked by everyone. He and the control number clerk became good office friends.

One day, he told her that one of the authorized users, located in another city, was in need of "another block of control numbers" and asked him to pick them up for him. She quickly complied. He

Continues

Continued

used those numbers to submit numerous fictitious invoices, stealing over $900,000.

She was not charged with fraud. It was clearly evident that she was tricked into giving out the necessary control numbers. She was completely unaware that the numbers were not going to the authorized users named. In ordinary circumstances, she could be disciplined for being negligent. However, the entity involved could not demonstrate that she had been properly instructed in her responsibility, nor could they show that her training had been refreshed. No action was taken against her. However, with her participation in the man's scheme, she became a "conspirator" in the sense that the crime required her cooperation.

The perpetrator was prosecuted, convicted, and given a one-year prison sentence with a daytime work-release opportunity. The sentence was offset by his pre-trial incarceration and he served far less than one year for his crime.

Proving conspiracy is usually very difficult, particularly if it cannot be demonstrated that stolen assets were received by the suspected conspirators. However, the auditor or examiner must proceed—when compelling evidence is discovered—to look for fraud. He or she must take the view that if it walks like a duck, and quacks like a duck, it must be a duck.

Consider, for example, a government case revealed in September 1982. No fraud was ever reported here, and indeed there may be no fraud involved. However, consider the evidence that was reported and decide for yourself. If this were your company making these errors, what would you have done? Would you suspect fraud?

U.S. General Services Administration San Francisco regional office leasing specialists missed a renewal date on a 10-year lease of 187,000 square feet of office space at $9.50 a square foot, causing the lease and its favorable rates to expire. Renewing the lease at the current market rate of $22 to $35 a square foot is expected to cost the government more than $24 million.

Continues

Continued

Additional relevant facts:

1. An option had been missed on the same lease five years earlier.
2. The same office missed renewal option dates on two other San Francisco buildings and one in San Jose, California in the past four years, resulting in millions of dollars more in losses.

Please note that in the illustration, the entity failed to renew a lease at favorable rates five times, costing millions of dollars, from which failures the leasor profited handsomely. Each failure was extremely suspicious and should have occasioned extreme measures to search for evidence of fraud and measures to tighten internal control procedures to preclude subsequent failures. It has been said that in the British army, they joke that "experience" enables you to recognize a mistake the second time you make it. Apparently the entity involved didn't recognize a mistake the fifth time they made it and this was about only one leasing office.

In the early stages of any search for fraud, or for any internal control custodian considering appropriate internal controls, it is somewhat irrelevant whether or not there was intent on the part of all participants to commit fraud. What is important is that the examiner or auditor proactively searching for fraud should expect that there will be conspiracies to defraud, either true or pseudo, and should design detection search procedures accordingly.

Fraud Involving Kickbacks

The term *kickback* is a slang expression that literally means "giving back a portion of ill-gotten profits to the party that was influential in making them possible." A kickback normally involves three parties: a vendor (the perpetrator), the customer (the victim), and the influential third party (usually the customer's employee). The mechanics of a kickback are very simple. A vendor or supplier usually instigates a kickback by giving, or offering to give, something of value to a key employee of a customer, in return for directing business to them. The employee then favors the vendor with an order for products or services. The employer is the victim who pays for the cost of the items purchased, usually at an inflated price which—at a minimum—covers the cost of the kickback. Hence, it is the employer who always pays the cost of kickbacks.

Kickbacks are accepted by persons in positions which allow them a choice of vendors or contractors. They range from insignificant gratuities, such as periodic luncheon parties, to property or cash in very significant amounts. Interestingly, where *quid pro quos* of insignificant amounts are involved, most inside conspirators would argue that a *quid pro quo* was not involved, that the victim lost nothing because the gratuity received did not influence their purchase judgements. Of course, these same people would be at a loss to explain why the vendors or contractors gave them, and only them, gifts of value. It is not normal to give gifts and expect nothing in return. It is simply not done.

In our experience, we have seen gratuities that have ranged from simple luncheons, prostitutes, television sets, trips to Europe, job offers, ownership shares in real property, and in one instance, a mountain vacation home.

It is useful to regard kickbacks as falling into two groups: unilateral kickbacks and bilateral kickbacks. The terms are not in general usage, and the authors chose them to identify the two groups separately for discussion purposes, and to be able to focus the reader's attention upon the more dangerous of the two: the bilateral kickback.

Unilateral Kickbacks.   As the term implies, these are gratuities given by vendors and contractors to employees of their customers, for no apparent reason other than in the hope—some say expectation—that the employees receiving the gifts will favor them with profitable business. They are termed unilateral because there is no formal *quid pro quo* agreement between the donors and the employees receiving gifts. The gifts are usually of relatively low value—seldom worth more than several hundred dollars. The gifts usually involve other than cash. Most often they include entertainment, including lunches and dinners at fine restaurants, liquor, and small electronic appliances. Occasionally, they include vacation trips, cruises, and even prostitutes.

There is rarely a clear conspiracy between the donors and the employees receiving the gifts, such as where one says to the other, "I will give you this in return for that." However, let's be realistic. Vendors simply don't give valuable gifts without the expectation of something in return. Where a vendor does make an overture to an employee by giving him a valuable gift, without a *quid pro quo* understanding, and the employee doesn't reciprocate in return, there is unlikely to be another gift in the future. In some cases, vendors are very open about the gifts they are prepared to give in return for orders. The *quid pro quo* arrangement for large orders works in reverse as well. Vendors often understand the penalty for not giving a suitable gift when they receive a large order.

A good friend named Marty used to tell us about his experiences with kickbacks. Marty was the off-line general freight agent for a western railroad, and always regretted the second Wednesday of every month when he was scheduled to visit a major midwest fertilizer manufacturer. The object of the visits was to solicit the movement of hundreds of tons of fertilizer on his employer's rail lines. There was an unwritten understanding, however, that the tonnage shipped on a given rail line was contingent upon how lavishly the company's freight traffic department employees were entertained.

The freight traffic department was so large, and the luncheon so extravagant, that it had to be accomplished in two shifts. The first shift always left on schedule at around 11 A.M. and the second shift was always ready to go when the first shift returned. Poor Marty had to accompany both shifts and eat, drink, and be merry with the people he was courting on both shifts. For salesmen like Marty, this story is likely to strike some responsive chords with salespeople. Although the monthly gala was never openly demanded by the company's freight traffic people, railroad traffic studies showed a significant loss of product tonnage shipped, and related revenues, in any month following a missed date. The missed dates were intentional on the railroad's part to attempt to determine if the lavish luncheons were really expected. It was decided they were and that the railroad could not afford to miss too many. Marty eventually developed bleeding ulcers and died in middle age.

Another acquaintance of ours was a manager of a large wholesale food distribution network. He was frequently showered with gifts ranging from tape recorders and television sets to expensive trips. On several occasions he was flown to Alaska on salmon fishing trips, all expenses paid by a food vendor. On other occasions he and his entire family were given all expense paid trips to Europe for two weeks and Caribbean cruises. The trips were worth thousands of dollars.

When considering unilateral kickbacks, it is usually assumed that the vendor or contractor giving the gifts is the culprit, and the employee the innocent beneficiary. However, we would be hesitant to even suggest that this is so. In fact, for going concerns, we dare say that the *quid pro quo* arrangements that commonly exist are analogous to asking which came first, the chicken or the egg? It would be difficult to determine who started it all. The truth is more likely to be that somewhere along the line, gifts were given and accepted. Donors are fearful of stopping, so they continue. Employee recipients are loathe to reject free gifts and accept them without thinking. The costs of the gifts are considered a normal cost of doing business and routinely included in the prices charged by the vendors.

Our advice to entities is that they review their own operations with the objective of determining whether or not their employees are protecting their personal interests or their employer's. Employers who do not object to their employees accepting kickbacks, without reasonable limitations, are asking for trouble.

Lest there be any doubt, it is the considered advice of the authors of this text that all entities should forbid all kickbacks to their employees, regardless of amount. Entities should view all kickbacks as a return of their profits to their employees. Perhaps we're old-fashioned, but we believe that all compensation of an entity's employees should be a matter of the entity's judgement of an employee's contribution to the firm. A bribe, pure and simple, is a vendor's compensation of an entity's employee for the employee's "contribution to the vendor's firm." Our question to all entities is "Do you really want to allow this?" Numerous successful businesses today are forbidding the acceptance of any gifts by their employees, regardless of value, and their wishes are being made known to their suppliers. Wal-Mart Stores, Inc., for example, has a policy which forbids its buyers from accepting so much as a cup of coffee from vendors. One retail consultant speculated that it's probably helping them keep costs down. What is Wal-Mart concerned about? Obviously, they wish to avoid the situation a competitor experienced. In 1995 the J.C. Penney Co. discovered that one of their buyers, earning $56,000 a year, made up to $1,500,000 in kickbacks from vendors. The Penney buyer was involved in what are known as bilateral kickbacks.

Bilateral Kickbacks.   These fit the dictionary definition of kickbacks in that they are "2. (slang) A percentage payment to a person able to influence or control a source of income . . ." (The American Heritage Dictionary, Second College Edition. Houghton Mifflin Company, Boston 1985). Bilateral kickbacks, however, are by far the more pernicious of the two types. Whereas many entities often take a somewhat permissive attitude towards unilateral kickbacks, no entity would be likely to approve of bilateral kickbacks. A bribe is a bilateral kickback, and in the world of commerce, bribes are a serious form of international fraud. In 1997, German authorities reported that the German economy loses the equivalent of $29 billion a year from inflated contracts and tax evasion associated with kickbacks. For U.S. companies it has been illegal to offer bribes to foreign companies for 20 years. However, it is not illegal for French and German firms to bribe foreign firms. In fact, the bribes have been tax deductible.

A kickback is called bilateral because it involves a *quid pro quo* agreement between two parties, usually a vendor or contractor and an employee or agent of a victim, to literally defraud the victim. The kickbacks themselves almost always involve large amounts of cash (in the thousands or even millions of dollars). Bilateral kickbacks may be involved in just about any acquisition transaction, influencing the selection of one vendor versus another offering possibly a better price. However, they are probably best suited for acquiring products or services that are not easily compared with competing products or services. Commercial leased space, janitorial services, custom-manufactured products, and the like are just a few examples.

If two office sites are being considered for leasing, for example, one at 123 Main Street, and the other at 456 Clark Avenue, it is extremely difficult to compare the space at one location with the other and make a convincing argument that they were comparable properties. Accordingly, if the space at 123 Main is rented at $28 a square foot, and the space at 456 Clark was available at $20 a square foot, there is no one who can give an unqualified answer that the space at 456 Clark is a better buy and should have been rented, or maintain that perhaps the leasing officer received a kickback of eight dollars a square foot to steer the lease to 123 Main Street. The eight dollar per square foot price difference may have been used to finance a kickback, but proving it is extremely difficult. The 123 Main Street property may have a better layout, it may have a better view, it may be in a better neighborhood, it may be quieter, it may be on a lower floor, and so forth, and so forth. Each reason offered adds to the justification for the additional price paid.

Consider also a simple item such as the acquisition of janitorial services. For example, who can say with any degree of certainty what it should cost to clean the office space at 226 South Main Street? Conceivably, the cost of janitorial services could run anywhere from $1.25 a square foot to perhaps $2.25. If 1,000,000 square feet are involved, for example, bilateral kickback conspirators could easily raise an entity's janitorial costs by $100,000 or more a year, just by charging 10 cents a square foot over what honest negotiators might conclude to be reasonable. Twenty-five cents a square foot would generate up to $250,000 a year in kickback cash.

An interesting article appeared in the November 23, 1988 *Wall Street*

Journal, "Travel Agent's Games Raise Ethics Issue" by Robert L. Rose, describing travel agent bilateral kickbacks resulting from their choice of, for example, one airline over another for client travel. The following are pertinent quotes from the article:

> A survey by Louis Harris & Associates Inc. found that 24 percent of agents usually use overrides in choosing a carrier. . . . Fears over how this affects service have prompted a growing number of companies to hire auditors to check on travel agencies. One auditing company, Topaz Enterprises of Portland, Oregon, says the biggest agency mistake is booking one airline when another has a cheaper fare. The average cost of that mistake: $113. One of the reasons: commission overrides.

> If I go to an agent and ask for his or her unbiased opinion between cruise ships for me, it's important to know whether the agent is working toward a fur coat."—Ed Perkins, editor of the *Consumer Reports Travel Letter*

Travel agents who select one airline or cruiseline over another at the expense of their clients in return for gratuities are participants in bilateral kickback fraud.

On the subject of kickbacks, it may interest many readers to know that they are likely to have been a recipient of kickbacks. The frequent flyer programs conducted by many airlines create tempting opportunities for employees flying at the expense of their employers and many regard them as kickbacks. Such programs could be defined as fraud should a traveling employee choose to take unnecessary trips, over higher cost airlines, and over circuitous routes for the purpose of accumulating frequent flyer miles.

The detection of kickbacks in questionable contract arrangements of significance, however, is often difficult to detect. Sometimes the "*quo*" in *quid pro quo* is impossible to identify, which tends to eliminate—for the participants—the likelihood of prosecution or some form of penalty for giving or accepting a bribe. However, what will occur if you are patient is that the reward for participation will be delayed until a future time. Sometimes a suspect will come into ownership of unexplained stock in the company involved. Often the reward will be a future job promise at an appropriate salary, often for doing nothing! One such individual, whom we cannot name, engineered a multi-million-dollar sweetheart contract with a large U.S. corporation. Although we searched for one, no motivation was apparent at the time the deal was discovered. However, within a year or two, he accepted a lucrative job offer in Europe with the same company that received the suspicious contract. In other examples that occur some-what frequently, it is common knowledge that some military procurement officers go to work for the same defense contractors to whom they had previously been instrumental is awarding lucrative contracts. For them, the unanswered questions will always be, are they being compensated for past favors, or are their skills truly needed? In instances where we have been in defense contractors' plants, rooms full of idle military officers, hired ostensibly for their defense experience, but with few if any job responsibilities, were always painfully obvious.

We believe that nothing in life is free. All gratuities—regardless of amount—are paid from the giver's profits, and none are given without expecting something in return. Accordingly, we recommend that all entities establish a policy of no gratuities, from anyone, and make it known to all employees that infractions will lead to disciplinary action or prosecution for fraud.

Employer Attitudes on Kickbacks.   Employer attitudes with regard to their employees acceptance of gratuities vary widely. Some adopt a zero policy, allowing no gratuities regardless of amount. Others, such as Sony Corporation, had no restrictions on gifts to their employees. In a previous example we told of a food distributor executive who accepted trips to Alaska and Europe from grateful suppliers. His employer was aware of the gifts, and apparently saw no problem in the executive being rewarded by suppliers. Assuming that he was correct and this particular man could be trusted to protect the company's best interest despite the free trips and the many other gratuities, his mistake in allowing it to continue was perhaps in the precedent it set. There were many people in the organization who were aware of the free trips, and undoubtedly wanted similar gratuities. Could they too be trusted to protect the employer's best interests when there is much to be gained?

There is one other very important consideration in adopting such a liberal policy. Should it ever be discovered that the employee has acted contrary to the employer's best interests, in return for a gift of some kind, it would be very difficult to prosecute or even to discipline the employee. By allowing a too liberal policy on the acceptance of gratuities, an employer literally forfeits his right to argue successfully that the employee was guilty of a *quid pro quo* not in the employer's best interests.

Most entities do establish limits upon the level of gifts that an employee may accept. Usually they stipulate that an employee may not accept cumulative gifts of over a specified monetary value, such as $300 a year. Any limitation set is usually provided for the purpose of sparing an employee the embarrassment of not accepting a lunch proffered to discuss business and are normally not intended for the purpose of setting limits on gifts having no direct connection with business. The employee is responsible for staying within any set limitation. Should it be discovered that they have accepted more than the limited amount, most have penalties ranging from a reprimand to termination. Regardless, a limitation—such as $300 a year—gives the employer an option for action.

Detection. The likelihood of detecting kickback fraud in proactive examinations ranges from difficult to impossible. However, it is worth spending a reasonable amount of time searching for it as a deterrent effect. The examiner must proceed under the presumption that the vendor or contractor who gives sizeable kickbacks to receive favors is in need of a favor. That is, he or she would not be successful in open competition. His prices may be excessive, his quality may be substandard; for whatever reason, he feels that he needs to buy his advantage. Accordingly, the examiner must look carefully at things such as unit prices charged for supplies. Do they appear excessive? A good example is a case where the auditor was conducting an audit involving the acquisition of a large number of small tape recorders, such as those used to transcribe memoranda. The auditor, at a location in New York City, was reviewing an invoice for a large number of the recorders by a large entity, and was disturbed by what appeared to be excessive unit prices for such a large purchase. At lunch that day, he visited a small office supply store and inquired about the price of an identical single tape recorder. The merchant quoted a price almost $100 cheaper.

This disclosure was not necessarily sufficient evidence to charge the buyer with kickback fraud. However, it was evidence of the possibility of fraud, negligence or incompetence. With the initial disclosure, the auditor should have proceeded as though he had found evidence of fraud and reviewed other similar acquisitions made by the same individual. The disclosure of multiple purchases at excessive prices would indicate— particularly if the same vendor was involved—the strong possibility of fraud. At that point, the auditor or examiner should proceed as though he had found evidence of fraud and seek investigative assistance and the advice of prosecution counsel. If prosecution for fraud is ruled out, management might wish to reconsider the buyer's competence to continue buying for the entity.

Fraud Involving Unbalanced Contracts or Purchase Orders

Unbalanced contract fraud normally involves contracts awarded on the basis of competition and a low total bid, convincing many entities that by contracting in this manner they are protected from fraud. In addition, the contracts always involve multiple line items, each item is priced separately, and the contracting entity reserves the right to delete any item or even vary the quantity ordered (especially where products are involved). The contractor submits his or her bid in such a manner that his or her aggregate bid is lowest to legitimately win the contract award. His or her bid may or may not include a profit and may even contemplate a loss, but his or her pricing of individual items is unbalanced in such a manner that some of the line items are overpriced and some are underpriced. The object of unbalancing his bid is that should one or more of the underpriced items be eliminated, or orders minimized, and the overpriced items retained or orders increased, his or her profits will increase substantially.

This is usually a complex and involved fraud, and we hesitate to give a simple illustration for fear that readers will assume that when a contractor unbalances his or her bid, the fraudulent intention is painfully obvious. However, with the forewarning that a real world case will *never* be this simple and openly apparent, please consider the following hypothetical illustrative example.

Assume that Corporation X solicits price proposals for the construction of two structures, Building A and Building B. Assume that the structures are estimated to cost about $2,000,000. In the competition to select a contractor, three contractors submit bids. Two submit bids to construct Building A for $1,100,000, and Building B for $1,000,000. Their aggregate bids are $2,100,000 to build both structures. The Third Company submitted a bid of $1,250,000 for Building A and $650,000 for Building B. The Third Company is awarded the contract for their low aggregate bid of $1,900,000.

To Corporation X officials, the bidding process has been successful. Three contractors have competed for the contract and their bids are all close to the estimated cost and to each other's bids, which is typical of a very competitive marketplace. The contract is awarded to the low bidder and he is directed to begin construction of building A immediately, with construction of building B to begin when building A is completed.

If you were with Corporation X, would you be content with the contract for $1,900,000? If not, why not? Ordinarily you should be satisfied with a price of $1,900,000, given that the other two bidders bid $200,000 higher at $2,100,000. *Bear in mind that were Corporation X to select a contractor other than the Third Company, they*

Continues

Continued

would have to have a valid reason. Otherwise, the Third Company has grounds to sue for the award.

If this contract were to be examined for fraud at this point, there is nothing that could be legitimately criticized. The contractor is legally obligated to build both buildings at the lowest price, in this case $1,900,000.

Shortly after the Third Company began construction of Building A, Corporation X announced plans to move the manufacture of its best-selling product Widgets to mainland China. This resulted in a reshuffling of their U.S. manufacturing and storage sites, and the conclusion that Building B was no longer needed. Since Corporation X had the contract option of deleting any line items in the contract, they chose to delete the requirement for Building B, at a savings of $650,000.

Reconsider the cost of constructing Building A. Had one of the two high bidders been selected for the contract award, the corporation's cost of Building A would now be $1,100,000. However, the corporation selected the low bidder and their cost of Building A will now be $1,250,000, or $150,000 higher that the low bidders. What has happened here?

What has undoubtedly happened is that the Third Company knew that Corporation X's move to a Chinese manufacturing facility was imminent and Building B would never be built. It is very likely the information source was an insider at Corporation X. In anticipation that Building B would be deleted as a contract requirement, the Third Company took advantage of the inside knowledge and unbalanced the bid, underpricing the building to be eliminated and overpricing the building to be constructed.

Detection. There is literally no way that this fraud type can be effectively detected and prosecuted. Although a post-active examination will reveal that blunders were made, it would be very difficult to make the discovery of blunders into a case of fraud—even though it may involve fraud.

In the illustration given, prevention is the preferable course of action. Corporation X should not have used this contract type for major construction items. If it wished to have two buildings constructed, it should have contracted separately for each building. Had it done this, the contractor would not have dared to unbalance his bid, for fear that Corporation X would have accepted the low-priced building and another contractor for a lower price on the construction of the other building. Readers should consider this a requirement to be included in their internal control systems. Be warned, however, that this contract type is unavoidable for many contracts for the provision of items of personal property. A manufacturer of end items would be likely to find this sort of contract useful for acquiring nuts and bolts, for example, to be used in his end-product assembly. If he or she were unable to accurately predict the end-item sales, the manufacturer would be interested in a supplier contract that would allow him to vary the requirement. In doing so, he or she becomes a potential victim of unbalanced contracting and must watch for signs of it.

When unbalanced contracts are used in the real world, they will never be as simple as depicted in the foregoing illustration. The unbalanced bids will not be so easily seen. However, the formula is always nearly the same. To make the fraud work, there is almost always a conspirator who is working for the intended victim, in a capacity in which he or she can influence contract performance. Or, the conspirator may have access to confidential information that would allow him or her to predict that the quantities of certain line items are likely, or not likely, to be required. For example, an imminent end-item engineering change might make "part X" obsolete. If so, that information can be used to unbalance a bid. A subcontractor supplying "part X" could under-price it while over-pricing other items that will be delivered.

Unbalanced contract fraud is somewhat similar to what has been described as contract rigging fraud. A prominent difference is that in unbalanced bidding fraud, a contract change is not required. The basic contract is written to allow variations in line-item quantities at the contracting entity's discretion. Often, they are used when the contracting entity has good reason to think that they *will* probably change the contract quantities of items purchased. Also, contracts subject to unbalanced bidding are written more often to purchase personal property than real property. If an entity cannot predict how many of an item they will be purchasing, it writes a contract in which the quantities are more or less variable. It may specify in the invitation for bids that it intends to purchase between 10,000 and 20,000 of "part X." There may be hundreds of different items obscuring "part X" for which the bidder is required to offer prices.

In the illustrative cases provided toward the end of this text, more complete case studies will illustrate different variations in unbalanced contract fraud. Note especially the one which involves interior painting. This is a different sort of unbalanced contract that is common.

Non-Repeating and Repeating Fraud

All fraud can be classified as being non-repeating or repeating. The terms non-repeating fraud and repeating fraud are self-descriptive. In an act of non-repeating fraud, the perpetrator initiates whatever is necessary for the fraud to occur, the fraud occurs, the perpetrator collects, and the entire deed is finished—unless, of course, the perpetrator chooses to do it all over again. In an act of repeating fraud, the perpetrator initiates whatever is needed to cause the fraud to begin to occur. The fraud then continues to occur automatically, without further intervention by the perpetrator, usually until the perpetrator initiates whatever action is necessary to end it. The period during which a repeating fraud can occur is unlimited, determined only by the perpetrator. Most fraud is of the non-repeating type.

Both types have advantages and disadvantages as far as detection is concerned. For the perpetrator, the advantage in non-repeating fraud is that the longer the time interval after the crime is committed, the more unlikely it is that the crime will be discovered. After a year has passed, it is often extremely unlikely that fraud will be detected. Unless, of course, a fraud-specific examiner is on the trail of a suspect and digs through old material for additional incriminating evidence. Auditors tend not to look at older transactions; as evidence ages, it tends to deteriorate and detection opportunities diminish. However, when there is repeating fraud, the examiner has an additional fresh opportunity to detect the fraud every time it repeats.

For fraud examiners who select payment transactions to test for fraud, they will usually find support for the transactions in the period in which the payment was made where non-repeating fraud is involved. Where repeating fraud is involved, however, the examiner may find him or herself having to seek transaction verification in one or more periods far in the past. For example, assume that the examiner, in the process of verifying monthly annuity payments, selects a payment of $1,000 to Mary Jones. The selection is from a negative payments system, so called because once the payment is set up, no further action is required to cause the payment system to automatically pay the designated amount, every month in perpetuity, until stopped. Once the examiner selects the $1,000 payment, he or she may have to return to source documents processed many years before to verify it. In so doing, he or she may note that the source files indicate that the original annuitant's name was Mary Smith. Is this evidence of fraud? Not necessarily. A check of the interim transactions may reveal that Mary Smith got married and changed her name to Mary Jones. Upon learning this, does the examiner stop further examination? Perhaps, and perhaps not. The marriage claim may be phony and inserted only after a death notice was received for Mary Smith. Please note that we do not claim that proactively examining for fraud is easy.

The variety of repeating frauds is limited only by the creativity of the perpetrator, and some of them are very creative. In one instance, a bank computer programmer had adjusted a computer program to skim a few pennies off the service charges debited to every customer's account. No customers ever complained, because the loss for any one account was minuscule and the service charge computation difficult to verify with average daily account balances entering into the computations. Once begun, the fraud, which accumulated only a few cents per customer, produced thousands of dollars for the perpetrator, each month, automatically, without any further initiating action required by the perpetrator. The pennies deducted from each customer's account were credited to a personal account set up by the perpetrator, which she drew checks against to collect her fraud proceeds. Discovery was most accidental. It occurred when the bank decided to award a prize to several customers selected at random. One of the lucky customers happened to be the phony account set up by the perpetrator.

Fraud on the Books or Off the Books

For detection purposes, it is also useful to know whether or not fraud is recorded on the books or not. Obviously, the most exhaustive examination of accounting transactions will not disclose fraud which involves assets which do not appear on the books. In the following paragraphs, we will discuss the two groups of fraud which appear on the accounting records in one form or another, and the fraud which involves assets which do not appear on the accounting records. In proactively searching for evidence of fraud, it is important to be mindful of how and where the fraud you're looking for is located.

On-the-Books Fraud Which Involves an Entire Transaction.   This is one of the two ways that fraud is recorded on the books—as an entire transaction, or combined with and obscured by another transaction. It includes all instances of fraud where the complete transaction is fraudulent. For the most part, it includes all duplicate payment fraud, multiple payee fraud, and shell payments. Fraud which involves an entire transaction on the books is the easiest fraud to detect because the entire transaction is either good or bad, and the fraud usually lacks the sophistication necessary to elude an experienced fraud examiner. The significance of the foregoing will become clearer as the next definition is discussed.

An illustration of fraud on the books which involves an entire transaction would be a fraudulent *duplicate* payment of $500 to a vendor. The $500 item would appear in the accounting records as a stand-alone, separate $500 transaction, perhaps in a check register or accounts payable register. If an accountant selects it for a fraud-specific proactive review, the entire transaction would have to stand by itself, and a skilled examination of supporting documentation and related particulars would stand a very good chance of detecting fraud in this grouping.

On-the-Books Fraud Which Is Obscured by a Legitimate Transaction. This type of fraud is included as an integral part of a larger legitimate transaction. Fraud in this group is surely the most significant and constitutes the vast majority of fraud. It is also very difficult to detect, for the examiner must look beyond the host transaction to discover the nature and amount of the fraud. For example, literally any purchase of any item can include a sum of money that will flow to a perpetrator. A kickback is an excellent example. If an item that would ordinarily sell for $50,000 includes a 10 percent kickback, the selling price will most probably be at least $55,000. The host item being purchased will usually be very legitimate, and all of the customary checks and balances will be in order. However, the price is inflated due to the kickback, which is likely to be fraudulent. Accordingly, the examiner must be sensitive to what the fair price of an item should be. The best way of accomplishing this is to carefully examine all bids received if the contract was advertised. If a contract was not advertised, the examiner might look to past contracts, noting unit prices paid. Also, where the examiner has suspicions that he or she cannot prove, it may also be a good idea to keep a confidential file of the people who are involved. If the same names appear in subsequent suspicions, after a time they will tend to corroborate prior suspicions, and the individuals involved can be monitored more closely.

Fraud Which Is Not On The Books. Many entities have assets that are not recorded in the accounting records, for one reason or another. Obviously, if an asset is not recorded, no examination based upon a selection of accounting transactions will discover any theft of those assets.

The nature of unrecorded assets varies from entity to entity. Scrap inventories sometimes constitute significant inventories. Photographic laboratories sometimes generate significant quantities of silver reclaimed from photographic waste materials that may not be picked up in the accounting records. Vending machines are often a source of revenue to some entities, not recorded as a natural accounting event. A 1998 audit of an entity charged that an entity executive had not properly accounted for $40,000 in shared revenue. Accounts receivable are possible candidates for fraud involving unrecorded assets. If a receivable is written off to bad debts and subsequently collected, it may be possible to divert the payment and never reverse the writeoff.

An interesting example of fraud involving assets that were not on the books occurred many years ago. It involved a factory-subsidized employee cafeteria selling meals to employees at substantial discounts. Subsidy arrangements provided that the cafeteria manager would turn in the cafeteria's daily cash receipts to the factory controller for deposit, and the factory would pay the cafeteria's operating costs as well as a negotiated profit. The controller was responsible for determining that cafeteria receipts were an agreed percentage of operating costs. Meal prices were to be adjusted upward or downward as necessary to maintain the percentage.

After several years of the above arrangement, fraud was discovered, purely by accident. Take a moment or two to contemplate what the nature of the fraud was, before reading further.

During the period in which the cafeteria fraud was occurring, a seemingly unrelated event took place. One of the factory foremen received an IRS Form W-2 from the factory and was unable to reconcile the gross wages reported on it with his meticulous personal account of his gross wages received. The factory account was approximately $100 higher. When he checked with the payroll department he found that the extra $100 was a salary and meal reimbursement for an evening meeting that he had attended. However, he was unyielding in his belief that he had not attended the meeting, so much so that the payroll department looked up the check that had been issued to him. His endorsement on the check was found to be a forgery, and not the only one. It was also discovered that other similar forged checks had been issued to factory supervisors who had missed evening meetings. The forgeries were later traced to the factory controller, who was suspended pending a resolution of the discovery.

What does this have to do with fraud not on the books? Subsequent to the controller's suspension, the controller's secretary began to wonder what to do with the cafeteria cash receipts that were accumulating in his office. It was only then that it was discovered that the controller had been depositing the cash receipts to his personal account. *No factory accounting entry had ever been made to indicate the deposit of the funds.* Even though the amount of the fraud was enormous, and the company had been audited annually by a CPA firm, the fraud had endured for several or more years. And, it may have continued indefinitely, had the controller not gotten greedy and careless and had the foreman not done the unexpected and kept such careful records. The controller was prosecuted and convicted of fraud. However, as a respected member of the community who had been most generous to various local charities, he was given no prison sentence on the promise of restitution payments.

Detection. Discovering fraud not on the books, first requires that the examiner speculate on the nature of possible unrecorded assets which might be the objects of fraud, and then initiate appropriate examination procedures designed to disclose if fraud has actually occurred.

Chapter 5

Internal Control and Fraud-Specific Internal Control

INTERNAL CONTROL: WHAT IS IT?

This simple question will probably be answered differently, depending upon who is asked. All are likely to be correct, depending upon the different applications each person will consider when responding. Before any meaningful discussion of internal control can continue, it will be useful to take a few moments to explain several internal control definitions, particularly those relevant to this text. The first part of this chapter will provide and discuss the various definitions of internal control and the circumstances and periods of their origins and applications. The second part will discuss Fraud-Specific Internal Control. Chapter 6, Establishing and Operating an Effective Fraud-Specific Internal Control System: Seven Steps to Internal Control, will include a discussion on establishing and operating an effective fraud-specific internal control system.

FOUR DEFINITIONS OF INTERNAL CONTROL

It is worthwhile to consider the different meanings of internal control, and to establish exactly what meaning of the term is intended when used in workplace conversation and in this text.

1. *Internal Control prior to September 1992.* The condition sought by, and/or resulting from, processes undertaken by an entity to prevent and deter fraud.
2. *Internal Control subsequent to 1992.* A process, effected by an entity's board of directors, management, and other personnel, designed to pro-

vide reasonable assurance regarding the achievement of effectiveness and efficiency of operations, reliability of financial reporting, and compliance with applicable laws and regulations.—COSO (the Committee of Sponsoring Organizations of the Treadway Commission).

3. *Internal Control as defined in 1988 by the AICPA.* For the purposes of an audit of financial statement balances, an entity's internal control structure consists of the following three elements: the control environment, the accounting system, and control procedures.—Statement on Auditing Standards No. 55, April 1988.

4. *Fraud-Specific Internal Control.* A system of "special-purpose" processes and procedures designed and practiced for the primary if not sole purpose of preventing or deterring fraud.

Definition 1

This provides a general definition of what it many accountants have long considered the meaning of the term "internal control" up until 1992 (It would not be a surprise to find that meaning still to be popularly held). In September 1992, as a result of COSO's preemption of the term "internal control", considerably expanding its meaning to apply to a broad spectrum of management functions, it became necessary to retitle the popular understanding of the term as "fraud-specific internal control" (definition 4). There is no generally accepted reference source for definition 1. It appears that accountants have generally considered the term to be so self-evident in the past as to not have required formal definition. Accordingly, the first definition is provided as the author's simple restatement of what accountants have generally accepted the term to mean when used prior to September 1992.

In seeking a generally accepted reference for a definition of internal control around mid-century, *The Accountant's Handbook*[5], a popular accountants' reference source was consulted. However, it made only brief mention of the term "internal control"—not as definition or discussion subject—but as a term narrowly applied to the safeguarding of assets such as cash, cash sales, charge sales, and sales, devoting only approximately three pages.

Definition 2

The official definition of internal control changed considerably in September 1992 when COSO published the results of its in-depth study, which included the publication of a new definition, or conception, of internal control. In view of the endorsement of the COSO conclusions by its member accounting organizations, the COSO definition of internal control must now be considered the definition of choice, regardless of any other view, or of how popular they may be. The following remarks defining internal control have been excerpted from the *COSO Executive Summary,* September 1992, for the reader's information and better understanding:

> *Internal control means different things to different people. This causes confusion among business people, legislators, regulators, and others. Resulting miscommunication and different expectations cause problems within an enterprise. Problems are compounded when the term, if not clearly defined, is written into law, regulation or rule. . . .*

> *Internal control is broadly defined as a process, effected by an entity's board of directors, management and other personnel, designed to provide reasonable assurance regarding the achievement of objectives in the following categories: effectiveness and efficiency of operations, reliability of financial reporting, and compliance with applicable laws and regulations.*

> *The first category addresses an entity's basic business objectives, including performance and profitability goals and safeguarding of resources. The second relates to the preparation of reliable published financial statements, including interim and condensed financial statements and selected financial data derived from such statements, such as earnings releases, reported publicly. The third deals with complying with those laws and regulations to which the entity is subject. These distinct but overlapping categories address different needs and allow a directed focus to meet the separate needs.*

> —COSO Framework, Executive Summary
> September 1992, page 1

The COSO definition of internal control is all-encompassing, and as such it tends to lose specificity of meaning. However, they appear to recognize that aspect in their report and later refer to their definition of internal control as a core definition under which additional special-purpose definitions may be appropriate. For example, the COSO report goes on to state, under a section titled *Perspectives on and Use of Definition* (pp 101):

> Different perspectives on internal control are not undesirable. Internal control is concerned with entity objectives and different groups and interested in different objectives for different reasons. The common linkage of internal control to objectives provides the basis for establishing a core definition from which all other definitions can be extrapolated.

Special-Purpose Definitions. While an entity may consider the effectiveness of all three categories of objectives, it will likely want to focus attention on certain categories, and perhaps on only certain activities or objectives. By identifying and describing specific objectives, special-purpose definitions of internal control can be derived from the core definition.

Accordingly, consistent with the COSO determinations, when formally referring to internal control which focuses upon the detection and deterrence of fraud, this text will use the definition *fraud-specific internal control*, unless stated otherwise.

Definition 3

This definition is self-explanatory. It was issued by the AICPA in April 1988, and together with similar internal control pronouncements issued by the AICPA and others with similar objectives, has caused various degrees of misunderstanding, particular among AICPA members seeking guidance. However, with the issuance of the COSO report in 1992 and the core definition of internal control, it is acknowledged that there can be other special-purpose definitions of internal control. Although the AICPA has not yet declared their definition of internal control to be a special-purpose definition, it is very clear that it must be. The special purpose objective? To assure the integrity and accuracy of financial statement balances!

The AICPA on Internal Control. The AICPA, a COSO participating organization, has long advocated that "good internal control and surety bonds provide protection from fraud." (Statement on Auditing Procedure No. 1)

However, over the years the AICPA's guidance to CPAs—and the source of counsel provided to entities relying upon the advice of CPAs—has not been clear. For example, in April 1988, the AICPA issued Statement on Auditing Standards No. 53, which appeared to limit the suitability of internal control for preventing or discovering fraud to immaterial employee fraud, stating:

Defalcations by employees are often immaterial in amount and concealed in a manner that does not misstate net assets or net income. This type of irregularity can be more efficiently and effectively dealt with by an effective internal control structure and fidelity bonding of employees.

The AICPA's 1988 Statement went on to state that internal control was not likely to prevent or deter management fraud:

> Material irregularities perpetrated by senior levels of management are infrequent (and) may not be susceptible to prevention by specific internal control procedures because senior management is above the controls that deter employees or may override these controls with relative ease.

What was not clarified was the recommended audit procedure for dealing with employee fraud which is material in amount, or which does not misstate net assets or net income! The 1988 pronouncements did not appear to change the AICPA's previously announced position on *not* using auditing to discover fraud.

It would appear that AICPA guidance to practicing CPAs did little to detect or deter management fraud. Internal controls were not considered effective, and up until the 1988 statement, most auditors believed their AICPA guidance "entitled them to assume that management was honest unless information came to their attention that specifically contradicted that assumption."[6]

In addition, the 1988 Statement appeared to concede that certain types of fraud were audit (and internal control) resistant, seemingly in defense of not recommending auditing to detect fraud.

Forgery may be used to create false signatures, other signs of authenticity, or entire documents. Collusion may result in falsified confirmations or other evidence of validity. Also, unrecorded transactions are normally more difficult to detect than concealment achieved by manipulation of recorded transactions. However, the effect of concealment on the ability to detect an irregularity is dependent on the particular circumstances. For example, an attempt to mislead users of financial statements by recording large, fictitious revenue transactions late in the period without supporting documentation would be more easily detected than fictitious revenue transactions spread throughout the period, individually immaterial in amount, and supported by legitimate appearing invoices and shipping documents. Moreover, both of these irregularities might be extremely difficult, if not impossible, to detect if collusion of customers is added to the concealment scheme.

> —Quoted portions of paragraphs 5, 6, and 8 from Appendix AICPA Statement on Auditing Standards 53, April 1988, The Auditor's Responsibility to Detect Errors and Irregularities

Definition 4

The term fraud-specific internal control pertains to a system of special purpose processes and procedures designed and practiced for the primary if not sole purpose of preventing or deterring fraud.

FRAUD-SPECIFIC INTERNAL CONTROL

It is difficult to discuss fraud-specific internal control in other than general terms, for to be truly effective, each internal control system must be designed to be responsive to the entity it will serve. As every entity differs in various regards, the needs of each entity will differ, often in very significant regards. Large businesses have different needs than small businesses, private entities have different needs than public entities, manufacturing entities have different needs than service organizations, not to mention the myriad of variations in between each of them. Not only will manufacturing concerns require internal control systems significantly different from those required by financial institutions, retail sales businesses, or public entities, internal control systems which meet the needs of one manufacturing concern, financial institution, retail sales business, or public entity are not likely to suit the needs of another. Accordingly, each internal control system should be custom-designed to have the maximum effect upon fraud.

Regardless of the many differences in internal control system requirements of each entity, the principles of fraud-specific internal control system design remain similar. The second part of this chapter will focus upon the fundamentals of fraud-specific internal control system design. Individuals faced with evaluating and/or designing fraud-specific internal control systems will find the material presented useful. For language efficiency, please regard any subsequent usage of the term "internal control" in this chapter to mean "fraud-specific internal control."

All internal controls may be classified into one of two general categories:

1. *ACTIVE INTERNAL CONTROLS.* Controls which seek to prevent fraud from occurring. The operative word here is "prevent".
2. *PASSIVE INTERNAL CONTROLS.* Controls which seek to deter fraud by significantly increasing the risk of discovery.

Active Internal Controls

Active internal controls are probably the most common internal controls in use. They may be considered to be impediments to fraud. They are literally *fences* erected to restrict or deny a fraud perpetrator's access to valuable assets. However insurmountable they may appear at first appear to be, all of them are vulnerable to defeat by clever and determined fraud perpetrators, and often pose little more than a nuisance to a thief. Their most significant weakness, like a fence, is that once evaded—not if evaded—they have little or no continuing value in preventing or deterring fraud.

Think of them as you would a gate secured by a sturdy padlock. With the padlock in place, the assets are secure within any enclosure it controls. However, if someone obtains a duplicate key, or smashes, saws, or picks the padlock, its efficacy as a control is nullified and it has no further value as a control to either bar or deter access to the assets within. As with all active internal controls, once the padlock problem is solved, a perpetrator can come and go as he or she pleases. Active internal controls, like padlocks, are usually visible and available to be studied indefinitely. A would-be perpetrator is able to ponder them at his or her leisure, until he or she is comfortable with a plan to overcome them. Once able to do so, he or she may plunder the secured assets without further deterrence or risk of detection.

A few of the more common active internal controls include:

- Signatures
- Document countersigning
- Passwords and personnel identification numbers
- Segregation of duties
- Separation of functions
- Physical asset control
- Real-time inventory control
- Fences, padlocks, and all physical restraints
- Document matching
- Pre-numbered accountable forms

Signatures.   These are perhaps the most common active control in use. They are the mainstay of most internal control systems. They are also among the most trusting of internal controls. Signatures are considered active internal controls because transaction documents which require them are not valid unless they are signed. The control effect presumes that without the signature(s), whatever transaction a document may be authorizing cannot be executed, will not be accepted or otherwise processed, and whatever assets they are protecting are therefore secure. The signatures assure those accepting these documents that the documents are approved, and therefore the assets involved can be conveyed.

The popular internal control requirement for authenticating signatures is based upon the fact that every individual's signature is unique, like a fingerprint. Because of that characteristic, theoretically any document bearing an authorized signature positively authenticates it as having the approval of the signer. As most handwriting experts would undoubtedly agree, as with a fingerprint, given the opportunity for careful examination and sufficient time to examine a signature, using samples of the signer's handwriting—known to be authentic—it is possible to conclude, with near certainty, whether a certain person did or did not write the signature being examined. The problem is that most people who rely upon signatures (1) are not handwriting experts, (2) do not have sufficient opportunity to study the characteristics of a signature, (3) do not have samples of a signer's handwriting known to be authentic, and (4) usually do not have sufficient signature recognition points in a signature to do a decent job of analysis. Accordingly, it is a very simple matter for a fraud perpetrator who needs a signature on a document to provide a generally acceptable facsimile that will satisfy most if not all persons requiring a signature to release control over assets.

To illustrate the regard for signatures by financial institutions, we recently learned of an interesting variation of signatures used to authenticate a document. When asked to authorize an electronic funds transfer, the Fidelity Investments company requires the applicant to sign an appropriate document specifying the bank account to which he or she wishes the funds to be transferred. However, before the document will be accepted as bona fide, Fidelity requires that the bank named as recipient of the fund transfer, stamp and authenticate the document, verifying that the applicant has been positively identified. In reality, the maneuver accomplishes little in the way of internal control, other than to transfer liability to the bank if resulting transactions involve fraud.

The internal control merit of requiring a signature on a document is at the very least questionable. It is recommended that the use of signatures to release control over assets be considered carefully before adopting them as internal controls.

Document Countersigning.   This practice was adopted many years ago as a control device seeking to demonstrate—usually to a third party—that two or more designated individuals have concurred on whatever document is involved.

The requirement for two or more signatures on a document is considered an active control because without the multiple signatures that may be required, any document requiring them is not valid. The requirement for two signatures may have merit where fraud is not involved, to evidence the concurrence of two or more individuals in whatever action is being authorized. However, where fraud is involved, it is just as easy to forge two signatures as it is one.

Passwords.   These grew in popularity with the growing need for people to interact with computers. They are considered active internal controls in that if individuals cannot provide the correct password, they are denied access to whatever they are seeking to gain access to. A popular password type used by many entities is the Personal Identification Number (PIN). To be effective, confidentiality of the password or PIN must be maintained. When it is, it is an excellent control. The problem is, confidentiality is frequently lost, and with it the control value of the password. In order to remember their passwords or PINs, people tend to write them down somewhere convenient they can refer to when the password or PIN is needed. Thieves or perpetrators know this and can often come by the secret numbers with a little patience. Those who require passwords or PIN numbers—usually financial institutions—realize that people are careless with the security over them. To provide another layer of security, they will often ask the maiden name of the user's mother. However, the request for the mother's maiden name is so common that a clever perpetrator would surely anticipate it, and be prepared to respond correctly.

The naiveté of some financial institutions, however, is unbelievable. A bank in Northern Virginia once began a service where customers could gain access to their confidential account information by telephoning the bank and using their telephone instruments to tap in their account numbers and their supposedly secret social security numbers. Of course, every personal check they write displays their account numbers, and their Virginia driver's license number was the same as their social security number. Interestingly, the bank manager didn't agree that their new service compromised control over customer account information.

Segregation of Duties. This is an often used active internal control system feature which provides that no one person is assigned the sole responsibility for transactions involving the receipt or disbursement of valuable assets. The practice is considered an active control in that, theoretically, a transaction cannot be completed by a perpetrator acting alone without being detected. The concept is based upon the notion that it is unlikely that two or more persons would conspire to commit fraud. However, in recent decades, such is not the case. Much of the fraud that occurs now involves conspiracy, which makes any dependence upon segregation of duties somewhat arguable. Nevertheless, internal control designs should incorporate segregation of duties whenever practicable to increase the level of difficulty in perpetration. Just don't rely on it!

A case which illustrates how the segregation of duties may have made theft of assets more difficult involves the justice system itself. In the way of background: Wisconsin motorists charged with traffic offenses are given the option of appearing in court to plead their cases, or to acknowledge their offenses and clear their liabilities by mailing in whatever fine was cited by the arresting officer. At some point, it was discovered—quite by accident—that perpetrators in one or more county clerk offices who were receiving payments of traffic fines through the mail were stealing a portion of the cash and checks received. They were clever enough to hide their thefts by posting credits to the clerk's traffic fines receivable accounts, with explanations such as "the judge has reduced the fine," a circumstance which often happens legitimately. In larger organizations, a problem such as this might be reduced by a control system feature which restricted responsibility for opening the mail to certain persons, who would then not be allowed to generate accounting entries reducing receivable accounts. This may have made the eventual discovery of their thefts more likely. However, it is likely that the volume of cash received by county clerks' offices would not allow the separation of duties. However, the thefts that were discovered accidentally by auditors could as well have been discovered by intentional searches. The audit function, performed as a *passive* internal control, would very likely have totally suppressed further instances of the fraud. We were told that future audits of county clerk offices will search for this type of fraud. Such searches will be, in effect, a most effective passive internal control and should be continued indefinitely, regardless of whether or not they defect fraud.

Separation of Functions. This is an internal control system design feature which provides for the division of transaction processing in such a way that different organizational activities process transactions in such a manner as to corroborate each other. By dividing functions in such a manner that different organizational units are involved the possibility of fraud is greatly diminished. The following two simple illustrations involving cash receipts and inventory receipts illustrate this control.

Cash receipts. Where an entity receives large amounts of cash in the mail, the control system may provide for mail to be opened by one or more persons working under constant surveillance—or apparent surveillance—by a video camera, a supervisor, through one-way glass, or other means. To minimize any theft of cash, their task should be limited to (1) separating the cash from any other documentation that may be included in each envelope, (2) counting the amount of cash in the envelope, (3) recording the amounts counted on a receipt to be included with the documentation, (4) depositing the cash at regular intervals, and (5) forwarding all documentation to the accounting department, where it will be reconciled with batch bank deposits and general ledger postings. Ordinarily, there should be no unexplained discrepancies between cash total receipts, the amount of the deposits, and the credits to destination accounts (e.g., accounts receivable, sales, un-applied cash, etc.). However, in large systems, glitches must be expected and reckoned with. For example, when the Internal Revenue Service processes its millions of incoming tax returns, large amounts of cash are received. Essentially, it follows the foregoing procedure, with the exception that the envelopes received are opened by machines (the top edge is worn away), and the opened envelopes are returned to the mail baskets for processing. This allows some of the cash receipts to fall out of the open envelopes before it can be counted and credited to the remitting taxpayers. After each mail basket is emptied, cash is often found in the bottom of each basket. It is counted, credited to "found cash," and is used to reconcile any batch disparities between amounts claimed as having been included by taxpayers and amounts found in each envelope.

Inventory receipts. Control over sales, inventory receipts, storage, and shipping usually benefit from a separation of functions.

For example, one fraud case that comes to mind involved a puzzling inventory shortage revealed in several consecutive physical inventory counts. At first, inventory losses were thought to result from inadequate physical warehouse security, but regardless of the measures

Continues

Continued

taken to strengthen security and stock issue procedures, the shortages continued. Finally, one day, quite by accident, an alert auditor noticed articles of merchandise identical to missing inventory items for sale in a surplus store. A freight delivery service driver had been delivering less stock to the warehouse than was loaded on his truck for delivery, and dropping the remainder off somewhere else. The entity's employee, his conspiring partner, would annotate the receiving document as though the entire order had been delivered. In other words, if the entity had ordered 1,000 widgets, the driver would only deliver 900, but 1,000 would be noted as received. From the receiving document, the entity's accounting department would take note that 1,000 had been delivered, increase the book inventory by 1,000, and pay for 1,000. The warehouse would place the 900 in storage without counting or otherwise noting the quantity received. Subsequent physical inventory counts would notice the shortages, but when investigating them, it was never assumed that the inventory shortages had never been in the warehouse.

In this instance, internal control would be improved were the warehouse employee responsible for placing the merchandise received in storage locations, required to recount and verify the quantities received, sending his or her copy of the receiving document directly to the accounting department. However, all of these recommended improved procedures are wholly dependent upon people doing their jobs as required. In actual practice, they don't! People get tired, are overworked, some are lackadaisical, and fail to see the need to count or recount stock, or to be precise in their counts. Accordingly, a good internal control system should periodically check incoming shipments to verify that everyone is doing what they are supposed to be doing.

Physical Asset Control.   This practice basically provides that any movement of assets requires documents authorizing the movement. Control is vulnerable to document and signature forgery.

Real-Time Inventory Control.   This term refers to the management of book inventories on a real-time basis. To take advantage of the control, the inventory control system must be suitably automated and inventory unit quantities ideally should display bar codes for easy and accurate readings. Inventory is scanned when entering and leaving control areas. One clear advantage, in addition to improved accuracy in inventory record keeping, is the ability to physically verify line-item inventory quantities at any time. The system is vulnerable to manipulation.

Fences, Padlocks, and All Physical Restraints. Basically, these involve physical controls designed to restrict access to valuable assets, often with no supplemental protection. Entities sometimes, with incredible naiveté, tend to rely too heavily upon physical protection of assets, although most physical restraints are relatively easy to overcome. Many entities are incredibly naive in their control expectations.

An example that stunned government auditors involved a U.S. government narcotics custodian. Perhaps unknown to most Americans, the government maintains huge stockpiles of narcotics in the event of war or natural disaster. In several storage facilities, the auditors became concerned that billions of dollars worth of narcotics were not adequately safeguarded. One building, located in a rather deserted area open to the public, was secured only by a heavy-duty padlock. Upon hearing the auditors' complaint, the custodian of the narcotics requested an opinion on the adequacy of the physical safety of the narcotics from the U.S. Drug Enforcement Agency (DEA). After inspecting the facility, DEA approved the padlocked facility as adequate. However, in the opinion of the auditors, anyone with a small tool could have broken the lock and stolen dangerous drugs with a street value in the billions of dollars. What it appears to have prevented the theft, was the fact that few people were aware of what was stored inside the nondescript building. Not even the police!

In another example of incredible internal control naiveté, the same government narcotics custodian received permission from the U.S. Treasury to store narcotics at a very secure site maintained to store precious metals used for coinage. Deep in the Treasury's vaults, the custodian stored billions of dollars not only in narcotics, but in diamonds as well. Incredibly, the custodian's employees were free to come and go into the vaults as they pleased, with no record ever being made of their entry. While they were in the vaults, however,

Continues

Continued

a Treasury guard waited out of sight in a corridor until they exited, at which time their bodies were scanned with a hand-held metal detector to protect against any unauthorized removal of the precious metals. No precious metal losses were ever detected, but missing and unaccounted for were 200,000 vials of injectable morphine left over from the Vietnam war, several 40-pound cans of morphine sulfate—a refined substance used to make injectable morphine—and unknown quantities of the diamonds.

Document Matching and the Use of Pre-numbered Accountable Forms.   These are commonly used in internal control systems to restrict the introduction of non-authorized forms and control documents, and to assure the receipt and processing of all forms in a sequence known to have been issued.

Active controls appear to be more widely used than passive controls, perhaps because they are the easiest to conceive and justify. Designing an active control is essentially a matter of placing an impediment between would-be perpetrators and the goodies. However, a control system substantially defended by active controls may be described as suffering from the "Maginot syndrome[7]." The alternative is to rely on a cost-effective combination of passive and active controls.

There are significant disadvantages to active internal controls:

- Most are vulnerable to human failure. Most active controls are operator-dependent. If the people who are charged with maintaining control features are poorly trained, naive, inattentive due to distractions or illness, or otherwise negligent even for a brief interlude—the control function must be protected even for the few minutes required for the operator to visit a restroom—the best active control can fail. Most active controls are vulnerable to conspiracy or pseudo-conspiracy[8].

- They are vulnerable to perpetrator evasion. Most perpetrators can be considered expert in those operational areas they consider for fraud. Before attempting fraud, they can be expected to have studied the active controls in use. They have become aware of their vulnerabilities and determined ways and means of defeating them.

- They are costly. Active controls are positive controls and must function continuously, all of the time, without interruption to be effective. This often requires the investment of significant resources.
- Many adversely affect productivity. Consider the delays encountered in checking authorizations, reviewing transactions, routing documents for countersignatures, giving passwords, segregating document processing, and the like. If active internal controls are not efficiently designed, the negative impact on productivity is all the greater.

Passive Internal Controls

Passive internal controls, although having the same objectives as active controls, differ conspicuously by seeking to stop fraud from occurring indirectly, through deterrence measures, versus directly through measures designed to prevent it. They are generally an economical and very effective fraud deterrent. In a manner of speaking, if designed properly, they induce a state of mind in the would-be perpetrator that strongly motivates him or her to decide against executing a fraudulent act. While not attempting to physically prevent a perpetrator from committing a fraudulent act, they create sufficient risk in a fraudulent act to convince a perpetrator that he or she "doesn't want to go there!"

An analogy that might improve understanding of the difference between active and passive controls might involve the two alternatives a chicken farmer might consider to protect his flock from thieves. The first alternative, which would be comparable to an active control, would be to build a fence around his chicken coop to make it difficult for any thieves to get at his chickens. He might even electrify it to improve its invulnerability. The second alternative, comparable to a passive control, would be not to build a fence at all, but to make it known that he planned to visit the chicken coop at frequent unannounced intervals with a 12 gauge shotgun.

The advantages and disadvantages of each of the farmer's alternative controls directly relate to those that any entity may expect in the ordinary course of business. Take note that whereas a fence is expensive and seemingly formidable, there are numerous ways that it can be breached. Anyone having a taste for chicken will not be deterred for long. However, the advantages of the farmer visiting the chicken coop with a 12 gauge shotgun are many. First of all, the control is very inexpensive. After first having announced and established his nightly visits, the farmer can vary the frequency intervals, or even discreetly discontinue them at any time without any loss of benefit. The deterrent will still be there. The would-be chicken thief must consider "Is it worth the possible cost to me—risking my life—to steal something that is only worth a few dollars?"

The following is an excellent example, not unlike the forgoing example, involving the employment of a passive control, and, incidentally, a significant departure from generally accepted practice.

News item: Los Angeles gets new subway honor system

There will be **no** turnstiles or ticket takers on the Metro Red Line. Tickets for the $1.10 fare can be purchased at subway stations from ATM-like machines with talking video screens. Fare inspectors will make spot checks, asking riders for proof that they purchased tickets. Violators will be subject to fines up to $250.

AP—LaCrosse Tribune
January 29, 1993

Note that the Los Angeles transit system does not require a passenger to display a ticket to enter and ride a train, which is commonly required where active controls are in use. If someone wishes to steal transportation by not buying a ticket, they are free to do so. They need only to walk aboard a train. However, a perpetrator who did not purchase a $1.10 ticket would be subject to a $250 fine if required to display a ticket in a random inspection they could not avoid. The risk decision a would-be perpetrator must make, is "Does avoiding a $1.10 fare justify risking a $250 fine?" Los Angeles is obviously betting that although some people will ride without paying a fare, the revenues lost will be more than offset by the convenience to passengers and the savings in the cost of collecting fare cards. This sort of passive control system has been practiced successfully for many years in European cities such as Athens and Düsseldorf.

Custodians who may be considering passive controls should expect criticism from persons who are comfortable with the more reassuring active controls, and should be prepared to offer counter-arguments. Although unknown, it is not unlikely that the behind-the-scenes argument experienced by those who favored the Los Angeles Metro passive fare collection system, resembled the following:

Proponents of active controls may have argued that the Los Angeles Metro passive control system is undesirable and ineffective in that it does not prevent unticketed passengers from riding free, with a resulting loss of transportation revenue. They may have argued that although onboard inspectors may detect some riders without tickets, many will not be detected. To prove their argument, they may have even conducted tests which demonstrate that in perhaps 100 attempts, as many as 99 of their agents were able to enter and ride Los Angeles Metro trains without purchasing tickets. Their conclusion: $108.90 for every 100 passengers would be lost if a passive control were used! Their recommendation: Bar entry to anyone without a ticket and increase revenue. The reader should wonder, do the results of such a test serve to defeat the passive system being discussed?

Proponents of passive controls probably argued that the Los Angeles Metro's passive control system is effective. They would probably argue that for the small cost of a $1.10 ticket, riders who might consider not purchasing a ticket will be deterred by the $250 fine. They will also argue that any study which might find that 99 out of 100 riders were able to board and ride trains without purchasing tickets is questionable, but is, nevertheless, an argument for system proponents. Even if 99 riders were able to ride free, it is true the system would lose $108.90 in revenue. However, the one who was caught could pay a fine of $250, for a net profit of $141.10. In fact, 227 passengers could ride free for every one caught before the system would lose money. Proponents would be tempted to recommend that more passengers not buy tickets. Of course, if the tests did disclose that this was happening, a greater frequency of ticket-checking would bring an end to that practice very quickly.

Proponents of the passive controls also may have argued that the statistical study conducted by those favoring active control was flawed in that those persons testing the system encountered no risk. Those who may have been caught faced no $250 fines! Without bona fide risk, such a test would be worthless. There is no way that anyone could convincingly argue that, for example, a large number of normal passengers would risk a $250 fine to save a $1.10 fare.

Los Angeles Metro officials demonstrated unusual insight and courage in adopting the passive control. In contrast, the Washington, DC Metro system—to assure that rider revenue is fully collected—is burdened with an expensive, cumbersome fare monitoring system which requires riders to (1) purchase machine-readable ticket cards, (2) enter into a turnstile to gain admittance to the trains, (3) enter into turnstiles again when they exit the system, (4) be barred from exiting if the ticket fare remaining on their card is insufficient, (5) have to return to ticketing machines to pay additional revenue, and (6) only then be allowed to exit the system.

Take note of the advantages of passive controls here, in comparison to active controls. The traditional active control for assuring that all passengers have purchased tickets has always been to restrict the entrance of passengers until they displayed evidence that they had purchased a fare. This often required a person to be positioned at each entrance, who either collected tickets as passengers boarded a bus or train, or required that everyone display a ticket. The system was designed to prevent anyone who didn't have a ticket from riding. There was no penalty for anyone attempting to board without a ticket. They simply were denied entry, and yet, who hasn't seen bus passengers sneaking in via the rear door or subway passengers jumping over the turnstiles? The active systems are costly and often delay transportation until all ticketed passengers can be boarded. The Los Angeles Metro system, much to their credit, employs a passive system. By not requiring that all passengers provide evidence of a fare payment prior to boarding, the trains are not slowed by the need to take tickets and the system requires fewer operators to maintain it. However, anyone riding without a ticket is considered to be a thief and subject to a penalty when discovered. Spot checks can be intensified or relaxed depending upon the rate of compliance noted. Persons familiar with the European system report that it is rare to see an inspector bother a passenger to display a ticket; but, they also report that few people would dare ride without one. Incidentally, riding a commercial transportation vehicle without paying a fare meets the definition of fraud.

The U.S. Internal Revenue Service tax collection system relies upon passive internal controls to assure taxpayer voluntary compliance with tax laws. As many taxpayers are undoubtedly aware, it is possible for them to evade the payment of taxes simply by falsifying data on their tax returns. They can even claim refunds to which they are not entitled. This is possible because the IRS does not audit or verify the data on every tax return—which an active control system would require—before accepting a tax return or making a refund of tax payments. In other words, a taxpayer could very easily commit tax fraud, and possibly not have their tax fraud detected. The IRS did not chose this passive system without careful deliberation. It is quite likely that they at one time did consider checking every tax return and soon discovered the futility of it. The cost and effort involved would far outweigh the benefits. However, it would be equally foolish to forego all control. If no tax returns were examined, tax fraud would surely increase. Accordingly, passive controls are the ideal solution, selectively auditing tax returns to a extent sufficient to inject enough risk into tax fraud to suppress it. As with most passive controls, it is possible for the IRS to monitor and estimate the extent of tax revenues lost to fraud and to occasionally decrease the intensity of their audits without loss of control effect.

Many custodians and managers feel uncomfortable with the use of passive controls rather than active controls; however, the concept is accruing more and more converts. There are many advantages to their use, the principal one being that the control can be intermittent without any loss of control effect, as long as the would-be perpetrator *believes* that the control is functioning.

Among the principle differences between active internal controls versus passive internal controls are:

- Cost. Whereas active controls are expensive, passive controls are relatively economical. Whereas active controls require continual attention, passive controls require relatively little maintenance and can be intensified or relaxed—based upon test results—at an entity's whim without appreciable loss of deterrent value.
- Efficacy. Whereas active controls are visible or predictable and can be avoided, passive controls are invisible and not predictable, and hence cannot be avoided. Once the mental deterrent is established in a would-be perpetrator's mind, it endures without additional reinforcement.

A few of the more common types of passive internal controls include:

- Customized controls
- Audit trails
- Focused audits
- Surveillance of key activities
- Rotation of key personnel

Customized Controls.   These are unique controls designed to serve a specific internal control purpose. Every entity with an internal control problem seemingly without a solution is encouraged to give thought to a unique and possibly unorthodox control. If it appears to address a control problem area, then by all means, try it.

The following is considered an excellent example of the perfect custom control. It involves a government agency. The agency, accustomed to delaying for long periods of time between repainting its office space, would contract to have two coats of paint applied to improve appearances and longevity, at significant extra cost. Once, quite by accident, they discovered that some painting contractors were cheating by applying one coat of paint while charging for two coats. Perceiving the need to control this situation, the agency was at a loss as to ways and means of effecting control. Short of having someone oversee the painters, an impractical and expensive option that was quickly rejected, it had no practical way of enforcing the contract provision that two coats of paint be applied. Further, was the agency ever to have reason to believe that a painter cheated by applying only one coat, a question arose as to how they would prove that this was true, should they decide to prosecute or otherwise pursue a claims action. It would be a judgement call—the painter's word against the agency. Finally, the perfect passive internal control was conceived.

It was decided that in future painting contracts, painters required to apply two coats of paint to an interior surface would also be required to include a prescribed slight tint to the first coat. The control was brilliant in all regards. It was simple, efficacious, and practically cost-free. Subsequently, proving that a painter had in fact applied two coats of paint was a simple matter of selecting an obscure part of a painted surface and scratching the paint. Using a loupe, it was possible to examine the scratch and to see two colors, if two coats had been applied.

Audit Trails. Particularly in automated systems, these are frequently used passive internal controls. They are considered passive in that they do nothing to prevent a fraudulent act. However, since they are a record of every change made to a permanent record, it is possible for an auditor to review changes made and trace any accounting entries back to a source. Such a feature, theoretically at least, insures that a record cannot be changed without the changer being identified.

Accordingly, any computer fraud which involves changes to records is subject to discovery. One example of a master record change that involved information entities are very concerned with, for example, are changes to an annuitant's address, or an annuitant's name in a financial payment system. In a common fraud of the past, perpetrators have intercepted the death notices of annuitants and changed the name or address. Thus, they have been known to continue the deceased's annuity payments indefinitely. Incidentally, a creative internal control sometimes used in cases such as this, is one where the annuitant insurer offers a small death benefit stipend of perhaps $1,000 when notification of a death is received. The award provides an incentive for the estate of a deceased annuitant to notify the insurer of the death, and to expect $1,000 when it is confirmed, which in turn effectively stops the monthly annuity payments. The $1,000 awards are considered a cost-beneficial passive internal control.

Focused Audits.   Conducted with internal control objectives, these audits are considered the best passive internal control measures an entity can employ. The term *focused audit* as used here, simply refers to an audit or examination that has a very narrow concentration (focus), and is used to achieve specific internal control objectives. The objectives may be to probe areas that have been previously determined to be vulnerable to fraud, but for which internal controls have been declined due to reasons such as unfavorable cost versus benefit estimates, and the failure to previously detect any significant fraud. The focused audits are used to assure the custodian that the areas remain benign. Focused audits are also used to achieve psychological objectives, to instill the perception that sensitive areas are being surveyed and that perpetration is not without risk. Focused audits should not be confused with ordinary internal auditing, although in some instances, the examination objectives may be similar and the differences subtle. The primary differences between focused audits and internal auditing are:

- Focused audits may be performed by management accountants, or literally anyone who may be asked to do so by the custodian of the internal control system. From time to time, the custodian may have his or her own staff perform directed examinations, or the accounting department or the internal audit department. Internal auditing is performed by auditors under the direction of a director of auditing.

- Focused audits are usually non-discretional and are performed as required by the internal control system design. Internal audits are substantially discretional and responsive to changing priorities of the parent entity.

A previous example involving the theft of traffic fines mailed to county clerk offices illustrates the use of focused audits as an economical but effective way to control future thefts through both deterrence and detection.

Surveillance of Key Activities.   This practice is often employed as a passive internal control. Although it does nothing to physically prevent fraud from occurring, it can inhibit fraud if would-be perpetrators are aware that they might be watched. Surveillance may be accomplished from behind one-way glass or other vantage points where the supervisor cannot be seen by those being watched. Videotaping sensitive activities may also be used. As with all passive controls, someone does not have to be watching, only that the subjects of the surveillance be aware that someone *may* be watching.

Rotation of Key Personnel.   This includes the requirement that employees take the vacations they have earned. Often, the secrecy of a fraudulent act will depend upon the physical presence of the perpetrator to manipulate data and records. If it is possible to rotate key employee assignments within the entity periodically, preferably without notice, a control effect is achieved very economically.

Passive Control Summary

Passive Controls seek to deter a fraud perpetrator by making his risk of discovery unacceptable. Passive controls remedy many of the disadvantages of active controls.

- Whereas active controls are costly, passive controls are not. In fact, they do not need to be operating continuously to achieve their control effect.
- Whereas active controls are highly vulnerable to human failure, passive controls are not. Most passive controls are not people-dependent. Accordingly, operator training, naiveté, corruptibility, or negligence is normally not a significant problem.
- Whereas active controls often adversely affect productivity, passive controls do not! Normally, they do not involve time-consuming practices such as repeatedly reviewing authorizations, examining every transaction, routing documents for countersignatures, giving passwords,

segregating document processing, and the like. Accordingly, output productivity is rarely affected.

• Whereas active controls are highly vulnerable to perpetrator evasion, passive controls are not! Properly designed passive controls cannot be evaded. There is no way for the fraud perpetrator to be assured of risk avoidance, regardless of his skill in operational areas being considered for fraud.

Can You Rely on Internal Controls?

Yes and No. If internal controls are well crafted, and if the personnel responsible for enforcing them are well trained and conscientious, the controls may be relied upon for reasonable fraud protection. However, they should not be totally relied upon. They must be continually tended. As time passes, it is normal to expect erosion of control effectiveness as entity missions change, personnel change, attitudes change, accounting systems change, and as would-be perpetrators have an opportunity to consider them for loopholes. It is well to heed the Murphy's Law which advises "It is impossible to make anything foolproof, because fools are so ingenious" (anonymous)[9].

An internal control custodian must periodically test the efficacy of internal controls and re-evaluate their adequacy. Internal control users should never underestimate the cunning of fraud perpetrators! No matter how effective an installed control appears to be, you can safely assume that someone will (1) searching for a way to evade it, and (2) will find a way to evade it. After months of seemingly unproductive work, clerks charged with the day-to-day maintenance of internal controls tend to get careless. Accordingly, subsequent to installation, internal controls must be periodically monitored and evaluated to determine their continuing efficacy. Over-confidence can be disastrous.

About Perpetrators

When crafting and adopting internal controls, it is well to keep in mind that most fraud perpetrators steal to enjoy the fruits of what they steal. Most are not gamblers, they prefer minimal risks. Those who do take risks are often detected. It is the ones who don't take risks that entities must worry about. In a 1996 conference at the Harvard Faculty Club, scholars discussed "Risk Aversion as a Behavioral Problem." The conversation applied to investing, but their observations provide interesting insights into how people handle risk. Richard Thaler, professor of economics at the University of Chicago, discussed a phenomenon called "myopic loss aversion," maintaining that people tend to feel the pain of financial loss more acutely than pleasure of financial gain. "In studies, people are given $10 and asked to bet on a coin toss. If it's tails, they lose all $10. If it's heads, they win. The question is: How much money do they have to win before they agree to the bet? Answer: About $25. Thus, people feel pain about 2.5 times more severely than pleasure, according to these studies.[10]"

Accordingly, when it is not possible to conceive of internal controls which prevent fraud—that have acceptable cost-benefit ratios—the next-best controls are those which put anyone attempting fraud at risk. Bear in mind the meaning of the word *deter* ". . . to prevent or discourage from acting, as by means of fear or doubt.[11]"

As a prelude to fraud, a would-be perpetrator will normally scrutinize his or her risk exposure in an area very carefully. Thugs contemplating armed robbery are said to case the joint to assess their risk exposure. It is the same with would-be fraud perpetrators. Among the things the would-be perpetrator will look for is the frequency with which auditors select a given area for examination. If auditors rarely work in an area being watched, it signals to the would-be perpetrator that the risk of discovery—even accidental—is minimal, and his chances of discovery equally minimal. However, the greater the time and frequency that auditors work in an area being observed, the greater the risk a perpetrator will see in a fraud attempt. And, he or she will be very likely to reconsider his fraud plans. Accordingly, auditors should be required to invest a reasonable amount of exposure time in all areas at risk, a strategy of risk psychology. Since a would-be perpetrator has no idea what the auditor may be looking for when he or she searches through files, the mere presence of the auditor is often sufficient to deter fraud. It is not even necessary for the auditor to do useful work as long as he or she appears to be doing useful work. A favorite audit tactic is to direct auditors who have idle time between programmed reviews—which happens quite frequently—to rummage through document files in areas with high fraud-profiles, if necessary with no particular audit objective in mind. This is called show time, or showing an audit presence. Often, the auditors are not given any audit objectives other than to make it appear that vital records were being examined. To the observer, the mere fact that auditors were looking for something in the lease files, for example, would not go unnoticed, and would signal to any would-be perpetrators that risk of fraud-discovery was present. If the auditor is able to do useful fraud-specific work in the process, it is a bonus.

Before leaving the subject of fraud perpetrators, it is interesting to note a common misunderstanding that perpetrators fit the criminal profile often seen on police "wanted" posters. When we search for individuals who may be fraud perpetrators, we often tend to look for unsmiling, unattractive, elusive, perhaps disagreeable people. The problem is that most perpetrators turn out to be some of the nicest people we know, and because of that trait, tend not to be suspected of fraud. Be advised, suspicion is often a most vital first step toward detecting fraud. Therefore, don't be prejudiced in selecting those whom you might suspect. You might just miss the grand prize. For example, a gentleman in Chicago who was suspected of stealing over $900,000 in phony invoices was highly regarded in the victim's office. By most accounts, he was a really nice man, often treating many of his office co-workers to lunch at fine Chicago restaurants. Spending far in excess of his moderate income, he would volunteer explanations that he had recently inherited money from a deceased aunt and effectively extinguish any suspicions that may have otherwise arisen. His fraud endured for several years before it was accidentally discovered when he got careless. In another instance, a company controller in a midwestern state— after years of very lucrative fraudulent activity—pleaded guilty to charges of stealing huge sums from the entity he worked for[12]. The jury, selected from the community he resided in, found it difficult to believe the charges that were levied against him. He was known as a benefactor of the community and to have given large sums to local charities. He regularly attended church on Sundays—a modern day Robin Hood. After pledging to make monthly restitution payments to his former employer, he was freed without a prison sentence.

Chapter 6

Establishing and Operating an Effective Fraud-Specific Internal Control System: Seven Steps to Internal Control

There are seven steps that must be considered in the establishment and operation of an effective fraud-specific internal control system (hereafter called "internal control system"). They are:

1. The appointment of an internal control custodian and sufficient staff resources dedicated to, and responsible for, the employing entity's internal control
2. The determination of internal control requirements
3. The design of needed internal controls
4. The installation and de-installation of internal controls
5. The training of operators and monitoring of their competence
6. Periodic testing of internal conflict efficacy
7. Fraud-specific auditing

APPOINT AN INTERNAL CONTROL CUSTODIAN WITH SUFFICIENT STAFF RESOURCES

The custodian will be responsible for designing and overseeing the operation of the entity's internal control system. This is the first step that should be taken toward achieving internal control objectives. Someone has to be responsible! If the entity involved is not sufficiently large to justify the appointment of a dedicated custodian and staff, or it is felt that the need is not sufficient to do so, a competent individual—not likely to have a conflict of interests or significant opportunities to commit fraud—should be named and given explicit instructions to dedicate a certain proportion of his or her time to this task. However it is done, a specific allotment of personnel resources should be budgeted or dedicated as well. Failure to appoint a custodian and sufficient staff resources will result in imperfect internal control and imminent failures.

In a large entity with a high fraud-risk index, the internal control custodian's role should have as high a profile as the chief internal auditor, and the custodian should report directly to the chief financial officer, or equivalent. Too frequently, the installation and operation of internal controls is approached on a piecemeal basis. For example, physical inventory counts may consistently reveal shortages, causing alarm, and the assignment of someone to improve internal controls. Responsibility is often assigned as an additional duty to a chief accountant or an organization head. This practice is particularly undesirable because it fails to address an entity's overall needs and priorities, concentrating only on those problem areas which cause alarm and failing to address other areas in need of control. In addition, by assigning remedial responsibility on an *ad hoc* basis as needs may arise to whomever may have jurisdiction over the area affected, the entity overall ends up with questionable internal controls designed by people who have little training in internal control design and operation, a questionable overall system with overall responsibility indistinct.

Many entities simply assign internal control responsibility to the chief accountant. Although chief accountants are ordinarily a good choice as far as centralizing internal control responsibility, they tend to be a poor choice in this situation, not because they are not qualified, but because most chief accountants are already carrying staggering workloads. Oversight of an internal control system as an additional duty often results in insufficient attention to internal control. Assigning internal control responsibility to organization heads may end up being comparable to assigning the fox to guard the chickens. Internal control responsibility is too critical to accomplish any other way than by giving the task to someone who makes it his or her prime responsibility, is independent of areas to be controlled, can acquire the training and experience to do the job competently, has no clear conflict of interests, and who has adequate time and resources available to administer it properly.

DETERMINE INTERNAL CONTROL REQUIREMENTS

This is the first and most critical objective of an internal control custodian. Among the first questions which all new custodians tend to ponder are where to begin and how to proceed. Those questions are very difficult to answer with any specificity because every entity's needs are different.

Many custodians tend to proceed—sometimes out of necessity—by fighting fires. They tend to panic and attend to the internal control needs of areas where trouble is being experienced, not realizing that more important areas may be in greater need and have a higher-risk exposure. If at all possible, this should be avoided. Instead, it is recommended that problem areas be controlled through focused auditing as an interim measure until more systemic internal controls can be devised.

New Internal Control Custodians

New internal control custodians should begin their assignments by performing a familiarization survey and becoming thoroughly familiar with all aspects of the entity they are responsibility for protecting. The functions and responsibilities of all organizational elements should be studied and fully understood. During this familiarization survey, the custodian should be sensitive to the vulnerability to fraud of each entity and area reviewed. During the familiarization survey, one of the first things that should be noted is the type of entity and the type of accounting system in use. It will determine at the outset whether the entity is at high or low risk of fraud.

Entities most vulnerable to fraud include those that normally have accounting systems that are cash-based or accrued expenditure based— as opposed to accrual-based—accounting systems. Entities that normally use this type of accounting system include governmental entities (federal, state, county, and local), public and private school systems (local schools, colleges, and universities), and institutions (e.g., hospitals, medical clinics). These entities normally have their operating resources appropriated or otherwise allowed by a governing body or supervisory group of some kind. Note: Any revenues these organizations may earn from operations normally flow to the governing body or entity treasury. Future budget authorities are appropriated from the same treasuries. It is normally impossible, or a useless exercise, for these entities to attempt to relate costs and revenues in the same manner that many private entities relate expense and revenue to determine profit or loss, or as a management tool to evaluate operational efficiency.

As a general rule, entities operating under cash-basis accounting systems are normally motivated to spend all the budget cash they receive and management (although they won't admit it) is not always appropriately concerned with fraud. Ironically, for cash-basis entities, money fraudulently taken usually justifies a like amount in their budget the next year!

For-profit entities may also be considered to be in a higher-risk category if they do not have a product or service which allows unit cost accounting, as are those which are able to practice unit cost accounting, but don't.

Unit Costing

This is a powerful fraud deterrent. Organizations which practice it have accounting systems which collect the unit costs of producing or delivering comparable products or services. Relatable costs per unit are developed which—when compared with each other—become the criteria of acceptable performance and make variations in unit costs apparent. Maintenance of unit cost accounting is usually done for the purpose of assuring that production or delivery costs are maintained within prescribed parameters. However, any cost variation, regardless of cause, would be likely to prompt an investigation. Realistically speaking, however, because the system has the capability to attract attention to a cost variation due to fraud, it is more likely that it would serve as an effective passive internal control, and deter perpetration.

For-profit entities which do not accumulate their operating costs so that their cost reporting has useful relevance in highlighting deviant costs— even though they may be using the accrual basis of accounting—are also at a higher risk of fraud than those that do. These include entities which engage in job order production—such as many manufacturers and contractors, service entities such as health care providers, insurance companies, and banks.

The following three examples illustrate the sort of fraud that occurs in the highest risk organizations and the difficulty in detecting it—and in one instance the difficulty in prosecuting it—when it is discovered. Note that the parent organizations of the perpetrators were unaware of the huge frauds that were occurring until the frauds were brought to their attention after being accidentally discovered.

In 1998, it was accidentally discovered that a former Employee of the Year for a state university had stolen over $158,000 from the university by padding time sheets and cashing bogus payroll checks. The discovery occurred accidentally when the employee's husband became a suspect in another crime and postal inspectors searching their residence found payroll check stubs under different names issued by the university and became suspicious. Over the seven-year period that the fraud occurred, it is apparent that the university did not suspect the sizable fraud (note the accidental discovery).

In a federal government case, a government office supply store operated for the convenience of various agencies located in the Washington, DC, area had noted unusually large quantities of Polaroid film being sold to an agency of the U.S. State Department. An employee, using a government credit card, had purchased over $350,000 of film over a year, in quantities so large that it was necessary for him to carry off his purchases in a pick-up truck. After a time, the agency managing the store became suspicious and queried the State Department agency involved, calling their attention to the large purchases. The investigation that followed revealed that the agency had not been aware of the purchases, even though they had routinely authorized payments totaling over $350,000. The employee had been selling the film to criminal outlets to support a drug habit (note the accidental discovery).

An older case involves a Veterans Administration psychiatric hospital. Over a period of time, the hospital's pharmacist had been reported leaving the hospital pharmacy on various evenings carrying large shopping bags. It was known that he also had an ownership interest in several pharmacies in a nearby large city, and it was suspected that he may have been stealing hospital drugs for resale in his pharmacies. In a special hearing he was accused, pleaded innocent,

Continues

Continued

and was released without any action taken on the suspected thefts, due to the hospital's poor internal control over pharmacy products and their inability to determine any losses.

In an attempt to assess the amount of drugs possibly taken, the auditors examined the hospital's reported drug expense for a three-year period. However, because the hospital was on the cash basis of accounting, monthly drug expense reported was actually the cost of drugs the hospital purchased each month, rather than the cost of drugs consumed in hospital medical care activities. Since drugs were purchased in accordance with monthly budget surpluses which varied wildly from month to month, rather than to replenish inventory, reported monthly drug costs varied wildly. It was impossible to determine the hospital's true drug expense, and to reconcile purchases and inventory in such a manner as to even approximate the amount that may have been stolen.

Under cash basis accounting, if appropriate internal control systems are not utilized to supplement internal control, inventory is an asset particularly vulnerable to fraud.

Entities at a much lower risk of fraud are those that normally manufacture and sell a product, or provide services, which are identical or very similar in nature thereby allowing unit cost (or standard cost) accounting. Of necessity, these entities also normally practice accrual basis accounting. Entities which may be included in this category are automobile manufacturers, electronics manufacturers, food purveyors, and the like, where they produce thousands of identical or nearly identical items, or portions, for sale.

Fraud Indexing—A System for Determining Internal Control Status and Priorities

For the internal control custodian faced with the substantial appraisal, or reappraisal, of an entity's internal control system, it is of utmost importance that he or she embrace some sort of system to guide them through completion. Whatever system is favored and used, it should guide the custodian through the process of collecting a subject entity's internal control requirements, evaluating them, and scheduling them for design and installation in such a manner that the most urgent requirements are addressed on a priority basis. For custodians who have not already embraced such a system, a fraud indexing system, as described in the following paragraph, is recommended.

The Fraud Indexing System. A fraud indexing system usually utilizes a set of two numbers ranging from 0 to 100 to express (1) fraud risk, and (2) existing internal control. By definition, a fraud index number of 50— expressed as FI-50—denotes a reference point or average condition. When used to refer to the fraud risk of a commodity, numbers above FI-50 indicate that the commodity is at a higher than average risk of fraud. Numbers below FI-50 indicate that the commodity is at a lower than average risk. The farther the rating number is from FI-50 indicates the degree to which the risk, or internal control, is above or below average. Hence, a fraud index set of FI-50/FI-50 would indicate that a commodity with this rating is at an average risk of fraud, and that the existing applicable internal control is also average. It is not expected that scores of FI-0 or FI-100 would ever be appropriate, and that scores above 75 or below 25 would be seriously considered, and reconsidered.

It is acknowledged that different custodians possessing different skill levels are likely to rate the same area of risk—or internal control—differently. One custodian may rate a given risk situation as FI-65 and another might rate it FI-75. This is acceptable, for it is not so much the actual valuation given to a risk, but the fact that someone has considered it and made a judgement, ranking the control at some point relative to other controls. There will always be differences of judgement in ranking controls. However, it is presumed that strong controls will always be rated above FI-50 and weak controls below FI-50, and ratings will be useful despite these gradation differences. It follows that an internal control system with many values above FI-50 is a relatively strong system, in less need of improvement. By the same token, one with many values below FI-50 is a weak system and perhaps urgently in need of improvement. In addition, the FI valuation system is intended to highlight which aspects of internal control require priority attention, that is, those with the highest risk FI numbers and those with the lowest internal control numbers.

To illustrate, assume that a custodian for a retail sales outlet observes that the store processes large amounts of cash each day which appear highly vulnerable to theft. Understandably, the custodian may rate it FI-75. This indicates to anyone looking at it that *We have serious internal control problem here.* Upon seeing it, a reader would be apt to ask *What are we doing about it?* The question would be automatically answered were the custodian to provide a second FI number indicating the strength of the internal controls in place. For example, if the custodian found the internal control over the mail order cash receipts to be excellent, he or she might rate it FI-75, in which case the "mail order cash receipts" item on his checklist would be reported as FI-75/FI-75. This dual rating signals that (1) there is a serious internal control risk area, and (2) applicable internal control is equally strong. There is no need to improve the control! An FI-75/FI-50 rating would signal that there is a significant internal control risk area, and internal control should be improved, but not urgently. And, lastly, an FI-75/FI-30 would indicate that the item is a significant problem area, and the internal control should be improved immediately. At times, the custodian will discover that some areas are over-controlled, in which case the custodian might rate the example just described as FI-40/FI-75. This might indicate that the theft risk is not considered to be relatively significant, and that the internal control(s) in place are excessive relative to the risk. Since internal controls are often costly and often have a negative effect on productivity, a FI-40/FI-75 situation signals that an internal control may be excessive and should be reconsidered, perhaps rewritten, and if appropriate, downgraded.

Be Cautious in Using Statistics to Determine the Need for the Efficacy of Internal Controls

In concluding the need for, or efficacy of, internal controls, a custodian must rely upon data generated from various sources. Be warned that it is very easy to be deceived by statistics which appear to be incontestable, or to interpret them incorrectly.

One of the things in life that mankind relies upon are statistics. Yet, one of the things that we can also rely upon is how otherwise intelligent people will interpret identical statistics to reach divergent conclusions. Internal control custodians will find it necessary to rely again and again upon statistics, and it cannot be overemphasized how easy it can be to be deceived by them. Consider once again the contradictory views taken by otherwise intelligent people based upon *identical* statistics relative to the very nature of fraud itself. Two extremely differing views exist with regard to the makeup of its largely unseen existence. The following two views of the fraud universe are based largely upon the same statistics.

View 1. Based upon careful research of thousands of fraud cases that are available for research, many distinguished scholars have concluded upon several fundamental characteristics of fraud. They are: most fraud perpetrators are careless, greedy, and inept to the extent that their incompetent ways eventually lead to critical mistakes leading to their accidental discovery.

Conclusion: Left alone, most fraud will ultimately reveal itself!

View 2. The careful research of the thousands of fraud cases that are available for research portraying that fraud perpetrators are careless, greedy, and inept to the degree that their incompetent ways eventually lead to critical mistakes and their discovery proves only one thing: that fraud perpetrators who are careless, greedy, and inept get caught! Those that aren't, don't get caught.

Conclusion: Left alone most fraud will not ultimately reveal itself!

The scholars that performed the research described in the first view made one vital mistake. Much of fraud is undiscovered, and the rest is confidential. Undaunted, they assumed that what was unseen was statistically typical of what they could see. A vital mistake. The authors of this text have many reasons to be confident that the fraud the researchers could not examine—because it was not available to them to be examined—was atypical of what they researched. Accepting this view significantly changes the conclusions that may be reasonably drawn from the same statistics. All fraud perpetrators are not careless, greedy, and otherwise incompetent. Only those that are discovered accidentally!

It appears that the auditing profession's opinion—that it was no longer necessary to practice proactive auditing to discover fraud in the expectation that fraud would in due course reveal itself—has its roots very early in the nineteenth century[13]. For the profession to take such an important position, it surely must have relied upon observations similar to those expressed in the first view. In any event, for over 50 years audits have not included procedures seeking to detect any fraud other than financial statement fraud that were generally accepted by the profession. This difficult to explain moratorium on proactive fraud-specific auditing continued to a significant degree, through the turn of the century. We believe this decision by twentieth century accountants was unfortunate, and surely resulted in a fertile breeding ground for fraud.

The following illustration involving the questionable interpretation of statistics is considered sufficiently important to include at this point to alert internal control custodians to how easily statistics can be misinterpreted.

A situation arose in 1996 when the Inspector General (IG) of the US Department of Transportation issued the following announcement:

The IG reported that her agents had tested the security controls at a number of US airports, and found them *badly deficient.* In 40 percent of their attempts, the agents were able to sneak phony bombs, guns, and knives past metal detectors (note: 60 percent were caught).

However, where the Inspector General concluded that airport controls were deficient, based upon the statistics she compiled, an experienced internal control custodian using the very same statistics would be very likely to conclude that the controls were successful. How can this be?

Consider first, that the system in use by the airports was a passive or risk control system. The IG's criticism was obviously based upon the expectation that airport control was an active control system which would be considered a failure were anyone able to smuggle a single weapon onto an aircraft. A passive system would be designed to deter people from smuggling weapons onto an aircraft. In a passive system the possibility that someone could smuggle a weapon aboard an aircraft is accepted. If you are new to this internal control reasoning, and troubled by it—please read on.

At this point it is expected that many readers will be sympathetic with the IG's views, which envision 40 out of 100 people bringing weapons aboard passenger aircraft. However, before proceeding, a somewhat humorous analogy is useful. It involves a Wisconsin farmer who had been troubled by burglars, and the conventional deterrents weren't working. Finally, in desperation, he posted this sign at the entrance to his property:

This property protected four nights a week by two guys called Smith and Wesson. You guess which four! I mean it!

The burglaries stopped! Similar to the airport security example, the farmer's property advertised to any would-be burglars that the house would not be protected three nights a week and could be burglarized at will, without fear. However, burglars did not take advantage of it. Why? Because of the deadly threat that awaited them should they be so unlucky as to select the wrong night. The same is true of airport security. Any would-be weapon smugglers were faced with severe penalties should they be in the theoretical 40 percent that would be likely to be caught. This is sufficient to deter the vast majority. Note carefully, what was lacking in the IG's tests of airport security were the severe penalties for the failures 40 percent of the time. The IG's agents took no risks in their smuggling attempts, hence their tests must be considered invalid. The real question is, when the stakes are high, as in a real world situation—not as in an IG's test where there is NO risk—would a smuggler attempt the high risk of failure?

For those readers who may still be unconvinced, and there should be many, please consider the alternatives. The IG did not say how the airport security should be improved, only that controls should provide assurance that weapons could not be smuggled through airport security gates. However, accomplishing this very desirable objective would be highly impracticable. To provide any degree of reasonable assurance would require highly objectionable positive controls, requiring thorough passenger and luggage searches, indeterminable delays in boarding flights, and significant additional security costs which passengers would have to bear.

This is a difficult decision that will confront internal control custodians from time to time: whether to attempt to design rigid and unpopular active internal controls or the relatively invisible passive controls. Unfortunately, it is difficult to test the passive or risk controls.

Incidentally, there was an irony in the IG's controversial tests. They were prompted by an airplane crash wherein a bomb was suspected and airport controls were tightened severely as a preventive measure. Later it was determined that an aircraft defect caused the crash—not a bomb.

If you can stand one last statistical story on this subject, we are reminded of the one about the airline passenger who worried that there might be a bomb on an aircraft. He asked a statistician friend, "What are the chances there would be a bomb on the plane?" His friend replied "One in a million." He then asked, "What are the chances there might be **two** bombs on the plane I might be on?" The friend replied "One in a hundred million." After that, given the better odds, he always carried a bomb with him whenever he flew.

Internal Control Requirements Inventory

Once a system, such as the fraud indexing system has been selected for use, the custodian's next step is to prepare an inventory of all entity assets, liabilities, and other major and miscellaneous considerations which need to be evaluated for purposes of internal control. The inventory is simply a listing of every internal control subject that may require internal control.

Each item on the inventory list should be reasonably homogeneous. For example, the asset "cash" must be segregated into its various internal control pertinent classifications of cash. The first subclassification is likely to be "cash receipts" and "cash disbursements." Cash receipts may be further subdivided to indicate each major source of cash receipts, such as over-the-counter sales, mail order sales, accounts receivable, scrap sales, cafeteria receipts, and so forth, each of which may require different internal control needs and for which different internal control measures must be considered.

Cash disbursements will present the biggest internal control problem for custodians, in that the necessary controls will appear endless at times. Would-be fraud perpetrators undoubtedly receive most of their ill-gotten gains through cash disbursements. Every sub-category of expense is a potential avenue for fraud. Consider, for example, the many ways just about any cash disbursement can involve fraud. A simple disbursement to blacktop a parking area can involve a defective delivery, a double payment, a duplicate payment, a shell payment, a rigged contract, and other types as well. It is literally impossible to design *active* internal controls which would have any serious prevention effect upon these frauds. What then, is the internal control custodian to do? Every avenue of fraud must be controlled! Having accepted the fact that he or she cannot prevent all of the common frauds, the savvy custodian will fall back upon passive controls. In doing so, the custodian will acknowledge that prevention is futile—at least from a cost-effective standpoint—and will seek the deterrent effects of passive controls. If he or she can create and install effective passive deterrents, all the better. As a last resort, he or she can elect to require post-active focused audit procedures (also a passive internal control) to determine whether or not the cash disbursement items in need of protection had been exploited. If any frauds are detected, further controls may have to be considered.

It is possible that inventories would have to be segregated by type of inventory, location, and internal controls considered separately for receiving, warehouse storage, and shipping. Any omissions or further subclassifications can be added at any time subsequent to the initial effort. Although over-simplified for explanation purposes, this is nevertheless the initial procedure recommended for beginning an internal control system. If there are any doubts in the custodian's mind regarding whether or not to include a control item, include it. It can always be eliminated later.

The next step after preparing the inventory is identifying each item to indicate its internal control importance and urgency. For custodians using the Fraud Indexing system, the numerical scores given each item do this task automatically. It is an easy matter to sort them with a computer. For this task, if the custodian has long experience with the entity, he or she may already be well aware of the most sensitive areas. If not, then the in-depth surveys of each area should provide insights into the importance and urgency of the various areas. The custodian should also access other information sources to collect trouble areas in need of controls. These information sources include internal audit reports, CPA reports, management studies of all kinds, notes of meetings, and the like, wherein problem areas will frequently have been discussed.

THE DESIGN OF NECESSARY INTERNAL CONTROLS

The design process begins by identifying those internal control areas most in need of improvement for priority attention. If the custodian is using the "fraud-indexing system," and if she has completed the inventory and has scored all items, this task is a relatively simple procedure. For example, all items with FI scores above 50 are considered first. Of the items identified, those with the higher internal control scores are eliminated. Remaining are the areas most at risk of fraud. Whatever system is used, the areas most at risk of fraud must be identified for priority attention.

To illustrate the foregoing, assume there is a "Cash Receipts" item, with a score of FI-75/FI-40. The numerical score indicates, without reading further, that there is a critical need for control here, and that the existing control is inadequate. It would certainly qualify for inclusion on the priority list for new control considerations. This process continues until the custodian is satisfied that the highest priority control issues have been similarly identified, and it is time to begin the difficult and often lengthy process of considering and designing whatever internal controls are necessary to bring the numerical FI scores into a relationship which the custodian considers to be an acceptable and cost-effective internal control.

Further assume, for illustration purposes, that the cash receipts item involved cash collections for a major department store. The entire scenario would work something this. During the survey, the custodian, or her representative, observed that the store's cashier received an average of $2 million in cash and checks each day, through the mail, the sales registers, and over the cashier's counters. Further, she observed that the six weeks before Christmas accounted for probably 60 percent of annual receipts.

The custodian felt that the sizeable cash receipts were very much at risk and worth a score of FI-75. In reviewing the control exercised over the large amount of cash taken in, the custodian became somewhat alarmed when she noted that cash handling was a laborious process, with questionable checks and balances, which delayed bank deposits pending reconciliations, and clearance of the frequent discrepancies arising in the reconciliation process. Many cash variances remained unexplained, and the entire system left numerous opportunities for theft and shortages difficult to trace. She scored internal control as FI-40. What her numbers signaled was that the need for control was high (FI-75) and the internal control present (FI-40) was inadequate to balance it.

After thoroughly reviewing the existing cash handling system, while interacting with the store's cashier, it was decided that cost-effective internal control could not be achieved with supplementary controls. The system had grown incrementally over the years, was basically not cost-effective, cumbersome, and difficult to reinforce. It was the cashier who suggested that an entirely new cash processing system be designed to reduce the need to handle incoming cash and checks, as well as the considerable clerical time involved. Rather than delay the deposit of cash and accumulate large amounts of it on hand, a new accounting system subset was designed. The new system involved segregating incoming cash by "payments on accounts receivable," "cash register sales," "other receipts," and bagging the monies collected for deposit in three accounts, depositing it at regular intervals, thereby reducing the opportunities for theft. The new system required that all cash receipts were to be deposited without counting or reconciling, as "amounts unknown" for each control period. Subsequently, the bank's count of the amount of cash in each bag was accepted as reported, and reconciled to accounting debits and credits posted to accounts receivable, cash register sales tapes, and other tallies. The new procedures, in their entirety, were considered stronger and much more cost-effective. The original FI-75 score for cash risk was reduced to FI-60, and the FI-40 score for the internal control of cash was reappraised as FI-60, signaling that the internal control problem area was now considered to be balanced.

Evaluation Tools

Custodians may find the following reference material useful in evaluating and/or designing internal controls. It provides approximately 200 pages of specific evaluation tools for risk assessment and is useful for preparing an inventory of areas subject to internal control.

INTERNAL CONTROL—INTEGRATED FRAMEWORK

Evaluation Tools, September 1992
Committee of Sponsoring Organizations of the
Treadway Commission
AICPA Product code: 990002

Copies of this document may be ordered from
American Institute of Certified Public Accountants
Order Department
Harborside Financial Center
201 Plaza III
Jersey City, NJ 07311-3881
Telephone 1-800-862-4272

Master File and Custodian's Daily Log

When a custodian is appointed and given responsibility for an entity's internal control system, it is a good idea to keep a record of everything that has been done. To accomplish this, we recommend two permanent records be maintained.

The first—a custodian's daily log—should be maintained by a custodian as a personal record, or diary, of day to day activities pertinent to internal control matters. The log, which may maintained as a personal computer file (password protected), should be used to indicate starting dates for various activities, personnel responsibility assignments, and notes (personal and otherwise) of literally anything that may be important for reference purposes at some future date. The language may be casual, and include reminders of target dates, due dates, and literally any information he or she wishes to save for his or her personal use. The value of such a journal will become particularly relevant when inevitably it becomes necessary to recall past events, fix responsibility, or review any aspect of the custodian's activities. The log is particularly important to allow a smooth transition of custodians. The role of custodian is not normally a permanent assignment, and every care should be taken to record noteworthy events so that a newly appointed custodian may be well informed.

The second record recommended is an internal control master file. A master file should be maintained as a formal record documenting everything that is pertinent to the internal control system. It too is a chronological record documenting the appointments of custodians, the up-to-date status of internal controls, records of internal control inventories with FI scores if utilized, programs for the review and evaluation of internal controls, when internal controls were installed or de-installed, what internal control studies and work papers are available and where they may be located, approval dates, target dates for completion of objectives, a record of internal audit reports bearing upon the internal control system, training program requirements including refreshment progress, and like information. Future management, custodians, or auditors should be able to review the internal control master file of an entity's internal control accomplishments (or non-accomplishments), and have all of their questions answered with regard to the internal control in the subject entity. All internal control active and passive procedures should be documented for ease of reference.

Involvement of Experts

Rarely, if ever, will an internal control custodian and staff possess the necessary technical skills for originating and designing creative controls for a multi-faceted, complex organization. Most will probably be professional accountants with insufficient knowledge of technical operations to create truly unique, effective controls.

Accordingly, custodians, regardless of professional discipline, should acquire the necessary disciplinary skills in the operational specialty areas in which the controls will serve. This can be accomplished by consulting with experts as needed and generating an atmosphere of cooperation with the entity's organizational elements upon which the controls will be focused. Also, when the need is significant, considerable task familiarity can be gained by enrolling in short, technically-oriented courses (such as commercial real estate leasing, for example) to gain a rudimentary knowledge of the subject area. There is normally no need to maintain confidentiality over the custodian's proceedings, and the entity's organizational elements should be very much involved in the process of internal control evaluation, design, and operation.

An excellent illustration which employed a very non-traditional but supereffective internal control was mentioned elsewhere in this text, however, it is worth repeating here.

The federal government accidentally discovered that some painting contractors were charging for applying two coats of paint to redecorate government office space, but were only applying one coat. Painting specialists were asked to develop an internal control to cope with the fraud. After careful consideration, they developed a simple, cost-effective, invisible control:

"Subsequent painting contracts requiring two coats of paint shall provide that the first coat include a slight tint."

That's the control! In future contracts that included the requirement, all that had to be done to verify that painters had indeed applied two coats of paint was to select an inconspicuous location anywhere on the painted surface—at any time after the painting had been completed—and make a small scratch, then inspect the scratched area with a magnifying glass to see if one or two colors were visible!

Please note from this illustration that internal control may involve literally anything which provides the desired control. In this case, the tinting of the first coat of paint was the ideal internal control. It is classified as a passive control in that it does not prevent a painting contractor from attempting to defraud the contracting entity. However, in defrauding a victim in this manner, the painter is aware that he or she is in dire peril of discovery and should be disinclined from doing so. The cost of the control is negligible, it is invisible, does not impair productivity, and any fraud will be discovered when the victim chooses to make a scratch test. Further, should the fraud be discovered, the fact that one coat of paint was applied can be easily proved. Readers should take incidental note here that the failure of the victim to discover that two coats of paint were applied does not prove fraud. One example only proves that the painter delivered one coat of paint, and that the victim is entitled to a reduction in the agreed upon contract price. It does not prove that the painter intended to defraud the entity. However, if the painter has performed in similar contracts in the past, the entity may perform scratch tests on those walls as well. Should it be discovered that all walls painted appeared to have received only one coat of paint, the additional examples make a strong case for proving that the painter acted with intent to defraud and prosecution may be considered.

Approval of Finished Design Segments

It is advisable for internal control custodians to solicit and obtain comments on approved internal control design segments from an objective third party. If the entity involved has an internal audit department, their participation in the approval process would be highly desirable. It is presumed that the affected organizational elements have already been involved in preparing the design. If they have not, they definitely should be invited to comment, but not as objective parties.

INSTALLATION AND DE-INSTALLATION OF INTERNAL CONTROLS

Installation of Internal Controls

After an internal control is conceived, designed, and approved, it must be installed. Like the blueprint for constructing a building, the design is only the plan for achieving internal control objectives, not the control system itself. It must be fully implemented as designed to be effective. This process is, at times, considerably more difficult than it might appear at first. Often, many people are involved in procedural modifications, and there is a tendency for people to resist change. In fact, installing controls is often an arduous, frustrating, and time-consuming process, usually requiring major and minor alterations to existing controls and accounting system processes, compromises, personnel assignments, training, overcoming resistance by operating personnel, and various other installation delays.

It is quite easy to set aside the installation of internal control design features because of installation difficulties or competing needs, only to forget about them, or to make changes when implementing the design to accommodate installation problems. Any deferrals should be carefully noted in the custodian's daily log and master file to assure that installation will be resumed when appropriate. Because internal control designs are often not completely installed, it is advisable for custodians, management accountants, and auditors who seek to periodically evaluate systems of internal control to compare the approved internal control system designs that should be available in the master file with the actual controls that may be in operation. It should never be assumed that they are one and the same.

De-installation of internal controls that are no longer necessary, or which have been superceded by new controls, is often overlooked. From time to time, specific internal controls become no longer necessary. To the degree that they are redundant, the procedures calling for them should be rewritten—if necessary—and the actual controls in operation canceled. This includes properly instructing the personnel who may have been involved that the specific processes they have been previously instructed to follow are no longer necessary and should be stopped.

TRAINING OF OPERATORS AND MONITORING OF OPERATOR COMPETENCE

These tasks are extremely important aspects of every internal control system and they are an ongoing responsibility. Operators charged with administering features of internal control systems must be trained (1) at the time a new feature or internal control process is first approved and implemented, (2) as each new operator, or substitute operator, is assigned the responsibility for a feature, and (3) periodically, to refresh their sensitivity to, and their understanding of, each process they are responsible for. Operators must understand and be impressed with just how important their roles are.

One of the principal reasons internal control systems fail to prevent or deter fraud is human failure. The competence and vigilance of the people who must operate an internal control system are often its weakest links. Some operators fail to fully realize the significance of their assigned tasks; they tend to be negligent at times, and aren't suspicious when the office "Mr. Nice Guy" suggests an expeditious shortcut around a control point. The best designed and implemented system in the world is vulnerable to failure if internal control personnel are not adequately trained and impressed with the importance of their roles. There is little that can be done to prevent a willing operator from becoming a conspirator with another to commit fraud and overcome an internal control. It is quite another matter when an operator is duped into becoming a pseudo-conspirator. A pseudo-conspirator is one who doesn't quite understand the importance of their control function and fails to perform their duties precisely as expected by the internal control design. Consider the following case example:

A very important internal control feature of a large accounting system provided that only certain individuals were authorized to enter source documentation underlying financial payments. Those individuals were periodically provided a group of control numbers, one of which

Continues

Continued

had to be affixed to each source document input into the payment system. Over a period of time, a friendly gentleman became acquainted with the control clerk. From time to time, he would tell her that one of the authorized users had asked him to pick up a group of new numbers as a favor. Innocently, the clerk would comply with his request and issue the numbers, which he used to perpetrate a fraud that aggregated at over $900,000. The man was eventually prosecuted but she was not, because it could not be demonstrated that she had been adequately trained, had an appropriate operating manual specifying the required control procedures, or that her training had ever been refreshed.

All operators charged with internal control responsibilities must be provided with all necessary internal control manuals specially written for their job purposes in language they can understand.

- Regular operators must be properly instructed in the precise mechanics of the control roles they are expected to fill, *by competent instructors.* A record of this training, with all particulars, should be filed in the custodian's log and/or the master file. If training is inadequate, the internal control system will not function as intended and control objectives will not be accomplished. Control procedures must be explained to operators by instructors who themselves are adequately trained. In addition, written procedures fully describing the operator's duties should be issued for reference purposes. Too often, training is provided orally by supervisors who themselves are not adequately trained and who do not fully understand control features. The result is a poorly trained operator who does not fully understand what is expected of them, and is not fully effective.

- Operators must be properly impressed with the *importance* of the control roles to which they are assigned. The norm is often an operator who knows what he or she must do, but doesn't know why. As a result, the operator may be inclined to take shortcuts and otherwise improvise, with a resulting loss of control.

- Substitute operators required to take the place of regular operators during their absences—vacations, illnesses, rest periods, lunch periods, or other emergencies—must be as well trained and impressed with their control duties as are regular operators. Fraud perpetrators who are deterred by competent and effective regular operators who are properly trained will be inclined to wait for the poorly trained or lax substitutes, and for the opportunities they provide.

- The job requirements of internal control operators can be very boring, requiring long periods of seemingly meaningless tasks. Since internal control functions usually do not produce observable accomplishments, there is a human tendency for operators to grow indifferent, careless, and/or to omit control procedures. Without a way to measure their productivity and make their jobs interesting, many will find it difficult to pursue their responsibilities conscientiously, hour after hour. Accordingly, ways and means should be sought to prevent this from happening. If possible, in addition to routine internal control duties, attempts should be made to provide the operators with other more interesting assignments to break up dull routine and keep them alert.

From time to time, tests should be performed to assure that assigned internal control functions are performed as required. For example, bogus transactions may be inserted into a batch of documents being processed to see if the clerks catch it. If they do, they should be rewarded with cash awards and/or some other recognition. Make their jobs exciting and provide a way to earn merit recognition.

PERIODIC TESTING OF INTERNAL CONTROL EFFICACY

Periodically, an entity's operating environment or practices can be expected to change. New product lines are added or shed, new divisions are acquired or combined, organizational responsibility is changed, business increases or declines precipitously, or any one of many things happen to increase or decrease the entity's exposure to fraud. The custodian must be sensitive to these various changes as they occur, and examine operations that may be affected to determine whether or not the internal control system needs to be altered.

FRAUD-SPECIFIC AUDITING

Fraud-specific auditing is discussed in Chapter 6 and—although it is not always thought of as an internal control—it is the very best internal control procedure that an entity can adopt! Fraud-specific auditing can be effectively used to accomplish the following internal control objectives:

- To monitor areas perceived as *weak* from an internal control standpoint, where active internal controls are declined for cost vs. benefit reasons. That is, it is believed that any fraud that may be occurring is *less* than the cost of conventional internal control. Periodic "point-specific" proactive audits are scheduled to reassure the internal control custodian that the areas continue to have a favorable fraud vs. cost-of-internal-control ratio. Note: A point-specific audit normally has a very narrow focus and is directed at generating statistical information relative to the general occurrence of a specific fraud. It stands a high probability of detecting (only) the specific fraud that is being sought. As with all audits, point-specific audits accrue a secondary objective of deterring fraud.
- To determine whether or not an elected internal control is effective. Tests include whether or not the design of a control is effective and if it is being properly conducted.
- To deter fraud by creating risk of detection as a passive internal control.

Whenever proactive auditing is practiced, a fraud perpetrator cannot avoid the risk of detection. Anytime an auditor is working—regardless of what his or her audit objectives may be—the auditor's activity is a threat to would-be perpetrators. Even if their fraud is well covered, at the very least the auditor could get lucky and that is a risk. The auditor is performing *fraud-specific auditing,* or if he or she is actively involved examining records where a perpetrator may be considering fraud, the auditor's activity will be noticed, and will deter all but the most carefree perpetrators, who, if they are truly careless, are likely to commit fatal errors. As an auditor discovers evidence of fraud, his or her presence becomes all the more intimidating to would-be perpetrators. It is important to note that regardless of how penetrating or competent an audit may be, the deterrent effect is undiminished.

It is unfortunate that many entities measure results realized from fraud-specific proactive auditing in terms of the amount of fraud detected, and fail to recognize the deterrent effect. If no fraud is discovered in the effort, it is often presumed that the auditing effort was not beneficial, the cost of it was not justified, and the effort is not repeated. Those who hold this view couldn't be more in error. Evidence of fraud which has been performed skillfully is very difficult to detect; deterrence is the most effective protective action an entity can take.

Management accountants are advised to use auditing freely for these purposes. They should be aware that use of the term *auditing* does not necessarily mean a function that only professional *auditors* can perform. For internal control purposes, most management accountants are fully competent to perform audit testing of internal controls. If their skills are supplemented by periodic training in fraud-specific evidence, the accountants may become more competent than auditors in that they have expert knowledge of the entity's financial management system. The problem that management accountants face in proactively detecting fraud is that, based upon the management accountants we have known, they usually are an overworked lot with many competing demands on their time. This makes it difficult for them to devote valuable time to what are often called fishing expeditions.

Chapter 7

Computer Fraud 101

Any reasonable coverage of computer fraud could easily fill one or more textbooks by itself, and to a significant extent would require advanced skills and experience on the part of the reader to appreciate the intricacies of the automation involved. However, no text for accountants would be complete without at least minimal discussion on the menace of computer fraud and how to cope with it.

Like all fraud, computer fraud ranges from minuscule amounts to huge sums. Among the smallest are the occasional insertion of a fictitious employee on an automated payroll system. The largest may involve millions of dollars in bogus wire transfers between banks. However, computer crime is often very significant. For example:

> HIGH TECH SUCCESS: Thieves working with computers steal an average $500,000 each time they strike, dwarfing the average $23,500 taken in all white-collar crime and the $250 grabbed in armed robberies, Brigham Young's W. Steve Albrecht tells a Peat Marwick conference.
>
> —The Wall Street Journal, November 22, 1988

Despite appearances to the contrary, which tend to intimidate many accountants, there is nothing magical about automated data processing. An automated system is simply the marriage of an administrative application well known by accountants, with a computer-based processing system for the purpose of producing specified results. The application may be an accounting system, inventory control system, or literally any of thousands of administrative processes.

In the early days of system automation, accountants tended to withdraw from the automation process. Entities wishing to automate an administrative system, or to upgrade their automated systems, usually turned the responsibility over to computer system design engineers. These folks, who usually knew their craft very well, often knew very little about the administrative accounting systems they were attempting to automate. They knew nothing about the management needs to be served by the new systems, including internal control opportunities. As a result, they often converted the old processing systems to function on modern computer hardware systems. The results came to be known as unsophisticated conversions. Others called them disasters. The new systems didn't work any better than the old systems they were replacing—the opportunities available with the new computers were usually unrealized—and the systems just worked faster with greater volumes processed. The same old limited data outputs were still there, the same internal control inadequacies were still there, and the odds in favor of fraud *not* being detected improved, as the high speed and voluminous, impersonal nature of automated processing made detection much more unlikely.

As time went by, however, many accountants became more involved in the design of automated systems and began to play an important role in automated system design. With a greater awareness of computer processing capabilities, accountants began to assume a responsibility for the design of the front end of newly automated systems. Using flow charts and the like, they structured the manner in which an application was to function, complete with internal control features. Once completed, they yielded design responsibility to the system design engineers, who married the new enhanced designs with suitable hardware and software (the technical component). The result was a sophisticated automation that was the best of all worlds, or at least it should have been.

The apparent complexity of automated systems, with networks of computers capable of processing enormous volumes of data at blinding speeds, has tended to intimidate some accountants from pursuing computer fraud protection and detection activities. Although there are aspects of automated systems that are best left to computer sciences system specialists, in most respects, the accountant is arguably the most qualified to engage in fraud protection and detection activities.

Consider, for example, that all automated data processing systems involve two distinguishable components:

1. The non-technical component—the application itself—does not directly involve any equipment processes. If the application is an accounting system, the non-technical component involves the chart of accounts to be used, source documents, a description of transactions that would result in postings to the accounts, the reports that would be issued by the system, and so forth.

2. The technical component, which involves the automated processes—usually hardware-specific—is designed to execute the application, whatever it may be. It includes the hardware and hardware schematics needed to process the operating system, audit trails, and so forth.

To conceive, structure, and conceptually design applications, as well as to conduct post-implementation examinations of a system's functioning, *the accountant is king!* This includes any design features intended to protect against fraud. He or she is expert in accounting matters, including the operating application, and therefore best suited to fraud detection involving the non-technical component of an automated system. On the other hand, the technical component of an automated system requires expert knowledge normally not possessed by accountants and must be left to those who do possess it. In some instances, accountants have chosen to specialize in the computer sciences, and their involvement results in the best of both worlds. The technical component involves the external and internal functioning of the computer hardware necessary to execute the operating system.

Accordingly, accountants are encouraged to actively participate in the design or design modification of all automated systems, to the extent they are able. Similarly, in seeking to discover fraud, accountants are advised to acquire all available system flow charts that may apply to the subject area they are interested in, which they can interpret and study for the purpose of detecting system processing weak spots.

In one example, the entity involved had become concerned with serious inventory shortages disclosed by a series of physical inventory counts. Warehouse security was strengthened and several internal control changes made, all to no avail. The shortages continued to be disclosed in subsequent physical inventory counts. Frustrated, and without any new ideas for controlling the losses, an unrelated event provided the answer. The missing merchandise had never been received in the warehouse, even though perpetual records showed otherwise. Investigation disclosed that the entity's receiving procedure was defective, and the defects could have been detected had the receiving procedure been reduced to a document flow chart. The cause of the shortage? A receiving department employee had conspired with a freight delivery driver to steal from incoming

Continues

Continued

shipments. For example, if 100 of something were shipped, the driver would drop off 20 before he arrived at the entity's receiving dock. The receiving person would verify the shipment as 100 received, rather than the 80 that were actually delivered. A review of the applicable transaction flow chart would have disclosed that the receiving dock copy of the receiving report went directly to the accounting department, who updated the inventory record to indicate that 100 had been received. No corroboration or quantity confirmation was received from the warehouse storage location.

TECHNICAL COMPUTER FRAUD

Technical computer fraud is normally beyond the capabilities of most accountants and is the province of specialists. Some large organizations have internal auditors who are highly trained in computer sciences, and who regularly review a computer's processes for errors and fraud, and who examine all changes to software, master records, and similar entries which provide an opportunity for computer fraud. In some instances, accountants have acquired advanced training in computer sciences and are effective in blocking or detecting computer fraud. Where entities possess this capability, they are usually reasonably protected from computer technical fraud.

AUTOMATED PROCESSING SYSTEM VULNERABILITIES

Automated accounting systems tend to facilitate fraud for several reasons. The principal reason is surely the impersonal functioning of the computer. It cannot discern whether the processed data is true or false, unless it has a program which enables it to do so. Nor can it discern when it is a party to fraud. Computers do not have a sense of right or wrong as their human counterparts do. In short, they can be manipulated by anyone having access to them, and they will obey a manipulator's instructions to the letter.

Another reason is the huge transaction volumes processed by computers. In another era, an accountant examining transactions as they were processed had a chance of suspecting a transaction as it passed through the hands of clerks and accountants involved in processing it. Today, the high volumes of transactions that flash through automated processing cycles leave little opportunity for recognition of glaring errors that had little chance of survival in the old days. The high-speed, high-volume, impersonal nature of automated data processing often works to the advantage of the fraud perpetrator. To illustrate, a number of years ago, government auditors were testing an automated payroll system by processing bogus payroll checks made out to Mickey Mouse. No one questioned the fact that the bogus checks had been made out to the cartoon character. In addition, the sheer volumes of transactions often frustrate accountants and auditors seeking to make the simplest tests. In one fraud case, the auditors wished to visually examine all transactions over $100,000 for one year and asked the accounting department for a printout that would serve our needs. The accounting department asked if we really wanted what we asked for, suggesting that a printed listing in standard format would tower over eight feet high. In instances such as these, accountants and auditors are left little choice but to devise examination processes that are themselves automated.

Contributing further to the problem of detecting fraud is the proliferation of computers within many entities. With networking, personal computers are available to practically every level of a company's operations, from top management to sales, from bookkeeping to maintenance. Furthermore employee use of personal computers to work off-site is commonplace. One does not have to be an employee familiar with the company's operations to gain access to data process files. Horror stories of maverick hackers appear almost weekly in national business publications.

Normally, most entities need not concern themselves with technical computer fraud as their automated operations utilize off-the-shelf software than can be expected to be free of any fraud threat to them. Larger entities, however, which have customized computer systems, must be concerned that on-site computer programmers have many opportunities to design computer program routines to enable fraud. Larger entities, of course, usually have internal controls which minimize those opportunities, such as requiring all programs, or program amendments, to be approved by computer-competent auditors.

Sometimes an automated system actually offers a particular advantage to a perpetrator he or she wouldn't ordinarily have in a non-automated system. Two cases come to mind which involved what might be called skimming, the theft of very small amounts, so minuscule that they are unlikely to be noticed, but which are material in the aggregate. Without an automated system, skimming would be impractical for the perpetrator.

In the first example, a bank programmer wrote a computer routine that added a few cents to the service charges added to the accounts of many customers each month. The fraudulent computer routine provided cautions designed to minimize the chances of detection. For example, no excess charges were made to those customers whose service charge fell below a certain criteria set by the perpetrator. To illustrate, only accounts with total charges over $5 might be selected by the automatic computer routine, and then the extra charges would only be a few pennies, depending upon how large the service charge might be and whether or not it might be noticed. It never was! Once the fraudulent routine was installed, it began to function. To collect her proceeds, the perpetrator established a fake customer account to which the pennies skimmed from each customer's account were deposited. She periodically wrote a check against this account to collect her ill-gotten gains.

The fraud could just as easily be adapted to skim pennies from interest-bearing accounts. The fraud was discovered by sheer accident. In either case, the bank's discovery of either fraud scheme would be unlikely without an examination of the technical programming of the automated system. In both cases, the bank's gross service charge income and the bank's gross interest cost would be corrected and computed, not likely to arouse the bank's concern had they employed routines designed to corroborate gross interest expense or service charge income. The customers would be unlikely to complain. There would be only a few pennies involved in each account, and the individual charges or interest are almost impossible to verify to the penny, given the average account balance formulas used by most banks.

A European international bank suspected that they were the victims of a skimming fraud involving its role as a clearing bank for international checks. As with all banks, it experienced overs and shorts in the daily cash balances processed, due to various acceptable reasons, such as small daily carry-overs. Normally, the banks watch the overs and shorts closely, but otherwise don't become overly concerned as the overs and shorts usually end up offsetting each other and are

Continues

Continued

accepted as a cost of doing business. However, the subject bank began to get concerned when the daily reconciliation reported only a balance or shortage condition. The overages had ceased to appear! After an appropriate time, the bank suspected fraud. However, neither the bank or its auditors had no idea of the fraud's mechanics, or perhaps more importantly, how the perpetrators were getting the money out of the bank. Sorry, we are not aware of the results of their investigation, but thought the scheme was a worthy one to pass on in illustration. In this case, undoubtedly, investigators with considerable computer programming skills were engaged to cull through the computer's routines to identify the fault.

AREAS OF VULNERABILITY

Computer systems are considered to be vulnerable to fraud or misuse in several key areas. The *AICPA Audit and Accounting Manual* cites many of these areas of vulnerability and suggests possible controls to offset the inherent risk:

- The computer functions are not fully segregated from users. For example, a using department may create source documents, enter them into the system, operate the computer, and produce output. This environment poses risks such as deliberate concealed errors, unauthorized master file changes, inadvertent input errors, and lost or corrupted data. Some controls to offset these risks include transaction and batch control logs, independent review of logs, use of passwords and other access supervision, rotation of user duties, a requirement that master files be altered only with applications programs that generate an internal log of all changes made and by whom, and periodic comparison of vendor programs with the company's version.
- The location of computers in the user's area gives rise to the following risks: unauthorized use of data files, unauthorized modification of programs, and misuse of computer resources. Controls suggested to offset these risks include password-protected menus, periodic review of usage history reports, and physical control over the system hardware, such as locks and read-only terminals.

- Lack of computer department segregation of duties presents the following risks: unauthorized access to master files and programs, concealment of deliberate errors, and programs that are not representationally faithful to management's objectives. Controls to mitigate such risks include limited access to source code, periodic comparison of programs in use with authorized program versions, password protection to limit access to an as-needed basis, and management review of logs.

- A lack of technical computer knowledge by computer supervisory personnel raises potential risks such as the inability of a supervisor to recognize failure to meet management objectives and the inability to test and review the system effectively. Controls to offset these risks include use of documentation and checklists and recruitment of outside personnel to review program modifications.

- Use of utility programs that bypass the system log to make master file and program modifications leads to several risks: unauthorized access to data and programs, undetected changes to files, and processing and concealment of unauthorized transactions. The primary means to control these risks are to require all program and master file modifications to be made through the relevant application program and to limit access to system utilities.

- Diskettes pose a variety of risks because of the relative ease of concealment resulting from their size and data capacity. Risks include processing the wrong data files and bypassing error logs. Controls include restricted access to the control diskette library and the use of read-only terminals.

- Terminals located throughout the company premises and offsite pose the risk of unauthorized access and unauthorized data entry. Controls include read-only terminals, terminals that can access only certain programs and files, and the physical security of hardware and access logs.

- Readily available vendor software encourages suboptimization of management objectives. This happens because users find it more convenient to use programs that are already familiar to them, even though such packaged software may fall short of management objectives. Such programs often are not tested by authorized personnel before they are used and accepted. About the only control over this risk is to require that all user-acquired software be tested by system personnel to ensure that it complies with management objectives.

EXAMPLES OF COMPUTER FRAUD

Perhaps one way to heighten one's sensitivity to the problems that can be created by the use of computers, especially now that personal computers are readily available to company personnel, is to survey seven examples of computer crimes that have been perpetrated.

1. Officials of a bank in Los Angeles discovered that an employee used the bank's computer to embezzle $21.3 million, the largest electronic bank fraud in U.S. history at the time.

2. An individual in California stole $10.2 million from Security Pacific Bank with one telephone call. The perpetrator gained access, through a ruse, to the wire transfer room at Security Pacific Bank. While in the room, he was able to obtain three vital pieces of information: (1) the security number used to authenticate each day's transfer orders (this code is changed daily); (2) the personal code used by one of the bank's security officers to identify himself to the system; and (3) the account number of an account that had a large balance on deposit. With this information, the perpetrator was able to initiate the wire transfer of $10.2 million from the Security Pacific Bank to a bank in Zurich, Switzerland. The bank did not discover that the $10.2 million was missing for approximately two weeks.

3. An insurance company bilked financial institutions of millions of dollars through the creation of fictitious policies that were subsequently used to collateralize large loans to the insurance company.

4. A senior employee in the bookkeeping department of a local bank, over a period of six years, embezzled over $250,000 and concealed the embezzlement through false entries into the bank's computer system.

5. An employee of a large New York bank programmed the bank's computer so that when computing interest on customers' accounts, every fraction of a cent was credited to the employee's personal account.

6. Seven workers at a state welfare officer in Miami were convicted of stealing $300,000 in negotiable food stamps by falsifying data fed into the agency's computer.

7. A company bilked $190.4 million from 19 lending institutions. The institutions were induced to purchase notes secured by false leases. In purchasing the notes, lenders were led to believe that the notes were secured by valid and binding leases and that payments on the notes would be made from rentals of data processing equipment due each

month under the terms of the leases. In most cases, the equipment did not exist. In others, the equipment was found not to be leased or records were altered to reflect higher rentals.

COMMONLY EMPLOYED BUSINESS SECURITY MEASURES

The following are eight commonly employed business security measures:

1. Strictly controlled access to the computer room and the central processing unit
2. Access through remote terminals limited to information retrieval only
3. Segregation of employee functions, such as data entry, operation, programming, and system analysis
4. Periodic review of data processing security
5. Supervisory review of all program modifications and changes
6. Frequent unannounced audits of computer outputs
7. Requirement that all data processing and accounting employees take annual vacations
8. Security codes for access to both the computer room and computer terminals, particularly those in remote locations

EXAMPLES OF AUDIT TESTS

Several years ago, U.S. General Accounting Office auditors made a study of the controls in a federal agency's automated payroll system. They found system weaknesses which, they believed, would result in fictitious payroll checks if exploited. Without the knowledge of the system's operators, they provided the necessary input they believed would generate a payroll check to a fictitious employee named Donald Duck to test their theories. It worked. With check in hand, the auditors reported the weaknesses and provided recommendations for strengthening the system. Management reacted by minimizing the auditors' finding, saying that "when the check was handed out, someone would have noticed Donald Duck's check and would have caught it at that time."

In another interesting example, auditors in the U.S. General Service Administration's Kansas City Regional Office were evaluating the security of a national purchasing and inventory control system when they noticed that a number of important internal controls were missing. They were convinced that the system was vulnerable to fraud. However, from prior experience they were aware that the system's designers were fiercely proud of their system and thin-skinned. It would be hard to convince that system controls needed to be tightened.

After considerable internal debate as to what course of action to take, the auditors decided to attempt to exploit the weakness to prove their conclusions. Before doing so, however, they took pains to disclose their plans to the agency's security staff, to assure that their actions would not be mistaken for a serious attempt at fraud—a distinct possibility. This kind of pre-test disclosure is a must for anyone who may be considering a "live" test designed to exploit a perceived system weakness—in the event the test is detected while it's in progress. If this precaution is not taken, the testers may find it difficult to prove that they were only testing.

> For the test, a purchase order was input into the system over an unsecured computer terminal, ordering 96 general mechanics tool kits at a cost of $97,200 from the General Tool Company, a fictitious vendor. Thirteen days later, the same computer terminal was used to advise the system that the 96 tool kits had been received and were in the warehouse. Six days later, on June 18, the auditors created an invoice for the phony tool kits, mailing it to the responsible government. The invoice indicated that $97,200 was due and offered a 2% prompt payment discount if paid in 20 days. On July 5th, a government check for $95,256 was mailed to the vendor's indicated address: P.O. Box 17732, Kansas City, MO. Box 17732 had been rented by the auditors. A few days later a second fictitious order for tool kits was successfully placed and a check issued. The weakness had been proved.

The example given had an interesting sub-plot that surely illustrates at least one of Murphy's laws: If something could go wrong, it probably will. Recall that the auditors notified the security office prior to engaging in their attempt to test the system. In so doing, the auditors' attempt was almost blown. It seems that one of the subordinate security staff personnel saw an opportunity to ingratiate himself with the department that was the focus of the auditor's test, and which happened to be hiring for a position this individual was interested in. He went to the department manager and told of the auditors' plans, but was unable to provide all details—only that he heard that the auditors were using a post office box. On the auditors' second test of the system, the target department received the forgoing information too late to prevent the check from being issued. But—as an official "US government agency"—it was able to retrieve it from postal officials. The postal service later apologized to the auditors, indicating that if they had shared their test with them, they would have denied the entity involved any access to the contents of the box. The security employee was later fired for his breach of confidence. The department manager lied under oath when deposed on the details involving her informant and was severely embarrassed.

Automated systems most vulnerable to fraud are financial disbursement systems. They include, primarily, payroll systems and those making regular monthly annuity payments. Many so-called computer frauds, however, are not necessarily unique to the computer era. They were present in payroll and annuity disbursing systems that existed prior to automation, which means that you do not necessarily have to be a computer expert to find them.

In one case that occurred before computers came into use, a large insurance company utilized metal "address-o-graph" plates to mechanically imprint monthly annuity checks mailed to annuitants. Someone had managed to insert extra metal plates into the inventory of plates used to prepare the monthly checks. Note that the basic system is quite like that used in an automated system, the difference being that instead of printing checks from a digital master record, the checks were printed from a physical master record, which was manually fed to a check imprinting machine. The bogus plates resulted in the preparation of annuity checks to bogus annuitants. The fraud is made relatively easy because most disbursement systems required to disburse the same amount over a relatively long period of time are on an exception basis. Once the data is in the master payment file, no other action is needed to cause additional checks to be issued. Theoretically, fraudulent disbursements could continue indefinitely.

It is impossible to give a complete and comprehensive picture of the many ways to commit fraud in a cash disbursing system in this relatively brief guidebook. However, consider some of the following possibilities:

- In an annuity payment system, annuitant Jones dies. The death notice is mailed to the paying organization. Employee A of that organization intercepts the death notice and substitutes a change-of-address notice. Future checks are mailed to her address.

- In an automated payroll system, employee Jones leaves the company. Employee A delays the termination order and changes the mailing address, perhaps for one or two checks.
- Employee A has the opportunity to input fictitious annuitants or payroll names into the computer without independent confirmation.

To prevent the foregoing, at the very least, you are advised to:

- Carefully review the data input controls of any automated payment systems, with the objective of reducing opportunities for inserting false data into the master payment records.
- Have an ongoing program for selectively reviewing actual input. One of the controls that every automated system should have is a record of *every* change to the master record. The processing program should provide for it. The changes may be serially numbered to make tampering more difficult and should be available in a format that can be used by auditors—on paper for smaller systems, or microfilm for larger systems.
- Examine all changes to program software.
- Always presume that someone has found a way to compromise the controls. Have an ongoing program for selectively test-checking outputs.

Audit efforts should be clearly apparent for their deterrent value. There are literally countless things that a computer audit program can do to protect system integrity. Every system is different. Protective measures are limited only by your own creativity.

Chapter 8

Fraud Case Studies

"Chance favors the prepared mind"

—a Pasteur maxim

THE MERITS OF CASE STUDIES

Fraud case studies are included in the *Accountants Guide to Fraud Detection and Control* in an attempt to provide real world opportunities for readers to experience actual cases of fraud as accountants, auditors and/ or investigators experience them. An attempt was made to select cases which would provide a cross-section of the sort of fraud cases the average accountant is most likely to encounter in his or her work environment (difficult fraud cases have been reserved for other more intensive training opportunities). It is firmly believed that fraud case studies, properly structured for learning effect, become embedded in a reader's mind, forming subliminal mental images. Once accomplished, it can be expected that, at some subsequent time, should the reader confront similar circumstances, he or she will experience a *déjà vu* recognition of fraud indicia and proceed accordingly. Case studies are unquestionably the next best thing to actual experience.

CASE STUDY SELECTION CRITERIA

The selection of case studies involved several considerations. It was first deliberated whether to use actual cases or fictional cases. The use of fictional cases—based upon actual facts—was chosen as being of greatest value to the reader. This is a departure from the practice followed by most fraud texts and was considerably more difficult for the authors. Actual cases don't require the authors' experience and only a bit of research of court records and other data available in the public domain is required. Readers would understand the essence of the case that was prosecuted.

The question is, other than being interesting, what would readers learn from this that would be useful in their professions? Very little!

Actual cases that find their way to the public domain as the result of prosecution often lack many of the details useful in fraud detection. Prosecutors are loathe to present unnecessary details to juries and only present enough to accomplish prosecution objectives. Relevant case details are often not publicized. There seldom is a description of how the case was discovered, how evidence was detected, or the problems confronted. Also, the majority of prosecuted cases may be said to be atypical of the greater universe of cases which are never prosecuted. As discussed in a previous chapter, prosecuted cases tend to be the products of fraud perpetrators who were so inept and/or greedy that their cases were discovered accidentally, and are not particularly suitable for learning purposes. Knowledgeable accountants are less concerned with incompetent perpetrators— who cooperate by revealing themselves—than they are with the majority of perpetrators who are competent, conservative, and who never reveal themselves.

The inclusion of actual cases known to the authors which were never prosecuted for one reason or another was out of the question. To include them would reveal confidential information proprietary to the victims and risk slandering the suspects involved. Unfortunately, the very best cases— the 40 percent of all fraud that is never discovered—could not be included due to a failure on the part of the perpetrators to cooperate. Also, when using actual cases, the author is compelled to include as accurate a representation of the actual case as possible. This makes it difficult to isolate the illustrative circumstances that are useful to the objective of the case study.

Accordingly, it appeared to be the best of all choices to include case studies that are fictional. However, all of the case studies were inspired by one or more actual cases, making them legitimate learning vehicles. Most of the actual source cases were never prosecuted for various reasons. All names and irrelevant details have been changed, any resemblance to actual cases is coincidental and unintentional.

THE PROBLEM WITH CASE STUDIES

Regardless of the care taken to structure the case studies included in the *Accountants' Guide to Fraud Detection and Control,* it is not possible to even begin to realistically simulate a real world fraud environment, for what should be obvious reasons. For one thing, as a real world accountant or auditor selects a topic to perform a pro-active examination for the presence of fraud, he or she often has no indication that fraud is present in the subject selected to be examined. In most proactive examinations, evidence of fraud will not be found. To simulate these circumstances, it would be necessary to include case studies which included no fraud. Additionally, for case studies which do include fraud, to make the case study realistic it would be necessary to include volumes of irrelevant information which would distract the reader. For obvious reasons this was considered impracticable and unwanted. Lastly, it was decided to keep the cases unrealistically simple for improved understanding of topics involved rather than to make them realistically more complex and lose the reader's comprehension of a case study's subject objective.

ABOUT THE CASE STUDIES SELECTED

The case studies included in subsequent pages provide practical illustrations of the mechanics of fraud and some of the many variations in which fraud can manifest itself. As each case is read, it is suggested that the reader ponder the circumstances given and consider the fraud possibilities. This is the approach you will have to use in actual proactive examinations. Usually, more than a single answer is possible and desired. The reader should attempt to test his or her skills by jotting down the fraud possibilities before checking the possible solutions that are provided. Remember, there are no incorrect answers. If you can conceive of an opportunity to commit fraud, within the context of the bare circumstances presented, jot it down, together with whatever speculation you deem appropriate based upon what you have read. Only reasonably plausible fraud possibilities are to be considered. This is roughly the process that a fraud accountant, auditor, or investigator follows when beginning his or her search for evidence that the fraud they have conjectured upon is bona fide.

CASE STUDIES: THE H2O-PURE CORPORATION

The H2O-Pure Corporation is an old line Wisconsin company whose main products are "the purest, best-tasting water in the world" and water-dispensing equipment. H2O-Pure water, pumped from wells sunk deep into the earth, is pure and sweet, and has been estimated to have last seen sunlight when it fell to the earth as rain before Christ walked the earth, more than 2,000 years before. Many of its customers are convinced it has curative powers. Its customers include individuals, beverage bottling plants, institutions, pharmaceutical companies, and general businesses worldwide. H2O-Pure's sales are strong and are growing rapidly.

Located on 500 acres of the eastern shore of the Mississippi River, the plant layout consists of approximately 25 buildings and an aging infrastructure which accommodates all general and administrative services, manufacturing operations, shipping, receiving, and warehousing functions. H2O maintains sales and distribution facilities in Newark, Fort Lauderdale, Chicago, Fort Worth, Seattle, and San Diego. H2O-Pure annual sales recently topped the $1 billion mark, earning $100 million in profit. H2O-Pure employs approximately 1,000 people. Their company logo bears the motto: *"H2O-Pure* 'is' *water."*

John Lorren is H2O-Pure's CEO (Chief Executive Officer). At a business conference in New Orleans, he became convinced that the company's profit on sales was abnormally low, considering H2O-Pure's dominance of the premium water industry. Customers were willing to pay a premium for H2O-Pure water, and yet the company was earning only 10 percent profit on gross sales. Upon returning to La Crosse, Mr. Lorren called a meeting and expressed his concern over the lower than expected profits and established an executive task force to study and report on what H2O-Pure's profit should be, given their premium product and market dominance, and to recommend the necessary steps to achieve that percentage. The company was contemplating an IPO (initial public offering) of stock next year to generate capital for plant expansion and renewal and wished to present the best possible face to the financial market.

Executive Task Force Report

John Eastman, Chairman of the executive task force created by Mr. Lorren, presented the results of their study at the September 17th weekly management meeting. Although the report was quite lengthy it included the following highlights and recommendations:

I. Net profit on gross sales should be 20%. It was recommended that all necessary efforts be taken to attain that goal within three years. Mr. Eastman recommended that actions needed to achieve the 20% profit objective should include—but were limited to—the following subjects:
  A. Plant modernization. Much of the present plant was constructed prior to World War II and was badly in need of expansion, renovation and renewal, to realize economies identified and productivity-enhancing efficiencies.

1. Included in a list of high-priority new construction items was the addition of three new storage buildings. The existing structures were said to be inadequate for optimizing inventory levels to meet seasonal product demands, for efficient inventory handling, and for the increased sales anticipated in the next three years. Recommendation: Fund and build three new storage warehouses.
2. A new archive to replace the records storage facility damaged by fire.
3. A secure location for the storage of computer back-up records.

B. Fraud. Mr. Eastman was particularly concerned with H2O-Pure's exposure to fraud. He related that industry experts have estimated that fraud at the average business or public entity could easily equate to two percent of the entity's gross sales. Given the facts that H2O-Pure has no internal audit department (they are audited annually by an independent public accounting firm), that their accounting systems are somewhat antiquated and only partially automated, and their internal controls are questionable at best, Mr. Eastman expressed concern that the two percent fraud criterion was not unreasonable and that it would be unreasonable to presume that H2O-Pure was not experiencing significant fraud. He expressed concern that with $1 billion in sales, fraud could be costing H2O-Pure more than $20 million a year. At that rate, H2O-Pure could afford to expend a significant sum in the expectation that an appropriate effort would cut that loss in half.

Recommendation 1. Review productivity enhancing improvements and report to H2O-Pure's Management Board for approval, construction priority, and budget authority.

Recommendation 2. Review and fund the chief accountant's capabilities for providing an adequate level of fraud-specific internal control and fraud-specific proactive examination activity to limit and otherwise control the possibility of fraud.

Recommendation 3. Fund and establish an internal audit department directing that a substantial portion of their resources be expended—at least initially—on proactive fraud-specific examination activity.

Recommendation 4. Supplement accounting staff to assure that 20 percent of their resources are directed to proactive fraud specific examinations and the development of a fraud-specific internal control system.

FRAUD CASE STUDY NO. ONE: THE TANK

In accordance with the directions of the H2O-Pure Management Board, eight new accountants have been hired. Two—Bradford (Brad) B. Brown and Timothy (Tim) T. Smith—are temporarily assigned to the performance of proactive fraud-specific examinations. Brad and Tim were both outside hires, have had no prior experience in fraud-specific examinations, and know little about H2O-Pure, but they have attended several fraud-specific training courses and have been given considerable discretional authority to perform the roles assigned to them.

They decided to begin their job assignments with the primary objective of searching for evidence of fraud as well as learning about the inner workings of H2O-Pure. In what was intended to be primarily a learning experience, they selected 10 payments for plant maintenance during the prior six months. They had no reason to believe that payment transaction number 8, 9, and 10 would involve the fraud that they were looking for.

Tim and Brad performed the following customary audit verifications. They examined the requisition that originated transaction number 8. It requested the contract for the maintenance on the water tank atop building number 12, and was issued by the Plant Maintenance Department. The work required to be preformed was:

1. Drain 5,000-gallon water tank atop Building 12.
2. Scrape and clean interior surfaces of tank.
3. Repair and rehabilitate interior surfaces as may be necessary. Apply one coat of rust proofing Z-25 Primer to all interior surfaces. Coat all interior surfaces of tank with Z-26 Sealant (a high-quality elasto-meric waterproofing material).
4. Paint outside surface of the tank. H2O-Pure Corporation will provide the paint.
5. Refill tank with 5,000 gallons of water.
6. Perform and complete all work during plant vacation shutdown period August 1–14.
7. Estimated cost: $5,500.

The two accountants noted that the requisition was properly signed by Mr. Blake, the building manager, and countersigned by Mr. Henry Ford, the Plant Maintenance Department Director. Mr. Blake was interviewed and confirmed that the renovation was needed, and in fact was long overdue. They examined the contract issued to the Aztec Company by the purchasing department, requiring the renovation of the building 12 water tank. Work requirements were exactly the same as those listed in the requisition, as shown above. The two accountants then examined the procedure for selecting the Aztec Company to perform the required work. Aztec had competed for the contract and had submitted the low bid of $5,000. Six other companies had submitted bids of $5,400, $5,500, $6,000, $6,300, $6,500, and $7,000.

Tim and Brad examined the receiving report attesting that the services had been satisfactorily delivered in accordance with the H2O-Pure contract. Mr. Blake had personally signed the report. As a result of their examination, as described above, Tim and Brad had confirmed that the water tank project had been properly authorized. The contract had gone to the low bidder, thereby assuring H2O-Pure of a fair market price, and contract requirements had been fully performed to the satisfaction of the H2O-Pure Corporation. Assuming that they had exhausted the possibilities for fraud, Tim and Brad closed the file on transaction number 8 with a finding of "no fraud," and proceeded to examine transaction number 9.

Reader Requirements

Review the facts as stated. Do you agree with Tim and Brad? If so, proceed to Chapter 9, "Fraud Case Studies—Solutions" for a discussion of the solution. If you think Tom and Brad could have done more, take a few moments to think and jot down what additional examination procedures you would have recommended, and—for each recommendation indicate the purpose or objective of the procedure recommended. In other words, write "I would do this (specify what) and this (specify what) to determine some condition (specify what)."

FRAUD CASE STUDY NO. TWO: THE OTHER TANK

Tim and Brad, the H2O-Pure accountants, prepared to examine transaction number 9, selected at random for examination. However, they had a problem in that the five days they had been given to perform proactive fraud-specific examinations was about to run out. They decided to expedite their activities. It was Tim who suggested that they skip the time-consuming examination of documentation supporting transaction number 9 and perform a quick examination to determine if the work was actually done properly. In other words, they decided to search for defective delivery fraud.

Transaction number 9 was very similar to transaction number 8. It involved a payment of $6,000 to the Anderson Company for the rehabilitation of the water tank atop building number 17. The Anderson invoice was examined and it was noted that the company had performed services on the building 17 tank that were very similar to those that had been required on the building 12 tank. Both accountants agreed to limit their examination to a determination of whether or not the rehabilitation services had actually been performed satisfactorily and agreed that an inspection of the tank was in order.

Neither Brad nor Tim felt competent to inspect the tank. An engineer who was employed in the H2O-Pure product design department was competent to do the task required, and he agreed to help them. They all went to Building 17, where the engineer took an elevator to the roof, climbed the tank side ladder, and flipped the top hatch cover aside. He then reached into the water that filled the tank, to examine the side surfaces.

When he returned to the ground, he reported to Tim and Brad. "No problem boys. The rehabilitation was not only done, it was done well. The side surfaces are smooth as silk, indicating a good job of scraping the old surface, and the waterproof coating has been very nicely applied, and is adhering nicely. The contractor has every reason to take pride in his work."

With this news, Tim and Brad closed the file on transaction number 9 with a notation "no fraud detected." They were satisfied that the H2O-Pure Corporation had received fair value for the $6,000 payment they made. They prepared to examine transaction number 10.

Reader Requirements

Review the facts presented and speculate on whether Tim and Brad acted properly. If you disagree, speculate on what additional work they might have performed, given the time constraints they were operating under. Keep in mind that we are not looking for an exhaustive examination.

FRAUD CASE STUDY NO. THREE: THE PARKING LOT

It was in October that Tim noticed that the H2O-Pure employee "north parking lot" had been newly resurfaced. When he returned to his office he decided to perform a fraud-specific examination of the transaction. The contractor's invoice had just been received, and upon inspecting it he observed the following particulars:

Contractor: First Class Paving Company
Invoice #:   . 89-6344
Invoice Date: 15 October
Amount Due: $300,000

Tim retrieves the work order from the maintenance file, and observes that it specifies:

Advertised procurement: Resurface Employee Parking Lot #2 with 4″ layer
   of bituminous concrete.
No repairs to parking lot surface are necessary.
Seal finished surface with Formula X.
                               Signed: Sam Diego, Grounds Manager

In the file, Tim finds that the RFP (Request for Proposals) that was sent out to six interested contractors is exactly the same as the work order shown above, with the additional notation for bidding contractors "Parking lot is 250,000 square feet (500′ × 500′)". The RFP is signed by the H2O-Pure grounds manager, Sam Diego.

Tim reviews the advertised procurement and finds that it has been conducted properly; there is no evidence of bid tampering. The First Class Company's bid of $300,000 is low. The other bids ranged from $325,000 to $375,000. Immediately subsequent to the contract award to the First Class Company, the next lowest bidder, the Blacktop Company, had protested the parking lot award to the First Class Paving Company. In their complaint, they indicated that they had proposed an extremely low bid, with little or no profit in the hope of getting future H2O-Pure business. They contended that there was no way that the winning contractor could perform the work at the $300,000 price bid and make a profit. Something was wrong, they claimed. However, the auditors reviewed the bid award process and everything appeared to be in order. The H2O-Pure Corporation's response to the Blacktop Company included the statement that whether or not a winning contractor made a profit was not their concern. They said that the First Class Company would be held to the terms of the contract.

Based primarily upon the Blacktop Company protest, Tim decided to perform a defective delivery examination of the contract.

Reader Requirements

In pursuing a defective delivery fraud search, speculate on what you think the auditor should look for and provide reasonably explicit examination steps for him to follow.

FRAUD CASE STUDY NO. FOUR:
THE PARKING LOT REVISITED

Case study 4 is actually an extension of case study 3. Some exceptional readers may have solved it when speculating on the fraud types possible for case study 3. However, we doubt that very many readers have guessed what we are going for here. The fraud you are looking for is somewhat unique and actually happened in a very similar case. Readers may rule out all of the common frauds, such as double payment fraud, multiple payment fraud, and shell fraud.

All the information that is needed to successfully speculate on this fraud is given as stated in case study 3. For your convenience, the essential information is restated below:

> Tim retrieved the work order from the maintenance file and observed that it specified:

> Advertised procurement: Resurface Employee Parking Lot #2 with 4″ layer of bituminous concrete.
> No repairs to parking lot surface are necessary.
> Seal finished surface with Formula X.
> Signed: Sam Diego, Grounds Manager

> In the file, Tim finds that the RFP (Request for Proposals) sent out to six interested contractors is exactly the same as the work order shown above, with the additional notation for bidding contractors "Parking lot is 250,000 square feet (500′ × 500′)." The RFP is signed by the H2O-Pure grounds manager, Sam Diego.

Reader Requirements

You must speculate upon the solution to this case study. In doing so you must be reasonably explicit in regard to exactly what the fraud was, the amount of the fraud, and how the perpetrators would profit from this fraud. In lieu of the opportunity to gather the actual information you would ordinarily need to support your solution, please feel free to hypothecate the data needed to state the amount of the fraud. The precise amount of the fraud is not important to the solution. Also, speculate upon the name of the H2O-Pure employee who was probably a conspirator in the fraud, and why you think it is he. Readers who are successful in solving this case study will have demonstrated they have the right stuff necessary for finding fraud.

FRAUD CASE STUDY NO. FIVE: THE STORAGE BUILDINGS

On August 12th, the H2O-Pure Corporation decides to build three new identical storage buildings to ease the overloading of its existing warehouses and to meet the need for additional storage in the next few years that is expected to result from an anticipated substantial growth in sales. The storage buildings were approved by the Management Board. They in turn authorized the Contract Division to proceed with acquisition. The H2O-Pure Engineering Department prepared the specifications for the three storage buildings and estimated the entire project would cost about $1,200,000.

The Contract Division published their intention to build the storage buildings in area newspapers, requesting that contractors interested in building the structures make their interests known to H2O-Pure. Six area contractors requested bid packages and copies of the building specifications and general contract requirements were mailed to them, stating that all bids be submitted by 8 A.M., September 15th. Among other things, contract particulars provided that the contract award will be made upon the basis of the low total bid for all three buildings. Prospective bidders were informed that building A would be constructed first; notice to proceed on buildings B and/or C would be provided by the contracting entity when deemed appropriate. Also, H2O-Pure reserved the right to cancel the construction of any of the buildings at any time. The prospective contractors were advised that progress payments would be allowed at the 50 percent completion point for each building and at acceptance of each building, less a five percent hold-back, pending satisfactory completion of all buildings required.

The suggestion that the construction of the storage buildings be authorized separately was made by Della Ware, the Director of the Storage Division, who suggested that given some current uncertainty over the scope of H2O-Pure's warehousing needs at the current time, this method of contracting would provide flexibility for H2O-Pure to alter their plans for the number of buildings to be constructed and/or the building features. To facilitate contractor progress payments, the exercise of H2O-Pure termination options, and/or the pricing of changes in building designs or schedules, bidding contractors were required to include their unit costs of each building when submitting their bids. Management Board members all agreed.

On September 15th, four bidders submitted proposals to construct the buildings at the bid opening, as follows:

The Pence Company: $1,000,000
Baker Builders: $1,050,000
Cain Contractors: $1,200,000
Delta Builders: $1,300,000

As low bidder, the Pence Company was awarded the contract on September 16th. The Pence Company was directed to proceed with construction of storage building A immediately.

At the time of the award of the contract to the Pence Company, Brad Brown, in his role as a proactive fraud-specific examiner, reviewed the contract actions. He obtained the bid proposals submitted by the four contractors, and took interest in the unit prices they have offered for buildings A, B, and C.

Pence Company   A = $500,000; B = $250,000; C = $250,000
Baker Builders: A = $350,000; B = $350,000; C = $350,000
Cain Contractors: A = $400,000; B = $400,000; C = $400,000
Delta Builders: A = $440,000; B = $430,000; C = $430,000

He is concerned with the wide variation in unit prices for identical buildings. He feels that identical buildings should be identically priced. He has heard of fraud types called front-end loading, where contractors attempt to shift their costs and profits to the first contract item(s) to be completed. The alleged purpose of contractor front-end loading is to assure them of substantial profits in the early stages of a contract should the unlikely happen, such as the contracting entity deciding to cancel the remaining contract items, as H2O-Pure reserved the right to do; or if the contractor defaults on the contract for any reason, he will have received his profit and costs up-front. Of course, if there were unbalanced bidding, it would suggest that the Pence Company is either heavily betting their profits that building B and/or C will be canceled, or someone inside H2O-Pure has information that building B and/or C will be canceled, and has shared it with Pence to allow them to profit handsomely on Building A. Who could that be? The problem is that the Pence Company is clearly the low bidder, financially sound, dependable, and unlikely to default. Brad feels there is little he can do at this stage to change the contract and does not share his paranoid suspicions with others. Only H2O-Pure itself can enable the contractor to profit unduly from his unbalanced bid. However, Brad is determined to maintain a watch over future events in this contract, and to observe who the initiators are.

On September 20, the Pence Company begins construction of storage building A.

At the meeting of the management board on October 20th, Della Ware briefs the board on the excellent progress the Pence Company is making on construction of building A. Completion is expected around mid-December, plans are being made to move stock from the old annex building currently used as a warehouse into the new structure. Robert Baker, a board member, asks about plans for beginning buildings B and/or C. Della explains she was about to brief the board on that item. She points out that with the new sales forecasts predicting substantial world-wide sales, previous storage requirement forecasts had to be revised. At the next board meeting, she promised to brief the board on the revised storage estimates. However, for the time being, she recommended that the construction of buildings B and C be terminated. She points out that they had foreseen this possibility and the current construction contract allows them to cancel with few if any problems. The Pence Company would not be happy, she said, but they could favor them with a contract on the new buildings or annex renovation work that was planned. The board approved the cancellation of buildings B and C.

Reader Requirements

Comment whether or not Brad should be concerned that the contractor's bid for building A is $100,000 to $150,000 higher than the prices offered for an identical building by each of the other bidders. If you think he should be concerned, explain why, and offer a course of action you would follow.

If you believe there are fraud possibilities in this case, explain. Be explicit in describing what you think they may be. Be fraud-specific in your thinking and jot down a few notes justifying your reasons. What would you do, if anything, after building B and C were canceled?

FRAUD CASE STUDY NO. SIX: LEASE VARIABLE COST "PASS THROUGH"

Tim, the H2O-Pure accountant turned fraud-fighter, has decided that he needs a break from the cold Wisconsin winters and turns his attention to an H2O-Pure location which is a bit more hospitable. San Diego, the site of one of H2O-Pure's area offices, is Tim's place of choice.

H2O-Pure's San Diego office site occupies the penthouse floor in a high-rise modern luxury office building, overlooking the bay. The site is leased at a cost which varies slightly from year to year. Tim decides to examine the lease. It includes a feature Tim is not familiar with, a variable cost "pass through." Upon reading the lease, he learns that it is a long-term lease—for a ten-year period—and is in its fourth year. At the time the lease was written four years earlier, the long-term lease was desired by both parties to it. When constructing the building, the owner had a need to assure full occupancy of the building to the bank financing construction of the building. H2O-Pure anticipated rapidly escalating rental rates in the San Diego bay area in the next decade and desired the ten-year lease to hold down their rental costs and to lock in their location. The conservative management at H2O-Pure sought, and received, an escape clause which allowed them to terminate the lease should their space requirements in the San Diego area decrease dramatically. The clause simply required H2O-Pure to renew their lease every two years—a simple formality—to prevent it from expiring in the fourth, sixth, and eighth year.

The variable rental rate resulted from the lessor's unwillingness to predict or guarantee rental rates for the 10 years of the lease, given the unpredictability of building variable costs and inflation. Accordingly, H2O-Pure and the lessor came to an agreement on a two-part rental computation. The first part was basically a proration of the owner's predictable fixed costs over the lease period. Basically, this included his depreciation and financing costs. Once determined, it would remain the same throughout the lease period. The second rental component was the lessor's somewhat unpredictable variable costs, such as heat, light, power, cleaning, recurring maintenance, and so forth. The lease provided that H2O-Pure would bear their fair share of the lessor's "actual" variable costs each year. If the cost of electricity went up, so would H2O-Pure's share of it. Variable costs were to be estimated for each month's rental payment and were to be adjusted in the subsequent year by a lump-sum payment (by either the lessor or H2O-Pure) based upon the lessor's actual costs. The lessor agreed to make his records available for H2O-Pure's inspection each year.

Tim began his examination of the Bay Building lease with a review of the terms of the lease and the computation of rental cost provided by the Bay Building management for the third year. See Exhibit 8.1.

Reader Requirements

Please describe what you think would be appropriate were you examining H2O-Pure's Bay Building lease for Year 3. Include whether or not you suspect fraud. If yes, indicate the nature of the fraud you suspect. What additional steps would you take were you in Tim's place?

Exhibit 8.1

Bay Building Corporation
129 Bay View Drive
San Diego, California

Statement Date: January 28, Year 4

Tenant: H2O-PURE CORPORATION
Period: Year Three

RE-COMPUTATION OF YEAR THREE RENTAL COST:
  (SQ′ = square foot)

FIXED CONTRACT RATE CHARGES		ANNUAL CHARGE
Office space rented:	25,000 SQ′ × $9.75	$243,750
Parking space (32 cars):	8,000 SQ′ × $2.00	16,000
Total fixed rental cost	33,000 SQ′ × $11.75	$259,750

VARIABLE RATE CHARGES

Total space occupied	33,000 SQ′ × $15.00	495,000

Total Year Three H2O-PURE CORPORATION rental costs	$754,750

H2O-PURE RENTAL PAYMENTS IN YEAR THREE	
12 MONTHS @ $65,000	780,000

OVERPAYMENT (CHECK ENCLOSED)	$26,250

BASIS FOR BAY BUILDING VARIABLE RENTAL RATE
COMPUTATION:

Total Bay Building variable costs (itemized)	$3,750,000
Total Bay Building rentable office space	÷ 250,000 SQ′
Cost per square foot	$15/SQ′

FRAUD CASE STUDY NO. SEVEN: THE VENETIAN BLINDS

On January 11th, an H2O-Pure auditor—Suzie Wong—is randomly examining payment transactions as part of a fraud-specific audit she is performing. One of the transactions she has selected for a detailed examination is a $7,056 payment to the Brite Cleaning Company. She visits the H2O-Pure Accounting Department and asks for the work order requesting the service, the purchase order, the applicable receiving report, the contractor's invoice relating to the $7,056 payment, and the canceled H2O-Pure payment check. Since all of the documents requested are normally part of an accounts payable permanent file, she had no trouble getting the documents requested.

Returning to her desk, Suzie begins her review with an examination of the work order requesting the purchase and finds that it is for the cleaning of venetian blinds in all of the H2O-Pure offices. She examines the work order requesting the work and finds that it has been requested and signed by Mr. Cee Attle, the buildings manager. The work order is also annotated to indicate that the H2O-Pure CEO has complained about the filthy blinds and directed that they be cleaned immediately.

She next examines the purchase order for the cleaning services and notes that it is directed to the Brite Window Company, without any solicitation for bids. However, Suzie then notes that a solicitation is not necessary. It appears that the H2O-Pure Contracting Division has anticipated the need for cleaning venetian blinds, drapes, and windows, and has advertised for a window cleaning contractor several months ago. In response to that advertisement, an open-end contract has been written with the Brite Window Company, who is now obligated to respond to any H2O-Pure request for window cleaning services for the entire year, all services to be performed as negotiated in the contract. The purchase order Suzie examines refers to the parent contract. The purchase order requires the cleaning of 150 venetian blinds, all uniformly sized at $6' \times 8'$, at the contract rate of $1 a square foot. A two percent cash discount is allowed for payment within 10 days. Suzie notes that H2O-Pure paid the invoice in the 10 days allowed.

Suzie examines the receiving report, noting that it has been signed by Sam Bernadino, a supervisory cleaning engineer. She visits Sam, who she knows quite well. Mr. Bernadino is casually questioned about the cleaning work. He remembered acknowledging receipt of the services. He adds that "the Brite people always do a good job."

She examines the Brite Window Company invoice.

- There is a valid purchase order signed by a person authorized to order goods or services, and that the item and amount was within his or her purchasing authority. In the present case, Sam Bernadino is authorized to order building maintenance supplies and services up to $25,000 on his signature alone.
- There is appropriate evidence that the goods or services were actually received. In this case, Mr. Cee Attle, the building 12 manager, had signed the purchase order receiving block. There is no question that the signature was Mr. Attle's, which has a unique flourish.

- There is a bona fide invoice that claims payment for the supplies or services. The H2O-Pure manager, or designate, responsible for the expenditure must sign the invoice indicating that he or she has reviewed the invoice, and that all requirements for payment have been complied with. In this case, the invoice was signed by Mr. Cee Attle.

He explains that if all of the above documents, signatures, and initials are present, he initials the invoice and indicates on it whether or not the prompt payment discount can be taken, and if so expedites payment. In this case, he pointed out, a two percent discount was earned for paying the Brite Window Company bill within the 10 days allowed. The accountant accompanies Suzie on a tour of the building, noting that the blinds are now sparkling clean and a big improvement. He notes that the cleaner also replaced some of the draw cords, which had become frayed, at no cost to H2O-Pure. Suzie notes that the blinds are now very attractive. She too recalls how dirty they were. She asks the accountant if he knew any of the Brite Window employees who did the work. He replied that he did.

As Suzie prepares to conclude her review, she assembles and goes over her notes. In doing so, she realizes that she has forgotten to do something she had intended to do earlier. She does it, and finds a significant discrepancy which could be fraud.

Reader Requirements

Comment upon Suzie's examination. Express an opinion upon what it was that she forgot to do, and what she may have found. Be imaginative!

FRAUD CASE STUDY NO. EIGHT: THE PAINTING TERM CONTRACT

The Ten/Four Corporation plant had grown explosively in the 1970s and now sprawled over a 200-acre site in suburban St. Louis. Among Ten/Four's growing maintenance requirements, painting, plumbing, recurring maintenance, and general repair of its many aging buildings was a growing problem. Mary Kerry, the director of plant maintenance, supervised a small group of Ten/Four employees who were on call for emergency maintenance services. However, to accomplish recurring maintenance tasks on an as needed basis, it was decided a few years ago to utilize term contracts. As a result, most of the corporation's plant maintenance work is now performed by contractors who work more or less continuously at

Ten/Four under term contracts. To obtain the best price for the various trades involved, most of the term contracts are let through advertising for the lowest bidder.

Note: Term contracts are so named because they are written to arrange for contractor-provided services over a defined period of time, usually for a term of one year. Under a term contract, a contractor agrees to respond to a business entity's total requirements—on short notice—as the needs arise. The entity, in return, usually guarantees to give the contractor all of their business—as defined—for the term defined in the contract.

The contracts are advertised and let, or negotiated, in advance of the beginning of the term, and include all of the agreed necessary contract specifics needed to begin performance without delay. Most specifically, the price for a contractor's performance is all pre-arranged. For example, if a term contract provides that a contractor will receive $50 an hour for each hour worked, and the contractor works 100 hours, he will automatically receive $5,000. The contracting entity may or may not call for services under a term contract. However, in that event, the contractor is usually guaranteed a minimum term revenue—for example $100,000—regardless of his participation, in order to make his participation worthwhile.

Ms. Kerry, anticipating a significant need for plant repainting, both interior and exterior, set out to arrange a new painting term contract for the year ahead. She would be the first to deny that her actions were affected by the new CEO's remark that the aging dark blue paint that covered most corporate office walls was depressing. He suggested repainting them quickly, any color, just as long as it was an off-white. It was soon after this that Ms. Kerry initiated the search for a term-contract painter. In preparing the corporation's painting requirements, Ms. Kerry took into consideration that the painting was likely to be expensive. Many of the ceilings were over nine feet in height—a condition which requires painting contractors to erect and work from scaffolds, which increases the cost of the painting—and the old dark blue walls meant that it was likely that two coats of paint would be required if the finish coat was to be off-white.

The Ten/Four Corporation's intention to enter into a term contract for interior painting was advertised in area trade publications in the St. Louis area; interested contractors were instructed to contact Ten/Four Corporation purchasing agent Jerry Whyte. Eight qualified painting contractors expressed an interest in the term contract advertised and were provided with the following essential details and instructions:

Ten/Four Corporation Request for Proposal (RFP)

Effective January 1st through December 31st, of the next calendar year, the Ten/Four Corporation intends to acquire its total interior painting needs from a term contract. Accordingly, this RFP is issued to invite contractors who may be interested in performing under the contract to submit their price proposals. Interested contractors are requested to submit their proposals in accordance with the attached form, indicating unit prices and extended totals, for each category of painting.

The contract will require the contractor to respond to all requests for interior painting made by the Ten/Four Corporation Maintenance Division during the year.

Proposals must be submitted in accordance with the painting requirement categories and estimated square footage in the format provided below. Square footage indicated is provided only for the purposes of determining unit prices and for selecting the low aggregate bid. Because of the uncertainty of the corporation's painting needs, it reserves the right to vary the quantity and type of painting ordered, as well as to not order any painting if it so chooses. In the event that total painting ordered under the contract produces less gross revenue than the successful contractor's winning low bid, the Ten/Four Corporation will reimburse the difference. The corporation also reserves the right to order services in excess of those indicated for bidding purposes.

BIDDER PRICE PROPOSAL

BIDDER:

Category A Painting:
 Walls up to nine (9) feet high, 1 coat.
 _____ Price/sq. ft. × 1,200,000 square feet　　$_____

Category B Painting:
 Walls up to nine (9) feet high, 2 coats.
 _____ Price/sq. ft. × 200,000 square feet　　$_____

Category C Painting:
 Walls over nine (9) feet high, 1 coat.
 _____ Price/sq. ft. × 100,000 square feet　　$_____

Continues

Continued

Category D Painting:
   Walls over nine (9) feet high, 2 coats.
   _____ Price/sq. ft. × 12,500 square feet $_____

Category E Painting: Ceilings, 1 coat.
   _____ Price/sq. ft. × 250,000 square feet $_____

Category F Painting: Ceilings, 2 coats.
   _____ Price/sq. ft. × 4,000 square feet $_____

TOTAL PRICE PROPOSAL
**   (ADD CATEGORIES A–F)** $_____

In response to the Ten/Four RFP, four painting contractors submitted proposals. The following are abstracts of their bids:

BIDDER PRICE PROPOSAL

BIDDER: JULIET PAINTING

Category A Painting:
   Walls up to nine (9) feet high, 1 coat.
   $ .08 Price/sq. ft. × 1,200,000 square feet $ 96,000

Category B Painting:
   Walls up to nine (9) feet high, 2 coats.
   $ .14 Price/sq. ft. × 200,000 square feet $ 28,000

Category C Painting:
   Walls over nine (9) feet high, 1 coat.
   $ .10 Price/sq. ft. × 100,000 square feet $ 10,000

Category D Painting:
   Walls over nine (9) feet high, 2 coats.
   $ .16 Price/sq. ft. × 12,500 square feet $ 2,000

Category E Painting: Ceilings, 1 coat.
   $ .12 Price/sq. ft. × 250,000 square feet $ 30,000

Category F Painting: Ceilings, 2 coats.
   $ .18 Price/sq. ft. × 4,000 square feet $ 720

TOTAL JULIET PAINTING PRICE PROPOSAL $166,720

BIDDER PRICE PROPOSAL

BIDDER: KILO PAINTERS

Category A Painting:
  Walls up to nine (9) feet high, 1 coat.
$ .085 Price/sq. ft. × 1,200,000 square feet $102,000

Category B Painting:
  Walls up to nine (9) feet high, 2 coats.
$ .15 Price/sq. ft. × 200,000 square feet $ 30,000

Category C Painting:
  Walls over nine (9) feet high, 1 coat.
$ 0.95 Price/sq. ft. × 100,000 square feet $ 9,500

Category D Painting:
  Walls over nine (9) feet high, 2 coats.
$ .14 Price/sq. ft. × 12,500 square feet $ 1,750

Category E Painting: Ceilings, 1 coat.
$ .11 Price/sq. ft. × 250,000 square feet $ 27,500

Category F Painting: Ceilings, 2 coats
$ .185 Price/sq. ft. × 4,000 square feet $ 740

TOTAL KILO PAINTERS PRICE PROPOSAL $171,490

BIDDER PRICE PROPOSAL

BIDDER: LIMA PAINTERS

Category A Painting:
  Walls up to nine (9) feet high, 1 coat.
$ .05 Price/sq. ft. × 1,200,000 square feet $ 60,000

Category B Painting:
  Walls up to nine (9) feet high, 2 coats.
$ .30 Price/sq. ft. × 200,000 square feet $ 60,000

Category C Painting:
  Walls over nine (9) feet high, 1 coat.
$ .05 Price/sq. ft. × 100,000 square feet $ 5,000

Continues

Continued

Category D Painting:
  Walls over nine (9) feet high, 2 coats
  $ .25 Price/sq. ft. × 12,500 square feet $ 3,125

Category E Painting: Ceilings, 1 coat.
  $ .05 Price/sq. ft. × 250,000 square feet $ 12,500

Category F Painting: Ceilings, 2 coats.
  $ .25 Price/sq. ft. × 4,000 square feet $ 1,000

TOTAL LIMA PAINTERS PRICE PROPOSAL $166,720

BIDDER PRICE PROPOSAL

BIDDER: MIKE PAINTING, INC.

Category A Painting:
  Walls up to nine (9) feet high, 1 coat.
  $ 0.75 Price/sq. ft. × 1,200,000 square feet $ 90,000

Category B Painting:
  Walls up to nine (9) feet high, 2 coats.
  $ .145 Price/sq. ft. × 200,000 square feet $ 29,000

Category C Painting:
  Walls over nine (9) feet high, 1 coat.
  $ .10 Price/sq. ft. × 100,000 square feet $ 10,000

Category D Painting
  Walls over nine (9) feet high, 2 coats.
  $ .15 Price/sq. ft. × 12,500 square feet $ 1,875

Category E Painting: Ceilings 1 coat.
  $ .13 Price/sq. ft. × 250,000 square feet $ 32,500

Category F Painting: Ceilings, 2 coats.
  $ .18 Price/sq. ft. × 4,000 squafe feet $ 720

**TOTAL MIKE PAINTING, INC.,
  PRICE PROPOSAL** $164,095

The four bid proposals submitted:

Juliet Painting	$166,720
Kilo Painters	171,490
Lima Painters	141,625✔
Mike Painting, Inc.	164,095

The Lima Company was the low aggregate bidder with a total bid of $141,625, and was awarded the painting term contract for next year.

Reader Requirements

1. Discuss the method used by the Ten/Four Corporation to select the low painting term contractor for next year. If you disagree with the method used, you must suggest a method that you think would solve any criticisms you may have. Bear in mind that the Ten/Four Corporation is not able to accurately predict their painting needs for next year at the time the contract was advertised, hence the use of loosely estimated painting needs. It is not necessary to be critical of the method used.

2. If you have been critical of the method used to select a painting contractor, be explicit in explaining why. Bear in mind that your comments should be relative to any possible fraud that may follow.

3. If you have not been critical of the method used, do you see anything suspicious, or any possibilities for fraud in the data that has been presented above? Explain.

4. Do you agree with the selection of Lima Painters for next year's painting term contract? If you do agree, state why.

5. If you don't agree with the selection of the Lima Painters, explain why. Be realistic!

6. Given the particulars of this case, as stated thus far, does the possibility of fraud concern you to any significant degree? If 0 were to mean "no concern", and "10" were to mean "highly concerned", express your concern with a number.

7. If you believe that fraud is likely in this case, do you believe that conspiracy may be involved? Explain.

For the purposes of this case study, you may ignore the possibilities of fraud that could arise as the result of duplicate payments, multiple payments, and defective deliveries.

FRAUD CASE STUDY NO. NINE: THE ARCHIVE

You will recall that in Case Study No. Five, the H2O-Pure Corporation completed the construction of a new storage building. Soon after completion, the inventory that had been stored in the old annex building was transferred to the new building. This left the annex building empty and, at a subsequent board meeting, it was suggested that the building be demolished. However, there was considerable support for retaining the historically significant building and using it for some other purpose. The Vice-President for Administration, Ann Cestor, cited a growing H2O-Pure need for records storage, calling the board's attention to a 1988 fire which destroyed a sizeable number of important records. She noted that all area office records, contracts, and so forth were stored at the corporate location in La Crosse, and there has been an ongoing search to locate a safe site for all corporate documents, including computer back-up records. She noted that the annex building was conveniently located, of brick construction and structurally very sound—although in need of substantial renovation. She recommended that the building be modified to serve as an H2O-Pure archive. The required modification would most likely include air conditioning, humidity control, lighting improvements, suitable storage shelves, fire suppression devices, and so forth. In addition, she recommended a fireproof vault for computer backup storage and other sensitive documents. She reported the alternative was a new structure which would very likely cost over $3 million. The board unanimously approved Ms. Cestor's recommendation and ordered that design plans be prepared as soon as possible.

Tom Logan, head of H2O-Pure's Architectural Engineering Office (AEO) submitted a renovation design plan, together with an estimate that it would require approximately $1 million to accomplish the renovations required. However, the completed archive would be an attractive first-class facility. The H2O-Pure board quickly approved the recommendations and directed that actual renovation begin as quickly as possible.

Mr. Logan's design provided for the following eight major renovations features:

1. Construction of a security vault to accommodate sensitive documents
2. Installation of twin 48-inch fluorescent lighting fixtures throughout the building
3. Resurfacing and leveling the existing concrete floor—which was badly cracked and uneven—with a three-inch minimum concrete veneer

5. Resurfacing of interior walls and provision of partitions in accordance with specification drawings

6. Installation of suspended ceilings in accordance with specifications provided

7. Removal of expired 165°F fire suppression system water sprinkler heads and installation of new 165°F sprinkler heads, throughout the structure, as specified

8. Provision of new four-foot wide entrances and roll-up doors at each end of the annex

On July 17th, the H2O-Pure Contract Division issued an Invitation for Bids (IFB) to several large contractors who had responded to an H2O-Pure advertisement of the renovation and expressed an interest in doing the job. They were required to submit sealed bids by 12 noon CST, September 17th. The job requirements, including a complete set of blueprints prepared by H2O-Pure AEO architects, were included in the IFB package sent to each contractor. They were substantially the same as the seven items listed in AEO renovation plan submitted by Mr. Logan.

The bid opening on September 17 revealed the following offers:

Acme Builders	$ 711,000
Baker Contractors, Inc.	1,003,500
Henry Construction Co.	1,026,999
Boxer Contractors	1,045,987

Although the Acme Builders, of La Crosse, Wisconsin, had submitted the low bid of $711,000, it was rejected as non-responsive because Acme failed to name the subcontractors who would be used on the job, a stipulation required by the H2O-Pure IFB. Accordingly, the next low bidder—Baker Contractors—was awarded the contract to renovate the H2O-Pure Annex building. The Baker contract included a value engineering (VE) clause, standard on all H2O-Pure construction contracts, that gave a performing contractor the incentive to seek and identify opportunities for cost savings that could be achieved through changes in contract specifications. The standard H2O-Pure VE clause provided that for all specification changes resulting in cost reductions—approved by H2O-Pure—the recommending contractor would receive 50 percent of any savings.

Soon after the contract was awarded, Baker Contractors, Inc. began the annex renovation. By October 18th, only three weeks after they had started work, it was reported that they were well ahead of schedule.

On October 19th, it was discovered that several errors, or omissions, had been noted in the contract requirements that had been distributed with the IFB package and which had been incorporated as contract requirements. Five contract change orders were subsequently issued to correct the errors:

1. An archivist visiting the H2O-Pure renovation project questioned the specifications requiring 165°F fire sprinkler heads. He observed that although 165°F heads are standard in general fire suppression systems, 286°F heads were advisable for archival storage. He stated that the 165°F heads were absolutely unacceptable for the H2O-Pure archive. He noted that in the event of a minor fire, the 165°F sprinklers would be activated at a relatively low fire temperature of 165°F, resulting in significant water damage to stored records, even though the fire might be relatively non-destructive and quickly controlled. Baker Contractors, Inc., were directed to make the change and the contract price was increased $7,350 to include the cost of changing to the 286°F sprinkler heads.

2. The visiting archivist also discovered that renovation specifications provided that the warehouse doors to be installed at each end of the annex building would be too narrow at the four-foot width specified. After investigation, it was discovered he was right. The four-foot width was too narrow to accommodate H2O-Pure material handling equipment and pallets. Contract specifications were changed to provide for 96-inch wide entrances at both ends of the building. The price for installing two new doors was estimated at $10,000 each, or $20,000 for the two entrances. The change order also allowed the contractor any actual costs already incurred in building to the four-foot specification, or incurred in widening the wall space to 96 inches wide, plus all finishing of the door frames, and the surrounding wall surface. At the time the change order was issued, if the contractor had not yet completed the annex end entrance doors, some credit may have been appropriate to offset the costs of this change order. However, Mr. Logan determined that the four-foot doors had been completely installed when this change order was issued.

3. It was also discovered that the H2O-Pure specifications mailed to the renovation contractors failed to include the air-conditioning and humidity control system, essential to records and computer media storage. The change was particularly expensive because of the need to provide a complete air delivery system, as well as the cooling/humidifying equipment itself. Baker estimated the cost at $125,000.

4. The contractor recommended a fourth contract change when he noted that the lighting fixtures required by the contract were not of the type

normally used in archive facilities. The basic contract provided that two 48-inch fluorescent tube fixtures be installed throughout the storage area. Baker pointed out that single-tube, 96-inch fixtures are preferred for records storage facilities. In recommending the change, the contractor cited a standard requirement for federal and other records storage areas located throughout the country which provided that light fixtures for stack areas be "fluorescent, continuous strip (single tube), not more than nine inches wide including the maximum width of the reflector. The installation of single 96-inch fluorescent tubes would only cost $17,500, vs. the $35,000 cost of the 48-inch lighting fixtures—because fewer and simpler fixtures would have to be installed. Accordingly, Baker was allowed a $8,750 VE bonus for recommending the change, which was approved by H2O-Pure. This change order was written to provide for the lighting change Baker recommended, and to adjust the contract price by $17,500 because of the contractor's VE entitlement.

5. The Baker contractors also advised that the new concrete floor, which was a required contract specification, was unnecessary. They recommended that a bituminous concrete paving material be used instead. The substitute surface was priced at $60,000. The cost of the concrete surface which had been included was $100,000. The VE savings would be $40,000, half of which, or $20,000, would be Baker's share for recommending the cost-cutting change, in accordance with provisions of the value engineering clause. Tom Logan approved the change and it was written to provide for the change in the floor renovation.

The annex renovation was completed on March 3rd, and shortly thereafter H2O-Pure began erecting tall metal shelving structures to hold the many boxes of records. The Baker renovation work was inspected by Tom Logan personally on March 5th, and Baker's performance under the terms of the contract was approved as highly satisfactory. A check was issued to Baker Contractors, Inc. in accordance with their invoice, as follows:

BAKER CONTRACTORS, INC.
March 15th

Basic contract	$1,003,500
Change Order No. 1	
Removal of 286°F fire suppression system water	
sprinkler heads and installation of 165°F heads	+ 7,350

Continues

Continued

Change Order No. 2
    Removal of 48-inch wide entrance doors   +   1,850
    Enlarge door openings to 96-inches wide   +   5,600
    Repair wall surrounding door openings   +   2,700
    Install new doors   + 20,000

Contract Change 3
    Install air conditioning and humidity control system   +125,000

Change Order No. 4
    Substitute 96-inch strip lighting for 48-inch twin
tube lighting specified in contract.
        Cost of 48-inch fixtures included in contract $35,000
        Less: Cost of 96-inch fixtures   −17,500
        Savings $17,500

    Contractor's share of savings VE incentive
    $\frac{1}{2} \times \$17,500 =$ +   8,750

Change Order No. 5
    Substitute bituminous concrete floors in place of
        concrete specified in contract
    Contractor's Value Engineering cost savings incentive
        $\$40,000 \times \frac{1}{2} =$ + 20,000

Total amount of contract, as amended $1,194,750

Ten months after large sections of shelving had been erected and loaded, the metal supporting columns began to sink into the relatively soft floor. This created a dangerous situation resulting from the likelihood of loaded shelving units (weighing about 2,500 pounds) toppling over. Eventually, another contract with Concrete, Inc. was entered into to replace the bituminous surface with concrete. A structural engineer with Concrete, Inc. stated that in his opinion, asphalt was not strong enough to support the weight of fully loaded shelving and should not have been used for the job. No attempt was made to get the Baker company to correct the problem without charge, because Tom Logan stated that he was responsible for approving the asphalt floor-surfacing material used. In fact, Tom was not at all as alarmed at the prospect of the shelving toppling over as was Ann Cestor, the Bluebird archivist. Tom stated that shelves uniformly loaded would not become unstable until the top reached a lean of at least 12 inches. He continued, saying that the farthest lean measured so far was only 3 inches. To Ann Cestor's concern over the domino effect, Tom replied that it was unlikely, since the aisles were 30 inches wide and shelving units leaning toward each other would form a sort of tepee and stabilize.

What Is Required

From the information provided in the case study a number of questions, comments, and/or observations should occur to you. List them, being reasonably explicit, and compare them to those offered in the case study 9 solutions. Do not list the sort of simple fraud possibilities that have been discussed in Cases 1 through 6.

FRAUD CASE STUDY NO. TEN: THE MORTGAGE

You are an accountant examining the loan portfolio of the Sundown Savings and Loan Association. You have been reviewing loans for three days when you come to a $125,000 loan secured by an office building located at 12345 Old Orchard Road. You review the loan file and note that the loan, made on July 1, 1999, was recommended and approved by Harvey Goodfellow, president and chief executive officer of Sundown.

Upon further review of the loan file, you note that the Old Orchard Road building had been appraised by the Sundown appraiser at $140,000. You also note that the appraisal was based on recent sales of the building. It had been sold in November 1997 for $135,000, the new owner apparently taking a quick profit by selling it again in March 1998 for $150,000. The current owner, who borrowed the $125,000 to purchase the building, paid $155,000.

What Is Required

Comment on the foregoing. Do you think that the Sundown loan is well secured? Bear in mind the property has a relatively recent market value of $155,000. The facts given in the case study are correct, but you should be troubled by what you read. What troubles you, and what additional work can you do to dispel your concerns?

Chapter 9

Fraud Case Studies— Solutions

The solutions which follow supplement the previous chapter, *Fraud Case Studies*. All discussions which follow presume that the reader has read the applicable fraud case study and is aware of the basic facts and circumstances.

FRAUD CASE STUDY NO. ONE—SOLUTIONS: THE TANK

The average auditor or accountant, who has attended fraud detection lectures conducted by the authors over the years, would have been in agreement with the course of action followed by Brad and Tim. They too would have passed transaction #8 after the examination procedures performed by Brad and Tim, with no finding of fraud. However, Brad and Tim missed performing an examination which would have detected the fraud that occurred in the actual case that this case study was taken from. In addition, they also failed to perform several other examination procedures that would have discovered other fraud types that *may* have been present.

The reason Tim and Brad did not detect any fraud in their examination was because they literally did not look for fraud. Consider carefully what it was that they did. They looked to see if the purchase had been properly authorized and specified. They examined to determine if the contract had been properly let to the Aztec Company and correctly found that it had been advertised, and that Aztec was the low bidder. They examined the contractor's invoice and found that it had been correctly prepared. They examined the receiving report which attested to the fact that the work had been properly performed, in accordance with the contract.

Their mistake was that they trusted all the documents to be authentic representations of fact. In particular, they believed that the work had been satisfactorily performed when they examined the receiving report and found that Mr. Blake had signed the report. What they failed to consider was that perhaps Mr. Blake was involved in a fraud and had falsely attested that the work required had been done—exactly what had happened in the actual case this case study was taken from.

In "The Tank," Brad and Tim failed to adequately search for defective delivery fraud. They came close to it when they examined the receiving report, but in trusting Mr. Blake's signature, they failed. What they should have done was personally determine that the services had been delivered. Every successful fraud-specific auditor or accountant must be a bit paranoid to be successful. When it comes to accepting signatures authenticating the delivery of products or services, they must adopt an attitude of "show me!" to be certain, and even then, they can be fooled.

In the actual case this was taken from, the auditors were suitably paranoid. Because of recent experience, they were no longer accepting authenticating signatures at full value. After having selected a payment transaction similar to number 8, they physically visited the remote site of the tank involved. Accompanying them was an independent building technician who was competent to verify the satisfactory delivery of the service. Mr. Blake's real life equivalent also accompanied the examination team, and chuckled when he was told the auditors intended to inspect the delivery of the tank's renovation, noting that the tank was over a hundred feet in the air and full of water.

The auditors nodded to the technician who had accompanied them. He quickly entered the building, took the elevator to the roof, climbed the ladder attached to the water tank, and threw back the access cover. He rolled up his sleeve and inserted his arm into the water as far as it would go. Spreading his fingers, and pressing them to the wall of the water tank, he slowly dragged his hand up to the top of the tank. As he removed his hand, he held a handful of rust and paint scale, which proved that the tank had not been renovated in quite some time.

Note that the auditors, with the assistance of the technician, sought to prove one thing and one thing only: was there defective delivery fraud? Had the tank wall been renovated, the technician would have been able to detect it immediately. The handful of rust and scale proved that fraud had been committed, and that Mr. Blake had either been negligent in signing the receiving report or was a co-conspirator. A co-conspirator with whom? With the Aztec Company, of course. When they submitted an invoice for services performed, they committed fraud.

The Tank—Additional Discussion

Tim and Brad were not necessarily wrong because they failed to search for defective delivery fraud. They were wrong because they failed to search for any variety of fraud. The accountant or auditor cannot, as a practicable matter, afford to exhaust the possibilities for fraud for each transaction examined and must limit their search time for practical purposes. Accordingly, he or she must decide upon one or more of the fraud types they are going to search for before the search begins. In the case of transaction No. 8, Tim and Brad did not have a clear fraud quest in mind. Had they chosen one or more of the fraud types listed in the chapter on classifying fraud, they could not be faulted. Had they chosen to search for defective delivery fraud in examining transaction 9, they would have been on the right track, but their methodology was faulty in that they naively relied on the receiving report to determine if the contractor's service had been delivered properly.

FRAUD CASE STUDY NO. TWO—SOLUTIONS: THE OTHER TANK

Were Tim and Brad correct in closing their review after having positively determined that the renovation of the water tank atop building #17 had been satisfactorily delivered? Yes! Anyone performing fraud-specific examinations cannot possibly be expected to disclose all fraud that may be present in any given situation. If the building 17 tank had been the same as the tank in case study no. 1, the accountants would have found fraud. However, it wasn't. As a result they did not find the fraud that was present in case study no. 2. Tim and Brad should not be faulted for this, however, because they chose a bona fide fraud detection procedure as an expedient. The fact that they guessed incorrectly in choosing which fraud type to look for is not a culpable error on their part.

The Fraud

Had the accountants chosen to go one step further and look for multiple payee fraud, they would have found the fraud they were searching for. Although the tank renovation was well done, it was not the Anderson Company that did the work. It was the Star Company. Tim and Brad's decision to eliminate a review of the paperwork underlying transaction #9 did not affect the outcome of their review. It would have disclosed nothing. All of the paperwork justifying the Anderson Company transaction was forged. Mr. Blake, the building manager, was the Anderson Company's co-conspirator.

An internal control feature which would facilitate detection of shell frauds is the maintenance of an information file which, in this case, would be literally a record of all maintainable property. The record, usually automated, is maintained as a part of an MIS (Management Information System). It records, for all maintainable property, a record of maintenance performed on each item. For example, when the rooms were last painted in building 16, when the roof was replaced on storage building A, and when the water tank atop building #17 was last refurbished. Had such a record been maintained, Tim and Brad would have been able to refer to it quickly and see that the water tank had been refurbished twice in a suspiciously narrow time-frame. Of course, for this record to be reliable for this purpose, it would have to be maintained by an independent department of an entity, such as the accounting department. Would the MIS have been useful in disclosing the water tank case discussed in Case Study No. 1? No. In this case, the MIS would have only indicated that the tank had been renovated.

Another Fraud Possibility

Given the particulars described in this case study, there is another possibility for fraud that Brad and Tim could have searched for—duplicate payment fraud.

FRAUD CASE STUDY NO. THREE—SOLUTIONS: THE PARKING LOT

Tim's decision to perform a defective delivery examination was most appropriate. It is not unusual for contractors who have bid low to cut corners to improve their bottom line. In view of the Blacktop Company's protest, Tim's choice was wise.

Tim's first priority was to examine the receiving report which accepted the work performed by First Class. Mr. Sam Diego had signed the receiving report attesting to the fact that all requirements of the contract had been satisfactorily delivered. Sam wasn't too happy when he learned that Tim was, in fact, questioning his confirmation of the services received. Nevertheless, Tim went forward with his examination. In doing so, Tim took the unusual step of speaking with the officials of the Blacktop Company who had protested the contract award. He offered them the opportunity of inspecting the parking lot for the purpose of validating their claims. They accepted, and their representative, Mr. Clark, Tim, and Sam Diego visited the parking lot in question. Sam vigorously protested Mr. Clark's involvement, but was overruled. One of the first things Mr. Clark did was to comment that the refurbished parking area had not been sealed as required by the contract, a defect in the delivery. The second thing he did was to take test cores from random locations in the lot. The cores were drilled out of the parking lot's surface, and could be measured to determine the thickness of the blacktop layer applied. The various cores averaged two inches in depth. The First Class Company had applied only two inches of material when the contract required four inches, another defect in the delivery. Tim asked Mr. Clark if he would provide expert testimony to substantiate his findings, should it be required, and he agreed. Tim took possession of the cores.

Later, Tim computed the value of the difference between the two inches of material and the four inches required, and the value of the Formula X seal coating, as amounting to $30,000. H2O-Pure management was considering whether or not to prosecute the contractor for fraud, but was inclined to accept the contractor's refund offer of $60,000. Sam Diego admitted that he was negligent in approving the paving work accomplished and was admonished. Tim, however, was not content. He was developing an intuitive sense that many fraud-specific auditors acquire with experience and he was bothered that there was something they had missed, but could not put his finger on it.

FRAUD CASE STUDY NO. FOUR—SOLUTIONS: THE PARKING LOT REVISITED

There was no question in Tim's mind that Sam Diego was a conspirator in fraud in the parking lot defective deliveries. However, it was difficult to connect him personally to the alleged crime. Sam admitted he was negligent in inspecting the work done by the contractor and apologized profusely for his error. It is unlikely that a person in Sam's situation would ever be prosecuted for his involvement in this crime based upon the evidence disclosed at this point. If prosecuted, just about any jury would give Sam the benefit of the doubt and find him not guilty. H2O-Pure Management gave him the benefit of the doubt, admonishing him to be more careful next time. Tim, however, was not convinced. To him, Sam looked like "the cat who had swallowed the canary," which caused Tim to rethink his involvement in the case, and to consider what he may have overlooked. After struggling with his suspicions, finally, *voilà,* there it was. He had an idea.

Tim borrowed a measuring device from the H2O-Pure Engineering Department. It was basically a wheel with a footage meter attached. Taking it to the parking lot, he began at the eastern edge of the lot, and rolled the device until it reached the western perimeter. The distance? 400 feet! Traversing the lot from north to south, his measurement indicated it was 400 feet. He double-checked his measurements with no variation. The lot was not 250,000 square feet based upon the 500 × 500 foot dimensions advertised; but 160,000 square feet based upon the actual measurements— a difference of 90,000 square feet.

The question left unanswered here is whether or not the misstatement of the parking lot's measurements was intentional or not. Also, if the mis-measurement was intentional, was Sam Diego aware of it? Consider here that the misstatement of the lot's dimensions is not the only possible crime. There is also the two inch versus four inch thickness deficiency, and the failure to apply the top coating. We advise that an accountant finding themselves in this situation "think fraud" and continue their examination into other questionable things that Sam Diego may have done. If he is a perpetrator-conspirator, it is likely that this is not his first venture into fraud. Another example or two will compel most prosecutors to proceed with an indictment.

Note: It is not unusual for busy contractors to not recheck the measure-ments of a lot such as the H2O-Pure parking lot. This case was taken from a real case that occurred in Southern California, and no one rechecked the incorrect measurements.

Incidentally, if you came up with other possible frauds given the circum-stances stated for this case, you are not incorrect. It is possible for other frauds to have occurred, and a good fraud-specific examiner would not be wrong to check them out. It is not unlikely that the transaction examined could have resulted in the discovery of a shell fraud, a multiple payment fraud, a duplicate payment fraud, or a rigged contract. Of course, the parking lot case study could also be a rigged contract, in that the First Class Paving Company could have lowered their bid by about $90,000, because of their knowledge that the parking lot was only 160,000 square feet in area, as compared to the 250,000 square feet that were advertised, and which other honest contractors would be bidding in accordance with.

FRAUD CASE STUDY NO. FIVE—SOLUTIONS:
THE STORAGE BUILDINGS

The apparent front-end loading of bid prices offered by the Pence Company for the three storage buildings that concerned Brad is suspicious but is not necessarily conclusive. Conceivably, when a contractor prepares to construct three buildings on adjacent sites, he or she will incur higher costs at the beginning of the contract which will benefit of all three buildings. For example, the site may require earthwork that is best accomplished for all buildings before actual construction begins and the installation of underground utilities is often done more efficiently at the outset of the contract for all structures. It may also be advantageous to the contractor to purchase job equipment and supplies at the beginning of construction, hence the higher cost for the first item to be constructed. Accordingly, although the contractor may have a fraudulent intent in unbalancing his bid, more evidence than was given is necessary to conclude on this possibility. All that H2O-Pure needs to do is to allow the contract to go to completion, as written, to protect its interests.

Note: Many contractors in this situation would unbalance their bids to assure their profits in the event of the contracting entity's cancellation of other contract items. Whether or not this practice constitutes fraud is arguable. Technically, it is fraud, in that through this practice the contractor secretly obtains payments he or she is not entitled to. For a contract that will go to completion—the basic presumption for all contracts—the only loss for the contracting entity is that he or she will have to make progress payments earlier than they are actually earned by the contractor, and those funds will be at risk should the contractor default, or his or her performance be unsatisfactory.

Brad's concern over the variation in bids offered for identical buildings was legitimate. His course of action is uncertain. At the very least—from an internal control standpoint—he should have been critical of H2O-Pure's contracting procedure. If H2O-Pure had doubts about whether or not they needed all three buildings, they should not have contracted for three buildings in the first place. In effect, what they did was provide the Pence Company an opportunity for fraud, while forcing the other honest bidders to offer bids that contemplated the independent construction of each building, as though there were three contracts (which there should have been).

The other course of action that Brad should have considered invokes two primary attributes every fraud-specific examiner should employ, patience and intelligence. To be patient simply means that when seeking to determine and announce a perpetrator, the examiner must be content to wait, sometimes excruciatingly, until the circumstances are sufficient to announce his or her catch. Rarely will the fraud examiner be in a position to gather readily available evidence and point his or her finger at a perpetrator immediately. In this case study, it was quite evident early on that Della Ware's involvement is suspicious. However, the time is not appropriate for Brad to make his suspicions of Della made known. This is where the intelligence—as in intelligence system—attribute enters. Brad should put Della into a "suspicious character" category, and watch her activities in the months ahead. Also, he should be suspicious of the Pence Company. There is insufficient evidence for him to openly voice his suspicions; however, they too should be placed into his personal intelligence file and watched in the months ahead. Brad's observation of the cancellation of buildings B & C on October 20th should have added to the evidence he was collecting on Della Ware and the Pence Company. However, he still does not have enough to suggest punitive action. However, he certainly knows in his mind that Della and the Pence Company are conspirators in fraud. Now it's simply a matter of acquiring the evidence to prove it.

Important note: This case study was intended to provide an example of unbalanced bidding in an over-simplified manner to make the unbalanced aspect of the bidding very obvious to all readers. Admittedly, the case study is not real world difficult. Were this degree of difficulty incorporated in the case study, no one would understand it without a great deal more evidence to draw from. For example, let's assume that the contract described in the case study called for the construction of three *very different structures* A, B, and C. Further assume that the low bidder offered construction costs of $600,000 for structure A, $800,000 for structure B, and $1,000,000 for structure C. Also assume that the bid for the first structure was unbalanced and inflated by $250,000. The bidding disparity is not quite as obvious as it was in the case study given. The fraud examiner would have no reason to suspect fraud until, perhaps, structures B and C were deleted or significantly changed. Proving it would be another matter and the best course of action would probably be to look for the Della Wares and the Pence Companies who may be manipulating the contracts.

Of course, the solution to the case study given is that the Pence Company and Della Ware are conspirators in fraud. It was Della who strongly advocated the need for the three storage structures, for reasons now obvious. There was never any intention in her mind of building the last two structures. The fraud netted the Pence Company at least $100,000 extra profit, a portion of which will be shared with Della Ware.

FRAUD CASE STUDY NO. SIX—SOLUTIONS: LEASE VARIABLE COST "PASS THROUGH"

Tim reviewed the Bay Building statement providing the computation of rental costs for H2O-Pure for Year 3. His first reaction was that the rates appeared to be high at about $40 a square foot of office space. However, upon reconsideration he realized that the location of the building with its fine view of the bay, easy access to San Diego's international airport, and the prime penthouse floor enjoyed by H2O-Pure made the rental rate more acceptable.

During his review of the lessor's Year 3 rental statement, Tim noted that the rate computations had also been reviewed by H2O-Pure's San Diego area office manager, Claire de Lune, whose signature, together with the word "approved," appeared in the lower left corner of the Bay Building statement. Satisfied that there was little potential for fraud in the transaction, Tim closed his review of the lease transaction with a finding of "no fraud."

That evening, however, Tim had a thought that caused him to reopen his review the next day. Retrieving the Bay Building Statement, he went directly to the item that had troubled him and there it was. The Bay Building management, in computing their variable cost rate had divided the total cost by the total rentable office space in the building, to arrive at $15 a square foot. In charging H2O-Pure for the variable cost portion of their rental rate, the Bay Building had applied the $15 rate to ALL 33,000 square feet of space that H2O-Pure rented in the building, including 8,000 square feet of parking space. They should have only charged the $15 rate to the 25,000 square feet of office space. Note that in computing the variable cost rate, the Bay Building divided their variable costs by the total office space. This would exclude any other space such as parking. Since parking space requires a very low level of maintenance anyway, this was appropriate. If it was fraud, the amount of the fraud was 8,000 square feet of parking × $15, or $120,000 in Year 3. Tim was elated with his finding; however, he was well aware that the lessor could always claim the extra charge was a random error. He wanted to call it deliberate fraud and he suspected that Ms. De Lune was a co-conspirator.

To strengthen his case, Tim decided to examine the computation of rental costs for Year 1 and Year 2. In both cases he found the same error, and in both instances Ms. de Lune had approved the statements. The overcharge in Year 1 was $98,000 and in Year 2 was $115,000.

Tim prepared his report to H2O-Pure management indicating his strong suspicion that fraud was involved. The H2O-Pure General Counsel agreed with Tim, but was extremely reluctant to seek prosecution. Rather, they discussed the matter with the Bay Building management, who quickly offered to repay the entire amount of the overcharges, plus any interest that had accrued. They also pledged to renew the lease at the end of the ten-year lease period, for an additional ten-year period, at the same terms as in the original lease, provided the matter remained confidential. H2O-Pure's counsel accepted their offer.

Authors' note: The particulars of this case study were taken from an actual case located elsewhere in the United States. The details were told to us by the lessee of the space involved, who was a shrewd businessman, and discovered the blatant overcharge. We have every reason to believe that it is true. His handling of the discovery is interesting. He requested a refund of all overcharges and requested other special favors (such as privileged parking, redecorating, and special signage) in return for his silence. He was convinced that the lessor had cheated other tenants in his building in a similar manner and was extremely fearful of their learning of his nefarious ways.

FRAUD CASE STUDY NO. SEVEN—SOLUTIONS: THE VENETIAN BLINDS

In re-examining her notes, Suzie Wong realizes that the Brite invoice specifies that the rate charged is in accordance with the annual H2O-Pure "requirements" contract with the Brite Window Company. It should be the lowest corporate rate currently advertised by Brite. She obtains the latest Brite advertisement and finds that the rate specified is $1 per square foot, as charged in their invoice. She is tempted to close her review at that point, but something tells her she should look at the actual contract between H2O-Pure and Brite.

On Monday morning, Suzie visits the H2O-Pure Contract Division and obtains the Brite contract. In a few minutes, she has confirmed that the contract provides, as the Brite invoice stated, that the cleaning rate would be in accordance with the lowest, latest Brite advertised corporate rate. As she verified earlier, that rate is $1 a square foot. She also learns something that the Brite invoice did not disclose—that H2O-Pure had negotiated an additional 35 percent discount off the latest published rate. Applied to the $7,200 invoice gross amount, the 35 percent discount would have reduced it to $4,680. There had been a $2,520 overcharge!

Suzie's next reactions are not only interesting, but noteworthy for all accountants and auditors. Whereas many auditors would quickly discuss the overcharge with management and suggest they seek a refund, Suzie did not. As an experienced fraud-specific examiner—and a bit paranoid as all good fraud examiners must be—she immediately suspected fraud. She had seen this sort of fraud before—where a vendor makes an "innocent" mistake, apologizes when confronted with it, and offers an immediate refund. She was determined it wouldn't happen again. She immediately began to plan an audit program designed to prove or disprove fraud.

For her audit program, she identified her suspects as the Brite Window Company, and Mr. Cee Attle. It was Mr. Attle who had signed the invoice and didn't notice that the discount had not been applied. She felt—correctly—that Mr. Attle was either negligent or a fraud conspirator. She also knew that this sort of fraud offered little risk for the perpetrating contractors in that they could always plead that they had erred, not committed fraud. However, although she knew that the plausible error excuse would have to be accepted if it was only shown to have happened once, she also knew that if she could show that the Brite people and Mr. Attle had "erred" several or more times, the excuse would wear thin and perhaps be beyond reasonable doubt.

Her basic assumption was that if the Brite Window Company was in fact a fraud perpetrator, they would have very likely been involved in fraud before, so she began to review all of their invoices for work in the last two years. Her hunch paid off; for every one of the prior eight invoices, the Brite Window Company had forgotten to apply the 35% discount. It was no surprise to her that Mr. Attle had signed off on all the invoices. She now felt she had eliminated any reasonable doubt as to whether or not the Brite Company had intentionally over-billed H2O-Pure. The total amount of the over-billing was $25,416, clearly a felony! Suzie prepared her report to management, indicating her finding of what she believed to be fraud.

Had Suzie found prior invoices representing work done by the Brite Window Company, but did not find any "mistakes" suggesting the possibility of fraud, she would have dismissed her suspicions and reported the finding to the department involved, suggesting they seek a refund of the $2,520. Had there not been any prior invoices by the Brite Window Company, Suzie was considering holding her finding confidential for several months while keeping a watchful eye out for new work by the Brite Company.

This case study was taken from a real audit case. However, the auditor who actually found the over-billing reacted in a manner typical of many internal auditors. He showed it to the manager of the department involved—very proud of his accomplishment—and suggested they seek a refund.

Within days, the contractor involved had issued a refund check with no questions asked. No other work was done to determine whether or not there were similar over-billings in prior periods and never for a minute did the auditor suspect that he may have found evidence of fraud.

FRAUD CASE STUDY NO. EIGHT—SOLUTIONS: THE PAINTING TERM CONTRACT

If you decided that the award to the Lima Painters was wrong, you are wrong, regardless of any data presented in the case study. In fact, there was little that the Ten/Four Corporation could do other than select Lima for the term contract award once they responded to the RFB with a low aggregate bid. The RFB process is a very serious one in contracting, and entities must have legitimate reasons for not selecting the low bidder if they have stated that will be the basis for awarding the contract and the bidder is otherwise responsive to the RFB. To do otherwise is legally actionable and a losing low bidder may sue an entity denying them a contract for capricious reasons (and they would probably win).

However, don't despair. If you decided that the award to the Lima Painters was wrong, you would have been right in theory. It is clear that in submitting their bid, they have an agenda to profit unjustly.

The details of this case are relatively easy to discern. By the same token, they were made easy for you to see, so that readers could understand more readily the gist of this case study. Be warned, however, that the details of this type of case in the real world will not be as readily discernable. Also, in this case study, as in the real world, identifying the problem is one thing, determining what can be done about it is another. If an accountant or auditor were to comment upon the profit perils in selecting a contractor such as the Lima Painters, their warnings would probably consign them wherever they keep people who have sighted UFOs. Their concerns would likely be regarded as pure and unfounded paranoia. In fact, were a fraud examiner to comment on the fraud potential, news of his or her comments might very well cause any such plans to be canceled, making their claims to be all the more ill-founded.

This case is a relatively realistic version of the fraud type previously described as involving unbalanced contract bidding, which can take a wide variety of forms. In this instance the successful painting contractor is Lima Painters, which was selected for its low aggregate bid of $141,625 (versus bids of $166,720, $171,490, and $164,095). Actually, if the bidders were held to the quantities of painting specified in the RFP's specified painting categories A through F, Lima Painters $141,625 bid clearly would have been the proper selection. There is no question that they have submitted the low aggregate bid. How can anyone argue with the low numbers indicated? As a matter of fact, however, were Lima Painters required to perform painting in accordance with its bid offer, it is very likely that they would lose money on the contract.

But in this case, their bid was offered only to win the contract award, not to perform in accordance with it. They have good reason to expect that the quantities of painting ordered will be changed to put their bid in the high-profit range. What Lima has done is to unbalance their bid so that any painting done in categories B, D, and E, will be highly profitable, while unit prices bid for painting done in categories A, C, and E are below the market prices (see bids by other painters). Also, note that painting categories B, D, and E all involve the application of two coats of paint, which undoubtedly will be needed to cover the old dark blue paint.

Lima's unbalanced unit prices can be seen best when compared to the other bids received:

Painting Category:	A	B	C	D	E	F
Juliet Painting	.08¢	.14¢	.10¢	.16¢	.12¢	.18¢
Kilo Painters	.085¢	.15¢	.095¢	.14¢	.11¢	.185¢
Lima Painters	.05¢	.30¢	.05¢	.25¢	.05¢	.25¢
Mike Painting, Inc.	.075¢	.145¢	.10¢	.15¢	.13¢	.18¢

Notice that Lima has bid high on all painting categories requiring two coats of paint (categories B, D, and F)! You should have considered this suspicious in view of the fact that the Ten/Four RFB estimated, for bidding purposes, that most of their painting would be of the one-coat variety.

What to Do?

The unbalanced Lima bid should very definitely be regarded as indicia of fraud, kept confidential, but shared with a suitable confidant in your organization, preferably someone on the audit committee. If you are correct, you will be able to predict what will happen next, which will enhance your credibility as a fraud examiner and set the stage for a course of action.

Presuming that you have discovered the first stages of a fraud, you should attempt to identify suspects, at the very least. It should be quite obvious that there is an inside Ten/Four conspirator who is either advising the Lima Painters to logically expect the entity to order two coats as a general practice, or who is sufficiently influential to cause the entity to order two-coat painting.

While we are attempting to identify suspects, we should be wondering why the RFB was based upon estimates of extensive one-coat painting, when a reasonable person would know that two coats would be required to cover the old dark blue surfaces with white paint. The most probable answer is that one-coat painting was used for estimating so as to set up the subsequent changes to two-coat painting. It should be relatively easy to determine who prepared the estimate and that person must be suspected! Once one or more suspects have been determined, the examiner should proceed along standard fraud case development program lines. Fraud perpetrators rarely commit fraud only once, unless of course they happen to discover the perpetrator's first attempt, which is unlikely. Standard procedure dictates that the examiner proceed to examine other transactions in which the suspects have been involved. If they are truly dishonest, the examiner will find other examples of fraud or suspicious activity, all of which can be combined to prove intent to defraud.

Regardless of the examiner's success in proving fraud, he or she should be making internal control system recommendations designed to improve the entity's contracting practices. For example, once an RFP is sent out and a contract is awarded on the basis of the numbers contained in it, capricious changes should not be permitted without a rigorous approval procedure. Those persons responsible for preparing the workload estimates for the RFPs should be held accountable for their estimates.

FRAUD CASE STUDY NO. NINE—SOLUTIONS: THE ARCHIVE

If this case study were written as a news article, it would have a correct solution and a number of incorrect answers. However, since it has been written as a teaching vehicle there is no correct answer, only possible fraud scenarios, any or all of which the fraud examiner may wish to consider in his/her examination. Accordingly, the solutions will be discussed in terms of possible fraud scenarios.

Scenario One

The first question that attracts the alert examiner is that of the low $711,000 bid Acme Builders submitted. In this study case, it is a red herring with no direct case significance. In the actual case, there was a low bidder eliminated for the identical reason. The contractor offering the low bid failed to name the subcontractors he planned to use which was a requirement of the IFB. His bid offer was simply non-responsive to the advertising entity's IFB. It is understandable for the fraud examiner to be concerned, particularly in that the low bid was $300,000, or 30 percent less than the next low bid. It is normal for you to question if this is this sufficient reason for the bidder to be disqualified, particularly if it was the only reason. The answer is Yes! In the actual case, it was the only reason and there was no question about eliminating the low bid as non-responsive.

As an interesting adjunct to this issue, in the real case, the second-lowest bidder awarded the contract (as was Baker Contractors in this case) did list subcontractors' names. However, for unknown reasons, the names listed were not made a contract requirement and the actual winning contractor did not use the subcontractors named!

The lesson here, however, is one of contract law. If the IFB, a formal contracting document, stipulates the bidder must submit a list, he must do so. If he doesn't, and if he doesn't state that he will not use subcontractors, he has failed to be responsive and must be rejected regardless of how low his bid is. There is no requirement that a contract has to follow through and be consistent with an IFB, and require that any subcontractors named and approved must be used, even though to do otherwise appears to be an exercise in futility. If the contracting entity were not to follow the procedure it itself had established, regardless of what the reasons may be, its deviation would very likely be actionable under law.

Very frankly, this item from the actual case is suspicious. The authors suspect the Acme bid was probably a legitimate bid, even though apparently unrealistically low and the others were not legitimate. Acme's failure to list the sub-contractors may have been simply an over-sight. However, their failure to provide the subcontractor list provided left the H2O-Pure contracting people with no legitimate alternative. They did have an "illegitimate" alternative that would have saved the corporation $300,000, however (one that is sometimes used in deserving cases). They could have declared that they had a change of heart (of convenience) on the design of the renovation project, and needed to change the IFB specifications before the contract was awarded. This would have been a valid reason for requiring all bidders to submit new bids. This is not recommended; the practice can be abused.

Another possible scenario here (and good fraud-specific examiners must think in terms of possible scenarios) is that the Acme bid was a legitimate bid and the other three were illegitimate. This sometimes happens in the real world. It is called contract rotation. Some contractors feel that the competitive process is self-destructive and cut-throat. To avoid it and to keep profits up, they have engaged in illegal conspiracies with other contractors; they agree before bids are submitted as to whose turn it is to get a given contract. If it was Acme's turn to win the contract award, then the other two contractors would bid slightly higher so as to allow Acme to be the low bidder, but close enough to Acme's bid to give the appearance of a competitive marketplace. Contract rotation would also explain why the $711,000 Acme bid in the case study appears unrealistically low. Be honest—how many of you readers felt that the low bid of $711,000 was faulty because it was out of line with the other three bids that were submitted? If you were, don't be embarrassed. Auditors frequently review all bids offered to make a determination of whether the winning low bid was realistic. If it falls within the ballpark of bids offered, it is usually assumed that this is proof of a bona fide price offering.

Scenario Two

The first contract change order provided for a change in fire suppression system sprinkler heads from 165°F to 286°F. In the actual case, the old facility being renovated did have 286°F sprinkler heads already installed that were well within their rated service life and did not require changing. Nevertheless, the IFB and the renovation contract inferred that the heads were 165°F heads that were old and had to be replaced. As in the case study, the actual case contract provided that new 165°F heads be installed. Later, the contractor would claim that he installed new 165°F heads in accordance with the contract requirements—the cost presumably included in his bid proposal—inferring there was no basis for a refund should the heads again have to be changed.

When the first change order was issued directing the contractor to remove the 165°F heads and replace them with the recommended 286°F heads, the contractor was entitled to be reimbursed for his cost of removing any of the newly installed 165°F heads and to be reimbursed for the cost of purchasing and installing the new 286°F heads now required by the change order.

At this point, let a degree of fraud-specific paranoia run through our minds for a moment or two and consider the question "What if the contractor (1) had been informed that the existing sprinkler heads in the annex building when he began work already were 286°F heads?, (2) that they were well within their lifetime service ratings, (3) would not have to be replaced for fire safety reasons, and (4) that the contract awarded would eventually be changed to require the installation of 286°F heads?"

Answer: He would know that he would have to do absolutely nothing and be in full compliance with the final contract requirements for the sprinkler heads. In addition, he would know:

- He would not have to buy 165°F heads, but would profit from any costs included in his bid for their purchase and installation.
- He would not have to remove the 165°F heads when the expected contract change order was received, but would be reimbursed for the costs of doing so.
- He would not have to purchase 286°F heads when the expected contract change order was issued, but could claim the costs of their purchase and installation.

In short, he would incur no costs for complying with the expected contract change order, but could charge for numerous costs.

This scenario would normally require the cooperation of an H2O-Pure employee who was aware of the type and condition of the fire sprinkler heads in the annex—someone such as Tom Logan. Tom could also arrange for an archivist to discover that the fire sprinkler heads called for in the contract were wrong for a records storage area.

Scenario Three

The second contract change order provided for wider doors (96″) than had been provided for in the contract specifications. As is true in most cases of this sort, the real question is if this an honest mistake or oversight, or was it intended. The first involves negligence, the second involves fraud.

If the fraud examiner suspects the latter, he or she should begin an examination program designed to search for evidence. Note that this examination phase is the result of the examiner's conception of a fraud scenario and the steps taken to prove or disprove the scenario envisioned. The first logical step seems to be to interview Mr. Tom Logan, who determined that the four-foot doors had been completely installed at the time the second change order was issued. He should be able to explain the circumstances of how he came to determine this fact and what record he made of the observation. Perhaps it was a progress report, which should be obtained and carefully scrutinized. These determinations are relevant in the event that other evidence is discovered which contradicts Mr. Logan's statement. His involvement as a perpetrator conspirator is strongly suggested.

Second, the examiner will most likely search for others who might be able to corroborate the completion, or non-completion, of the four-foot doors. In an organization as large as H2O-Pure, and with a project as large as the annex renovation, there surely must have been others who were aware of the entrance door work. Subcontractors, utility workers, plumbers, the visiting archivist who recommended the 96-inch doors, and others who may have worked in the annex during the renovation period should be sought out and interviewed regarding their contributions to the Annex project, and innocently questioned about project work, including the door replacement.

The lesson to be learned here is one of internal control: (1) carefully review line items in proposed contracts before awarding them; (2) do not change contracts unless absolutely necessary; and, (3) if it is necessary to change a contract, take pains to determine the status of related work at the time of issuing a change order.

Scenario Four

The third contract change order called for adding the air conditioning and humidity control package. H2O-Pure's failure to include the items in the original contract package indicates negligence, but there appears to be no criminal intent here. In larger construction contracts, building systems are sometimes omitted intentionally in the expectation that the bidding contractors will price their bids out as though the omitted packages were included. Many contractors price their bids on the basis of so many dollars per square foot of space, rather than itemize the cost of an entire building's systems. In such instances, the perpetrator contractor can reduce his bid to reflect at least a portion of the omitted system to be able to submit the lowest price. Later, he can discover that the building's specifications are deficient. With no options left to them, the contracting entity *must* provide for the missing system through a change order to the contractor involved. Of course, the contractor will profit handsomely as a result of his pricing of the change order.

Scenario Five

The fourth change order is a value engineering change recommended by the contractor calling for single 96-inch fluorescent tubes rather than the twin tube 48-inch tubes called for in the contract.

The contractor is correct in recommending 96-inch single tubes for an archive. Accordingly, he is entitled to half of the $17,500 savings. The question here once again is, was the contract set-up—that is, the 48-

inch fixtures wrongly required—to enable him to earn the $17,500 value engineering savings? We don't know. However, there is a pattern of possible fraud emerging in this case study which suggests that more is involved than simple error.

Scenario Six

The fifth change order is another value engineering change which gives the contractor a $20,000 bonus for recommending a cheaper material for the archive floor. Ordinarily, of itself, this change would not attract a fraud-specific examiner's attention. However, this one is different. In addition to being among other questionable change orders, the change in floor materials was not a good recommendation and proved to be unsatisfactory. In the actual case, the floor had to be replaced. Note again that Mr. Tom Logan approved the change order.

Scenario Seven

How many readers examined and understood the Baker Contractors invoice? Those who did noticed that for the fourth change order, the contractor added $17,500 as his bonus for the VE change recommended and approved. His price should be reduced for the H2O-Pure share of the savings! Also, the fifth change order is similarly in error. Rather than adding his $20,000 bonus, he should be reducing his price by $20,000, half of what he saved the H2O-Pure Corporation. His invoice is at least $75,000 overstated because of these errors. Notice, once again, that Mr. Logan approved this invoice and did not notice the overcharge.

Epilogue

Although all details, amounts, and names have been changed, all of the items included in this study were taken from an actual case. To our knowledge, the details of the actual case have never been released to the public and will in all probability never be generally known. However, after documenting the case, we were given to understand that there was an organized crime connection—the audit report was subpoenaed by a U.S. Attorney and the indictment and prosecution process prevented. The actual events and the bravado of the perpetrators of the allegedly criminal acts were truly incredible.

FRAUD CASE STUDY NO. TEN—SOLUTIONS: THE MORTGAGE

In Case Study 10, you are informed that the building had an apparent market value of $135,000 in November 1997 when it was sold. The building's resale four months later for $150,000 in March 1998 appears to make the appraiser's valuation of the building at $140,000 very reasonable. The subsequent sale of the property to the mortgagee for $155,000 appears a bit high, given the $140,000 appraisal. However, the loan of $125,000 is still $15,000 under the appraisal value and should be enough to protect the bank. What really happened here is that the property was purchased in 1995 for $50,000. The owners then engaged in what are known as "land flips" or "flipping" to give the appearance that the property was worth $140,000 in 1999. It is not. There is no legitimate evidence to indicate that the building is worth more than the $50,000 paid for it in 1995.

This is actually a very simple case study, but because of the high degree to which flipping was used in the savings and loan scandals of the late 1980s, we thought it worth including for those who may not have heard of the practice. Incidentally, flipping was not invented by the wayward savings and loan institutions. It has been around for a very long time. We can recall a Chicago office building that was purchased a number of years ago for around $4 million and subsequently sold to the government for about $14 million. There is little doubt that flipping was used to increase the appraised valuation. It is interesting to note that the government employee who was critically involved in the building's sale acquired a percentage ownership in the resold building.

Flipping simply involves a series of sales of a piece of property between associates, over a short period of time, substantially increasing the sales price each time the property is resold with fraudulent intent. Subsequently, when the property is sold to an innocent third party, his or her review of recent sales will confirm that the asking price is in the ballpark. For more information on land flipping, see the discussion at the end of "The Savings and Loan Debacle" and the section which follows it, "How High Can a Land Flip Go? in the following chapter.

Chapter 10

Custodial Fraud

This text has been written to respond to the primary professional needs and interests of the average accountant, as well as to conform to the practical limitations imposed by one text. However, the potential for fraud in the custodial industries—for example, the banking industry, the insurance industry, pension funds, the securities industry, and literally any investment or activity entrusted to possess, safeguard, and reinvest customer assets—is so awesome that this text would not be complete without brief mention of them.

Consider, for example, that in 1990 the government was guaranteeing depositary assets to the following extent:[14]

Assets	Taxpayer Liability
Insured checking and savings accounts, credit unions	$2,700 billion
Insurance for pensions, floods, war risk, crops, and overseas investment	1,300 billion
Government sponsored home mortgage, farming agencies, etc.	800 billion
Guarantees such as FHA and VA housing loans, student loans, small-business loans	600 billion
Agriculture and other direct loans	200 billion
TOTAL	$5,600 billion

Without the benefit of relatively recent experience, the probable reaction to comments suggesting that these assets were at risk would probably not be regarded seriously. However, experience has seen rampant fraud in savings and loans bank accounts that it is estimated will ultimately cost US taxpayers over $500 billion. Experience has also seen the failure of too many financial banks, worldwide, for all readers not to be concerned.

In considering whether or not to present this chapter, it was difficult to ignore the nagging thought that the extensive frauds occurring in the savings and loan association frauds (discussed below) could not have been executed without the knowledge or suspicions of the many accountants employed in the banks involved, who did not react in some manner to what was going on right under their eyes. In fact, many frauds committed by entities require the silent participation of accountants to do their dirty work. Accordingly, an additional objective of this chapter is to sensitize all accountants, regardless of employing industry, and to impart to them the thought that "it can happen to you!" The question is not so much if, but when. So, beware and react; it could be happening right now!

When discussing custodial fraud, what should worry readers most is the human tendency to rationalize a fraud if it is insured, especially when the guarantees are provided by the government.

THE SAVINGS AND LOAN (S&L) BANK DEBACLE OF THE 1980s

For examples of fraud on a grand scale involving depositary funds, one need only to look to the 1980s, and the scandal involving S&L bank operations, where outrageous fraud occurred, seemingly without limits. It has been estimated that fraud played a major role in 40 percent of the failed S&Ls. Ultimate losses U.S. taxpayers bore as the result of S&L bank failures were still being tallied at the turn of the century, but were estimated by the U.S. Comptroller General (GAO) in 1990 at as much as $500 billion. It is interesting to note that the U.S. government was both the unwitting **cause** of the S&L bank failures—(1) when the US Congress deregulated S&L bank activities in 1980 and 1982 and eliminated many long-standing requirements designed to restrict bank operations and (2) the **ultimate guarantor** of any bank losses, as the result of guaranteeing individual deposit accounts up to $100,000. Intended to protect individual investors and encourage saving, the $100,000 account deposit guarantees had a major contributory effect on the shenanigans and failures of the banks. The guarantees attracted many deep-pocket depositors who might otherwise have been unwilling to invest in risky S&L bank activities.

The deregulation of S&L banks by the U.S. Congress, which made the massive frauds which followed possible, were seemingly done with the best of intentions. The main objectives of the deregulation were:

- To allow the S&Ls to attract the additional money to sustain their lending operations.

- To raise depositary account guarantees from $40,000 per account to $100,000. There was no limit placed upon the number of $100,000 accounts a single depositor could have.
- To remove interest rate restraints[15].
- To stem the demise of S&Ls, suffering from overly restrictive regulations that required banks to have at least 400 stockholders—with no one stockholder allowed to hold over 40 percent of an S&L's stock. New regulations allowed a single person to own 100 percent of an S&L's stock. This allowed the many new single owners a free rein over bank operations, without interference from other more conservative owners. When the single owners were dishonest—and many were—there were literally no restraints over their activities.
- To increase loan activity.
  - 100% financing was allowed with no borrower equity required.
  - S&Ls were allowed to make loans on property located far from the lender's base territory.
  - Up to 40 percent of a bank's assets could be invested in non-residential commercial property. Previous investments were limited to residential properties only.
- To allow S&L banks to invest funds on their own behalf.

The results were chaotic. Congress, seemingly influenced by the contributions made to their political campaigns[16] by S&L banks, completely failed to foresee the opportunities for fraud that the deregulation presented to unscrupulous S&L operators. Without the restrictive regulations, the operations of many—not all[17]—of the S&Ls can be best described as incredibly reckless. If it were simply a matter of bad banking practices, the losses would undoubtedly have been far less than the eventual $500 billion cost. However, given the nefarious nature of many of the new S&L operators, the very naive deregulation measures gave many of them the opportunities to engage criminal fraud, with little or no restraint. William Seidman, chairman of the Resolution Trust Corporation (RTC), who subsequent to the turbulent 1980s was charged with resolving the affairs of the many failed S&Ls, estimated that fraud occurred in about 50 percent of insolvent thrifts and contributed to failure in about 40 percent of them.

Examples of Questionable and Criminal Practice in S&Ls

Example 1.   The government deregulation of S&Ls in 1980 and 1982—some called it "unregulation"—allowed S&Ls to generate cash through brokered accounts. Rather than being forced to depend upon the savings of local depositors, deregulation allowed S&Ls to go out and seek funds, and to provide generous incentives to invest. This attracted huge sums of cash from pension funds and others with pools of money to invest. The investments—broken down into $100,000 increments[18]—were risk-free to the providing funds; the interest rates were attractive; and, last but not least, the fund managers personally were often given commissions of several percent to attract the funds in their custody. It was the best of all worlds.

Once the deposits were received, they were often loaned out immediately on what were often illegal or questionable loans. For unscrupulous operators, the bottom line on a loan was irrelevant. The S&L would earn its profit at the time a loan was made. For example, a $1 million loan at an S&L commission of five percent would earn $50,000 profit immediately, and the $50,000 could be (and usually was) withdrawn and spent by the S&L managers immediately. Subsequently, if a loan went bad—an event which surprised no one—the government could be counted upon to reimburse the deficit.

Example 2. It was a not uncommon practice for unscrupulous S&L bank owners to make—literally—bad loans to themselves. When they subsequently defaulted, they got to keep the gross receipts from the loans, as well as the profit realized from writing the loans. Of course, the government reimbursed the institution for any losses on the loan—including the S&L's profit taken when the loan was written. Think about it! For a thief, wasn't this the best of all worlds?

This was the way it was done. The process usually began with the purchase of a piece of property, or a property already owned. By employing a process called flipping, the recorded property value is increased several or more times over its realistic market value. Next, a straw borrower is found who will act as the purchaser of the property. In return for his or her brief service, he or she will receive a small percentage of the property's value—say, two percent. He or she applies for a loan and is readily given up to 100 percent of the property's value (as determined by the current sales appraisal basis). The borrower refunds the money to his or her accomplices—the S&L owner/perpetrators—and disappears, subsequently defaulting on the loan. When the smoke clears, the perpetrators have gained several times the property's value, plus whatever commission income the S&L gained when the loan was written. The S&L gets the mortgaged property which is worth considerably less than the amount loaned.

For those not familiar with flipping or land flips, they involve a criminal practice wherein a parcel of real property is formally resold and recorded with each sale, within a circle of accomplices, several or more times over a relatively short period of time. Each time the property is resold, it is at a substantially higher selling price. When finally the property is resold to an unsuspecting buyer, or mortgaged, its current market value is likely to be appraised—on the basis of recent sales—as considerably higher than its true market value (which, of course, will remain undisclosed). Note: An appraiser valuing the property, as recorded, will confirm that the property has recently sold for prices in accord with the mortgage amount or asking price.

To illustrate, a parcel of land and building may be acquired at a fair market price of $100,000. The buyer, a short time later, resells the property to a second buyer—an accomplice—for $150,000. The second buyer, a day later, then sells it to a third buyer—also an accomplice—for $200,000. The third buyer sells it a day later to a fourth buyer for $250,000. The practice can continue, escalating the apparent market value to, let's say, $1,000,000. Each sale is recorded as a bona fide sale and serves as a basis for subsequent independent appraisals. The parcel, however, is still really worth only $100,000, the original and the only legitimate sales price. Since all parties to a sale of flipped properties are usually accomplices, no questions are raised about any discrepancies apparent between the appraised value and the apparent value of mortgaged properties. In one actual instance, a house worth only $50,000 was flipped to serve as collateral for a $487,000 loan. The borrower defaulted on the loan and the S&L involved was forced to sell the property at a great loss.

Of course, when the buyers of flipped properties are accomplices to the flipping, they have no intentions of repaying the amount borrowed, or possessing the properties they have purchased. They were usually well paid for their services and it is unlikely that they had ever even visited any of the properties they were buying.

HOW HIGH CAN A LAND FLIP GO?

The San Francisco Examiner *reported on what it said was a land flip orchestrated by San Francisco broker J. William Oldenburg at State Savings of Salt Lake City. Reportedly, Oldenburg bought 363 acres of land in Richmond, California in 1977 for $874,000 (he actually paid only $80,000 in down payment, the paper reported). In 1979, he hired an appraiser who appraised the land at $32.5 million. Just a little over two years later, the same appraiser decided the land was worth $83.5 million. In 1983, Oldenburg bought State Savings for $10.5 million. In*

1984, he sold the Richmond property to State Savings for $55 million, the Examiner *reported.*

> —*Inside Job: the Looting of America's Savings and Loans* by Stephen Pizzo, Mary Fricker, and Paul Muolo

Readers interested in an excellent well written book, which provides many details of savings and loan bank practices during the 1980s, as well as names, dates, and places, can find them in the book just cited[19]. Although the book is currently out of print, readers who can locate a copy will find it well worth their trouble.

THE SAVINGS AND LOAN BANK AFTERMATH

It is difficult to say exactly when the day of reckoning came for the S&Ls. One would think that it would have come quickly after 1980 and 1982, when the flagrant practices began appearing and savings banks began failing. Initially, it appears that the S&L bank failures and the resultant losses were so great that many S&Ls lost all their capital and should have been closed; but, the Federal Savings and Loan Insurance Corporation (FSLIC), lacking the funds needed to close them down and pay off their federally insured depositors, allowed them to keep operating. Additionally, it appears that the issue may have been played down to keep it from becoming an issue in the 1988 presidential election campaign.

Nevertheless, the bank failures became a flood after 1988 and could no longer be ignored. By early 1990, the FBI had been swamped by nearly 8,000 cases of potential S&L fraud and there were 13,000 tips on other suspected fraud cases pending investigation. (Source: Newsweek *Bonfire of the S&Ls* May 21, 1989)

Newspaper Headlines from the Era Illustrate the Chronology, Escalation, and Details of the S&L Scandal

1988 June 30 (*WSJ*)	"Documents Indicate Pressure Wright (MC Representative James-Texas) Put on Thrift Regulators Was Extensive"
1988 August 22 (*WSJ*)	"Texas Thrifts Rescue to Cost U.S. $5.5 Billion"
1988 November 4 (*WSJ*)	"Three Ex-Officials Indicted in Failure of Maryland"

1989 February 15 (*WSJ*)	". . . Says Raymond Vickers, formerly the chief appointed bank and thrift supervisor for the state of Florida, 'I haven't found a single bank failure that didn't involve a conscious conspiracy to defraud'."
1989 March 28 (*WSJ*)	"As S&L Crisis Grows, FSLIC Falters in Task of Property Disposal"
1989 July 6 (*WSJ*)	"Justice Agency Says Three S&L Ex-Officials to Enter Guilty Pleas"
1989 August 25 (*WSJ*)	"Two Former Officers of Guaranty Federal Indicted by Grand Jury"
1989 August 24 (*WSJ*)	"Prosecutors Allege Texas Thrift Fraud Paid for Executives' High-Style Living" "The prosecutors allege that . . . (two officials) . . . received millions of dollars in kickbacks in exchange for providing loans for land acquisition and condominium construction . . . the loans were based on fraudulently inflated appraisals . . . and went to borrowers whose financial statements had been falsified to make the institutions appear credit-worthy."
1989 December 22 (*WSJ*)	"Thrift Regulators Find It Is Tough to Recover S&L Bad Debt"
1990 January 24 (*WSJ*)	"Appraisers, Culprits in S&L Crisis, Are Now Key to S&L Recovery." "Fraud, Error Inflated Value of Real Estate and Helped Thrifts Make Wild Loans"
1990 April 3 (*WSJ*)	"FBI Staff Found Too Small for S&L Cases"
1990 May 2 (*WSJ*)	"Federal Jury Convicts Florida Thrift of Falsifying Data"
1990 July 19 (*WSJ*)	"S&L Bailout Could Cost $500 Billion, Says GAO"
1990 July 24 (*WSJ*)	"McKinzie Gets 20-Year Term in Thrift Case"
1990 July 9 (*WSJ*)	"Bush Administration Targets 100 S&Ls for Accelerated Probe on Fraud Charges"
1990 October 31 (*WSJ*)	"Fraud Played Major Role in 40% of Failed Thrifts"
1990 November 8 (*WSJ*)	"Columbia S&L Had $352 Million 3rd-Period Loss." "Skid in Junk Bonds' Value Sends Firm's Net Worth to Minus $709.8 Million"
1990 December 6 (*WSJ*)	"Thrift Aide Says Pressure by Senators Helped Delay Action on Lincoln S&L"
1990 December 21 (*WSJ*)	"Ex-Owner of Failed Vernon S&L is Convicted on 23 Federal Counts"
1991 January 18 (*WSJ*)	"Guaranty Federal Ex-Owners Get Long Sentences"

1991 April 3 (*WSJ*)	"S&L Figure in Texas Draws Five-Year Sentence"
1991 July 24 (*WSJ*)	"Ex-Lincoln S&L Aide Enters Guilty Plea on Fraud Charges"
1991 June 24 (*WSJ*)	"Former Official of Columbia S&L Is Found Guilty"
1993 July 9 (*LCT*)	"Ex-S&L Boss Gets 12½ Years"
	(Source: WST = Wall Street Journal; LCT = LaCrosse Tribune)

THE AUDITORS' RESPONSIBILITY DURING THE S&L CRISIS

Creditors held independent auditors responsible for failing to adequately disclose questionable S&L practices, and sued them successfully in many instances. The following news clips provide an idea of the extent.

1989 February 6 (*WSJ*)	"GAO Says Accountants Auditing Thrifts Are Hiding Behind Outdated Standards". (A General Accounting Office report last week alleged that six of 11 audits of collapsed Texas savings associations "did not adequately audit and/or report the S&L's financial or internal control problems. . . . Evaluating one assertedly faulty audit of a Texas thrift in 1985, the GAO report said the accountants took the word of one of the S&L's executives that a loan was collectible even though the executive 'was also one of the borrowers on the loan.' The borrowers later defaulted."
1990 August 3 (*WSJ*)	"The suit, filed by the Federal Deposit Insurance Corp. last week in federal court in Little Rock, Arkansas, seeks a minimum of $400 million in damages from the accounting firm (Deloitte & Touche) for allegedly faulty audits performed by one of its predecessors, Deloitte Haskins & Sells."
1990 December 6 (*WSJ*)	"California sought to revoke or suspend the accounting license of Ernst & Young, citing its Arthur Young & Co. predecessor's audit work for the failed Lincoln Savings and Loan association."
1991 February 7 (*WSJ*)	"Ernst & Young tentatively agreed to pay the government more than $40 million in connection with shoddy work a predecessor accounting firm did for the failed thrift unit of American Continental Corp."
1991 April 29 (*WSJ*)	"The California State Board of Accountancy said Ernst & Young agreed to pay $1.5 million to settle charges of professional negligence relating to its Arthur Young & Co.

	predecessor's audit of Lincoln Savings & Loan Association."
1992 January 2 (*WSJ*)	"The second largest U.S. Accounting firm and the No. 2 law firm agreed to pay a total of $87 million to settle investors' fraud claims arising from the collapse of Lincoln Savings & Loan Association." "The settlements with the accounting firm Ernst & Young and the Cleveland law firm Jones, Day, Reavis & Pogue are among the largest ever reached by professional partnerships sued over advice given to a client. The deals, announced in Tucson, Arizona, federal court, bring the total settlements in the case so far to about $180 million."
1992 March 3 (*WSJ*)	"Arthur Andersen & Co. agreed to pay as much as $30 million to settle investors' civil fraud claims stemming from the collapse of American Continental Corp.'s Lincoln Savings & Loan Association unit."
1994 March 15 (*WSJ*)	"Deloitte to Pay $312 Million to Settle U.S. Claims Related to S&L Failures"
1994 August 10 (*WSJ*)	"Peat Marwick to Pay U.S. $186.5 Million to Settle Claims Tied to Bank Failures"
1996 April 24 (*WSJ*)	"Arthur Andersen to Pay $10 Million to Settle Colonial Realty Case." (Source: WSJ = Wall Street Journal)

PENSION, WELFARE, AND SIMILAR FUNDS HELD IN TRUST

In 1990, the Inspector General of the Department of Labor reported that billions of dollars in the nation's trust funds were at risk. His semiannual reports proclaimed and documented a concern that appears to be going largely unheeded by the government. Readers who may have been concerned with the savings and loan excesses may have an unshakable sense of *déjà vu* when reading his comments.

Rather than attempt to paraphrase the concern of the inspector general, we offer direct quotations from the sources indicated.[21] Decide for yourself whether we are not again on the brink of a devastating financial catastrophe.

Source:
U.S. Department of Labor
Office of Inspector General
Semiannual Reports
October 1, 1989–March 31, 1990

Fraud and racketeering in pension and welfare plans are not the exclusive province of labor officials or ethnic stereotypes. Today, we face a new generation of racketeers disguised as attorneys, accountants, bankers, benefit lan administrators, investment advisors, and medical service providers (p. 1).

Skyrocketing health care costs have caused major insurance companies to all but abandon the small-employer market concluding that it represents an unacceptable risk. The vacuum of traditional group health insurance is being filled by self-funded plans commonly known as multiple employer welfare arrangements (MEWAs). Criminal investigations have disclosed that this environment has attracted an alarming number of fraudulent MEWAs that masquerade as legitimate providers of group health coverage. Through aggressive, deceptive representations, the racketeer operators of these schemes generate millions of dollars in monthly premiums from unsuspecting small companies and their employees. Structured as a modern day Ponzi scheme, the fraudulent MEWA typically pays small claims and defers major claims while dissipating revenue through a variety of embezzlements disguised as legitimate operating expenses. . . . The consequences of such fraud are tragic. Today, thousands of employers and their workers are held personally liable for unpaid medical bills even though they believed there was health coverage (p. 2).

The OIG continues to express significant concerns about the nation's private pension plans' vulnerability to fraud and abuse. Inadequate audit work by independent public accountants (IPAs) and a lack of effective law enforcement are the primary factors creating this climate of vulnerability.

The Employee Retirement Income Security Act (ERISA) was designed to make plan participants the first line of defense against fraud, abuse, and mismanagement by creating a reporting and disclosure system that would keep participants fully informed. Independent public accountants' financial statement audits, however, have too often failed to meet their client responsibility to plan participants to identify and disclose material violations of ERISA. Today there exists a gap between the independent public accountants' performance and expectations of the Congress and plan participants who thought they would receive clear, precise information to permit evaluation of the status and management of their plan assets.

This audit "expectation gap" in employee benefit plans also exists in other arenas as well and is a primary factor in fostering an environment conducive to fraud and abuse. In February 1989, the General Accounting Office reported that fraud and insolvencies within the savings and loan industry could in large part be attributed to the failure of the public accountants to identify and report on significant problems. The "scandalous mismanagement and rascality" causing these financial disasters were undetected by the public accountants despite the fact that the problems were recognizable . . . (pp. 3 and 4).

Typically, fraudulent self-funded MEWAs offer premiums well below the prevailing market rate for legitimate trusts and insurance companies and do so without any intention of meeting their total reimbursement liabilities. With the expectation of staying afloat for a period of time through aggressive selling and slow claims payment, these fraudulent MEWAs have become a variation of the classic Ponzi scheme (p. 43).

Case Example Excerpts

An Atlanta corporation administering the welfare plans trust for the Drivers, Warehousemen, Maintenance and Allied Workers of America Local 1 of White House, Tennessee, and the local's president were indicted on January 18, 1990, by a Federal grand jury in Atlanta on charges of making and receiving kickbacks and embezzlement. The seven-count indictment, which named four individuals and two corporations, was unsealed on January 23 after the arrests of the defendants by special agents from OLR, the FBI, the Georgia Bureau of Investigation (GBI), and the U.S. Postal Service.

The defendants are Harbor Medical Administrators of Georgia, Inc.; James Craighead, president of Drivers Local 1; Frank Buccheri, president, chief executive officer, and trustee of Omni Employee Benefit Trust of Atlanta; Catherine Steele, secretary and chief financial officer Omni Trust in Boston, Massachusetts, and Atlanta; and Southeast Group, Inc., a corporation set up by Buccheri to receive funds for himself.

Harbor Medical was a third-party administrator of Omni Trust. As a self-insured group health arrangement, Omni provides health benefits in 16 states to approximately 9,000 employees and dependents of nearly 300 companies that participate in the trust. Sherman Dixie Concrete Industries, Inc., a participant in the Omni Trust, employs approximately 100 members of Drivers Local 1 in the Nashville area.

The indictment charges that from December 1987 through November 1988, Craighead solicited and received $4,670 in the form of nine payments on a new Lincoln town car by Buccheri so that the union benefit plans would continue to use Omni Trust.

From about November 1987, through August 1988, Buccheri, Steele, Rowe, and Harbor Medical allegedly embezzled approximately $368,788 from the Omni Trust account by taking commissions to which they were not entitled . . . (pp. 45–46).

Laborers District Council Building and Construction Health and Welfare Fund in Philadelphia: . . . Mims was responsible for reviewing and approving claims for medical benefits filed by eligible members of the local. From September 1985 to January 1987, she processed fraudulent medical benefits claims, causing checks to be issued to the other defendants. The checks were cashed or deposited in various bank accounts and divided among the coconspirators (p. 46).

END NOTES TO PART 1

[1] In Albrecht's study (W. Steven Albrecht, Ph.D., CFE, CPA, Arthur Andersen &
Co., Alumni Professor of Accountancy and the Director, School of Accountancy, Brigham Young University), he noted that half of frauds are discovered
by accident, a third come from co-worker complaints and the rest (about one
in five) are discovered by audit. Joseph T. Wells, CPA, CFE, chairman of the
National Association of Certified Fraud Examiners, *Journal of Accountancy,*
February 1990.

[2] It is difficult to determine why public accountants withdrew from this responsibility and why they continue to withdraw. It is very likely that they did not
consider fraud to be a significant threat to client entities, and assumed that it
would eventually surface of its own accord, and that victims would be able to
recover losses through surety bonds or insurance. Accordingly, audit resources
could and should be devoted to more important tasks. This is consistent with
the popular belief that there was no essential difference between the characteristics of the fraud that had been disclosed (category 1) and the fraud not disclosed
(categories 2 and 3).

[3] The detection of fraud as an object of an audit has steadily eroded. This erosion
is evident in the descriptions of audit objectives in successive editions of
Montgomery's *Auditing* and in professional standards. In the first three editions
(1912, 1916, and 1923), Montgomery acknowledged that in the formative days
of auditing students were taught that the detection or prevention of fraud . . .
were the chief objects of an audit. . . . Subsequent editions gave less and less
emphasis to the detection of fraud until, in the eighth edition (1957), it was
described as a "responsibility not assumed," with the observation that, "The
American Institute has properly pointed out that if an auditor were to attempt
to discover defalcations and similar irregularities he would have to extend his
work to a point where its cost would be prohibitive. . . . In Montgomery, this
disavowal of responsibility clearly relates to the detection of defalcations and
similar irregularities (misappropriation or misuse of assets with no material
effect on financial statements) . . ."

 The position of the American Institute of [Certified Public] Accountants
in Statement on Auditing Procedure No. 1, *Extensions of Auditing Procedure,*
issued in 1939 slightly modified was carried forward in a codification of
auditing pronouncements issued in 1951:

In a well-organized concern, reliance for the detection (of fraud) . . . is
placed principally upon the maintenance of an adequate system of accounting records with appropriate internal control. . . . It is generally recognized that good internal control and surety bonds provide protection
much more cheaply (than audit examinations)

> —The Commission on Auditors' Responsibilities:
> Report, Conclusions, and Recommendations—An
> Independent Commission of the American Institute
> of Certified Public Accountants. 1975, pp. 33–35.

[4] This service should not be confused with any request for reactive audit service, where suspicions of fraud have arisen and audit service is requested to participate in the reactive investigation. Also, it should not be confused with the work that certified public accountants normally do when examining for fraudulent financial statement balances.

[5] *The Accountant's Handbook,* Third Edition, New York: The Roland Press Company, 1950.

[6] "The Auditor's New Guide To Errors, Irregularities and Illegal Acts," by D. R. Carmichael, CPA, PhD technical editor for the *Journal* and former AICPA officer. *Journal of Accountancy,* September 1988, pp 41–42.

[7] Subsequent to World War I, France sought to protect itself from their traditional enemy to the east (Germany) by constructing an impenetrable defense, called the Maginot Line. Located a short distance inland from the border with Germany, the Maginot Line was a continuous fortification constructed along a north-south axis stretching from Belgium in the north, to Switzerland in the south. Served by connected underground tunnels and vast stores of food and ammunition, the surface was saturated with seemingly invulnerable artillery and machine gun emplacements. The French felt most secure behind it. However, when World War II began with Germany's invasion of France, the Maginot Line was hardly a hindrance to the German army who had many years to study the fortification and consider ways and means of defeating it. When the time came, they simply picked the weakest point in the line, concentrated their forces on it, and overwhelmed it. Subsequently, their armored columns poured through the breach into the unprotected French countryside behind the line. The French, confident that the Maginot Line would protect them, had few defenses after it was breached, but most of the infamous Maginot Line was left intact.

[8] A pseudo-conspiracy has much the same effect as a bona fide conspiracy of individuals to override controls to commit fraud. The difference is that there is no fraudulent intent on the part of one or more of the parties to it. For example, a control clerk entrusted to limit access to the vault allows "Charlie Brown" entry because he assures her it is okay.

[9] *The Official Rules* by Paul Dickson, as extracted in *Time,* February 26, 1979, pp. 25.

[10] "Risk Aversion as a Behavioral Problem," *The Wall Street Journal,* May 31, 1996 (C1).

[11] *The American Heritage Dictionary* Second College Edition, Boston: Houghton Mifflin Company, 1982.

[12] Ironically, it was one of his petty fraudulent activities that resulted in his accidental discovery. He had been submitting false claims on behalf of supervisors who were entitled to time and meal allowances for attending evening meetings, but who were absent. He would intercept the checks after they had been prepared. He was discovered when one of the supervisors involved, unexpectedly, had maintained personal records of all his earnings during the year. The supervisor compared personal records with the year-end W-2 reports provided to him for income tax purposes and had inquired into the small discrepancy.

[13] The auditor's concern with detecting fraud was clearly expressed in works such as Dicksee's *Auditing,* first published in the nineteenth century, when the three-fold object of an audit was said to (include) the detection of fraud. The straightforward recognition, in early literature, of the detection of fraud as an object of an audit has been steadily eroded. This erosion is evident in the descriptions of audit objectives in successive editions of Montgomery's *Auditing,* and in professional standards. In the first three editions (1912, 1916, and 1923), Montgomery acknowledged that in the formative days of auditing, "students were taught" that "the detection or prevention of fraud" were the "chief objects" of an audit. Subsequent editions gave less and less emphasis to the detection of fraud until the eighth edition (1957), when it was described as a "responsibility not assumed," with the observation that, "The American Institute has properly pointed out that if an auditor were to attempt to discover defalcations and similar irregularities he would have to extend his work to a point where its cost would be prohibitive." In Montgomery, this disavowal of responsibility clearly relates to the detection of defalcations and similar irregularities (misappropriation or misuse of assets with no material effect on financial statements).

The ordinary examination . . . is not designed and cannot be relied upon *to disclose defalcations and other similar irregularities, although their discovery frequently results. In a well organized concern, reliance for the detection of such irregularities is placed principally upon the maintenance of an adequate system of accounting records with appropriate internal control. If an auditor were to attempt to discover defalcations and similar irregularities, he would have to extend his work to a point where its cost would be prohibitive. It is generally recognized that good internal control and surety bonds provide protection much more cheaply. . . .*

—The Commission on Auditors'
Responsibilities: Report, Conclusions, and
Recommendations (An Independent
Commission Established by the American
Institute of Certified Public Accountants,
pp. 33–34, 1978.

[14] Source: "Bonfire of the S&Ls, *Newsweek Magazine,* May 21, 1989.

[15] Before the 1980s, the S&L "motto was 3-6-3: offer three percent on savings, lend at six percent, and hit the golf course at three o'clock. . . . In 1980, it (Congress) allowed S&Ls to pay much higher interest rates. The effect: S&Ls competed by offering savings account rates as high as 13 percent." (Source: "Bonfire of the S&Ls," *Newsweek Magazine,* May 21, 1989).

[16] "Quid pro quos can rarely be proven but we do know this: never has so much money gone to such key legislators who worked so hard for measures that cost taxpayers so dearly." "Bonfire of the S&Ls, *Newsweek Magazine,* May 21, 1989.

[17] At the end of 1989, there were 2,898 S&Ls in the United States. One thousand two hundred seventy three were going strong. Source: "Bonfire of the S&Ls," *Newsweek Magazine,* May 21, 1989.

[18] The government allowed large investors unlimited numbers of guaranteed $100,000 accounts. "Bonfire of the S&Ls," *Newsweek Magazine,* May 21, 1989.

[19] Stephen Pizzo, Mary Fricker, and Paul Muolo, *Inside Job: The Looting of America's Savings and Loans.* New York: McGraw-Hill Publishing Company, 1989.

[20] WSJ, *The Wall Street Journal;* LCT, *La Crosse Tribune,* La Crosse, Wisconsin.

[21] *Semiannual Reports,* October 1, 1989 to March 31, 1990. U.S. Department of Labor, Office of the Inspector General.

Part 2

Investigating Fraud

John C. Wideman, Ph.D.

Chapter 11

Investigating Suspected Fraud

The purpose of this chapter is to provide the accountant and auditor with fundamental investigative procedures should they be interested in pursuing the development of evidence beyond the detection stage. Although the investigation of violent crimes differs in many ways from the investigation of white collar crimes, particularly fraud, there are many commonalities.

Top management has overall responsibility for an organization. Therefore, although this chapter is addressed primarily to accountants and auditors, it also aims to inform progressive top managers who are interested in learning about the activities of a very important control element of the organization, fraud-specific examinations.

Because of the accountant's strategic position within the company, he or she will often be the first person to arrive at the "scene of the crime." At a minimum, the accountant is often the first person to suspect that a crime may have been committed. The following material introduces the fraud-specific examiner to principles and techniques used by professional investigators. Perhaps more important, the material will provide fraud-specific examiners with information designed to assist them in preserving and documenting facts about a suspected fraud and its suspected perpetrator. The facts the fraud examiner preserves will assist in the accumulation of evidence and in the prosecution of the perpetrator if prosecution becomes appropriate. An investigator collects the facts and lets the facts tell whether a crime has been committed and who committed the crime. The object, sometimes ignored by investigators, is to make the shoe fit the foot and not vice versa.

An investigation begins with the detection of a possible crime. There will be times when something initially appears to be the result of sinister criminal activity when, after all the facts are gathered, it is determined to be simply the result of mistake, ineptness, or incompetence. Conversely, there will be times when suspects will encourage the investigator to believe that activities which are criminal in nature are only the results of mistake, ineptness, or incompetence.

The purpose of an investigative plan is to allow the investigator an opportunity to determine how to attack the problem in an organized manner. The investigative plan takes into consideration the following factors:

- The crime. What are the elements of this crime and what information must be collected in order to prove those elements?
- Materials. What types of materials will have to be reviewed to prepare the investigator and properly investigate the crime? Is there a "crime scene" that may contain physical evidence? Are there documents to be reviewed? Is there a process about which the investigator will have to learn (for example, chemical plant production, silver futures, sawmill operations)?
- Witnesses. Are there witnesses available? What are their relationships to the crime and the suspect, if there is a suspect? In what order should they be interviewed?

CASE ASSESSMENT

The first component of the investigative plan is to make an assessment of the case. This requires the investigator to evaluate the situation in terms of threat, risk, and vulnerability.

- Threat. Anything of value has some kind of threat to it. For example, if one lives in a high-crime, inner-city neighborhood, the threat of being mugged is considerably greater than if one lives in a small, close-knit farming community in the Midwest. We can identify the threat of being mugged by simply understanding that a mugging is more likely to occur in certain types of areas, at certain times of day, and if one exhibits certain types of behavior.
- Risk. Risk is the likelihood that a threat will occur to the object we are investigating. Certain banks, for example, have a higher risk factor because of their location. They are more likely to be robbed than other banks because of their threat factors (for example, isolated location, location adjacent to a convenient escape route, generally known periods when large amounts of cash are present).
- Vulnerability. A facility may have a high threat and high risk quotient, but a low vulnerability because of other factors. The bank in the isolated

location with known periods of high cash presence may be so heavily guarded and have such stringent security measures that its vulnerability is very low.

The investigator must then make a list of the threats, risks, and vulnerabilities within the situation, defining the parameters of the investigation. For example, if a situation is threatened, at risk, and vulnerable only to a certain group of persons at a certain time, it limits the initial population of suspects and witnesses and defines the kind of manpower required to resolve it. A simple example is the difference between losing a five-dollar bill in downtown Chicago around noon on a weekday and trying to figure out who picked it up, compared with the theft of $1,000 from a company safe between 4:00 P.M. and 5:00 P.M. when only two people could have had access to it. In the first case, investigation would be meaningless due to the value of the loss and the low possibility of identifying the person who picked up the five-dollar bill. In the second case, the investigation would be very focused, require low manpower expenditure, and probably be resolved within a short period of time.

INTERVIEWING

The investigator's main tool is the interview. All interview techniques should take into consideration a number of common factors. Nothing in the ordinary experiences of growing up prepares us for the process of obtaining accurate information from sometimes very reluctant people. The investigator must overcome his or her own reluctance to be insistent or to pry into certain areas. In normal society, people voluntarily tell things that reflect their moods, make them seem important to the listener, cause the listener to react in a certain way, or optimize their own positions. People rarely volunteer information that is detrimental to their own self-interests. In many crimes such as fraud, conspiracies, and other white-collar crime, the interview is often a significant means of collecting the facts needed to make the case. The reason for this is that people may agree verbally to commit certain bad or corrupt acts, but rarely do they reduce agreements to written form. Witnesses observe not only written acts, but a whole range of activities, including physical activity (Bill opening the safe drawer), associations (Joe and Bill always eat lunch together), conversations (I heard Joe tell Bill to open the safe), and other occurrences that the investigator cannot readily initial and place in a file.

There are essentially two general methods of influencing the state of mind of witnesses and suspects. The first is physical or mental abuse. Of course, this method is completely unjustified and illegal in our society and under our laws. The second method predominantly consists of systematic interviewing conducted in a humane and friendly atmosphere. The inhibitions of the person being interviewed are replaced by logic, and any natural incentives to cooperate are stimulated to the point that the individual feels that truthfulness will be beneficial in some way.

Personal Attributes of the Interviewer

Four of the most important qualities of an interviewer are:

1. Honesty, integrity, and the ability to impress upon all interviewees that the investigator seeks only the truth
2. The ability to establish rapport quickly and under a variety of conditions
3. The ability to listen to interviewees and evaluate their responses to questions
4. The ability to maintain self-control during interviews and not become emotionally involved in the investigation

It is the investigator's job to convince the interviewee to divulge information. In this respect, the investigator must keep in mind several guidelines, which reflect attitude and personality and avoid the obvious traps.

Interviewing

- Do not prejudge a suspect or witness.
- Subdue all personal prejudices regardless of whether they are social, racial, sexual, or of any other type.
- Keep an open mind, receptive to all information regardless of its nature.
- Try to evaluate each person and each piece of information on its own merit.
- Do not deliberately lie or make false promises to an interviewee.
- Refrain from trying to impress the interviewee unless such action is specifically part of an interviewing technique.
- Do not underestimate the mental ability of the interviewee.
- Avoid contemptuous attitudes.
  - Do not ridicule.
  - Do not consider success a victory, but simply the accomplishment of the interview objective.

- Do not bully. Remember that the person being interviewed is there at his or her leisure, not the interviewer's. The interviewee can get up and leave anytime he or she desires.
- Keep all promises.
- Do not belittle the interviewee, his or her situation, or his or her information.
- Avoid controversial matters to the maximum extent possible (for example, religion, politics).
- Be fair.
- Avoid creating the impression that the only thing of interest is a confession or a conviction.
- Do not shout or raise your voice unless it is absolutely necessary as part of a practiced, proven technique.
- Always maintain control of the interview. The interviewer is there to obtain information and therefore must remain in charge.
- Be serious about what you are doing. You can display warm, personable confidence and still maintain the seriousness of the situation.
- Be a good listener. The investigator's job is to learn, not to impart information.
- Be patient and persistent. You will rarely get what you are looking for early in the interview. Keep at it until all of the information available is obtained.

PEOPLE AND THEIR PERSONALITIES

Just because an interviewer shows up on a witness's doorstep or at the office does not mean that the witness will talk to the interviewer. In order to evaluate the situation, divide witnesses into several useful categories:

- Friendly. A friendly witness is one who is willing to be interviewed and make a statement. This witness is usually friendly to the interviewer's cause for one reason or another.
- Neutral. A neutral witness is one who may be willing to be interviewed and make a statement. This witness is neither friendly nor hostile to the interviewer's cause. It is simply a person who was in the right place at the right time.
- Hostile. A hostile witness is one who may be unwilling to be interviewed and make a statement. This witness is usually hostile to the interviewer's cause for one reason or another.

If a witness is willing to be interviewed and/or provide a statement, he or she is considered to be cooperative. If the witness is unwilling to be interviewed or make a statement, they are referred to as uncooperative. Friendly, neutral, or hostile witnesses can be cooperative or uncooperative. Please notice that nothing in the above definitions deals with the truth.

THE PREARRANGED INTERVIEW (OR APPOINTMENT)

The interviewer has several options for arranging and conducting the interview. The interviewer can contact the witness and request a convenient time for an interview, clearly advising the witness of the identity of the interviewer, who the interviewer represents, and why the interviewer is requesting the interview. This is a good way to get a feel for the outlook of the witness based on their reaction to our contact. This can be done through a telephone call and sometimes a letter. This is also a good use of the interviewer's time since usually it avoids making several trips to contact the person. A down-side to this is that sometimes people will make appointments with you and then, after reflection or talking to someone else, they will not be available and you will have to chase them around to contact them.

The Telephone Interview

You can conduct an interview over the telephone. This is quick, convenient, avoids long-distance travel, and conserves resources. It is not preferred, however, since it takes away valuable eye-to-eye contact with the witness. Also, it cannot be used if the witness is expected to look at some evidence or provide a signed statement at the time of the interview. The witness can also lie about his or her identity or hang up on you.

The Unannounced Interview (or Surprise)

This is sometimes the best answer. Find out where the witness is and go there, unannounced. The witness is usually surprised but cooperative, since few people want to offend another person to his or her face. It is difficult for the witness to avoid the interview if they are willing to be interviewed at all. Witnesses can, and do, refuse to be interviewed and shut the door in the interviewer's face. This also can bring in the witness who might be persuaded to be interviewed, but wants to avoid the interview.

Interviews are art. You can develop a style that suits you and your personality. Remember that you are attempting to get another person to cooperatively provide information to you. It is your job to persuade them to cooperate. An interview goes through several stages.

Initial Contact.   In the initial contact, advise the witness who you are, who you represent and why you are there. Next, advise the witness why he or she is important to this matter.

Establishing Rapport.   Always be friendly. Find some neutral matter with which to make small talk. For example, the weather, the person's house, some furnishing that is obviously a prize to the witness, outside landscaping, or the like. This is the ice-breaker. This presents you as someone who is friendly, interested in their welfare, and easy to talk to.

Background Information.   You will need to provide the witness some limited background information so that they know what you are going to talk to them about. It may be as simple as, "Mr. Smith you were a witness to a traffic accident that occurred last May 12th in Pittsburgh. I want to talk to you about what you saw." If the case is an involved matter, you may have to provide more information, including copies of documents for the witness to review.

Body of the Interview.   This is the meat and potatoes, where you ask all the questions concerning the matter at hand. Interviews are best covered chronologically. Human beings see almost everything in a chronological sequence and reconstruct their memories that way so the interviewer should start as far back in time as practical and bring the person forward to the present moment. Cover every topic with the six basic interrogatives: who, what, when, where, why, and how. When the witness can no longer provide an answer, go on to the next topic. For coverage of this aspect of the interview, see "Three Main Parts of the Interview" below.

Obtaining the Statement.   If you desire to have a recorded statement of some sort, this is the point at which you ask for it. Always get the information orally from the witness, then ask if he or she would mind putting it in the form of a recorded statement. It's a lot easier for the witness to say no before he or she gives you the information, than after. If the witness agrees, obtain the statement in the preferred format and style.

Closing the Interview.   Always leave the witness with a pleasant memory of the interview. Thank the witness for his or her time and cooperation regardless of the information provided. Leave an opening for further contact in case later information comes up or if you forget to ask something during the interview. Finally, confirm that you have the witness's correct name, address, telephone number, work, and information on how best to contact the witness. Leave your business card with the witness, so that if he or she remembers something or comes up with further information, the witness can contact you.

Generally, interviewees may exhibit any or all of the following characteristics:

- They have faulty perception.
- They have faulty memories, which vary in direct relationship to the amount of time that has passed since the incident.
- They do not know what it is the interviewer wants from them.
- They are generally reluctant to get involved.
- They are not impressed with authority; they may hate authority; they may hold a grudge against authority; they may be fearful of authority.
- They may have been intimidated by the suspect; they may be loyal to the suspect; they may be related to the suspect.
- They do not want to be inconvenienced.
- They have faulty logic.
- They mistake inferences for facts.
- They have differing levels of mental capacity, mental health, and intelligence.
- They conceal or distort information for personal reasons.

QUESTIONS AND HOW TO ASK THEM

If questions cannot be understood by the interviewee, information will not be forthcoming, or will be inaccurate. When composing questions, take the background of the interviewee into consideration. Persons of different ethnic, educational, and social backgrounds will have differing vocabularies. As a rule, the simpler a question, the better. The interviewer must be sure that he or she understands the words and manner of speech of the person being interviewed. Local idioms ("of a morning," meaning A.M.), uncommon words ("croaker sack," meaning a burlap bag used in frog hunting), trade expressions ("two ten net thirty," meaning deduct two percent if paid within 10 days, otherwise total amount due within 30 days"), regional accents ("hit were," meaning "it was") and imprecise sentence construction ("He ain't lie from nobody," meaning "He would not lie for anyone") can result in a misunderstanding unless the investigator makes sure that the words are completely understood. When asking a person to explain one of these matters, ask, "What do you mean by . . ." as opposed to "Do you mean . . . ," since people often will agree with an investigator just to agree, due to the investigator's authority or because the interviewee thinks the investigator understands.

A question is used to persuade the listener to make a predictable topical response. If the questioning process is not carried out properly, it may confuse, irritate, or intimidate the listener, reducing the flow of information.

Good questions have identifiable characteristics regardless of the topic:

- Good questions are short, simple, and confined to one topic. (Where were you on August 12, 1988, at 2:30 P.M.?) Do not use complex sentences (Did you go to the bank and kill Mary, or eat dinner?).
- Good questions are clear and easily understood. (What color is your car?)
- Good questions avoid sensational words. Avoid using such words as confession, drug addict, doper, stool pigeon, drunkard, child molester, rapist, embezzler. Try to use milder terms that do not evoke strong emotions.
- Good questions are precise. Do not ask, "What did you do?" when you mean, "What did you do about getting to the meeting last Thursday night at about 7:00 P.M. when your car had a flat tire on Route 29?"
- A good question requires a narrative answer. A question that results in a yes or no answer is usually a leading question and can result in a restriction of the information the investigator receives.

The Six Basic Interrogatives

Who, what, when, where, why, and how are the six basic interrogatives. If you start each question with one of these words, you will not be asking a leading question since each requires a narrative answer rather than just yes or no. Some schools of thought also include the interrogative, which. Couple the characteristics of good questions with the six basic interrogatives and you have the foundation of the interview.

Question Sequencing in Interviews

All things in a person's life happen in a chronological order. People are generally comfortable relating a story in a chronological order. Jokes, stories, movies, and the other information we share in daily life generally presented are in chronological sequence. One of the problems with interviews is that the interviewee is asked to describe an activity that took place in the past. The investigator should be aware that memory is reconstruction, not recollection. It is sometimes useful when asking questions to frame them in such a way that the interviewee can use a time-related reference point for such reconstruction (for instance, a birthday, a holiday, another significant event).

In using the general-to-specific questioning technique, the interviewer guides the interviewee from the general to the specific. It involves a narrowing of time-related information to a specific instant or event. The general-to-specific technique aids the witness in information reconstruction and can trap the suspect in a story that is difficult to change once he or she sees the ultimate direction the interview is taking.

In moving from point to point, try to use a transition to connect the thoughts. Phrase a transition question by using known information to proceed to the unknown. If the interviewee has a good grasp of the information, but is simply having trouble phrasing it properly or keeping it in sequence, the investigator might ask, "What happened next?" or "What did you do next?"

Another technique, the controlled-answer questioning technique is used to stimulate an interviewee to agree to talk or to give information. For instance, the interviewer might ask, "Since you were not involved in this situation, you won't mind answering a few questions, will you?" The technique can also be used to stimulate a suspect to acknowledge certain critical facts, which may ultimately result in a confession. For instance, the interviewer may ask, "Eddie and others have told us that you were at the bar on Thursday night with Mary, so you're not going to deny that, are you?" This is a stronger question than "Were you at the bar on Thursday night?"

THREE MAIN PARTS OF THE INTERVIEW

The interview consists of three main parts: free narrative, direct examination, and cross-examination.

Free-Narrative

This is a continuous account of an event or incident given with a minimum of prompting by the investigator. Its purpose is to get the witness talking and to obtain a quick account of what the interviewee knows. Remember, you will get only what the interviewee wants to tell you or what he or she thinks you need to know. The free narrative has the effect of involving the interviewee completely in the interview and overcomes any initial objection to providing a detailed reply to a question. One problem with free narrative is that many people digress or get sidetracked on issues that are immaterial to the investigation, but may be important to the interviewee. Do not be too hasty to jump in and try to redirect the narrative. Give the interviewee a little room to wander, because valuable information may come up in an unexpected context. However, once you see that the digression is not leading in a meaningful direction, politely interrupt and steer the interviewee back to the point where he or she left the trail. If the topic of the digression subsequently assumes importance, at least you know about it and can re-interview for more detail if necessary.

Direct Examination

When beginning the direct examination, start off with the soft, easy questions so as not to alienate the interviewee. People will answer difficult questions a lot sooner if they have been talking to the interviewer for a while than if they are asked difficult questions pointedly without a warmup period.

When asking questions, do not hurry. Remember to have patience. Everyone thinks and arranges information at a different speed. After you have talked with the interviewee for a while, you will know whether he or she is stalling or whether it just takes the person that long to answer a difficult question. There will come a time when you will have to help an interviewee remember. It is important not to suggest an answer or imply that any particular answer is preferred over another. If you have information that might be helpful in assisting the person to remember, divulge it a little at a time until the person reconstructs the information in his or her mind.

If a person seems confused, repeat the question after having rephrased it. Work with the question until the interviewee understands it and gives you an answer. If an interviewee uses terms like "we," "I heard," or "he told me," be sure to determine exactly who "we" and "he" are. Be sure to find out whom the witness "heard" it from. Be aware of persons using as their own the thoughts, sights, sounds, and facts learned from another. Obtain specific detail when dealing with interviewees. Some people are very accurate about time-distance relationships, others are not. The final phase of an interview is the cross-examination phase. At this point, the investigator has listened to the free narrative and filled out all the blank spots through direct examination.

Cross Examination

Discrepancies in the responses of interviewees, and even of suspects, may be the result of error as well as evasion. Cross-examination is designed to reconcile that problem. Cross-examination will usually address certain specific areas where there are significant discrepancies in information. Clues to those areas include:

- Attempts to evade answers. Be particularly alert if a person starts to answer your question and then goes on to tell you about something else. This usually indicates that he or she is trying to avoid answering your question.
- Vague answers.
- Conflicts of information.
- Inconsistent answers to the same or similar questions.
- Apparent lies.

Change the contextual matter of the question. For instance, the first time you might ask, "When did you first meet Joe?" Then you might later ask, "What were you doing when you first met Joe?" You might follow with, "What led up to your first meeting with Joe?" "Did you know Mary when you first met Joe?" "Who knew Joe first, you or Mary?"

Ask about known information as if it were unknown, and vice versa. If the investigator's delivery is smooth and casual, the interviewee will not know what the investigator knows and what he or she does not know. However, be careful about trying to bluff an interviewee, because the interviewee might just call the bluff. When conducting a cross-examination, it is important to have first obtained as complete an explanation as possible from the interviewee. Ask all necessary questions before any confrontation because the interviewee, upon being confronted with discrepancies, may terminate the interview.

A fourth aspect of the interview, if required, is the confrontation. This is the point at which the discrepancies are placed before the interviewee and an explanation is requested. This is a critical point in an interview. This is when you are essentially telling a person that he or she is either lying to you or just doesn't understand what he or she is talking about. Few people suffer through this moment easily. Continue to be patient and persistent, requesting an answer to the conflict. Do not let the interviewee off the hook without a resolution.

LISTENING TO ANSWERS

Ideally, the interviewer never draws conclusions. To do so makes the interviewer a prisoner of his/her case. The interviewer's job is to collect facts and information to provide to the ultimate consumer, the client. It is the client's job to draw conclusions from the facts and information. However, the interviewer cannot be blind to the world and simply accept *carte blanche* what someone says. To this end, it is good if the interviewer is familiar with logic and fallacies.

A British philosopher, Steven Toulmin, developed what he considers a model system for understanding how arguments are made. Examples follow each term.

The Claim

This is your bottom line, what the whole argument is about. This is your claim or belief and it should be as accurate as possible. "I believe that John Doe embezzled the funds."

The Data

This is the information that makes you believe your claim is true.

- "John Doe was arrested with more money than he could account for."
- "John Doe and, his wife, Jane Doe were separated pending a divorce."
- "John Doe had to support her and the children."
- "John Doe had a history of bad financial decisions and bad investments."
- "John Doe goes to the race track often."

The Qualifier

These are the words that indicate the strength of your argument. Keep in mind that absolutes such as "always", "never", and "absolutely" are difficult to back off from in the event a single exception is found. "John Doe *probably* stole the funds because he was in over his head in debt."

The Warrant

This is the assumption that you make which you expect your listeners to adopt. The warrant connects the claim and the data. "People in bad financial situations sometimes resort to crime to help themselves out of the situation."

The Backing

These are any facts which support the warrant.

- "The National Institute of Justice figures show that better than 80 percent of persons who embezzle are in serious debt."
- "The NIJ statistics also show that compulsive gamblers almost never make money, they lose money."

The Rebuttal

These are the exceptions which you must make to allow yourself "wiggle room." When that single exception is found, you are not cornered by your argument.

- "While it is possible that John Doe is innocent, the facts point strongly to the fact that he is the embezzler."

From this, we see that we must carefully think out what we are saying before we commit ourselves to a claim. Yet, this is rarely done in everyday life. Listen to some of the common talk among your co-workers or fellow travelers on the airplane or bus. Is their logic firm? Do they make absolute claims or claims without data, warrant, and/or qualifier?

Convincing a jury or another person of the correctness of a claim is a matter of logic and persuasiveness. We have no absolutes. If we did, guilt would have to be proven beyond any doubt instead of beyond a reasonable doubt. Therefore, we prove matters logically. The way we do it is persuasively. If you are interviewing witnesses, you will want to evaluate what they are saying, their logic, and their manner. Are you persuaded by what they say? Why?

In making the claim, people often fall afoul of fallacies. Fallacies are nothing more or less than mistakes in logic. There are a series of fallacies with which the reader should be familiar in order to recognize what a person is actually saying when he or she tries to persuade you with faulty logic.

Hasty Generalization

"All Bosnians are poor and ignorant." In this fallacy, all members of a class or group are defined by criteria which applies only to some members. This is commonly used in propaganda rhetoric.

Begging the Question

"It's an obvious, known fact that women are weaker than men." In this fallacy, the claimant assumes the truth of the argument that is trying to be proved. Begging the question is usually used when facts are lacking or hasty generalization precedes it.

Post Hoc Ergo Propter Hoc (Latin: After this, then therefore this)

"John Doe was seen at the race track on Tuesday evening. On Friday morning, the money was found missing." This fallacy is an attempt to link up two succeeding events which are not related. This is not to be confused with hindsight, "Oh, if only I had known Doc was a gambler, the money wouldn't be missing." Hindsight, sometimes true, is only conjecture based on avoidance.

Faulty Analogy

We use analogy to compare and contrast matters we are trying to understand. However, we need to be very careful about comparing the right things. A good example of faulty analogy is case citation by lawyers in court. Rare is the lawyer who has not been told by the judge or opposing counsel that his or her case citation is "not on point." In other words, the analogy is faulty because the case cited is not analogous to the situation in the present case.

Argumentum ad Hominem (Latin: Argument to the man)

This is really popular inside the Washington, D.C. beltway. Instead of attacking the claim or the proof, you attack the claimant. It is done every day in court as well. In court, it is called impeaching a witness. We may not be able to point out that the witness is incorrect, but if the witness has done something wrong in the past or has a vested position to protect, we bring it out in the hopes that the jury will dismiss the witness's statements (which are usually injurious to our cause.) This is used most particularly when we cannot defend against what is being said for lack of evidence to the contrary. For example, if there is only one witness to that crime and that witness is testifying against our client, then *argumentum ad hominem* may be all we have.

Argumentum ad populum (Latin: Argument to the people)

In this fallacy, the statement is couched in such a way that the audience will accept it. We may know of certain prejudices, emotions, or beliefs that the target audience holds. We appeal to those emotions and beliefs rather than to fact. In doing this, we use words which paint a verbal picture of what we want to say. We call our person a "patriot" or an "upstanding citizen." The opponent is a "sleazebag" or a "crook." These words carry definite pro and con meanings, but must be addressed carefully to the target audience. Some audiences may think a certain person was a great American, while others may consider that person a traitor. This fallacy must be properly addressed to the audience to be effective. This is also a standard of the propagandist.

When listening to an argument or evaluating another's claim, keep in mind the above factors. If you evaluate each claim accordingly and watch out for fallacies, you will rarely be led astray.

NOTE-TAKING

Investigator's notes are critical and deserve special attention. The content of the interview notes will determine the success of the investigation. These notes are the basis of all reports and, ultimately, the prosecution. During the interview, the investigator should take careful notes of what the interviewee says. Where possible, the investigator should use the exact words of the interviewee. These notes, made at the time of the interview as the words are being spoken, are called "contemporaneous notes."

There is no specific format for note-taking. They should be written on a standard 8½-by-11-inch, lined notepad. This type of notepad will also be useful if a statement has to be taken. As a general guideline, notes should be written so that another person, unfamiliar with the investigation, could read them and make sense of them. Do not let the interviewee rush you and force you to take less than adequate notes.

At the beginning of the interview, the investigator should write at the top of the first page of the notes the following information concerning the interview and the interviewee:

- Date, time the interview commenced, place of interview
- Full name, position, work and home addresses, work and home telephone numbers of the interviewee
- The names of any other persons present (other investigators, attorneys, supervisors, union stewards) and full identifying data regarding these other persons
- Anything unusual about the circumstances of the interview (for instance, the interviewee's physical condition, such as obvious injuries)

When the interview has been completed, the investigator should review his or her notes for completeness before excusing the interviewee. After a typewritten report is made, using the contemporaneous notes, the notes should be placed in the case file in the event that they are needed later.

Notes are typewritten into a form called a "memorandum of interview." This is simply an easier form of the contemporaneous notes to read. There are, however, several important guidelines in regard to the memorandum of interview.

Make sure that there is nothing in the memorandum of interview that is not also in your contemporaneous notes. It would be very embarrassing to be accused on the witness stand of adding information to the memorandum that was not given at the interview.

The memorandum should contain any useful narrative material indicating physical actions that took place. For example, if a document was shown to the interviewee, that document should be completely described in the report at the appropriate place.

The investigator's personal opinions, conclusions, or non-interview-related observations should never be placed in the body of the memorandum of interview.

TAKING THE WRITTEN STATEMENT

In order for the collected information to be useable, it should be reduced to written form. It may then be incorporated in a file and sorted accordingly. Long before that information is obtained, however, there are a number of steps that must be taken. For the purpose of clarity, we will define statements as follows:

- Verbal statement. This is a statement that is made orally by one person to another, but is not recorded nor memorialized.

- Recorded statement. This term is generally used to mean that the statement was preserved contemporaneously using an electronic recording medium, usually audiotape.

- Unwitting. This refers to the fact that the person being interviewed is not aware that his/her statement is being recorded.

- Witting. This refers to the fact that the person being interviewed is aware that his/her statement is being recorded.

- Written statement. This term refers to a verbatim statement that has been reduced to writing. It may be signed or unsigned. It should be in the handwriting of the person making the statement, but this is not an absolute requirement. A simple form for a statement is found in the appendix. The form can be expanded for a statement of any length.

- Affidavit. This is a statement taken under oath. It may be recorded or written, but there must be a person authorized to administer oaths present (e.g. notary public) at the time it is signed, sworn to, and adopted by the affiant.

- Memorandum. This is a non-verbatim, sum and substance recital of the interview in the words of one of the parties to the interview. Often this is referred to as a "memorandum of interview." It may or may not be detailed. It may or may not be an accurate reflection of what was said.

Our system of jurisprudence has adopted the theory that a statement made under oath carries with it some indicia of truth. This is a relic from our Judeo-Christian heritage wherein the name of God was invoked and person believed that God would punish a liar. Needless to say, the invocation of the name of God is not necessary today. Today, one may affirm an oath without reference to God. This has its good and bad aspects.

Probably the worst thing about taking information in the form of a sworn statement, or affidavit, is that it locks the witness into a story that may or may not be a true reflection of his or her memory. We have all made statements about something that has happened in the past, only to remember later that it was not the way we said it was. With an affidavit, however, a material change from one sworn statement to another may constitute false swearing or perjury. Changes in two sworn statements are difficult to reconcile and seriously damage the credibility of the witness. Of course, you may just want to lock some people into a sworn statement out of concern that they may change their testimonies later.

Let's examine several matters concerned with taking statements. Most people will talk more freely if they are not aware that what they are saying is later going to become a matter of serious consideration. This is even more true when recordation is concerned. So, how does the interviewer handle this?

In taking a statement in a situation where the interviewed person is a stranger and an unknown quantity in the equation of the investigation, it is better to obtain the information first without discussion of the fact that you would like the statement memorialized for later use. If you just talk to a person, you will usually get the information you need. You need not scare them by announcing up front that you want to have a sworn statement for use in a later trial. Interview the person first, then, after you have conducted a complete interview and have your notes, you might want to approach the subject of formalizing the statement in some manner. There will come a time in every investigation when the investigator will have to take a written statement. This statement is taken for the purpose of preserving the testimony of an interviewee. A statement should be taken only when, in the opinion of the investigator, it is absolutely critical. A statement is taken at the end of the interview after the investigator has obtained all the information from the interviewee. Although there may be exceptions, most persons are willing to put in writing what they have just told you orally. If you ask a person about a written statement before the interview is complete, he or she may decide to withhold information or become reluctant to cooperate.

Every statement, regardless of format, has certain common characteristics. The beginning of the statement, usually the first paragraph, should contain identifying data about the person giving the statement (for example, name, address, date of birth) and an acknowledgment of what the statement concerns (for instance, "I am giving this statement in connection with an investigation into the theft of $5,000 from the company safe"). In addition, the fact that the statement declarant can understand the statement should be included (for example, "I can read and understand the English language"). The next and all succeeding paragraphs should be directly applicable to the investigation, and each paragraph ideally should cover one topic. An example follows:

> I arrived at work on January 14, 1989, at 9:30 A.M. When I arrived at Smith and Associates, Incorporated, there were three other people already at work. Those persons were Mary Wade, Betty Compton, and Larry Boswell. When I walked into the office, I noticed that the safe door was open and the inside of the safe was empty.

The statement could then go on to describe the declarant's activities and other information in subsequent paragraphs.

After all the relevant information is written into the statement, there should be a concluding paragraph. This paragraph should be an attestation on the part of the person making the statement that the statement is true, accurate, and obtained under legal circumstances. A typical closing paragraph might look something like this:

> I have read this statement consisting of this page and two other pages. I have given this statement freely and voluntarily without any threats, reward, or promises of reward having been made to me in return for it. It is true, accurate, and correct to the best of my knowledge and belief.

The interviewee should carefully read the statement and initial any corrections that have been made. The object of taking a statement is to obtain information that cannot be changed at a later date should the interviewee be intimidated or bribed, or simply think better about becoming involved.

The statement should be typed or neatly handwritten. The usual practice is for the investigator to write the statement in the interviewee's presence, while the interviewee watches.

Statements serve several purposes. They can be used to refresh a witness's recollection. They can be used to impeach a witness who changes his or her story at a trial. They can be used to elicit information from reluctant witnesses. (People would rather be part of a group in doing something like this than do it alone.) They can be used as leverage with suspects to demonstrate that information has been obtained from other sources that supports the investigator's suspicions of guilt.

Sworn Statement

A sworn statement, or affidavit, is a statement taken from an interviewee before a person authorized by law to administer oaths. This authority is statutory in nature. If a sworn statement is to be taken, the person authorized to administer the oath should swear in the interviewee before the signature is placed on the document. The person giving the oath should then write in the jurat, or the authentication line. This is usually a line that states:

"Subscribed and sworn to (or affirmed) before me this 27th day of March, 1989, at Chicago, Illinois" (the appropriate date and location being placed in the proper places). This is then followed by the signature of the oath-giving individual.

In our system of government, more reliance is placed on sworn testimony than is placed on unsworn testimony. This does not mean that an unsworn statement is useless, since it is adopted by the person giving it with his or her signature. The least desirable statement is one that is unsigned and unsworn.

Question-and-Answer Statement

Question-and-answer statements, or "Q and A" as they are called, are verbatim statements. The Q and A shows the exact questions asked and the answers given. This type of statement is taken when the answers of the interviewee are critically important and a narrative answer will not be suitable. The body of a Q and A statement looks like this.

Q: What kind of weapon did Joe have that night?
A: It was a revolver.

Q: What make of revolver was it?
A: It was a Smith & Wesson.

Recording Statements

In over 30 years of conducting literally hundreds of interviews, it is the author's experience that people sometimes change their stories between the time you talk to them and the time they come to testify at trial. If you do not have some reliable record of that interview, the witness will insist that you misunderstood what he or she said or are lying about what took place during the interview. The situation then devolves into a "he said–she said" situation.

Of course, you have your contemporaneous notes of the interview. What do those notes show? They show what you put down after the witness made his or her statements to you. Did you accurately write what was said? Did you get the correct meaning of what was said? If the witness changes his or her statement dramatically at trial, you may be called upon as a rebuttal witness to show that the person has changed his or her testimony.

One way to avoid this difficulty is to record the conversation using a tape recorder. Many people will stop talking the minute they see a tape recorder. They fear being called to task for what they may say so they simply refuse to talk to you if you produce a tape recorder. If you have a tape recorder operating and the witness doesn't see it, then he or she may speak freely to you.

Immediately, everyone will begin to question the legality and the fairness of this procedure. We will address both topics. It is legal, under Federal law, to record a conversation between two or more persons, if you are a party to that conversation or have the permission of one of the parties to that conversation to record the conversation. (18 USC 2510 et seq.) You need not advise the other party that the conversation is being recorded. However, you should be aware that there are states where recording a conversation through electronic recording devices requires the knowledgeable agreement of both parties or all parties to the conversation (e.g., California and Maryland). Before you record a conversation in which you are involved with others, consult with an attorney who is knowledgeable of the law in your state. Care should also be taken when conducting telephonic interviews across state lines since the other state may not have the same law as your state.

Is it fair? What is fair? If the person is telling you the truth, then what does he or she have to fear from your recording the conversation? Nothing! Importantly, consider this scenario: You are a male investigator interviewing a female. She alleges that you made a pass at her or used suggestive language. How do you defend yourself? Or, you are a female investigator and are interviewing a male. He says or does something very inappropriate. How do you prove that you were the victim of unwanted sexual advances?

Recording the entire interview may be a personal protection for you and certainly backs up your version of the interview. In order to do this, you must take the appropriate steps to preserve the tape as evidence. As soon as possible after the interview, you should review the tape to make sure that the interview was recorded completely and accurately. Machines fail and batteries fail. Next, you should remove the record tab from the cassette. You should make a copy of the tape for use in preparing transcripts or playing for other persons. Finally, you should clearly mark the original tape with the name of the interviewee and the date of the interview. Your initials should be used in a large office where there may be a number of persons conducting these types of interviews. You should put the tape in a safe place to which only you have access. This way, the chain of custody of the tape is assured and you can testify that you made the tape and that the tape has been in your possession since its making.

For every tape, there is a transcript. Transcribing tapes is a long, boring, tedious task. Once it is accomplished, the tape and the transcript must be compared side by side. You must listen to the tape and follow in the transcript. If there is a mistake in the transcript, it must be corrected. There are usually words or parts of sentences on tapes which cannot be understood. These should be marked "unintelligible." "Mary said that he (unintelligible) the car after the accident."

If you are unsure of a word, you should indicate it as follows: "Mary said that he (painted?) the car after the accident."

This shows the reader of the transcript that you are reasonably sure that the word is correct, but you cannot be positive.

Tapes and transcripts are sometimes very critical in a matter. For instance compare the following sentences:

"Jim told me he never saw a spread sheet."

"Jim told me he never saw the spread sheet."

In the first sentence, there is a question as to whether or not a spread sheet even existed. In the second, there is no question that the spread sheet existed. In an interview, it is unlikely that you will catch all of these fine points of the English language. You are concentrating on the interviewee, what they are saying, how they are saying it, and what you are going to ask next.

CONTACT WITH THE PROSECUTOR

A prosecutor should be contacted when fraud is first discovered and the victim intends the crime to be prosecuted. Each prosecutor has different preferences with regard to the evidence needed to support prosecution. Different criminal statutes may apply and require different sorts of substantiating evidence to be gathered. Also, some prosecutors may be more demanding than others in their evidentiary requirements. For example, one U.S. Attorney, after successfully prosecuting a case of fraud, had this admonition. He advises that if possible he prefers documentation of more than one instance of fraud by the accused, as was the case in the evidence package provided to him for prosecution. He was concerned that one example would be insufficient, regardless of its significance, to clearly convince the jury that the defendant had clear intent to defraud. His concern was that juries sometimes tend to be overly sympathetic to a plea by a defendant's attorney that one instance of fraud does not a criminal make. Also, prosecuting attorneys often have varying degrees of investigative resources that may be available to assist in evidence gathering. U.S. Attorneys, for example, probably have the most investigative resources available because they have every federal law enforcement agency (there are over 80 of them) at their disposal. Prosecutors at state, county, or equivalent level however, are not as fortunate, and may depend more heavily on the victim's resources to accomplish any necessary investigative activities.

SUMMARY

The fraud investigator must patiently and persistently accumulate information to be used in the decision to prosecute a perpetrator, as well as in an actual prosecution of a fraud perpetrator. Interview questions should be phrased in such a way to elicit a narrative response. The interrogatives who, what, where, when, how, why, and which are useful in asking such questions.

The end product of the fraud investigator's efforts may be a memorandum of interview or a signed statement. In either case, the document should be supported by legible and complete notes taken at the time of the interview. These notes may be presented as evidence during a fraud trial. Their content, clarity, and consistency is of the utmost importance if the prosecution is to have a reasonable chance to secure a conviction.

Chapter 12

Proactive and Reactive Investigations

FRAUD CHOKEPOINTS:
VULNERABILITY AND THREAT ANALYSIS

If all we do is wait for somebody to do something wrong, we will fail to control the level of damage the company suffers and we will fail to provide an incentive against committing the fraud. We call what we do when we wait for crime to be committed *reactive investigation*. To this end, we need to be aware of where fraud can be conducted before it happens. The investigator needs to know as much about the weakness of the system as the employee does. When we go looking for fraud in the system weaknesses, we call this *proactive investigation*.

Proactive investigation is critically important to control the amount of loss. If the fraud is permitted to continue for years, the loss will be staggering and the chance of recovery will be reduced significantly. In effect, the money will be spent. Our best bet is to stop the fraud as early as possible to limit the loss and insure the maximum amount of recovery.

A second important factor is the message this type of investigation sends to the potentially corrupt person, employee or outsider. If the perpetrator feels that he or she will be caught early in the fraud, he or she is less likely to try it. The perpetrator will not get anything for the risk; it is not worth the expected gain.

To accomplish the proactive investigation, the investigator must, of necessity, know how the system works. This may require some study and effort. Once the system is learned, its vulnerabilities are assessed. How can someone steal from this system? Some of the flaws in systems include:

- Uncontrolled access to cash. Till tapping in retail sales is an example.
- False billing. No review of billings to determine legitimacy.

- Uncontrolled inventory. If someone steals a number of items from inventory, will anyone know it?
- Uncontrolled shipping points. Are items just dropped off at the business or are they counted when they arrive to make sure that the company receives everything it ordered and paid for?
- Inadequate security. Can someone come into the facility at night and take items without detection? Can employees easily take items home with them?

After the investigator has observed the flow of the business, he or she determines the areas of vulnerability. After vulnerability assessment, the investigator should determine the level of threat present. Threat assessment is an art. The investigator can generally determine existing threats, but has no way of knowing if the threats will materialize. Some, like employee dishonesty, can generally be evaluated. Some, like local criminal element activity, may not be so easy to evaluate. Like locks, security measures keep honest people honest.

With the vulnerability and threat assessments complete, the investigator is now in a position to evaluate the possibility of loss to the business. The company will ignore some *de minimis* losses. All shoplifting cannot be stopped, but if it is reduced to an absolute minimum, the loss may be acceptable to the business. There comes a trade-off between cost of prevention, customer inconvenience, and executive perception of the need.

Where the investigator can plug the leak, he or she should do so. It is certainly preferable to take the temptation and opportunity away from the potential crook than to wait until damage is done. The investigator can never be sure how much damage is going to be done before it is caught. Some fraud schemes that have gone on for years are continuing undetected today.

In taking action to reduce the probability of fraud at the point of possibility, the investigator needs to consider if he or she is creating a bigger problem than the one he or she is trying to correct. Before the corrective actions are taken, an impact study must be made to see what impact the corrections will have on the system. For example, if the possibility of fraud is remote and the corrective action will require a complete overhaul of the system, it might be better to leave the system as it is.

One problem that presents itself in all situations is what to do when fraud is discovered. Does the investigator rush in and stop it immediately, arrest the miscreants, and stop the action or, on the other hand, should the investigator carefully analyze the situation, identify all parties, record the activities, and seek the weak point to use against the persons committing the fraud? In some circles, people get excited and rush into a situation to stop the fraud immediately. If the losses are staggering and the losses must be stopped immediately, this might be the desired solution. However, those situations are rare. In most cases, it would be prudent to watch the action, determine the identities of the players, map out the scheme, and then present the findings to the responsible authority. Any prosecutor is going to assess the complexity of a situation before he/she decides to take the case. If the case is too complex for the average juror to understand, they may want to avoid it (e.g., complex economic schemes involving multiple levels of activity).

By identifying the players, you give the criminal investigators and the prosecutor an opportunity to evaluate which of the persons involved in the scheme they may want to approach. If an insider can be "rolled over" to cooperate with authorities, the case is infinitely easier to investigate and prosecute.

WORKERS COMPENSATION FRAUD

Each year, millions and millions of dollars are lost to business through the simple application of fraud to workers' compensation claims. Who pays for this? The employer. It is always in the employer's best interest to aggressively investigate and deal with workers' compensation fraud matters. Aggressive action serves several purposes:

- It reduces the company's exposure to loss. The faster the claim can be shut down, the less the loss.
- It serves as a warning beacon to those who are tempted to commit fraud. Don't kid yourself, the employee underground news network gets the message in a hurry when one of their own gets caught with his/her hand in the cookie jar.
- If the scheme is properly identified, the manner of the fraud may be used to make the necessary corrections in the system to prevent future fraud.

Often at the mention of workers' compensation fraud, the image immediately comes to mind of a person who claims to be injured, but who is really malingering. This is usually referred to as *claimant fraud*. There are, however, others in the system who might be taking advantage of a fraudulent scheme. If a person or entity is providing services to the injured worker and is committing a fraud, we call this *provider fraud*. If a corrupt employee is putting in false claims and receiving the benefits, this is *insider fraud*. If an employer makes fraudulent claims, we call this *employer fraud*. In other words, anyone who can get a check out of the system can commit fraud.

Injuries are of two types, objective and subjective. An objective injury is one that can be proven medically. For instance, a broken arm can be diagnosed through X-ray. A subjective injury is one that cannot be proven medically. For instance, a constant headache or a soft-tissue injury (strain) of the lower back. Either type of injury can result in a fraudulent claim aspect.

Claimant Fraud

Claimant fraud results from fraudulent activity on the part of the claimant. It can occur in any one of several ways.

Legitimate Injury Fraud.   A claimant is legitimately injured and has suffered an injury with objective symptoms. However, the claimant has access to records which will allow him or her to manipulate the system to obtain funds greater than those to which he or she is entitled. A case in point: Claimant A was issued a prescription for a certain drug to help with his legitimate claim. When A went to the drugstore, his prescription was given to him in a bag with the receipt on the bag. A altered the handwritten receipt, added other drugs and other amounts. A then submitted the receipt for reimbursement through workers' compensation and received a check for about four times as much as the sum to which he was entitled. This should have been caught by any sort of simple medical audit that would have recognized that the fake drug listings were not related to A's injury. It wasn't and A continued the scheme for many months before it was caught by accident.

A claimant may also claim an aggravated injury that does not exist. For instance, the injury may be legitimate and the claimant may be able to return to limited duty. However, the claimant would rather have the time off, so the claimant says that he cannot do even the limited duty work. This is extremely difficult to catch and usually requires a surveillance to show the claimant performing tasks inconsistent with his claimed injuries.

False Injury Fraud.   A claimant is not injured, but claims to have suffered injury so that he may claim benefits and take time off. In this case, the claimant makes up an incident and reports that he has been injured. The injury, of course, must be subjective. It is usually a soft-tissue lower back injury or a psychological injury. Doctors will usually report that they have no objective findings, but they cannot say that the person is not injured as medical science is not far enough advanced to properly diagnose the condition. A case in point: Claimant B, a truck driver, was delivering to another company. During the delivery, one of the resident company's forklift operators allegedly ran over B's foot with the forklift. B reported to his company that he was injured and went out on workers' compensation. B sued the other company for the tort. B, at deposition, claimed that he could not walk well and was limited in his personal activities. B was seen by a doctor and told the doctor that he could barely walk or use his foot. The day after the doctor's visit, B was videotaped by a surveillance team. The videotape showed B walking, carrying heavy objects, planting a tree and stomping a large paper bag flat. B insisted on taking the case to trial in spite of the videotape evidence. The jury gave him nothing. His company is still paying him compensation though.

Double-dipping Fraud.   When a claimant goes on workers' compensation, the idea is to return the claimant to some kind of productive work as soon as possible. We now know that if we let people lay around, they generally get worse unless rest is prescribed. However, if there are two unconnected systems for receiving income, a claimant can play both and not get caught. Claimant C was legitimately injured on the job. C, while on workers' compensation, filed for unemployment and did not list the company which was paying him compensation. He received checks from workers' compensation and a check from the bureau of employment security. It took a while to convince the state to compare its workers' compensation rolls with its unemployment compensation roles. In Chicago, in the 1970s, the rolls of those on welfare were compared with those employed by the U.S. Post Office in Chicago. Several hundred people were receiving welfare checks in addition to their substantial postal service benefits. This was done only after the U.S. Department of Health and Human Services agreed to run their tapes against the Post Office payroll tapes.

Another kind of double-dipping is the claimant who goes out on workers' compensation, and then holds down another job, receiving benefits from workers' compensation and a salary from the job. This situation is, at times, difficult. There is some case law extant which reports that it is all right for a claimant to engage in employment while on workers' compensation as long as his activities are not inconsistent with his claimed injuries. Once again, surveillance is recommended.

Employer Fraud

A couple of years ago, a group of people got together to decide how to defraud the workers' compensation system. They decided that they would form their own corporations regularly through the secretary of state's office. Once the corporations were formed, they listed themselves as employees of the corporations. After they paid the first premium, they filed workers' compensation claims for nonexistent injuries. Since they were the employers as well as the claimants, they certified their own claims as valid. The group used an attorney to help them set up the system. After one was caught, he gave up the others. All pled guilty except the attorney, who went to trial and was acquitted. The situation here is that the corporations were to be folded following the claims and the corporations would no longer have to pay their premiums to the workers' compensation fund. The cost of the claims would then be spread out among other employers in the same risk category.

Provider Fraud

A provider is anyone who provides service of some manner to a claim. It can be a doctor, a hospital, a nurse, an occupational therapy worker, or just about anyone who can make a claim against the system for money. There are a number of ways that providers can, and do, defraud workers' compensation systems.

False Billing.   The simplest fraud is to submit a false bill. The bill can be wholly false or partially false. Consider the following examples:

- Doctor H. bills workers' compensation for tests that he claims were performed at his office. However, it was later found that he did not have the equipment to conduct these tests and was just inflating his bill.
- Doctor J. bills workers' compensation for modalities of treatment that were not performed. He saw the patient and performed some modalities, but not all. For instance, hot packs, massage, and manipulation were a part of treatment, but he did not perform the shortwave diathermy which he claims to have performed. When the patient was interviewed, the patient described the treatments he had received and they did not correspond with the invoices from the doctor.

Visits Never Made.   The provider bills for visits never made.

- Doctor L. bills for office visits by the claimant for three days in a week. The claimant was actually seen only once. This was caught when the claimant made his claim for mileage reimbursement for travel to the doctor's office. The claimant's travel claim was matched against the doctor's invoice. The claimant was interviewed and denied having been seen more than once a week. The doctor's records, when subpoenaed, had been altered severely in an attempt to hide the fraud once it had been discovered.

- A vocational rehabilitation specialist falsifies an invoice reflecting meetings with the claimant to assist the claimant in finding employment that will not conflict with the claimant's injuries.

    A chiropractor's invoices were compared and according to them, he was seeing 40 patients in an eight-hour period and performing a complete set of modalities on each. A surveillance of his office, followed by a review of his invoices for the same period put an end to that scheme.

Drug Over-Prescribing.   One of the means by which the illegal drug trade obtains its product is through prescription by a licensed practitioner. This is a sinister system which is difficult to catch.

- Doctor M. prescribes controlled drugs to women in return for sexual favors. The visit is charged to insurance or compensation.

- Doctor N. prescribes controlled drugs to persons whom he never sees. They pay a $40 cash office visit fee and are given a prescription for the drug of their choice. Even though the person is not seen, the doctor charges insurance or compensation and pockets the cash.

- Doctor P. prescribed 10,000 Tylenol #4 with codeine tablets to a patient in a nine-month period. When interviewed, the doctor advised the investigator that the patient had intractable pain (from a very minor traffic accident). The doctor also stated that he had advised the patient of the possible bad side effects of taking that much Tylenol. The patient insisted, when interviewed, that he had taken each and every one of the tablets.

PROVIDER/CLAIMANT CONSPIRACY

When the provider and the claimant team up and conspire to defraud the system, it will be very difficult to catch. One case was caught by an undercover investigator visiting the doctor with a hidden camera. The doctor told the patient exactly how to act when the patient underwent an independent medical examination (IME). The doctor, of course, continued a long period of treatment for the patient and charged for the treatment, even though the doctor well knew that the patient was malingering.

SOURCES OF INFORMATION

Information concerning fraud schemes is obtained from a variety of sources, both reactive and proactive.

Co-workers, Neighbors, and Ex-spouses

A very common source of workers' compensation fraud is from co-workers, who know the claimant and see the claimant in the neighborhood; neighbors, who see the claimant, but are not associated with claimant's workplace; and, ex-spouses, who hate to see the claimant get by with anything. Sometimes, co-workers are reluctant to report wrongdoing by fellow workers because of the "worker vs. management" mentality. There is a feeling among some workers that any time anyone can get by management, it is a victory for the workers' solidarity. It is incumbent upon management to demonstrate to the workers how fraudulent claims increase overhead costs and reduce the amount of capital available for new jobs and pay increases. Of course, it is also incumbent on management to insure that workers' compensation matters are handled fairly and not routinely denied. An evenhanded treatment of claims and an aggressive prosecution of fraud will go a long way toward improving the worker–management relationship.

Fraud 800 Numbers

Some companies and workers' compensation organizations have obtained a toll-free number for reporting fraudulent activities. The toll-free 800 number allows workers from all parts of the state or nation to report fraudulent activity. The toll-free numbers also offer some anonymity to the reporting party since they can call from a pay phone. To be effective, the toll-free number and its purpose must be widely advertised, using all media possible.

The Claim File

A careful review of the claim file by a fraud-trained, experienced claims specialist is another sure way to detect fraud. Using the above information as a guide, the specialist can comb through the documents and look for indicia. It is also a good idea to conduct random, unannounced audits of claims by persons other than the claims handlers. Recently, one fraud specialist was talking with a government official concerning the vulnerability of that official's compensation system. When asked, a proto-typical fraud scheme was described in some detail, which involved an employee of the compensation organization. Approximately one month later, the official called to report that law enforcement had discovered a fraud scheme perpetrated by a compensation system employee almost exactly as the one described to the official a month earlier. This is not magic, it is common sense. With enough experience, anyone (including a crooked employee) can spot the vulnerabilities in the system.

TAKING ACTION TO COMBAT COMPENSATION FRAUD

There are few companies with an in-house capability to conduct investigations into potentially fraudulent activity. Law enforcement agencies are generally reactive in nature and will not want to put the time and manpower into an investigation that does not have a clear-cut criminal aspect. Many cases of workers' compensation fraud are matters of degree. The follow-up once a fraud is thought potential must be done by a skilled investigator.

Most companies have a law firm which routinely handles its legal matters. The first place to inquire about an investigator would be at this company. If the law firm is unable to assist in this, call around to connections in the same industry and find out who they use for their investigations. A final step would be to go to the Yellow Pages. Regardless of how the investigator is obtained, there are several matters which must be pursued before the investigator is hired.

- **Is the investigator licensed?** Most states, but not all, have a licensing division for private investigators. It may be the secretary of state or it may be a dedicated board. Have the investigator provide a copy of his license. This will show that at least the investigator has met the minimum statutory requirements for licensure.
- **Is the investigator insured?** Do not hire an investigator who does not have at least $1,000,000 in professional liability (errors and omissions) coverage. This is a very reasonable requirement and most reputable investigators carry that kind and amount of insurance. When hired, the investigator is acting as your agent in some respects. If he or she makes

a serious error, the injured party will go after the deep pockets, usually you if the investigator has no insurance.

- **What is the investigator's background?** Most investigators are very willing to send you a CV or a brochure about their company. Ask for it.
- **Do they have the necessary equipment?** The video camera is the *sine qua non* of workers' compensation surveillances. The newer cameras have optical image stabilization and significant zoom lenses. With them, you can get good, clear, non-shaky, identifiable video of activity by the claimant. If the investigator does not have a newer, usually 8 millimeter, video camera, move on to someone else. The product will not be acceptable otherwise.
- **How much is this going to cost?** Ask the investigator for his or her rates—all of them. Investigators all usually charge an hourly rate plus a mileage rate. It varies widely from place to place across the country. Some investigators charge for office time (writing reports, making copies of tapes, etc.), some do not. Some investigators charge for successful tape by the minute of tape, some do not. The professional investigator will discuss all charges and fees in advance of doing any work to insure that the client is not surprised when the invoice arrives. You should also set an initial budget, not to be exceeded by the investigator. This budget should be based on your exposure in the claim, the distance between the investigator and the claimant (travel time), and the type of injury that will be considered.
- **Once you have hired the investigator and the budget is established, then what?** The investigator will conduct the surveillance. You should establish mutually agreeable benchmark dates for initial results and completion. This again can vary depending on the circumstances. You should discuss this with the investigator and have him commit to dates acceptable to both of you. Some dates may be established by an upcoming deposition of the claimant, where the attorney will want the information for the deposition.

Surveillances are conducted at the leisure of the claimant. The investigator can do no more than follow the activities of the claimant and record them. If the claimant is outdoors and active, there is ample opportunity. If the claimant has decided to be a "couch potato" and not engage in any activity, then there will be no opportunity. One time where the claimant will be out and about is at a doctor's appointment, either his own doctor or an IME. If those can be properly planned, medical appointments offer a great opportunity to observe the claimant.

Generally, a surveillance should last as long as there is activity. If there has been no activity for about four hours, the investigator should try again at a different time on a different day. You should never receive an investigator's report which says that the investigator sat there for eight or ten hours and nothing happened.

Upon completion of the successful surveillance, the investigator must provide you with a report of all his surveillance activities regarding the claimant and a copy of the videotape. The investigator should always keep the original tape since he may be required to testify in court regarding the tape and its authenticity. If it has been passed around to others, the chain of custody of the tape may not be maintained and the tape may not be allowed in as evidence.

With the report and the tape in hand, you should review the file and determine if the claimant is clearly performing tasks which are incompatible with his reported injury and limitations. If so, your legal counsel should be consulted regarding the necessary measures needed to terminate the claim and proceed with prosecution of the fraud.

WORKPLACE FRAUD

It's 10 A.M., do you know where your worker is? The whole object of the worker-management relationship is eight hours of work for eight hours of pay. You expect the worker to be productive during the time he or she is at work. He or she expects compensation according to your employment agreement at the specified times. Are you getting what you are paying for?

In those businesses where the employees are all in a single location, the ability to supervise and maintain productivity is pretty good. However, in those instances where the employees spend a great deal of time away from the office, you may not be getting your full worth. This situation calls for work surveillances. A work surveillance is nothing more than checking on your employee to determine if the employee is doing what he or she is supposed to do. Or is he or she stopping home for a two-hour nap in the afternoon? Or stopping to see a friend? Or stopping at a bar and drinking?

Most supervisors can look at an employee's work results and get a feeling if the employee is working at a reasonable capacity. If the employee is not producing at a reasonable capacity, you might want to have a surveillance conducted of the employee while the employee is away from the office. In these cases, the employees routes, rules, and work should be given to the investigator. The investigator should then be able to follow the employee and record his activities on the job.

There are presently available recording devices which are linked to the U.S. government's global positioning system (GPS). These devices might be the answer for fleet operations. They are put on a vehicle and the main office can have a complete record, on a map if required, of every place the vehicle went, how long it was there and when it was there. This permits the supervisor to manage his or her fleet operations in a more efficient manner and reduces the temptation of employees on the road to do something other than their work.

Part 3

Prosecuting Fraud

Patrick C. Coggins, J.D., Ph.D.

Chapter 13

Rules of Evidence, Fraud Discovery, and Prosecution

INTRODUCTION

The rules which determine what constitutes relevant and substantive evidence in establishing the existence of fraud and the perpetrator's guilt are of paramount importance. The courts and its officers are well versed in them and fraud cases presented for their consideration must be in conformance. Often, however, the rules of evidence are voluminous and written in a "legalese" that is difficult for the layman to understand. It was with this concern in mind, with apologies to our lawyer leadership for any liberties taken, that the following text explaining the rules of evidence was written for non-lawyer accountants and auditors who are reading this book.

The rules of evidence are complex and have been the subject of hundreds of books and essays. The material that follows presents an outline to facilitate finding summary information quickly. The wording has been "delegalized" to the extent possible without denigrating the meaning and the context. As it is most likely, once evidence of fraud is discovered, that competent legal counsel will be called in to guide the evidence-gathering process, this chapter is not intended to be a substitute for such counsel. Rather, it is intended to guide the management accountant and internal auditor, those who are most likely involved in fraud discovery and control efforts, in completing their training and education on the topic of fraud discovery and control.

The ultimate decision to prosecute a suspected perpetrator of fraud must be made by top management either as a matter of policy (preferred by the authors), or on a case by case basis. All cases of suspected fraud should be documented as if it were the intent of top management to prosecute the perpetrators. Therefore, no discretion to prosecute or not to prosecute the suspected perpetrator of fraud is given to the management accountant or auditor within this text material.

Successful prosecution of fraud depends on the relevance and materiality of the evidence and, most important, whether the preponderance of evidence is proven beyond a reasonable doubt. Therefore, internal auditors and accountants can greatly assist the prosecution of fraud by ensuring that there is substantial documentation of fraudulent transactions. The following information is intended to provide the reader with general information related to evidence and evidentiary rules which should be considered in identifying, documenting, and confronting fraud within various entities in the private and governmental sectors.

The detection, documentation, and prosecution of fraud require vigilance and strong commitment on the part of all managers, executive staff, and employees of the company. Since a perpetrator could be anyone, including a valued and long-time employee, identification and confrontation should take place if and when there is clear and convincing evidence. Such evidence should, on its face, be non-speculative, but should point to the loss of property and the fraudulent conduct of the employee(s) in question. Once the individual is detected and successful prosecution is achieved, the entity must follow through with its own internal sanctions, which may range from suspension and probation, to restitution and termination. The culminating action of the entity should include preventive systems changes to ensure that opportunities to commit similar fraud have been eradicated.

WHAT CONSTITUTES FRAUDULENT CONDUCT?

Solicitation

Modern statutes refer to criminal behavior that solicits another person to commit a crime. Solicitation may also constitute criminal attempt when the crime is one requiring joint action of both parties; for example, soliciting another to give perjured testimony is punishable as a criminal attempt to perjure oneself. Under the Federal False Claims Act, solicitation of another to commit a fraud against the government is actionable under this act.

Conspiracy

Conspiracy is an agreement between two or more parties to do an unlawful act or to do a lawful act in an unlawful manner. A defendant could be prosecuted for conspiracy as well as the completed crime. For successful prosecution, an agreement between two or more persons either expressed or implied must be proven. Some fraudulent acts are committed by two or more persons.

Two More Persons. In *Gebardi v. U.S.* (USSC, 1932), the facts were that a man and the woman he transported were charged with a conspiracy to violate the Mann Act. The man made all of the arrangements; the woman voluntarily consented to go with him.

Congress intended by the Mann Act to exempt the woman of the substantive crime. Therefore, the woman could not be convicted of conspiracy to violate the Act. Since she is not guilty, neither can the man be guilty, since it takes two persons to commit a conspiracy (there must be an agreement).

The Model Penal Code would convict the man in the Gebardi case. It says if you agree with someone to commit a crime, you are guilty of a conspiracy even if the other person is not. Most courts, however, follow the Gebardi rule.

In *Regina v. O'Brien* (Canada, 1954), one party without the requisite intent, the facts were that A and B agreed to a kidnapping, but A never at any time had the intent to go through with it. A could not be held since he did not have the requisite mental state accompanying the commission of a prohibited act (*mens rea*). The issue uses whether B, who did intend to commit the crime, was guilty of conspiracy.

In this case the defendant was found not guilty because there was not the requisite meeting of the minds between two or more people to conspire to commit a crime. Under common law, a husband and wife were considered to be one legal person and could not, therefore, conspire with one another. Many courts have now rejected this view. If however, husband, wife, and a third party agreed to commit a crime, then there is a conspiracy and all are guilty.

False Pretenses/Misrepresentations

False pretenses consist of obtaining title to a personal property of another person by an intentional false statement of past or existing fact with intent to defraud that person. A misrepresentation as to what will occur in the future is not sufficient. A false promise, even if made with the present intent to perform, is also not sufficient. The victim must actually be deceived by, or act in reliance on, the misrepresentation. This must be a major factor (or the sole cause) of the victim's passing title to the defendant.

Larceny by trick consists of obtaining possession of personal property (with intent to deprive) by a misrepresentation of past or future fact; false pretenses requires that the defendant obtain title. Whether the victim transfers possession or title depends upon the victim's intent.

Extortion (Kickbacks)

Under common law, extortion consisted of the corrupt collection of an unlawful fee by "an officer under color of his office."

Under modern statutes, extortion often consists of obtaining property by means of threats to do harm or to expose information, or merely of making threats to do such things with intent hereby to obtain property. Modern extortion statutes cover several situations not previously covered. Actions which are involved in extortion are situations:

- Where the threats are not of the required physical harm or of sufficiently immediate harm
- Where the property obtained is not in the victim's presence

Receipt of Stolen Property

Receipt of stolen property consists of receiving possession and control (manual possession of property is not necessary) of personal property, knowing it to have been obtained in a manner constituting a criminal offense by another person with the intent to permanently deprive of the owner.

It should be noted that to receive goods and benefits from fraudulent conduct could result in criminal action against the beneficiary of these ill acquired gains.

Theft

Under many modern statutes, some or all of the above mentioned property offenses are combined and defined as the crime of theft.

Forgery

Forgery consists of making or altering (by drafting, altering, adding, or deleting) a writing (defined as a writing with apparent legal significance) so that it is false (defined as representing that it is something that it is not, not as merely containing a misrepresentation) with intent to defraud (although no one need actually have been defrauded).

If the defendant fraudulently causes a third person to sign a document which that person does not realize he or she is signing, forgery has been committed. But if the third person realizes he or she is signing the document, forgery has not been committed even if that person was induced by fraud to sign it.

Uttering a forged instrument consists of offering as genuine an instrument that may be subject of forgery and is false with intent to defraud. Some instances of fraud are accompanied by forgery of checks, documents and certificates resulting in the loss to the owner of the asset/property.

Malicious Mischief

Malicious mischief consists of the intentional destruction of or damage to the property of another. Malice requires no ill will or hatred. It does, however, require that the damage or destruction has been intended or contemplated by the defendant.

Embezzlement

Embezzlement consists of fraudulent conversion of personal property by a person in possession of that property where the possession was obtained pursuant to a trust relationship. Note: If the defendant claims that he or she intended to restore the exact property taken, it in no way excuses the defendant from embezzlement charges. *In re* Morgan (1992)[2], the motion under Section 329 of the Bankruptcy Code and Federal Rule of Bankruptcy procedure 2107, seeking review of payments made by debtors to their counsel, James D. Norvell.

The United States trustee reviewed the records of Mr. Norvell's client trust account and revealed that Mr. Norvell was improperly invading the account for at least a year prior to April 1999. Mr. Norvell, when confronted, agreed to repay the sum of $5,000 to both debtors and his former associate. Mr. Norvell was not free from further sanction which included a.) resignation from practice before the United States District Court, and b.) refraining from representing any party in a proceeding before any United States Bankruptcy Court. The further sanction is awaiting a referral to the State Bar of Texas, Northern District of Region 6, Texas. This matter can still be forwarded to the local prosecutor for embezzlement charges.

As in larceny, embezzlement is not committed if the conversion is pursuant to an open claim of right of the property. Embezzlement differs from larceny in that:

- Embezzlement can be committed only by one with valid possession of the property (although if he had mere custody, larceny can be committed).
- Embezzlement requires only fraudulent conversion, rather than taking and transportation.

ELEMENTS OF CRIME

In order to establish fraudulent criminal acts, the three elements of a crime must be established. The three elements of a crime are *actus rea, mens rea,* and *causation.*

Actus Rea is either the commission of some act which is prohibited by law, or negative acts, or omissions to act. If an individual omits some act where there is a legal duty to perform it, the individual is criminally liable (for example, cover-up).

The essence of the actus rea is that facts derived must point to the defendant's commission of a prohibited act under the law (for example, taking money without permission or knowledge of the owner, thus defrauding the owner).

On the other hand, mere omissions to act, if proven, could establish criminal intent and liability, especially where the individual had personal knowledge of the fraudulent act and conduct, provided assistance, was a co-conspirator who provided minimal or some assistance, but did not receive any of the benefits from fraudulent act.

Mens Rea is the mental state accompanying the commission of an act prohibited by law. The defendant's mental state must include specific intention to defraud or commit a crime. The mens rea, or mental state, of the suspected individual is critical to establishing that a crime has been committed. In most fraud cases, mens rea will be easily established by clear and convincing documentation that points directly to the actions, behavior, and control of the property in question in the hands of the suspected employee. Thus, if someone gave the employee permission to borrow or use the property for a period of time, the requirement of intent to defraud will not be easily proven.

Causation means that the defendant must have actually caused the result before he or she can be held criminally liable for the crime. Additionally, according to the "material factor rule," it is necessary that the facts indicate that the actions and behavior of the accused were materially responsible for the commission of the fraud. In the instance of causation of the fraud, under the general rule of *res ipsa loquitor* (the act speaks for itself), the property which was defrauded was under the control of the suspected employee(s), and this property could not have disappeared without their knowledge and control over its disappearance. Thus, it is essential to prove carefully through material evidence that the suspected individual had full control over and access to the defrauded property. For example, because the defendant had the keys to the safe or was responsible for counting the bonds each day, he should know about the loss of the contents.

PROCEDURES FOR DISCOVERY

It is of utmost importance that the following factors be taken into consideration when applying fraud discovery procedures:

- Wiretapping and other forms of electronic eavesdropping are prohibited by the USSC. However, the defense must prove physical invasion or trespass to limit the admission of information obtained by such means. A court order should first be obtained. In *Rathburn vs. U.S.*, (USSC, 1957) it was ruled that an employer can listen to any conversation conducted during the course of business on the employer's premises.
- The use of a private investigator to obtain incriminating statements (evidence) is permissible. In *Osborn vs. U.S.* (USSC, 1966) it was ruled that tape recordings might be admissible under certain circumstances.
- In *Baggio vs. U.S.* (1987), informants were permitted to be used to gather evidence which was later admitted by the court. It is essential that the agency/employer consider a court-appointed informant, or an informant from the U.S. prosecution or local state attorney's office. The other option is an individual competent to undertake such an operation, such as a private investigator.
- Internal auditor's reports are excellent documentary proof of fraud. In most instances, an internal audit will be required after the suspicion of fraud, or in the normal course of a regular audit if the internal auditor uncovers a fraudulent act.
- Confrontation is permissible in some instances in which there has been probable cause that directly links an individual's actions to a suspected fraudulent conduct. The suspect could be confronted about such suspected fraud. It is suggested that such confrontation be conducted in privacy with as few people present as possible. In all instances, it is

important to have two people perform the confrontation to ensure that there will be at least one available witness to the statements of the suspected individual.

- Confession, under the rules of evidence, could be admitted as a "hearsay declaration against interest." However, there are careful steps that should be followed in documenting an individual's confession to a suspected fraud.

    1. The individual should record in writing, on audio, or on videotape that the statements are being made voluntarily, willingly, and without any threats or coercion.
    2. The entire confession must be in writing or recorded fully.
    3. The text must be signed and dated by the declarant.
    4. The parties to such a statement should witness it or at least note in separate document that they were present and that the statements were voluntarily given and duly signed by the declarant whose confession was witnessed.

    Another option available to the employer is to turn the matter over to the company's internal security personnel and let them secure the confession. Since these are trained law enforcement individuals, they will follow appropriate procedures for securing a confession from the accused party.

- Coercion may be used by the employer to gather vital information from an employee suspected of fraud, by threatening to suspend or fire the employee. This method should be used carefully until and unless the employee is charged with fraud or there is substantial proof of such fraudulent conduct.

Other methods may be used by the employer whose establishment is experiencing losses as the result of fraud. Any legitimate method can be used to gather information in order to detect, document, and apprehend an individual suspected of fraudulent conduct. Deciding when to involve outside resources, such as private investigators or law enforcement officials, would in some cases determine the types of strategies that are ultimately used.

It is important that the strategy or procedure used to detect fraud cause as little disruption as possible to the normal operations of the business enterprise. Since in most fraud the scheme is carefully contrived, an investigation should proceed without giving notice to the suspected individual(s) that they are under surveillance and that their conduct and transactions are being monitored. Do remember that a suspected employee has fundamental constitutional rights which include a) the right to be represented by an attorney, b) the right to request all charges/accusations in writing, c) the right to be silent and avoid any self-incrimination, d) the right to request quick resolution of the matter and any other fundamental rights afforded by the constitution, statutes, and the employer's personnel policies.

RULES OF EVIDENCE

Liability Insurance. The courts have consistently held that evidence of liability insurance is not sufficient to prove malfeasance or misfeasance. This evidence of liability insurance basically will show that an individual has ownership of such insurance. Therefore, the limited admissibility of this evidence will be to show control and ownership of the liability insurance only.

Consequent Changes. Evidence of subsequent changes and other precautions an employer makes following fraudulent act are inadmissible to prove negligence or culpable conduct on the part of the employer. However, it may be admissible to prove ownership or control to rebut the claim that the precaution (against fraudulent act) was impossible. Additionally, this evidence might be useful in proving that the accused party had damaged the internal security of the operations, which resulted in the need for such subsequent changes.

Settlement Offers

It should be noted that offers to compromise and settle a matter of fraud are not admissible to prove that fraud was committed. Therefore, withdrawn guilty pleas and offers to plead guilty are not admissible. Some courts, however, have allowed admissions of facts which accompanied offers to pay restitution for the injured party's losses resulting from fraud.

Similar Acts

The evidence of any previous similar conduct, or acts resulting in fraudulent conduct, of the parties accused or of other persons in the same department, may be relevant if the evidence is probative of (substantiates) the material issue involved. Specific types of similar acts include the following:

- Previous tort claims. Evidence that the party has made previous similar false claims is considered relevant under a common scheme or plan theory to prove intent to defraud.

- Previous similar deliberate acts by a party. Similar evidence of conduct committed by a party (such as suspension or firing for similar fraud) may be introduced to establish that there was a motive or intent, when such motive elements are relevant.

- Prior contracts and course of conduct. A prior agreement of conduct between the accused and the employer may be admissible to show that the accused party was aware of the proper and acceptable course of conduct.

- Habit evidence. Under federal rule (406a) "evidence of the habit of a person . . . is relevant to prove that the person's conduct . . . on a particular occasion was in conformity with the habit."

- Evidence of industrial or business routine. Any evidence that will show the norms and standards of care and established business routines is relevant and admissible to show that a particular event occurred.

It is essential that the internal accounting standards and business procedures be fully understood by the internal auditor or other investigating parties. The documentation of fraudulent action and conduct will involve a full discussion of the variances and conformities to the business or industrial standards of conduct and care.

Real Evidence and Fraud

The issue of real evidence is important in the documentation and prosecution of fraud. "Real evidence" is the actual physical evidence that will be presented in court to prove that the conduct of the accused party was in violation of a criminal law related to fraud. The critical issue here is the authentication of the real evidence. The discussion that follows is intended to provide the reader with practical requirements that assist in the authentication of real evidence.

The following are specific kinds of real evidence:

- Reproductions and explanatory real evidence. This type of evidence includes photographs, diagrams, maps, models, charts, pictures of accused, and other reproductions. These are admissible if their value is not outweighed by the danger of unfair bias and prejudice to the accused party. However, it is necessary to ensure that these reproductions are authenticated through testimonial evidence that they are faithful reproductions of the objects they depict.

- Jury's view of the scene. The trial court in its discretion may permit the jury to visit the scene of the crime to view the conditions and circumstances surrounding the alleged criminal conduct.
- Demonstrations. The court in its discretion may permit experts to demonstrate or conduct experiments to amplify the conditions and circumstances related to the criminal conduct.

Documentary Evidence

Documentary evidence, such as an audit report or forged checks, must be relevant to the charges in order to be admissible. In the case of such written documents, it is generally viewed as only one aspect of the proof that a particular fraudulent act has been committed.

The courts continue to be consistent in their ruling that writings or other documents will not be received in evidence unless they are authenticated by proof that clearly shows that the writing or document is what the proponents claim it is. The appropriateness or relevance of the writing or documents may be admitted into evidence by the stipulation of the parties or in the pleadings.

Evidence of authenticity may be gained in a particular audit report or document by the following means:

- Direct evidence, which includes the following:
  — Testimony of an eyewitness to the actual execution of the writing or document, or to the commission of the fraudulent act.
  — Handwriting verification of the document by a handwriting expert.
  — Any evidence that the accused party has either confessed, admitted to its authenticity, or acted upon the writing as though it were authentic, with the intent to commit and carry through with the fraudulent act.
  — Testimony as to the authenticity of the writing or document of the fraudulent act by any person who can prove personal knowledge of the accused person's fraudulent action. For example, if a supervisor personally signed the checks for fraudulent invoices prepared by the accused party and under the signature of the accused party, such first knowledge of the fraudulent invoices would be admissible.
- Self-authentication of documents refers to the fact that some documents and writings prove themselves. These documents include:

— Certified copies of public records

— Official publications

— Trade inscriptions

— Newspapers and periodicals

— Acknowledged documents

— Commercial papers and other related documents used in the normal course of business

— Published guidelines and operational procedures of a company

- Circumstantial evidence may consist of a writing or document, which may authenticated by any of the following:

— Evidence that the writing is a written response to a communication sent to the claimed other author. This rule is called the reply letter doctrine. There is an analogous doctrine that is applied to telephone logs and telephone messages.

— Evidence that the writing is an "ancient document" (at least 20 years old under the Federal Rules of Evidence. There is some further clarity needed here because under federal rules all writings apply, whereas in most jurisdictions, there is limited admission of ancient documents to such items as wills and deeds.

A final note on authentication: the best evidence rule should be adhered in most cases. This rule, more accurately called the *original document rule* requires that the original writing and fraudulent documents must be produced if the terms of the proposed fraudulent act or documents are to be material and reliable as evidence of the facts purported.

The exceptions to the production of the original document include the following:

- Duplicates or photocopies are admissible if authenticated or certified by an official person (for example, the auditor) as being a true copy of his or her audit report.

- The writing is admissible if it is collateral to the litigated issue. The essence of the writing is of little importance to the matter in controversy.

- The writing is admissible if the fact to be proven has been authenticated independent of the particular writing.

- If it can be proven that it would be convenient to examine a voluminous collection of writings in court, the proponents may present their contents in the form of a chart or summary.

- Photocopies of public records are admissible. Again, efforts should be made to secure certification from the record keeper.

The proponent of secondary or duplicate copies of a writing should be prepared to provide some excuse or justification for the admissibility of secondary evidence, such as the following.

Testimonial Evidence

Competence of the Witness.   The auditor, accountant, or other individual is called upon to testify as a witness to shed light on the fraudulent issues being pursued. The witness's testimony normally conforms to four basic standards: the capacity to observe, the ability to recollect facts and situations, the ability to communicate things within one's knowledge and perception, and the competence to appreciate the obligation to speak the truth in response to all questions.

Opinion Testimony of Witness.   The courts are not anxious to admit opinion of evidence of lay witnesses unless there is proof that no better evidence can be secured. In most jurisdictions and under federal rules, opinion testimony by the lay witness is admissible if it can be shown that the evidence is rationally based on the witness's perception and personal knowledge and such testimony will be helpful to the determination of a fact at issue. The opinion of a lay witness is admissible to verify:

- The general appearance or condition of a person
- The emotional state of a person
- Any proximity sense perception
- The identity of voice, handwriting, or likeness of appearance
- The value of his or her own services
- The rational or irrational conduct and behavior of another person
- The intoxication of another person

Opinion Testimony by Expert Witnesses.   The role of expert witnesses will continue to be expanded, as we have seen in the fraud cases involving Wall Street brokers and other individuals. The expert, like a lay witness, will be subjected to cross-examination. The opinion of the expert witness must be supported by factual and reliable evidence and based on the personal observation of the expert, facts known to the expert at the trial, or information supplied to him or her outside the courtroom or in a hypothetical situation. The expert may state his or her opinion, providing the expert can establish that he or is she is:

- Qualified as an expert in the subject matter issue at hand
- Familiar with the subject matter, and the subject matter is deemed appropriate for expert testimony
- Capable, and it is reasonably probable that his or her opinion or conclusion is based on the subject matter and facts presented

The Hearsay Rule

The hearsay rule is important in documenting evidence for the prosecution of fraud. The Federal Rules of Evidence define hearsay as "statement, other than one made by the declarant while testifying at the trial or hearing, offered in evidence to prove the truth of matter asserted." Generally, if a statement is hearsay and no exception to the rule applies, then the evidence will be excluded upon appropriate objection. Hearsay statements include oral statements, writings, and assertive conduct. Under the Federal Rules, nonassertive conduct is not hearsay, but under the common-law definition of hearsay, statements may include nonassertive conduct.

Hearsay exceptions include:

- Former testimony, which is admissible in a subsequent trial providing the following tests are met:
  - It is shown that the declarant is unavailable at the subsequent trial.
  - The former testimony of the declarant must have been given under oath or sworn affirmation.
  - The former action must involve the same or identical subject matter and cause of action.

  It is essential that all statements secured in any investigation are in writing and sworn statements. There must be convincing evidence that the witness is unavailable to testify.
- Admission by a party opponent involves a statement made or any act or conduct that amounts to prior knowledge by one of the parties to an action of one of the relevant facts being tried. It should be noted that an admission may be inferred from conduct or facial expressions. Another aspect of admissions may occur vicariously when:
  - An admission of one partner, relating to matters what are clearly within the scope of the partnership business, is binding upon co-partners.

— Admissions of one conspirator are made to a third party in further-
ance of a conspiracy to commit a crime at a time when the declarant
was participating in the conspiracy.

These statements are admissible against co-conspirators.

It should be noted that vicarious admissions may not be used where
a principal-agent relationship exists unless the matters were within the
scope of agency. Generally, admissions of a party are not receivable
against his or her coparties merely because they happened to be joined
as parties.

- Declarations of physical or mental conditions, excited and contemporaneous utterance. There are four instances in which such declarations
are admissible due to their reliability:

  — State of mind statements are admissible if they prove a person's
  intent to perform a certain action and such an action was carried out.

  — The excited utterances made during or soon after a startling event
  are admissible when such evidence shows that a startling event did
  occur and the declarant had firsthand knowledge.

  — Personal sense impressions are admissible if the individual had
  firsthand presence and impression of the facts.

  — A declaration of physical condition is admissible if it includes personal knowledge of a person's present bodily condition and is based
  on a spontaneous declaration. Additionally, statements of a person's
  past bodily condition may be admitted to show personal knowledge
  of the condition in question.

- The *Business records* exception to the hearsay rule is critical since it
includes any business records such as audit reports, financial statements,
and business policies. Additionally, any correspondence could be admitted to show that a transaction was completed.

The general rule is that such business records will be admitted as
evidence if they were prepared in the normal course of business and
professional services. The records must be authenticated and, most important, the entrant of the information recorded and such recordings must
have been within the duty of the entrant.

The proof of a fraudulent transaction must be linked to the time period
of the alleged fraud. The maintenance of good business records of all the
monetary transactions or other business activities are helpful in documenting fraudulent conduct. In addition, the auditor's report forms a solid basis
for identifying the existence of fraud in an entity. Any opinion as to the

estimated time frame of the fraudulent conduct could be useful in subsequent investigation and prosecution.

Privileges

The prosecution of fraudulent conduct is sometimes stymied by the accused person's Fifth Amendment right against self-incrimination. This constitutional right provides the individual with the privilege of declining to answer any incriminating or other questions, and protects him or her from being compelled to testify.

Other privileges provided to suspected individuals are as follows:

- The Attorney-client privilege is a long-standing privilege that protects the communication and work products of the attorney and client, providing a bona fide relationship exists. The client is the holder privilege, therefore only he or she can waive this right. Once the accused worker has engaged an attorney, communication between attorney and client will be protected under this privilege.
- Husband–wife privileges include protection of the confidential communication between a husband and wife during a valid marriage. One spouse cannot be compelled to testify against the other in any criminal proceeding. In federal courts, the privilege belongs to the witness spouse, thus the privilege must be claimed by that spouse. A general exception to this rule can be made if there is an action between the spouses and either spouse waives his or her rights.
- Clergymen's, psychologists', and physicians' confidential communications are privileged in many jurisdictions. This privilege, like the attorney-client-privilege, belongs to the client and can be waived by the client alone. There are, however, cases in which the court compelled the production of medical records notwithstanding this privilege. The clergyperson enjoys a strong privilege, and courts find it more difficult to compel any disclosure of the confidential information by a clergyman. It is up to the discretion of the clergy as to what information is disclosed.
- Accountant and auditor privilege exist to protect confidential communications and documents and is similar to the attorney-client privilege. The client may waive this privilege. There is a sufficient number of cases to suggest that the accountant auditor-client relationship could be breached by a court order compelling the disclosure of communication and audit reports when these confidential communications are material to the prosecution of a case or amplification of a fact in issue.

As in all cases, there must be a formal relationship between the parties, and the interaction and communication must have been conducted in the normal course of business.

- Professional journalists generally have no journalist-client privilege; therefore, a journalist can be compelled to disclose any confidential communications and information. Resistance could result in a contempt of court citation.

- Governmental privileges follow the general rule that government can protect the identity of an informer, or official information not otherwise open to the public, by claiming a variety of privileges that include national security, governmental privilege and privacy, and freedom-of-information laws.

Business and industry should remember that the freedom-of-information and privacy laws, both federal and state, provide protection against the disclosure of any personnel records or trade and business secrets. These laws provide very detailed procedures for the prohibition against certain protected disclosures. When faced with a subpoena or request to release confidential information, it is advisable to secure legal advice on the extent of such disclosure.

Summary

The documentation of evidence of fraud must be clear, convincing, and beyond a reasonable doubt if it is a criminal prosecution. If it is a civil matter or under the Federal False Claims Act also known as the Whistle-Blower Law, the burden of proof is lower, merely a "preponderance of evidence" which is required in civil litigation. Real evidence is crucial, and the best evidence will be original documents, and direct evidence of the fraudulent conduct and behavior.

AUDITOR'S/MANAGEMENT ACCOUNTANT'S ROLE IN FRAUD EVIDENTIARY PROCESSES

The auditor's role is very important in this evidentiary gathering process. The auditor must use vigilance while conducting the audit to identify suspected fraud, report it to the appropriate authorities, and stop worrying about being a whistle-blower. The fiduciary and ethical responsibility of the auditor is to identify and report both suspected and actual documented fraud.

Once fraud has been identified, the entity should pursue its further documentation vigorously by any means, including private investigator, legal wiretaps, informants, and careful surveillance of the suspected employee(s). When fraudulent conduct has been established and perpetrators duly identified, it is essential for the entity to be decisive in prosecution and to begin by using suspension, probation, demotion, restitution, and termination actions. Prosecution of a fraud serves as an excellent deterrent. Merely the suspension and firing of an employee alone are insufficient to send a chilling message to other workers—that fraudulent actions will neither pay nor go unheeded. The auditor's fiduciary and ethical responsibilities require vigilance and full disclosure of fraudulent behavior. In this period of malaise and public skepticism, related to audits of the thrifts and savings and loan institutions, it is important that public confidence in the auditor's work be restored. To this end, fraud must be identified and reported in a timely manner.

EVIDENCE AND FRAUD CASE STUDY

John, the manager of a Western Union office, had the combination to the safe. The only other copy of the combination was sealed in an envelope at the company's main office. John had a spotless employment record for 15 years. He had received all the highest employee awards. John was in need of extra cash to pay off gambling debt. He abstracted $10,000 from the company safe. A subsequent audit revealed that the funds were missing. John confessed to taking the money. While the company was conducting its investigation, it was discovered that Tim, a maintenance worker, had removed $300 from a cash register. Tim was caught because he was the only person in the building at the time of theft.

Instructions for Case Study

1. Identify the crimes that were committed by John and Tim.
2. How would you go about obtaining the documentation that will help the prosecutor to secure convictions against John and Tim?
3. Are you convinced that all elements of a crime have been met by the conduct of John and Tim?
4. Assume you are the prosecutor. What arguments would you put forth based on an analysis of the facts and evidence? Identify all the facts with which potential evidentiary question might be associated. Be sure

to discuss the relation of appropriate evidentiary rules to these facts and what variations in the facts might affect the rule's application.

5. Assume you are the defense attorney. What arguments would you put forth based on analysis of the facts and evidence? Identify all the facts with which potential evidentiary questions might be associated. Be sure to discuss the relation of appropriate evidentiary rules to these facts and to discuss what variations in the facts might affect the application of the rules.

6. Assume you are the judge who will be responsible for hearing the facts and ruling on the case. What analysis of the facts will concern you?

7. After responding to all the preceding questions, rule on the motions and the appropriateness of the application of the rules of evidence by both the prosecutor and defense attorney.

Purpose of Exercise

The purpose of this exercise is to provide the reader with experience regarding the application of evidence and evidentiary rules to the prosecution of a case of fraud. Role-playing is also an excellent learning tool for understanding the broad dimensions of fraudulent conduct.

Sample Answer for Case Study

Question No. 1: Identify the Crimes That Were Committed.   These are possible crimes. Ultimately the prosecutor will decide which crimes apply to this case and facts in question.

Crimes by John	Crimes by Tim
1. Embezzlement	1. Theft
2. Theft	2. Larceny

Note: There is no conspiracy, even though these actions occurred in close proximity. Do not confuse employer policies with other criminal charges.

Question No. 2: Obtaining Evidence to Prosecute John and Tim

1. The best evidence will be an eyewitness or a whistle-blower/informant.
2. The video camera's report of these incidents of John and Tim could be useful.

3. A series of interviews (recorded) with John and Tim separately will be important to establish any inconsistencies, admissions, and information regarding the removal of the money.
4. The audit report is crucial in establishing the fact that $10,000 and $300 are unaccounted for during the period in question.
5. A review of the employment record will also be useful in the preparation of charges against John and Tim.
6. John's confession is relevant and, if recorded, will be crucial details in building a case against him.

Question No. 3.   The three elements of a crime were met by John's conduct.

• Actus Rea. The facts indicate that both John and Tim removed money without any permission and with intent to defraud their employer.
• Mens Rea. The facts indicate that both John and Tim intended to take their employer's money and hoped they were not caught. Their mental states appear to be established.
• Causation. The facts indicate that because the money was taken by John and Tim, their action caused the defrauding of the money from their employer.

Question No. 4.   The prosecution must prove beyond a reasonable doubt that John and Tim did take the money.

1. The confession must be presented as voluntarily, knowingly and without any coercion. A videotaped confession is best, an audio tape confession is good, or a written signed statement is also useful.
2. The prosecution must be leery about potential challenges to the confession. Other documentary evidence including the audit report, statements of the defendant(s), and witnesses to the crime will boost the case of the prosecution.
3. The prosecution should be familiar with the company's procedures regarding access to the safe and the internal procedures to protect the company from fraud, embezzlement, and theft of assets.
4. Linking the embezzlement of the money to John's gambling habit and debt will require careful investigation and evidence as to when and how much of the gambling debt was settled/paid around the time of the loss of $10,000.
5. The case against Tim is circumstantial and will require confession, a witness, or video cameras capturing Tim's act of taking the money.

Question No. 5 The Defense Argument.

1. The defense could argue that there is insufficient evidence to convict John and Tim beyond a reasonable doubt.
2. No one saw him take the money. Tim did not confess to the act of theft. Thus, there will need to be direct evidence.
3. John's confession was done under coercion and threats of being fired. Therefore, it is inadmissible. John is now willing to retract his confession.
4. While John admits to having the gambling debt, the monies used to pay his debts were not acquired from the safe of the company.
5. The audit is correct and shows the missing $10,000 and $300, respectively. But this audit alone is not sufficient to conclude who took the money, but merely that the money is missing.

Question No. 6 Judges.

1. The judge(s) must be concerned about evidence and whether the prosecution has proven its case beyond a reasonable doubt.
2. Tim made no confession; there needs to be more convincing and direct evidence on the part of the prosecution to convict Tim.
3. John's confession should be examined to ensure that it was not coerced or defective (e.g., was it in writing, witnessed, or, if recorded, was it authenticated for voice, accuracy, non-tampering, and clarity of sound?)
4. The judge(s) should also examine the basic information regarding the gambling debt to establish valid connections regarding dates of debt and dates of payment in relation to the proximity of the embezzlement/theft of the moneys.
5. The judge(s) will be limited by the presentation of facts, the laws, and cases related to the matters at hand

Question No. 7 The Final Decision.

1. Since this is a simulation, the judges in the role-play will render a decision on the basis of the facts presented and the side (prosecution or defense whose arguments are more convincing).
2. The possible decision in a court of law could be as follows:
   - With respect to the case against Tim, unless there is more proof of the theft or a confession by him, it will be difficult to secure a conviction.

- With respect to John, unless his confession is rule excludable, then the evidence of his control and custodial care of the missing money will be hard for him to overcome. Thus, he could be convicted for embezzlement of the $10,000.

IMPLICATIONS FOR EMPLOYERS

The employer should always consider a three-prong approach to dealing with fraud namely: legal action, restitution, and sanction. The employer must ultimately decide on a course of action which involves all three, or two or one of the remedies. Let's discuss each one.

Legal Action

Turning over the matter to a local prosecutor will still require substantial company resources to assist in the prosecution of the case. Of course, the publicity will serve both as a deterrent and a distraction as the public becomes aware of this matter. The cost or prosecution will be borne for the most part by the local prosecutorial entity, local, state, or federal. The position of this text is that such prosecution should be done as frequently as fraud is detected.

Restitution

A wise employer seeks restitution at any stage of the investigation and prior to turning the matter over to the prosecutor. Each restitution should be done in writing, and witnessed and verified as to the amount provided by the perpetrator.

Employers who fail to secure restitution prior to the case being referred for prosecution should advise the prosecutor that they desire full restitution of their fraudulent losses. Negotiation of a lesser amount should be a matter for you, your legal team, and the prosecutor to decide at any stage of the proceedings. Bear in mind that if the word gets out that fraudulent acts by employees result in only partial payment of the loss, this fact can hurt full recovery.

Sanctions

A vigilant employer will apply a series of sanctions once there is proof that a fraud has been committed by the perpetrator, for instance, an employee. These sanctions could include: suspension pending court resolution of the charges or immediate termination where there is proof beyond a reasonable doubt. Clear documentation of the sanctions should be in the employee's records. In some instances, a leave of absence without pay will suffice until the matter is resolved. Of course, if conviction or proof of fraud results, then termination should follow closely. Another option is probation if the employee is vindicated, but there are still unresolved questions as to questionable professional conduct. The probationary period should be for a specific time period and the expectations and conduct of the employee should be made clear in the document.

Chapter 14

The Legal Cases in Fraud

"Many employees who steal, embezzle are repetitive, checking a potential employee's references and criminal record can weed out a would be embezzler"[1]

Is it possible to reduce the amount of embezzlement cases nationwide that costs companies over $40 billion every year (Risinit, 1999)? In 1997, FBI statistics revealed that there were 17,000 arrests for embezzlement. In commenting on embezzlement, Case said, "It's at all levels, just different types. At the white-collar level, it's fraud and paperwork, and at the lower levels, it's outright removal of cash".[2] Embezzlement goes beyond these types of wrong-doings to include fraud related to the use of property. For example, a local embezzlement case found a Yonkers, New York man guilty of using his company's limousine for trips to Foxwood Casino in Connecticut. These sections will focus on three broad areas, namely:

1. Understanding the Rules of Evidence, the legal evidentiary requirements for documentation, investigation and prosecution of fraud
2. The lessons to be learned from the court cases with respect to prevention, prosecution and restitution related to fraud
3. An examination of the ethical issues related to fraud
   - Protection of whistle-blowers
   - The role of statutes in restitution and prosecution in fraud cases such as RICO law and bankruptcy court laws
   - Evolving Ethical Principles for the Profession

This chapter will provide the reader with a good sense of the implications for fraud, discovery and control. The emphasis will be on the fact that "crime and fraud do not pay". These acts will be detected and vigorously prosecuted by the employer and prosecutorial arm of the local, state or federal government. The legal cases are merely a reminder of the reality of an experience with the courts.

PUBLIC AND PRIVATE FRAUD AGAINST INSTITUTIONS

This section deals with fraud committed against public and private institutions with clear consequences for the perpetrators of fraud. The recent institutional cases such as *Lynons v. U.S.* (1999),[3] in which a church president embezzled millions and was convicted and the case of Medicaid fraud by the Columbia Hospital Group (1999)[4] where several top executives were found guilty of embezzlement. Arney, a Wichita employee of Canford Business College in 1999, was indicted and convicted for embezzlement of $146,704 from federal student loan programs. More recently, the conviction of several executives in the embezzlement trial at the Aids Institute of San Juan, Puerto Rico of $2.2 million dollars illustrates fraud.

CRIMINAL PROSECUTION OF HEALTH CARE FRAUD

In the health care industry, medical professionals are going to jail in record numbers as the federal government attempts to crack down an estimated $12 billion a year in fraudulent Medicare claims. In 1996, Congress passed legislation that increased the spending for investigations and prosecutions of health care fraud. Over $150 million in new funding in 1997 and $47 million served to increase the FBI involvement. Those targeted in the new investigations are doctors, hospitals, nursing homes, home health care agencies, suppliers, medical supplies companies, and billing companies.[5]

The top ten states with the largest number of health care fraud prosecutions by the U.S. Attorney's Office are:

State	No. of Cases Prosecuted	Percent Conviction
1. Florida	345	85
2. Texas	196	89
3. California	171	86
4. Pennsylvania	145	97
5. New York	135	57
6. Illinois	63	96
7. Missouri	61	80
8. Michigan	59	80
9. Georgia	57	47
10. West Virginia	50	90

In reviewing the above chart, only Georgia with 47 percent and New York with a 57 percent conviction rate for fraud, fall below the national conviction rate of 87 percent in 1997. The reasons might include conviction and failure to produce convictable evidence beyond a reasonable doubt.[6]

LEGAL CASES IN FRAUD

The cases which follow deal with embezzlement and misuse of public funds.

The PEOPLE of the State of Illinois,
Plaintiff-Appellee,
V
Raymond J. Gornik, Defendant-Appellant.
No. 3-91-0404
Appellate Court of Illinois
Third District.
April 7, 1992
Rehearing Denied May 22, 1992.

Facts

Raymond J. Gornik, School Superintendent, defendant, was convicted of official misconduct for using monies in an institute fund account for purposes other than those specified in the statute with respect to the expenditure of funds for public school related activities. Defendant was charged with 52 counts of official misconduct (Ill. Rev. Stat. 1987, Ch. 38, pars. 33-3(b)(c)).[7] Much of the state's case consisted of testimony by former employees of the superintendent's office who identified various payments authorized by the defendant that were made from the institute fund account. These payments were the bases of the charges against the defendant and included: expenses related to defendant's attendance at a political seminar; consulting fees to the defendant's brother on matters unrelated to teachers' institutes or workshops; tuition payments for members of the defendant's office staff; donations to various organizations, including the Will County Sheriff's Police Benevolent Fund, the Al-Hamid Temple, the United Pentecostal School, the Guardian Angel Home of Joliet, the Joliet Chamber of Commerce July 4th Celebration, the Joliet Drama Guild, the Joliet Breakfast Lions Club, the Kiwanis Charities and Kappa Alpha Psi Fraternity; tickets for high school football playoff games;

tickets to annual dinner meetings; membership dues in the Joliet Chamber of Commerce and Industry; bottled drinking water for defendant's office staff; two Will County sesquicentennial medallions; rental of parking spaces for defendant's employees; annual membership dues in the Illinois Association of Regional Superintendents of Schools and the University of Illinois Alumni Association; tickets to Chicago White Sox baseball game; and other expenditures unrelated to teacher's institutes or workshops. Two of the defendant's former employees testified that they had questioned the defendant about the propriety of some of these expenditures. In addition, one of these same employees testified that defendant had stated on many occasions that the donations he was making were "going to get me lots of votes."

The defendant testified that he asked the county for an audit shortly after he took office. He later asked the state on numerous occasions to perform an audit but it was never done. The defendant also testified about the various expenditures from the institute fund account. He felt that they were proper and justified and were for educational or education-related programs. For example, defendant stated that he made donations to the United Pentecostal School and the Guardian Angel Home of Joliet because they were doing a "tremendous job" with young people. He provided parking spaces for the women on his staff as a protective measure so they would not have to walk around after dark looking for their cars. The defendant did not feel that he was doing anything improper or illegal. The superintendent's office was audited shortly before the defendant took office and no one had indicated to the defendant that such expenses were improper. Following closing arguments, the defendant was found guilty of 48 counts of official misconduct.

Rule of Law

IL Statute 33-3. Official Misconduct. A public officer or employee commits misconduct when in his or her official capacity, he or she commits the following acts:

- Knowingly performs an act which he knows he or she is forbidden by law to perform.
- With intent to obtain a personal advantage for himself or another, he or she performs an act in excess of his or her lawful authority.

The money was deposited in an account designated as the institute fund. Section 3-12 of the School Code provides in part:

IL Statute 3-12. Institute fund. "All examination, registration, and renewal fees shall be kept by the regional superintendent, together with a record of the names of the persons paying them. Such funds shall be the institute fund and shall be used by the regional superintendent to defray administrative expenses incidental to teacher's institutes, workshops or meetings of a professional nature that that are designed to promote the professional growth of teachers or for the purpose of defraying the expenses of any general or special meeting of teachers or school personnel of the region, which has been approved by the regional superintendent." Ill. Rev. Stat, 987, ch. 122, par. 3-12.

Discussion of Legal Issues

1. Whether the prosecution proved their case beyond a reasonable doubt because the institutional fund contained money from other than those provided by statute?
2. Whether the state proved beyond a reasonable doubt that defendant knew he was forbidden by law to expend the fund in the manner alleged?
3. Whether the evidence seized at his office, primarily records related to the improper expenditures should have been suppressed.

Issue No. 1. The defendant was charged with 41 counts of official misconduct and fraud under Section 33-3(b) of the Criminal Code of 1961 (Illinois. Rev. Stat. 1987, Ch. 38, par. 33-3 (b)). The defendant argued that the state did not prove him guilty beyond a reasonable doubt because the institute fund contained money from other sources than those provided for by the statute. The court found that the facts support the state's case in that the expenditures of those funds by the defendant for purposes other than those authorized by statute were acts forbidden by law and holds the defendant liable.

Issue No. 2. The defendant contended that he did not know the acts were forbidden. The previous administrations spent the funds in ways not authorized by law. Furthermore, he did not attempt to conceal his actions. Therefore, there was no fraud or embezzlement. The court found that in prior cases the essential elements of the crime of fraud beyond a reasonable doubt since the two defendants testified that they warned the defendant about fraudulent expenditure of funds. The court found that the defendant had full knowledge of his fraudulent acts. *People v. Collins* (1985), 106 Ill.2d 237, 87 Ill. Dec 910, 478, N.E. 2d 267).[8] Two defendants testified that they warned the defendant about fraudulent expenditure of funds. The defendant Gornik in this case admitted he knew that expenditures of funds received by his office for "teachers' certificates, bus receipts, and GED testing" were restricted by statute. Thus the defendant's argument of not knowing the law was unfounded.

Issue No. 3. The defendant contends that the evidence seized at his office, primarily records related to the improper or fraudulent expenditure of funds should have been suppressed. The affidavit signed by Will County Sheriff on February 14, 1990 quoted that the basis for the search established probable cause based on information on an article by a local reporter. Using the Freedom of Information Act, the reporter established that the defendant fraudulently used public funds to pay for various political, charitable, and personal expenses, including tickets to the White Sox baseball games, alumni dues, and political seminars.

The defendant acknowledged that no motion to suppress was filed nor was any objection made by counsel during the trial or post-trial motion. The court found that under the plain error rule (134, Ill.2d r.615(a)), the court will not consider a defendant's claim unless it is presented to the trial court (*People v. Speed* (1982) 106. Ill. App. 3d.890.62 Ill. 686, 436 N.E.2d 712).[9] To preserve an issue, it must be raised at trial and a written post-trial motion raising the issue was required (*People v. Steidl* (1991), 142 Ill. 2d 204, 154 Ill Dec 616, 568 N.N. 2d 837).[10] The evidence seized in this case was in fact trustworthy and there was no indication that if the state was alerted to any alleged deficiency in the search warrant, it could not have introduced more credible evidence to establish probable cause. Because these issues were not raised, they are waived.

Holding/Decision

Justice Slater, on behalf of the appellate court and Justices Barry, P.J., and Stouder, J., concurred. The Illinois court held that:

1. The prosecution did prove their case beyond a reasonable doubt as provided by criminal and education statutes.
2. The state proved beyond a reasonable doubt that the defendant knew that he was forbidden by law to expend or illegally use the funds for his own purposes.
3. The evidence seized at his office, primarily records related to the improper expenditures, should not be suppressed since the defendant failed to raise the suppression issues at trial or failed to show that these

records were not official business records of his employer and records required to be kept as a matter of the proper execution of his duties.

Therefore, the conviction on misuse and fraudulent use of the state funds for personal and political benefits were upheld.

To successfully secure a conviction for misconduct and fraud, the prosecution (employer) must prove beyond a reasonable doubt

1. The audit was performed to establish the facts of wrong-doing.
2. The records needed for prosecution should be seized (secured) promptly—with a warrant/subpoena or voluntary.
3. The defendant does not have a claim to privacy of records stored in his office if those records are recorded or kept as part of the official job responsibility.
4. The evidence required to secure this conviction had to be direct, clear, and convincing from records and the witnesses who testified against the defendant.

Implications for Internal Controls/Fraud Prevention

1. Good Faith/No Intent to Defraud is not a Defense. While the defendant maintains that he was acting in good faith and he believed the expenditures were proper, there was also evidence that the defendant was motivated by self-interest. As our supreme court stated in a related context:

"Almost every example of official conduct could be classified as 'mixed politicians' are experts at making their self-dealing appear to be in the best interests of their constituents. To allow instances of self-dealing to go unpunished merely because the benefit the public official receives is 'incidental' or because the municipality receives the lion's share of the benefit would effectively prohibit the State from prosecuting all but the most egregious cases of official misconduct." *People v. Scharlau* (1990), 141 Ill.2d. 180, 199, 152 Ill.Dec. 401, 410, 565 N.E.2d 1319, 1328.[11]

2. Public Officials have no immunity from prosecution for fraud embezzlement. The plain rule in this case is that public officials, including School Superintendents, have a fiduciary responsibility to expend funds entrusted to them in honest, statutory, appropriate and legal sound ways that protect the integrity of the office and the internal controls set forth by local accounting rules and statutes. The expenditure of public funds for personal benefits like baseball tickets, political seminars, etc. will be viewed as embezzlement, fraudulent and actionable under existing criminal statutes.

EMBEZZLEMENT OF PUBLIC HOSPITAL FUND

U.S. 11th Circuit Court of Appeals
U.S. v. Fischer[12]
United States of America, Plaintiff-Appellee,
v.
Jeffrey Allan Fischer, Defendant-Appellant.
Nos. 96-3587, 97-2877 and 98-2091
United States Courts of Appeals,
Eleventh Circuit
March 4, 1999.

Appeal from the United States District Court for the Middle District of
Florida (No. 95-239-CR-Orl-22), Anne C. Conway, Judge.
Before Anderson and Hull, Circuit Judges, and Hancock, Senior District
Judge.

Facts

A jury convicted appellant Jeffrey Allan Fischer on 13 counts, including
violations of 18 U.S.C. §371 (conspiracy), 666 (fraud and bribery involving
an organization receiving federal funds), 1341 (mail fraud), 1343 (wire
fraud), and 1957 (money laundering). Fischer appeals his convictions and
65-month sentence.

$1.2 Million Loan. At trial, the evidence established that in 1993,
Fischer, as president and part-owner of QMC, arranged for West Volusia
Hospital Authority ("WVHA") to loan $1.2 million to QMC. Fischer
negotiated this loan with WVHA's chief financial officer, Robert Caddick.
On June 30, 1993, Fisher and Caddick executed the loan agreements
between QMC and WVHA. As security for the $1.2 million loan, Fischer
pledged QMC's accounts receivable and a $1 million letter of credit
QMC had obtained for this purpose through a foreign bank, First Asia
Development Bank ("FADB"). However, QMC's accounts receivable
already were pledged to another QMC creditor. In addition, the $1 million
letter of credit did not appear to be legitimate and even if it were, its terms
severely limited WVHA's ability to collect $1 million.

Furthermore, questions were raised about WVHA's authority to loan
money to QMC. The question arose both before WVHA loaned the $1.2
million to QMC and later, when WVHA's board of directors discovered
the loan had been made. WVHA, a local government agency funded by

a bond issue, was authorized to invest its excess funds only in instruments backed by the federal government.

Nonetheless, WVHA made the $1.2 million loan to QMC on July 2, 1993. QMC used the $1.2 million to repay creditors and to raise the salaries of QMC's five owner-employees, including Fischer. In addition, Fischer had QMC lend at least $100,000 to a company owned by the FADB representative who had assisted QMC with the $1 million letter of credit. Fischer also had QMC open options-trading accounts using these loan proceeds.

In a short time, Fischer lost about $400,000 of the loan proceeds through his options-trading on QMC's behalf. In February 1994, WVHA auditors disclosed the $1.2 million loan to QMC in the annual audit report. Through this report, WVHA's board of directors and the chairman of WVHA's finance committee first learned about the $1.2 million loan. Shortly thereafter, the board asked that the loan be called. The due date for the loan was July 1, 1994.

On July 1, 1994, QMC did not have the funds to repay the loan. Later that month, Fischer persuaded FADB to send QMC a $1.2 million draft to repay WVHA. QMC endorsed this draft and presented it to WVHA, which in turn presented the draft to its bank. However, FADB refused to honor the draft when presented by WVHA's bank. Thus, WVHA was unable to collect the $1.2 million owed by QMC.

$10,000 Kickback to Caddick. The evidence indicated that in June 1993, Caddick requested a $10,000 loan from QMC at the end of one of Fischer and Caddick's initial meetings about the possibility of the $1.2 million loan. After the QMC received the $1.2 million loan from WVHA, QMC paid $10,000 by check to Caddick's mother, Stella Greenfield, August 1993. This $10,000 check, paid with Fischer's approval, was marked "consulting fees"—even though Greenfield never performed any services for QMC. Greenfield sent the proceeds of the $10,000 check to Caddick, pursuant to Caddick's instructions.

In January 1994, a QMC bookkeeper sought an invoice to correspond with the earlier $10,000 check to Greenfield. The bookkeeper received an invoice dated August 1, 1993. A notation appeared on the invoice in Fischer's handwriting, indicating that the payment was for a "loan origination fee."

Another attempt to cover up QMC's $10,000 payment to Caddick apparently was made after QMC defaulted on the $1.2 million loan from WVHA and that default became the subject of an investigation and widespread publicity. In this cover-up attempt, Caddick allegedly approached

QMC's vice-president, Charles Kramer, with a "contract" for programming services Caddick purportedly had performed for QMC. Caddick allegedly asked Kramer to sign and backdate the "contract" to create a retroactive justification for the $10,000 payment. However, Kramer refused.

Rule of Law

Scope of 18 U.S.C. §666.

The statutory prerequisite for a conviction under the 18 U.S.C. §666 is that the organization or agency affected by the fraud, unauthorized conversion, bribery, or other prohibited act "receives, in any one-year period, benefits in excess of $10,000 under a federal program involving a grant, contract, subsidy, loan, guarantee, insurance, or other form of federal assistance." 18 U.S.C. §666(b). In the present case, the primary issue is whether WVHA received benefits under a federal assistance program for purposes of §666(b). The court found that a receipt of between $10 and $15 million in Medicare funds qualified as receipt of benefits under a federal assistance program and that the government presented sufficient evidence to satisfy the requirements of 18 U.S.C. §666(b).

1. Whether Fischer, President of West Volusia Hospital Authority (WVHA) has received and violated 18 U.S.C. §666(a)(1) and (a)(2)?
2. Was there sufficiency of the Government's Evidence under §666(b) to convict Fischer of mail fraud, embezzlement and money laundering?
3. Was the target recipient analysis required for a conviction of fraud?

Discussion of the Issues in Fraud

Violation of 18 USC §666(a)(1) and (a)(2).   To establish that Fischer had violated 18 U.S.C. §666(a)(2), the government was required to prove that WVHA was an agency receiving in any one period, benefits in excess of $10,000 under a federal assistance program. 18 U.S.C. §666(b). At trial, the government introduced evidence that WVHA was the county agency responsible for operating two county hospitals. The government also introduced testimony from WVHA's director of finance that "most health care organizations collect a majority of their funds from programs that are funded by the federal government." Asked to give an example of how much money WVHA specifically collected in 1993 from the federal government under the Medicare program alone, WVHA's director of finance testified that WVHA had collected between $10 and $15 million dollars in Medicare in 1993. Thus, according to the testimony of WVHA's director of finance, even if the hospital charges the patient an increased amount of services, the hospital is paid only a fixed amount from Medicare for those services.

This court previously addressed the scope of §666(b) in *United States v. Copeland*, 143 F.3d 1439 (11th Cir. 1998). At issue in Copeland was whether Lockheed, a prime contractor for the United States Department of Defense, qualified as an organization receiving benefit for purposes of §666 by accepting bribes from individuals including co-defendant Winders. Id at 1440. In turn, defendant Winders had been convicted of violating 18 U.S.C. §666 by giving bribes to co-defendant Copeland. Id. On appeal, the defendants argued that their convictions under §666 should be reversed because the government had failed to prove that Lockheed met the requirements of §666(b). Id. In reviewing the defendant's claims in Copeland, this Court examined the statutory language and construed §666(b) as requiring that the benefits an organization or agency receives from the federal government be linked to some form of federal assistance. Id. at 1441. Specifically, this court recognized that engaging in contractual relationships with the federal government would fall within the scope of the statute, if those contractual relationships constituted some form of federal assistance.

In the Fischer case, the court established that he received bribes and that since this hospital was not a commercial entity like Copeland, Lockheed. In Fisher's case, the funds were received under the federal program, thus the statute applied to Fischer and his conduct can be prosecuted under federal fraud statutes.

Sufficiency of the Government's Evidence Under §666(b).   The evidence in the present case contracts sharply with the evidence in Copeland. Whereas Lockheed received federal dollars through purely commercial transactions, WVHA, as an agency responsible for the administration of two hospitals, actually received payments from the federal government. In fact, WVHA finance director's testimony indicated that the $10 to $15 million WVHA collected under the Medicare program in 1993 was paid directly to WVHA for providing health care services to covered individuals.

Section 666(b) provided that the benefits an organization receives under a federal program can be in form of "a grant, contract, subsidy, loan, guarantee, insurance, or other form of federal assistance." 18 U.S.C. §666(b) (emphasis added). Because WVHA received payments under a federal assistance, WVHA received a type of benefits expressly covered by §666(b). Thus the statutory prerequisite for Fischer's convictions under §666 was satisfied.

In this case, the court determined that WVHA is an agency receiving benefits within the meaning of §666(b), thus the illegal embezzlement of funds by Fischer is covered by the statute which prohibits anyone receiving federal funds from committing "fraud, theft, and undue influence by bribery related to the money distributed to health care providers."

"Target Recipient" Analysis Not Required.   Fischer's main argument that the Medicare funds received by WVHA are not benefits for purposes of §666(b). This concept relies on a narrow construction of "benefits" that does not consider the context in which the term appears. Fischer primarily bases his argument on a district court decision in *United States v. Lahue,* 998 F.Supp. 1182 (D. Kan. 1998). In Lahue, the court concluded that a group of physicians who received Medicare funds and, more specifically, funds under Medicare Part B, as payment for their services had not received benefits for purposes of 18 U.S.C. §666(b). Id. At 1186–87, 1192.

The Court

The court declined to adopt the Lahue analysis. It first noted that in this case, the testimony of WVHA's finance director indicated that in 1993 WVHA received $10 to $15 million from the Medicare program. The finance director's testimony did not clearly establish whether WVHA received funds directly from the Medicare program or received funds as an assignee under Part B or even Part A of the federal program. Thus, there is a possibility in this case that WVHA received funds directly from the Medicare program without having been assigned the right to receive those funds by a patient. However, even if WVHA received funds as an assignee, the plain language of §666(b) does not distinguish between an organization, government, or agency that receives benefits directly under a federal program and an organization, government, or agency that receives benefits as an assignee under a federal program.

The language of §666(b) does not require that the "organization, government, or agency receiving . . . benefits" be the target recipient of the federal program at issue. Instead, the language focuses on the source of the benefits, requiring that the benefits have been received "under a federal program involving a grant, contract, subsidy, loan, guarantee, insurance, or other form of federal assistance." 18 U.S.C. §666(b).

Thus, in context, the use of the term "benefits" serves to emphasize not that the recipient must be a target recipient, but rather that the funds must have been received by the organization, government, or agency as part of an assistance program, rather than a purely commercial transaction—the federal government's purchase of goods from a contractor, for example. See *United States v. Copeland,* 143 F.3d 1439 (11th Cir. 1998).[13]

Decision/Holding

Fischer contends, *inter alia,* that his convictions on two counts under §666 and on related conspiracy counts should be reversed because the government did not prove the statutory prerequisite that the agency affected by Fischer's wrongdoing "received, in any one-year period, benefits in excess of $10,000 from a federal program involving a grant, subsidy, loan, guarantee, insurance, or other form of federal assistance." (8 U.S.C. §666(b).) After review, the court affirmed Fischer's conviction and sentence which included a 65-month sentence.

Implications for Internal Controls and Fraud Prevention

Beware if your business is receiving federal funds; the federal statutes are very clear about detecting and prosecuting fraud. The courts already have held that the government is not required to prove a direct link between the federal assistance and the fraudulent conduct in the issue. *United States v. Paradies,* 98 F.3d 1266-89 (11th Cir. 1996).[14] (A direct "connection to federal funds" is not required for a conviction under §666). Instead §666(b) requires the government to prove that WVHA is an agency that receives "benefits in excess of $10,000" under a federal assistance program, as we have already determined that the government has done. See 18 U.S.C. §666; *United States v. Copeland,* 143 F.3d 1439 (11th Cir. 1998). Thus, here the government was not required to prove a direct link between the Medicare funds received by WVHA and either Fischer's fraudulently obtaining and converting the $1.2 million loan from WVHA or Fischer's bribing an agent of WVHA in connection with $1.2 million loan.

The government can introduce into evidence past acts of fraud as in the case of Fischer by showing that Fischer had a pattern of fraudulently obtaining money and then using that money to speculate in the securities market. The government further introduced evidence that Fischer embezzled $2 million of his clients' money and thereafter lost $2 million speculating in the securities market. This past conduct of fraud can be introduced by the government.

Employers who do routine criminal background checks could uncover prior fraudulent behavior of employees who will have access to or directly handle large financial transactions.

Internal audit checks based on sound internal control processes mentioned in this book would identify, deter, and prevent fraud in the business or organizational entity.

PROSECUTION OF EMBEZZLEMENT AND FRAUD

The following section explains successful prosecutions of fraud against business owners with a fiduciary responsibilities.

Charles Esskuchen, Defendant
vs.
State of Florida, Prosecutor
Circuit Court,
Volusia County, Florida
April 26, 1999.

Facts

Charles Esskuchen, a Deltona businessman, was charged with 77 counts of racketeering, fraud, and illegal securities sales for using his mortgage and lending company to swindle investors of several million dollars. Esskuchen was accused of accepting money from new investors to pay previous ones. From January 1, 1995 through December 31, 1996, Esskuchen companies, ENC Mortgage and Lending Inc. and ECN Corporation, were used as depositories for money he and his staff collected from 150 people who invested amounts ranging from $5,000 to $1,000,000. The state sought 20 years and restitution of the defrauded funds.[15]

Issue

Did the state prove beyond a reasonable doubt that Esskuchen had committed fraud?

Holding

In his decision, Judge McFerrin-Smith found that Esskuchen was guilty as set forth by a jury, which convicted him of 77 counts of racketeering, fraud, and illegal security sales to swindle investors. The court ordered a sentence of nine and a half years in prison for one count and a concurrent five years for the remaining counts, plus 20 years' probation. The judge also ordered restitution to the investors. A restitution hearing was scheduled to determine how the forfeited money would be repaid to investors.

Implications for Prosecution and Prevention of Fraud

1. The defendant lost his plea to stay free while he made restitution. The court in its decision was clear that the investors trusted the defendant. His conduct, which included a lavish lifestyle, was his own doing, thus, the defendant must accept the consequences.

2. The court followed previous precedents by using a sentence which included jail time of over nine years, 20 years' probation after the prison term is served, and restitution of funds to the investor. On the later point of restitution, the defendant expressed that even while he was on trial one of his businesses, a skating center, was sold for $875,355.75. All of the defendants' assets will be liquidated by the court and the proceeds distributed to the investors (victims of this fraud).

3. The fundamental concern is that fraud always takes a bite out of the assets of innocent citizens. In this case, a retired physician who lost nearly $800,000 dollars, blamed his wife's death on the defendant's fraud. These angry statements were expressed in court. Another victim, Julia Fletcher, 73-years-old, said in court papers, "an Ocala investor lost $100,000 dollars she invested from her dead husband's life insurance policy."

4. Is nine and a half years' jail time, 20 years' probation and restitution a just punishment for defrauding over $8 million dollars from investors who invested from $5,000 to $1 million dollars? As one investor said, "I think he got what he deserves. I wish he could have gotten more time but we have to take what we can get sometimes."

5. The unequivocal message is that securities fraud will be vigorously prosecuted. This prosecution is necessary because it is a crime and the public policy requires that the court protect the investments of citizens from unscrupulous investors.

EMBEZZLEMENT FROM BEST WESTERN INN

Martin J. Donohue, Appellant,

v.

State of Florida, Appellee.

No. 88-1069.
District Court of Appeal of Florida,
Fifth District.
August 24, 1989

Appeal from the Circuit Court for Volusia County; Uriel Blount, Jr., Judge; James B. Gibson, Public Defender; and Barbara C. Davis, Assistant Public Defender; Daytona Beach, for appellant.

Robert A. Butterworth, Attorney General, Tallahassee, and Colin Campbell, Assistant Attorney General, Daytona Beach, for apellee.

Sharp, Judge.

Facts

Donohue appeals from a judgment and sentence after a jury found him guilty of second-degree grand theft in connection with the embezzlement of funds from the Best Western Deltona Inn. The judgement and sentence was affirmed, except for those portions of the sentence which imposed costs and require a probation officer to determine a repayment schedule of $14,400 in restitution ordered by the court.[16]

Rule of the Law

FN1. 812.014 (1) and (2) (c), Fla. Stat. (1985).

FN2. Likewise, the determination of the amount of restitution is a nondelegable judicial determination. *Fresneda v. State,* 347 So. 2d 1021 (Fla. 1977)[17]; *Balance v. State,* 447 So. 2d 974 (Fla. 1st DCA 1984).[18]

Discussion of Issues

Can the probation officer determine the repayment of the restitution?

Both sides agreed that costs were improperly imposed without prior notice to Donohue, and that this portion of the sentence should be quashed. *Wood v. State,* 544 So. 2d 1004 (Fla. 1989); *Mays v. State,* 519 So. 2d 618 (Fla. 1988). The sentence provides that restitution of $14,400 is to be paid "at a rate to be determined by your Probation Officer."

A probation officer may monitor a probationer's economic circumstances during the probationary period, notify the court when a probationer appears to have the ability to commence restitution repayment, and furnish the court with a recommended repayment schedule. However, the determination of the probationer's ability to pay is a nondelegable judicial responsibility. *Balance v. State,* 447 So. 2d 974 (Fla. 1st DCA 1984); *Fletcher v. State of Florida,* 405 So. 2d 748 (Fla. 1st DCA 1981).[19]

Holding/Decision

Thus, "we squash the imposition of costs and that portion of the sentence directing Donohue's probation officer to set a restitution repayment schedule, and we remand the sentence to the trial court to make appropriate corrections in accordance with this opinion."

The case was Affirmed in part; Quashed in part; and Remanded with directions. Cobb and Cowart, J.J., Concur.

Implications for Prosecution and Prevention of Fraud

1. The appellate court upheld the defendant's conviction on embezzlement and grand theft. The only portion of the sentence that changed was the fact that the trial court ordered the probation officer to determine a restitution plan consistent with court guidelines.
2. Employers and victims of fraud should insist that as part of the sentence, the court and only the court will be involved in the delicate process of setting a restitution repayment schedule. This means that the court will supervise the collection of all assets of the convicted defendant and the court will determine an equitable distribution of assets towards the restitution repayment schedule.

BANKRUPTCY FRAUD OVERVIEW

The following personal fraud cases were secured from Bankruptcy Cases— Bankruptcy Fraud, second, third, fourth quarters, postings, 1998. These reports come out of the United States Trustee Program's statutorily mandated duties, which include policing the bankruptcy system for criminal activity, undue delay, and abusive filings. Below are some cases of fraudulent activities of debtors and professionals. This is an area of fraud that reaches to the fiduciary responsibility of the accountants, attorneys, and individuals that file bankruptcy papers with the court. As quiet as it's kept, the convicted persons in bankruptcy fraud are attorneys, accountants, paralegals, businesspersons, and citizens from all backgrounds. The cases that follow focus on accounting and financial statements fraud. See Exhibit 14.1 for a summary.

Exhibit 14.1.   Cases of Bankruptcy Fraud

State/ Region	Defendant	Charge	Sentence
Minnesota (Reg. 12)	Allen Hamilton Bates	Fraudulent statements, no accountant has books	Guilty: Fine $5,000. 200 hours community service Five years probation.
New York (reg. 2)	Donna Quinn, Esq.	Embezzlement of client funds	Guilty: three years probation Six month home confinement 100 hours community service. Restitution $231,606.29 plus 17,166.85 interest earned.

Bankruptcy Fraud—Why Should Accountants Be Concerned?

The review of over 250 fraud cases in 1998 resulted in the prosecution and conviction for bankruptcy and other related fraud. This area of fraud is presented for the accountant reader because the financial statements, filing petitions, and court papers are often prepared by an attorney with help from the accountant. Petitioners file financial statements prepared by their accountant in which might be concealment of assets. It is essential that management accountants and fraud auditors pay close attention to this new frontier of fraud with a close eye. When prosecuted, it often results in a) incarceration b) monetary fines c) restitution of defrauded funds and d) sanctions to the perpetrator which could include disbarment from practice of law and other professional sanctions which limit the professional's ability to practice in the profession. These cases of fraud reflect some of the cases that were prosecuted and the convictions that were secured. (United States Trustees Program, Department of Justice http://www. USDOJGov/bffist 98.htm. page last updated on August 26, 1998).[20]

Minneapolis, District of (Region 12): Accounting Books/Fraudulent Declarations (Jan. 1998)

On January 16, 1998, Allen Hamilton Bates, a nationally known actor from Minneapolis who has appeared in *The Fugitive, Untamed Heart,*

Chain Reaction, and *Only the Lonely,* pleased guilty to one count of bankruptcy fraud for making false declarations and statements in his bankruptcy schedules and testimony. According to the charging documents, Mr. Bates falsely declared in his bankruptcy schedules that no accountant was in possession of his books and records. In fact, essentially all of Bates's books were in possession and control of an accountant who had both kept and supervised the keeping of his books and records in the prior six years. An investigation of these books and records revealed that Mr. Bates also failed to disclose his right to receive several hundred thousand dollars in residual fees from pre-petition productions.

As part of the plea agreement, Bates was fined $5,000, and ordered to perform 200 hours of community service, and placed on five years' probation. It should be noted that this case was generated with the investigation of the Federal Bureau of Investigation and the office of the United States Trustee in Minneapolis.

New York, Northern District of (Region 2): Embezzlement of Client Funds (Jan–March 1998)

As a result of a referral by the United States Trustee, Donna M. Quinn, Esq. pled guilty to the post-confirmation embezzlement of $231,606.29 while serving as the attorney for the unsecured creditors committee in the U.S. Commstruct, Inc. Chapter 11 case.

She was sentenced to three years' probation, six months' home confinement, 100 hours of community service, and ordered to pay restitution in the amount of the embezzled monies she had not returned prior to her detection. On the United States Trustee's motion pursuant to 11 U.S.C. §§543 and 329, the court directed Ms. Quinn to disgorge $54,868 in attorney's fees and expenses received in the U.S. Commstruct Inc. and related cases. The motion was filed prior to the criminal prosecution and had been pending for over a year. The Chapter 7 trustee in the now converted case has reduced the order to a judgement and is seeking its execution against Ms. Quinn's assets with the hope that additional assets will be available to pay creditors. (http://www.usdoj.gov/ust/bf1st98.htm, 1998)[21].

These cases are discussed in detail below and could be reviewed by referring to the United States Trustee Program/Department of Justice http://www.Usdoj.gov/ust/bf2nd/98.htm and 3rd 98. Htm, 1998.[22]

This next case is critical in defining the role of the accountant in the detection of fraud. The Loewenkenherz case demonstrates the role of the accountant in discovering that the trustee was involved in theft and embezzlement of the assets entrusted to him.

Oklahoma, Northern District of (Region 20): Embezzlement and Bankruptcy Fraud

Rick Loewenkenherz, a former Chapter 11 trustee, was convicted of bankruptcy fraud under a plea agreement and was sentenced to 15 months in prison, three years' supervised release, and ordered to pay restitution in the amount of $30,000. (See Exhibit 14.2.) Mr. Loewenkenherz is an attorney who was appointed and served as a Chapter 11 trustee in two cases prior to the authorization of the United States Trustee in the Tenth Circuit. On the eve of final distribution in the cases, Mr. Loewenkenherz misappropriated the funds. The theft was discovered by the accountant and attorney for the trustee and brought to the attention of the Assistant United States Trustee in Tulsa, who made the criminal referral. The Tulsa staff, working closely with the FBI and United States Attorney, assisted with the investigation and sought the removal of Mr. Loewenkenherz. In one case, the United States Trustee moved for conversion of the case and then served as Chapter 7 trustee. In proposing distribution of the remaining funds as well as the claims against the former trustee, the United States Trustee entered into an agreement with the Internal Revenue Service, the largest creditor, to assign the bond claim and any rights to restitution against the former trustee, thereby allowing the cases to be closed.

Implications for Prosecution and Prevention of Fraud

1. The Oklahoma case of Loewenkenherz was a classic case in which the accountant and the attorney for the trustee discovered the theft of funds. The matter was then referred for criminal prosecution. This discovery underscores the focus of this book in that whenever an accountant or auditor reviews the books and financial records of an entity, it is essential to look for the ever-present factors of fraud and embezzlement.

Exhibit 14.2 Cases in Bankruptcy

State	Defendant	Charges of Fraud	Sentence
Oklahoma (Reg. 20)	Rick Loewen-kenherz	Bankruptcy, theft, embezzlement	Guilty: 15 months in prison; three years supervised release. $30,000 restitution.

2. The Loewenkenherz case reminds the management accountant and the fraud auditor about their responsibility to detect fraud in every aspect of the accounting practice including auditing, preparation of financial statements, and the review of accounting records upon whose statements a third party relies on for accuracy and truth.

Texas, Northern District of (Region 6): Fund Account/Client Account Fraud

In Morgan's Chapter 11 case, the U.S. Trustee filed a motion under section 329 of the Bankruptcy Code and Federal Rule of Bankruptcy Procedure 2017, seeking review of payments made by the debtors to their counsel, James D. Norvell. During discovery regarding the matter, the U.S. Trustee obtained and reviewed records of Mr. Norvell's client trust account. These records revealed that Mr. Norvell was improperly invading the account and had been operating out of trust for a period of at least a year. When confronted with this evidence, Mr. Norvell agreed to refund the sum of $5,000 to both the debtors and his former associate, resign from admission to practice before the U.S. District Court, and refrain from representing any party in a proceeding before any U.S. bankruptcy court. The bankruptcy court has now approved this agreement. A referral regarding the matter has been forwarded to the State Bar of Texas for sanctions against the attorney.

Ohio, Northern District of (Region 9): Accounting Systems False Filing Fraud

The Sixth Circuit Court of Appeals affirmed the order of the U.S. District Court supporting the denial of accounting fees in the amount of approximately $90,000 sought by Delphia Accounting Systems, Inc. In the Chapter 11 case of *Beaver Office Products, Inc. Delphia Accounting Systems, Inc. v. Donald M. Robiner, United States Trustee, et al.* Delphia Accounting Systems, Inc. received preferential payments from the debtor pre-petition, but failed to reveal the receipt of these payments in its affidavit filed under Bankruptcy Rule 2014. Delphia also received post-petition fee payments.

Texas, Western District of (Region 7): Fraudulent Accounting Practices

In the case of The Care Group, Inc., Case No. 98-13247-FM, a publicly traded company that was de-listed from NASDAQ in June 1998, and 19 of its subsidiaries filed for protection under Chapter 11 on September 15,

1998. The Austin Division was the proper venue for filing based upon the location of the order filler, headquartered in Austin. The debtors offer home health care for critically ill patients. The filing was prompt when, during the course of an annual audit, it was discovered that the CFO had been misrepresenting the aging of nonexistent accounts receivable, leaving the companies in default with its secured lender, and with no operating capital. The debtors sought joint administration of the cases, which the court approved.

Implications for Prosecution and Prevention of Fraud

While there are over 220 more cases in the realm of bankruptcy fraud, it is essential to discuss these final cases that pertain to the accounting profession in particular.

Norvell Case.   Norvell was convicted for co-mingling client funds and improperly invading $5,000.00 client funds. This misconduct was unearthed when an audit of Norvell's books was done.

Delphia Case.   This case indicates the court's disdain for an accounting firm's deliberate attempt to conceal and defraud the bankruptcy court by receiving certain fees without court authority. Additionally, there was evidence of preferential payments from the debtor prepetition. This is a clear signal of a $90,000 denial of fees, a severe sanction by the court against the accounting firm.

Exhibit 14.3   Accounting-Related Fraud and Bankruptcy

Client	Charge of Fraud	Sentence
Novell	Co-mingling of client fund account	Guilty. Restitution of $5,000. Resign from admission to practice before U.S. District Court/U.S. Bankruptcy Court
Delphia Accounting Systems	Bankruptcy fraud and concealment of payments	Guilty. Denial of $90,000 accounting fees. Sanction for fraudulent accounting statements.
The Care Group Inc.	Fraudulent accounting system	Court Grant Chapter 11 debtors reorganization.

The Care Group Inc. Case.   The Chief Financial Officer (CFO) of the corporation has been misrepresenting the aging of non-existing accounts, leaving the company in default with its secured lender and with no operating capital. This case raises the question: why wasn't this fraudulent conduct on the books uncovered by routine and annual audits of the firm? In order to uncover the fraud it took an investigation by the court and audit of the books to uncover this fraudulent behavior.

FRAUD IN GOVERNMENT OPERATIONS

The premise of the author in this section is that government fraud is widespread in every branch of the government including the IRS, the military sector, federal, state and local governments, the White House travel office, and even the Post Office services. The central themes in the cases that are presented include:

• How successful are the prosecutions of governmental fraudulent acts?
• How many of these prosecutions of governmental frauds result in restitution?
• Is there evidence of a prosecutional strategy which includes jail terms, restitution, sanctions, or fines?

Case of an IRS Agent

In a Washington Associated Press release in November, 1999, it was reported that Internal Revenue Service employees stole at least $5.3 million sent in by taxpayers over a recent two-and-a-half year period including one scheme in which a check to the IRS was altered to read "I.R. Smith" according to an audit by the General Accounting Office (GAO). The chief of the IRS Service Centers, Jimmy Smith said, "he has no quarrel with the GAO findings. The problem is among a tiny fraction of the 25,000 employees who handle the payments and refunds for about 200 million tax returns." Despite Mr. Smith's reassurance that theft and embezzlement are rare, the GAO report documented that at least $5.3 million in theft and embezzled IRS funds were taken during January, 1995 to July, 1997. This report included one instance where an employee of the IRS stole a check for $590,000. Duplicate checks with forged signatures and payees were made in the name of the perpetrators. Several of the checks were cashed before being discovered by the taxpayer and reporter to the IRS. Another IRS employee, a tax examiner with the ability to adjust taxpayer accounts, used the payments to fraudulently issue 10 refund checks to herself using her maiden name. The total embezzled was $269,000.[23]

Implications of Fraud for Prosecution and Prevention of Fraud

1. While these are rare occurrences of fraud in the IRS operations, the fact that they occurred and continue to occur signals the need for better internal controls against fraud.

2. The GAO's audit clearly identified that the IRS was lax in its internal controls which deter fraud at its 10 service centers.

3. The IRS must go beyond surveillance cameras to proper tracking of receipts to establish a check and balance system that includes an independent audit team at each center that audits receipts, contacts taxpayers to verify payments and assessments, and a system that routinely checks the accuracy of reporting by tax examiners and other IRS agents.

This case of IRS fraud is a reminder that even government agencies are not immune from fraudulent acts by employees. Some other cases of governmental fraud include:

- Air Force Staff Sgt. Robert L. Miller, former pay official in Kellering, Ohio, stole $435,000. He was convicted in 1999.

- Air Force contracting specialist, Mark Krenido, sent $504,461 in checks to a phony corporation that was based in a post office he operated. He pleaded guilty to embezzlement in 1996.

- Civilian worker, James Lugas, who worked at the now-closed Reese Air Force Base in Texas, was imprisoned for collecting $2 million for a lavish lifestyle, including six Corvettes that were seized by law enforcement officials in 1992.

- In a $2.2 million embezzlement case involving now-defunct San Juan AIDS institute, 11 people were charged with crimes of conspiracy, money laundering, and theft of federal funds. Five pleaded guilty and were sentenced by trial courts in Puerto Rico in 1999.

- Betty Igl, a postmaster fired in Dousman, Wisconsin, was accused of mailing fliers for a charity she founded without paying about $10,000 in postage. She mailed the materials twice a year for two years. The government has not decided to file federal criminal charges as of March 7, 1999.

- The White House travel office director was acquitted of embezzlement, 1995. This was a case with much national attention. A case that Independent Counsel Judge Starr vigorously prosecuted without any convictions.

The cases that follow will demonstrate the seriousness of fraud against the government but in no way represents all of the important cases of fraud. These cases require proof of intent to defraud. Sloppy accounting is not fraud against the government.

Bates v. United States

No. 96-7185

Argued October 7, 1997

Decided November 4, 1997

CERTIORARI TO THE UNITED STATES COURT OF APPEAL

FOR THE SEVENTH CIRCUIT

Facts

James and Laurenda Jackson owned and operated Education America, Inc., a for-profit consulting and management firm for technical and vocational schools. In 1986, the Jacksons acquired the Acme Institute of Technology, a not-for-profit technical school, and appointed petitioner Bates, then vice president of Education America, to serve as Acme's treasurer.[24]

In 1987, James Jackson, as Acme president, signed an agreement with the Department of Education that authorized the school to receive student loan checks through Title IV Guaranteed Student Loan (GSL) program. See 20 U.S.C. §1070 et seq. Acme's participation hinged upon both its continued accreditation by an approved accrediting association and Jackson's promise to comply with all applicable statutes and regulations. Under the GSL program, banks and other private institutions lent money to Acme students for tuition and other educational expenses. The federal government administrated the program and guaranteed payment if a student borrower defaulted. Acme would receive a loan check from the lender, endorse the check, and credit the amount against the student's tuition debt. If a GSL student withdrew from Acme before the term ended, the governing regulations required the school to return to the lender, within a specified time, a portion of the loan proceeds. The lender would then deduct the refund from the amount that the student owed. If Acme did not repay the lender, the student—and, if she defaulted, the Government—would remain liable for the full amount of the loan. In late 1987, pursuant to decisions made by the Jacksons and Bates, Acme initiated a pattern and practice of not making GSL refunds.

Bates gave priority to the payment of a management fee to Education America and salaries to the Jacksons, and instructed other Acme employees not to make the required GSL refunds. Bates, as Education America's vice president, wrote a letter that stated the unmade refunds were solely the responsibility and decision of the corporate office. By March 1989, Acme's refund liability had grown to approximately $85,000. Acme subsequently lost its accreditation, and, in 1990, the Department of Education notified the school that Acme was no longer eligible to participate in the GSL program. A few months later, Acme ceased operations. In 1994, Bates was indicted on 12 counts of "knowing and willfully misapplying" federally insured student loan funds, in violation of 20 U.S.C. §1097(a)(1988ed.) and 18 U.S.C. §2. Agreeing with Bates that conviction under §1097(1) for willful misapplication required an allegation of the defendant's "intent to injure or defraud the United States," the District Court dismissed the indictment because it lacked such an allegation. The Seventh Circuit vacated the judgement and reinstated the prosecution, concluding that §31097(a) required the government to prove only that Bates knowingly and willfully misapplied the Title IV funds.

Rule of Law

Title 14 Federal Guaranteed Student Loan (GSL) program 20 U.S.C. §1070 et seq. requires that participating institutions provide evidence of accreditation by an approved accrediting association for continued receipt of funds. Recipients are obligated to return any funds not spent or provided by the government within reasonable time. Failure to respond is actionable in district court.

Discussion of Legal Issues

Issue No. 1.   Was the District Court correct in its decision that dismissal was in order where the prosecution fails to allege that the defendant "intended to injure and or defraud the United States"?

This case concerns the meaning of 100 Stat. 1491, as assessed, 20 U.S.C. §1097(a) (1988ed.), which declared it a felony "knowingly and willfully" to misapply student loan funds insured under the Title IV of the Higher Education Act of 1965. The United States acknowledges that §1097(a) demanded allegations and proof of the defendant's intentional conversion of loan funds to his own use or the use of a third party. The question presented is whether §1097(a) demanded, in addition, allegation and proof that the defendant specifically intended to injure or defraud someone—either the United States as loan guarantor, as the District Court read the measure, or another. We hold, in accord with the Court of Appeals, that specific intent to injure or defraud someone, whether the United States or another, is not an element of the misapplication of funds proscribed by §1097(a).

Issue No. 2. Did the government only have to prove that Bates knowingly and willfully misapplied Title IV funds?

Despite the contrasting language of §1097(a) and (d), Bates relies on decisions interpreting 18 U.S.C. §656, which proscribes willful misapplication of bank funds. An "intent to defraud" element, originally included in the text of §656, was dropped from the text during a technical revision of the criminal code. In view of that history, courts have continued to hold that an "intent to defraud" is an element of the offense described in §656. Assume, without deciding, that §656 is correctly read to retain an "intent to defraud" element. §1097(a) never contained such requirement, one present from the start and still contained in §1097(d). Neither text nor history warrants adoption of Bates' construction of §1097(a) to set a trap for the unwary. As construed by the Seventh Circuit, §1097(a) catches only the transgressor who intentionally exercises unauthorized dominion over federally insured student loan funds for his own benefit or for the benefit of the third party.

Holding/Decision

Specific intent to injure or defraud someone, whether the United States or another, is not an element of the misapplication of funds proscribed by §1097(a). The text of §1097(a) does not include an "intent to defraud" requirement and this court ordinarily resists reading words into a statute that do not appear on its face. In contrast, 20 U.S.C. §1097(d), enacted at the same time as §1097(a), has an "intent to defraud" requirement. It is generally presumed that Congress acts intentionally and purposely where it includes particular language in one section of statute, but omits it in another.

The decision was affirmed. Justice Ginsburg, J. delivered the opinion for a unanimous court.

Implications for Fraud Prosecution and Prevention

1. **Unwise use of funds: A defense.** The measure does not render felonious innocent maladministration of a business enterprise, or imply that merely unwise use of funds is actionable. Furthermore, a 1992 amendment adding "fails to refund" to §1097(a)'s text does not demonstrate that the deliberate failure to return GSL funds, without an intent to defraud, became an offense within §1097(a)'s compass only under statute's current text. The added words simply foreclose any argument that §1097(a) does not reach the failure to make refunds. *Chief Commissioner v. Estate of Sternberger,* 348 U.S. 187, 194. Nothing in the text, structure, or history of §1097(a) warrants importations of an "intent to defraud."

2. **Refund and Restitution.** The refund and restitution of funds will not bar prosecution for fraud. However, this act will be considered as a mitigating factor in the decision of the court.

FEDERAL SENTENCING GUIDELINES FOR EMBEZZLEMENT AND FRAUD

U.S. 9th Circuit Court of Appeals
United States v. Berlier,
948 F.2d 1093 (9th Cir. 1991)
United States Court of Appeals, Ninth Circuit.
Argued and Submitted April 11, 1991.
Decided October 31, 1991.

Facts

The government appeals a downward departure from the guideline sentence in this case of a repentant white collar embezzler who made restitution and pled guilty.

David Joseph Berlier's pre-sentence report calculated the adjusted offense level at 16, less two levels for acceptance of responsibility, leading to a level of 14. The resulting sentencing range was 15–21 months imprisonment and a fine. At sentencing, the district courts departed downward from this guideline range and sentenced Berlier to straight probation and a fine. The government appeals under 18 U.S.C. 3742(b) (1988), arguing that none of the reasons given by the district court was a proper ground for departure.[25]

Rule of Law

We review departures from the sentencing guidelines under the three-step process established in *United States v. Lira-Barraza,* 941 F.2d 745 (9th Cir. 1991) (*en banc*). First, examine whether the trial court had the legal authority to depart. Id., 941 F.2d at 746. A trial court may depart from the guidelines if "the court finds that there exists an aggravating or mitigating circumstance of a kind, or to a degree, not adequately taken into consideration by the sentencing commission. . . ." 18 U.S.C. 3553(b) (1988). Whether the commission adequately considered a particular circumstances is a question of law that we review *de novo.* See Lira-Bazrraza, 941 F.2d at 746. The court reached the steps in the Lira-Barraza process because it held that there was no circumstance that would warrant departing from the guidelines. Therefore, the district court did not have the legal authority to depart from the guidelines.

Discussion of Issues

1. Did the trial judge impose a sentence within the intent and scope of the embezzlement statute?
2. When does the court have justifiable and legally defensible reasons for downward departure from the sentencing guidelines?
3. Was a lack of a prior record sufficient legal grounds to depart from the sentencing guidelines and give defendant straight probation, a fine, and restitution?
4. Was Berlier's prompt total payment of restitution sufficient grounds for departure?
5. Was Berlier's acceptance of responsibility a legal bases for downward departure?
6. Was the court justified in using the test of keeping the family together as a basis for downward departure?
7. Is incarceration unjust and counterproductive in this case?

Effect of Embezzlement Statute.   Berlier argues that we should affirm his sentence because the trial judge imposed a sentence within the range specified in the embezzlement statute, and the more lenient range of sentencing authorized by the embezzlement statute preempts the authorization of a maximum sentence of a $1 million fine or 20 years in prison or both, but does not specify minimum sentence. See 18 U.S.C. 657 (West Supp. 1990). Berlier argues that the statute's failure to specify a minimum sentence implies that the minimum sentence is no prison term, and that this minimum of no imprisonment controls the minimum sentence specified in the guidelines. Berlier concludes that it was therefore proper for the district court to impose a sentence without a prison term.

In *United States v. Sharp*, 883 F.2d (9th Cir. 1989), this court held that when a court departs from the Guidelines, the court may not impose a sentence below the minimum specified in the statute governing the particular offense. Id. At 831 ("[W]hen a statute requires a sentence different than that set by the guidelines, the statute controls.") (emphasis added); see also *United States Sentencing Commission, Guideline Manual,* 5G1.1(c) (Nov. 1989) (U.S.S.G.) (a guideline sentence may not be less than the statutorily required minimum sentence). Sharp stands for the proposition that a statute controls over the guidelines when the two conflict. When there is no conflict, however, the guidelines control. See 18 U.S.C. 3551(b) (1988) (requiring that an individual found guilty of an offense "shall be sentenced" according the provisions of 18 U.S.C. 3553, the sentencing guidelines section). To hold, as Berlier suggests, that the silence of a statute regarding a mandatory minimum creates a conflict with the guidelines and requires the guidelines to be preempted would invalidate guideline sentences in the majority of cases. This could not have been the intent of Congress.

Since the embezzlement statute does not require a sentence different from that in the guidelines, no conflict exists between the embezzlement statute and the guidelines. Thus, the guidelines alone determine Berlier's sentence.

Downward Departure.   The district court listed the following reasons for departing from the Sentencing Guidelines: (1) Berlier's lack of prior record; (2) Berlier's prompt total payment of restitution; (3) Berlier's acceptance of responsibility; (4) the effort to keep the family together, the challenges that Berlier's and his family faced, and the manner in which they overcame those challenges; (5) how unfair and counterproductive a period of incarceration would be given the effort these people have made to put their live back together; and (6) the totality of the situation. Each factor was analyzed to decide whether the circumstance was adequately considered by the Sentencing Commission.

Berlier's Lack of a Prior Criminal Record as a Mitigating Factor.
The Commission considered criminal history and provided that first-time offenders should be classified in Criminal History Category I. See U.S.S.G. 4A1.1, 5A. Berlier justifies the downward departure by arguing that be-

cause category I can include persons who have been repeatedly arrested without conviction or who have had conviction records sealed, the Commission did not adequately consider the difference in degree between such persons and a person like him who had "an absolutely clean prior record." The express language of the guidelines demonstrates that the commission did adequately consider situations such as Berlier's and that Berlier's lack of criminal history cannot form the basis for a downward departure: "The lower limit of the range for a category I criminal history is set for a first offender with the lowest risk of recidivism. Therefore, a departure below the lower limit of the guideline range for a category I criminal history on the basis of the adequacy of criminal history cannot be appropriate." U.S.S.G. 4A1.3.

Berlier's Prompt Total Payment of Restitution. Berlier received a two-level reduction in his offense level for acceptance of responsibility, based in part on the fact that he made full restitution. The Sentencing Commission explicitly included the payment of restitution as a factor to be considered in granting the reduction for acceptance of responsibility. See U.S.S.G. 3E1.1, comment. (n. 1(b)). Nevertheless, Berlier argues that his responsible actions and hard work in making restitution are sufficiently unusual to allow a downward departure.

Berlier has made no showing that his payment of restitution is a degree not adequately considered by the Commission. Berlier received sufficient credit for this circumstance when he received his two-level reduction for acceptance of responsibility for his fraudulent conduct.

Berlier's Acceptance of Responsibility for His Fraudulent Conduct. The district court also cited Berlier's acceptance of responsibility as a basis for downward departure, even though Berlier had already received the two-level adjustment provided for in the guidelines for acceptance of responsibility. This circuit has not considered "super-acceptance of responsibility" generally or extraordinary circumstances relating to one of the enumerated factors in law can support a downward departure beyond the two-level downward adjustment. However, nothing in the record before us suggests that Berlier took any action beyond what is normally encompassed within the acceptance of responsibility finding. Acceptance of responsibility, therefore, cannot form the basis for downward departure in this matter.

The Effort to Keep the Family Together and the Manner in Which the Family Overcame Its Challenges. Berlier argues that his efforts to keep his family together are sufficiently unusual to justify a downward departure. The guidelines expressly state that "[f]amily ties and responsibilities . . . are not ordinarily relevant in determining whether a sentence should be outside the guidelines." U.S.S.G. 5H1.6, P.S. The commission considered family ties and how those ties could be affected by prison sentences, and declared that family ties ordinarily should not be a factor in departing from the guideline sentence.

Incarceration as Unjust and Counterproductive to All Parties.   To the extent that this factor refers to the degree of Berlier's family ties, it is subsumed within our analysis in the previous section. The district court did not identify any separate circumstances that were not adequately considered by the Commission. In the absence of such identification, a general statement about the injustice of imprisonment in this case is not a sufficient basis for departure.

Permissible Grounds for Departure from Sentence Guidelines.   Berlier does not argue that the court may base a departure on a combination of factors, each of which would have been impermissible as a ground of departure considered alone. Rather, he argues that the factors in this case are permissible grounds for departure, but that even if no one factor, taken alone, would justify the departure, the factors considered together justify the departure.

Holding/Decision

This court recently observed by the way of dictum that "a unique combination of factors may constitute the circumstance that mitigates." *United States v. Cook,* 938 F.2d 149, 153 (9th Cir. 1991). In the present case, there are no "unique combination of factors." The factors in this case, even viewed together, do not justify a downward departure. All of the factors were considered by the Commission in preparing the guidelines and in preparing the commentary to the guidelines. Thus, even had the Cook dicta been law, it would not have affected the decision in this case. The district court erred in departing downward from the guideline sentencing range, and we remand for resentencing within the appropriate guideline range.

Implication for Fraud Prevention/Prosecution

Restitution and remorse for the embezzlement will not be used as mitigating circumstances that induce the court to refrain from following the sentencing guidelines which include a jail term or fine. Of course, in this case, the convicted embezzler wanted to avoid any jail term. Where there is downward departure from the sentencing guidelines, it is necessary that the prosecutor agrees with the departure. As in this case, the judge's decision was reversed on appeal and the case remanded for compliance with the sentencing guidelines. The government agency prosecuting the fraud must be clear about its role in the sentencing phase. The time to express any desires to the prosecutor is before the judge makes a ruling on the sentence. Communicate any desires in a timely manner to the prosecutor.

A deterrent note about fraudulent conduct against the government can best be described in the *United States v. Berlier* (1991) case, which basically demonstrated that the government prosecutors will challenge the leniency of the trial court judges by appealing the sentence part of the conviction. Prosecutors argue that the intent of the sentencing guidelines is to provide judges with limited flexibility. In this case the embezzlement statute provides a maximum sentence of a $1 million fine or 20 years in prison, but does not specify a minimum sentence [see 18 USC .657 (West Sapp. 1990)]. *United States Sentencing Guidelines Manual* (USSG) 5 G1.1(c) (Nov. 1989). The suggestion here is that a sentence cannot be less than a statutory required minimum. The issue is whether the Court can give a minimum sentence of probation and a fine. The answer in the Berlier Appeal is no.

Implications for Internal Controls and Deterrents

The sentences for convicted embezzlers seem to be consistent in the cases referenced in this book, namely:

- **Prison term.** Jail time, however small the number of months, is given unless the prosecutors agrees to a plea bargaining for probation.
- **Fine.** A fine is routine for the punishment phase of the conviction. Even if restitution occurs, a fine is still possible.
- **Restitution.** The Berlier case stands for the ultimate restitution goal of 100 percent. Berlier paid 100 percent of all the funds he embezzled, yet he was convicted, fined, and put on probation.
- **Sanctions.** The range of sanctions are severe and should be overlooked.
  a. Probation for years following incarceration.
  b. Barred from performing ones current business or professions. In the case of an attorney or accountant, conviction of fraud before the bankruptcy court could result in the individual being barred from future practice before the bankruptcy court and or the district court.

c. In case of sweepstakes fraud, the owner of the entity might agree to a non-fraudulent way of doing business and agree to a bond to refund victims of such fraud.

A Final Note: Successful prosecution of government-related fraud can serve as a deterrent if this is publicized more to the public.

FRAUD IN BUSINESS AND INDUSTRY

One fraud study found trouble at small firms. An Associated Press article (Sun Sentinental, March 1999), asserted that "when it comes to cooking the books, small companies are the biggest culprits." Half the companies in the fraud study wound up either closing their doors or reorganizing in bankruptcy court. In 300 cases of fraudulent financial reporting that the SEC tackled between 1987 and 1997, the chief executive officer was involved almost 75 percent of the time. Also 68 percent of the directors were either company executives or family members whose ties put them in a conflict of interest situation.[26]

The professors from North Carolina State University, the University of Tennessee, and Kennesaw, Georgia State University took a random sample of 200 of 300 cases in which SEC took action because of fraudulent reporting. These researchers warn investors in small companies to look for warning signs of fraud. "A weak and unexperienced board of directors that has an unusually large stake in the company's stock is a sign of potential fraudulent conduct," according to John Flaherty, Chairman of the Commission of Sponsoring Organizations of the Treadway Commission (Fraud Study Report, 1999).[27]

CREDIT CARD FRAUD

The issue of fraud in industry is part of the many operational issues that this business considers with respect to internal controls. On July 6, 1999, Chrystal Jones, 27, an employee of the bank, was convicted after she pleaded no contest to theft and fraud, taking over customers' credit card accounts and using them to buy items worth nearly $90,000. The facts also showed that Ms. Jones had a co-conspirator named Marissa Levine who also embezzled about $65,000. Together, the embezzled amount is about $165,000. This First, USA Lake Mary Bank in Florida had internal controls which ultimately caught the embezzlement schemes.

Jones was convicted for grand theft and fraud and received one year in county jail, probation of 25 years, and restitution, which was unique in that the court required 100 percent restitution by requiring the perpetrator to work and pay back the money during the 25-year probation period. Additionally, Jones turned over one of the objects of her purchases from the embezzled monies. For example, she turned over to the court four vehicles, a 1997 Toyota 4 Runner, a 1998 Acura, a Chevy van, and a 1995 Hyundai Sonata, which was surrendered by her sister.[28]

Implications for Fraud Prosecution and Prevention

This Jones case raises several issues that should be of concern to Business and Industry namely conspiracy theories. Should we look for conspirators in our investigation of fraud?

The Facts

1. Rene Stutzman, *The Orlando Sentinel,* July 7, 1999 reported in the Jones case that the family members were aware of the fraudulent conduct. The family benefited from airline tickets and automobiles. Unless, there is a direct or provable act in the commission of the fraud, it will be hard to prosecute relatives.

    However, Jones did not act alone, she had a co-conspirator, an employee who aided her and benefited from the embezzled funds. Of course, an employee can be prosecuted much easier than the relatives.

2. Implications of the federal or state RICO (Racketeer Influenced and Corrupt Organization) Act, Florida's Statute 895-06, provides another legal strategy to recover embezzled funds since the statute reaches any identifiable assets wherever they are located, regardless of who is the holder of the assets.

3. Restitution can be secured whether it is a state or federal prosecution of fraud. Both the federal and state prosecutors have access to the RICO statutes which aid in locating and seizing assets to fulfill restitution and court penalities.

IMPLICATION OF THE RICO STATUTES: FEDERAL, STATE, AND FRAUD PROSECUTION

Typical State Statute (Florida)

F.S. 895.02—Definition "Racketeering activity" means to commit, to attempt to commit, to conspire to commit, or to solicit, coerce, or intimidate another person to commit any crime which is chargeable by indictment or information under the following provisions of the Florida Statutes:

4) Section 409.920, relating to medic aid provider

6) Part IV of Chapter 501, relating to telemarketing

7) Part 517, relating to sale of securities and investor protection

23) Chapter 812, relating to theft, robbery, and related crimes

24) Chapter 815, relating to computer-related crimes

25) 817, relating to fraudulent practices, false pretense, fraud generally, and credit card crimes

28) Chapter 831, relating to forgery and counterfeiting crimes under RICO that a convicted perpetrator could be charged with

As you can see, the defendants could have been charged under the Florida RICO Statute because the fraudulent activities of credit card fraud through use of computers related directly to:

23) Chapter 812, relating to theft, etc.

24) Chapter 815, relating to computer-related crimes

25) Chapter 817, relating to fraudulent practices generally and credit card crimes

28) Chapter 831, relating to forgery

Once the defendant voluntarily agrees to make 100 percent restitution of embezzled funds, this could forego the use of RICO and avoid the penalties therein.

Criminal Penalties (FS 895.04) (1979)

(1) A person convicted of engaging in an activity in violation of the provisions of 895:03 is guilty of a felony of the first degree and shall be punished accordingly to statutory provisions.

(2) The court can impose a fine not exceeding three times the gross loss caused, plus court costs and costs of investigation and prosecution.

(3) The court shall identify anything of pecuniary value in the form of money or anything else, the primary significance of which is an economic advantage. All property or service value over $100 will be counted for the purpose of forfeiture.

(4) Forfeiture. (e) (2) (a) All property, real or personal, including money used or derived from the scheme shall be subject to civil forfeiture. Upon entry of final judgement in favor of the state, the title of the state to the forfeitured property to the state.

(5) The Active Role of Business/Industry in the RICO Proceedings. The business or entity should make a decision immediately upon the referral of the fraud for prosecution that:

a) It desires to have 100 percent restitution of the losses to be a part of the sentence or plea bargaining and that any negotiations regarding the recovery and destination of assets should be done in consent with the business and industry.

b) The failure to take this affirmative action will result in the forfeited property becoming the legal title and property of the state or governmental entity. At this point, the business and industry will not be able to recover any of those assets unless there is a voluntary negotiated settlement with the state entity.

The cases which follow are merely samples of cases on fraud where prosecution was successful and RICO or voluntary restitution was secured. There is also evidence that a prison term, a fine, restitution, and sanctions including probation constitute prohibition against future involvement in the business activity and continue to be a consistent pattern of results.

The Federal Statutes

18 U.S.C. 1961, 1963, (1978). Chapter 96 Racketeering action means:

[1961] Section A) any act or threat involving murder, kidnapping, gambling, arson, robbery, bribery, extortion dealing in obscene matter or dealing in narcotics or other dangerous drugs which is chargeable under state law and punishable by imprisonment for more than a year. B) Any act indictable under any of the following provisions of Title 18 United States Code:

Section 201—relating to Bribery, theft, embezzlement
Section 1341—relating to mail fraud
        1343—relating to wire fraud
        1344—financial Institution fraud
        1503—relating to obstruction of criminal investigators
        1513—relating to retaliating against a witness a victim or an informant
        1956—relating to the laundering of money

18 U.S.C. 1962—Criminal Penalties. (a) Whoever violates any provision of Section 1962 of Chapter 96 shall be fined under this title or imprisoned for not more than 20 years (or for life if the violation is based on a racketeering activity for which the maximum penalty includes life imprisonment) or both and shall forfeit to the United States irrespective of any provision of state law:

(1) Any interest the person has acquired or maintained in violation of Section 1962.

(2) Including any a) interest in b) security of c) claim against or (d) property or contractual right of any kind or has an influence over the activity or property: any enterprise which the person has established, operated, controlled, or participated in the conduct of in violation of section 1961 or 1962.

(3) **a)** Any property constituting or derived from any proceeds which the person obtained directly or indirectly from racketeering activity or unlawful debt collection in violation of Section 2.

    b) Property subject to criminal forfeiture under this section includes real property including things growing on, affixed to and found in land; and tangible and intangible personal property including rights, privileges, interest, claims, and securities.

    c) All rights, title and interest in property described in (a) and (b) give rise to forefeiture under this section.

    d) "Any such property that is subsequently transferred to a person other than the defendant may be subject to a special verdict of forfeiture to the United States unless the transferee establishes in a hearing that he/she is the bona fide purchase for value of such property who at the time of purchase/acquisition was reasonably without cause to believe that the property was subject to forfeiture under this section." (18 U.S.C. 1961, 1970) and (Public Law 101-73, Title IX, Section 968, Aug. 9, 1989, 103 Stat. 506).

    e) Forfeiture

    Upon conviction of a person under RICO, the court shall enter a judgment of forfeiture of the property to the United States and shall also authorize the Attorney General to seize all property ordered forfeited upon such terms and condition as the court deemed proper.

Implication of the RICO for Business and Industry

1. In addition to federal or state fraud charges, the perpetrator can be charged under the state or federal RICO Acts which specifically cover acts spelled out in 18 U.S.C. 1961, 1962 namely:

Section 201, relating to bribery and theft

Section 1341, relating to mail fraud

> 1342 relating to wire fraud
> 1344 relating to financial institution fraud
> 1956 relating to money laundering and Title 29 U.S.C. 186–
> Section 501(c) relating to embezzlement of Union funds and
> Title 11 U.S.C. Section (D) relating to fraud including the sale
> of securities.

2. The federal RICO statute (18 U.S.C. 1961 Section 1513), relating against a witness, a victim, or an informant. This provision coupled with the Whistle-Blower Statutes provides protection to persons who come forth with information regarding existing fraud. This provision is very good for the business or government entity in identifying and prosecuting the fraudulent acts in the business or identity.

3. Forfeiture of ill gotten gains from fraudulent act(s) will result in the application of RICO forfeiture sections which recovers the funds or property from the perpetrator(s).

THE CASES OF FRAUD AND RICO

Case No. 1—Application of the RICO Statute-Securities Case.
Kidder v. Brandt
United States Court of Appeals
Eleventh Circuit (No. 97–2123)

Kidder, Peabody & Co., Incorporated, Plaintiff Appellant v. Robert Brandt, as trustee, Selma Brandt, John H. Gary, Donna L. Gary, Irwin Goldstein, et al., Defendants–Appellees. December 22, 1997.

Kidder Peabody & Co., Inc. ("Kidder") is a securities broker. Around 1987, a group of individuals (the "defendants") purchased shares in a limited partnership through Kidder. As a condition of purchasing securities through Kidder, each of the defendants agreed to submit any dispute or claim arising out of or relating to their Kidder accounts to arbitration. That agreement specified that the NASD Code would govern any arbitration claim they brought.

In 1994, the defendants filed a seven-count arbitration complaint against Kidder alleging, among other things, that Kidder had violated RICO, 18 U.S.C. 1962. Before any action could be taken on that complaint, Kidder filed suit in federal district court, based upon diversity jurisdiction, seeking a declaration that the defendants' claims were ineligible for arbitration and an injunction forbidding the defendants from pursuing their claims in arbitration.

Kidder filed a motion for summary judgement contending that the "occurrence or event" which gave rise to the defendants' claims did not occur within six years of the date defendants filed their arbitration complaint as required by Section 15 of the NASD Code. The district court granted Kidder's motion in part and denied it in part. Relevant to this appeal, the district found that the "occurrence or event" which gave rise to defendants' RICO claim was a "pattern of racketeering activity" which began more than six years before the defendants filed their arbitration complaint but ceased inside the six-year window. Based on that finding, the court denied Kidder's motion with respect to defendants' RICO claim. As to that claim, the court entered summary judgement for the defendants, declaring that the RICO claim was eligible for arbitration. Kidder filed a motion to alter or amend the judgement which the court denied. Kidder appeals from the district court's order on summary judgement and its order denying Kidder to alter or amend the judgement.

Rule of Law

This case involves a claim arising under the Racketeer Influenced Corrupt Organization Act ("RICO"), 18 U.S.C. 1962. The issue before us, however, involves less the intricacies of RICO law and more Section 15 of the National Association of Securities Dealers Code of Attribution ("NASD Code"). That section provides that no dispute, claim, or controversy is eligible for arbitration where six years have elapsed from the "occurrence or event giving rise to the act or the dispute, claim or controversy." This appeal turns on the definition of the quoted language.

Issue No. 1

Did the court erroneously interpret and apply Section 15 of the NASD Code to the facts of this case?

The district court found that the "occurrence or event" giving rise to the defendants' RICO claim was a pattern of racketeering activity, "at least a portion of [which] allegedly occurred within the Section 15 time frame." On the basis of that finding, the court concluded that the defendants' RICO claim was eligible for arbitration.

Kidder argues that under Section 15 the defendants' RICO claim was not eligible for attribution, unless all of the predicate acts upon which that claim were based occurred within six years of the date defendants filed their arbitration complaint. Specially, Kidder states: "Defendants' Federal RICO claim is eligible for arbitration only if each act or fact which forms each of the elements of their Federal RICO claim—including those underlying the pattern element—took place within the six-year period preceding the initiating of arbitration. "If Kidder's interpretations of Section 15 is correct, the defendants' RICO claim was not eligible for arbitration because the district court found that some of the predicate acts supporting the claim took place outside the six-year window.

Kidder asserts that its interpretation of Section 15 is supported by our decision in *Merrill Lynch, Pierce, Fenner & Smith, Inc. v. Cohen,* 62 F.3d 381 (11th Cir. 1995). However, in Cohen, we did not define the phrase "occurrence or event giving rise to the . . . claim." Instead, we merely recognized, under facts similar to those here, that "[I]t is not a foregone conclusion . . . that the purchase date is the relevant occurrence or event giving rise to the Cohen's claims, as neither 15 nor any other provision of the NASD Code so provides." Id. At 385.

Issue No. 2

Does the six-years rule in any way bar the claims of the defendant under the RICO Act?

The interpretation of Section 15 in Cohen is inconsistent with Kidder's position. In that case, the Cohens began purchasing securities from the defendant in 1985. They alleged that from 1985 through 1991 the defendant had misrepresented the value of their investments in statements it sent to them. The Cohens filed an arbitration complaint in 1993 asserting a claim for breach of fiduciary duty. Because the existence of a fiduciary duty was one element of the Cohens' claim, they had to prove that the defendants owed them a fiduciary duty. That duty was born when the Cohens purchased securities from the defendant in 1985, more than six years before the Cohens filed their arbitration complaint. Under Kidder's interpretation of Section 15, the Cohens' claim would have been ineligible for arbitration because one of the acts upon which their claim was based occurred outside the six-year window. However, the court did not adopt that interpretation of Section 15. Instead, the court recognized that if the defendant had made misrepresentations within the six-year window, the Cohens could have claims for breach of fiduciary duty that would be eligible for arbitration. "Each misrepresentation [e.g., the statements the defendant sent out] might be an event or occurrence giving rise to a claim for breach of fiduciary duty." *Osler v. Ware,* 114F.3d91, 92–93 (6th Cir. 1997) (plaintiff who opened securities account in 1984 and filed arbitration complaint in 1993 could have an arbitration claim based on defendant's misrepresentations made within the six-year window); *Paine Webber Inc. v. Hofmann,* 984 F.2d 1372, 1381 (3d Cir. 1993) (misrepresentation could be the act or occurrence giving rise to arbitration claim).[29]

Holding/Decision

Issue No. 1. The court held the occurrence or event-giving rise to a claim for purpose of Section 15 of the NASD Code is necessary to make the claim viable, the occurrence or event after which a complaint was made. The last occurrence or event must be established and all the elements of a chain. The court did erroneously interpret and apply Section 15 of the NASD Code. The appellant court found that the district court upon remand to identify the occurrence or event which created a viable RICO claim for the defendants. If the occurrence or event which made the claim viable took place more than six years from the date the defendants filed their arbitration complaint, the claim was ineligible for arbitration. But the court does not foreclose RICO claims during the six-year period.

Issue No. 2. The district court found that the "occurrence or event" which gave rise to defendants' RICO claim was a "pattern of racketeering activity." Because a "pattern of racketeering activity" is, by definition, a composition of multiple distinct "occurrences or events," it is surprising that the district court failed to identify precisely the last "occurrence or event" necessary to make the defendants' RICO claim viable. Therefore, the case is remanded to the district court with instructions to identify if the occurrences or the claim viable took place more than six years from the date the defendants filed their arbitration complaint, the claim is ineligible for arbitration.

For the reasons set forth above, we vacate the judgment of the district court the case is remanded with the instruction that the district court make detailed findings of facts concerning the occurrence or event-giving rise to defendants' RICO claim.

Implications for Fraud Prevention and Prosecution

1. **The arbitration rules.** The cases of securities fraud should be followed carefully to avoid conflicts with the RICO Statutes. Section 15 of the NASD Code has different requirements for resolution of wrongdoing. *Kidder v. Brandt* also signals that where there are multiple claims of wrongdoing, such as "a pattern of racketeering activity," the claims arising out of this action may not be foreclosed by an arbitration process and agreement.

2. **The statute of limitations.** This is a critical rule for filing of the complaint. Accordingly, investors and victims must be diligent to discover the fraud that has been committed and in the case of securities,

the claim should be brought within six years from its occurrence. The bottom line is for victims of fraud to file civil, criminal, or administrative complaints in a timely manner.

3. **The RICO Act.** This act is useful in stamping out securities fraud. Familiarity with the rules and procedures for filing complaints under the statute is an essential part of the prevention, identification, and prosecution of fraud. In each referral for criminal prosecution, the employer is advised to raise the issue of the application of the RICO statutes to the set of facts being presented to the prosecutor.

A CASE OF RICO—STATE PROSECUTION
Sun City Oil Company Inc.
v.
State of Florida, Appellant/Cross-Appellants.
No. 87-449
District Court of Appeal of Florida,
Fifth District.
March 17, 1998
522 So.2d. 474, 476, 1988

Facts

Defendant Sun City Oil Company was charged with racketeering violations, embezzlement, and grand theft with failure to remit fuel taxes. The Circuit Court Judge Rom W. Powell, Orange County, Florida, dismissed the information. The state appealed the dismissal of 57 counts.[31]

Rule of Law

1. Embezzlement—5
   Criminal statute section.
   146k (5)
   Embezzlement statute requires proof of criminal intent. (West's F.S.A. section 206.56.)
2. Indictment and Information—132 (5)
   210k 132(5)
   State charging embezzlement and grand theft based on same taking could not be required by motion to dismiss to elect between repugnant counts. (West's F.S.A. sections 206.56, 812.014)

3. Indictment and Information—132 (3)
   210 K 132(5)
   Motion to require state to elect between repugnant counts must be made
   before introduction of evidence by defense.

4. Criminal Law—29 (5.5)
   110 K 29 (5.5)
   Formerly 110K29 (5), 110k29. Embezzlement information could charge
   as a separate crime each distinct month that monies were not reported
   and paid and did not need to charge all alleged embezzlement in one
   count (West FSA §206.56).

Issue No. 1

Did the court erred in dismissing the seven counts including embezzlement?

The trial court correctly determined that section 206.56 requires proof
of criminal intent. The State had failed to present sufficient evidence of
embezzlement and theft. The court cannot convict for both embezzlement
under section 206.56 and theft under section P12.014 for the same taking.

The trial court prematurely dismissed the counts based on the grand
theft statutes because the state cannot be required to elect between repugnant counts by a motion to dismiss. A motion to require the state to elect
must be made before introduction of evidence by the defense.

Issue No. 2

Can the state proceed under grand theft and RICO Statutes or should all
counts be brought under Section 206.56?

The trial court erred in requiring the state to charge all the alleged
embezzlement under section 206.56 in one count. The state may charge
a separate crime for each distinct month that monies are not reported and
paid. The court concluded that if the state elected to proceed under the
grand theft statute, it might also prosecute under the RICO count, because
grand theft is one of the predicate crimes on which a RICO violation may
be based. On the other hand, if it elects to proceed under section 206.56,
the RICO count should be dismissed because a violation of that statute is
not one of the predicate crimes listed in section 895.02. That this omission
was intended by the legislature and was not an oversight is indicated by
the fact that violation of the statute relating to evasion of payment of
cigarette taxes is listed as a predicate crime. Had the legislature intended
to include evasion of payment of fuel taxes in the long list of predicate
crimes, it would have said so. We reject appellees' contention that they

may not be prosecuted for the underlying predicate acts in addition to the RICO violation. See *Carroll v. State,* 459 So.2d. 368 (Fla. 5th DCA 1984).

Holding/Decision

The District Court of Appeals under Judge Orfinger, with concurrence from Justices Dauksch and Cobb, said: "We affirm the trial court's dismissal of the counts charging embezzlement of fuel taxes, with leave to amend to allege the requisite criminal intent, and we reverse the trial court's dismissal with prejudice of the counts charging the RICO violation and grand theft. We also reverse the trial court's determination that the embezzlement counts must be reduced to a single count. The cross-appeal is dismissed. Supra."

The case was affirmed in part, reversed in part and remanded.

Implications for Fraud Prosecution and Prevention

1. The embezzlement information could charge separate crimes for each distinct month that monies were not reported and paid and the state did not have to charge all alleged embezzlement in one count.
2. The state can prosecute defendants for grand theft and racketeering but not embezzlement and racketeering procedures with respect to the pattern of wrong-doing.
3. This is a case that stands for the proposition that the embezzlement of funds could result in charges with the racketeering statute. Unlike the grand theft statute, RICO has far reaching provisions embodied in the forfeiture of assets sections of the statute. The net results could be the loss of substantial assets of the business, plus court costs, fines, incarceration, and other sanctions.
4. The good news is that the use of the RICO Acts in the prosecution of fraud increases the chances of restitution to close to 100 percent.

PARTNERSHIP FRAUD IS ACTIONABLE

U.S. 9th CIRCUIT COURT OF APPEALS
IN RE BUGNA, 33 F.3d 1054 (9th Cir. 1994)
IN RE RANDOLPH C. BUGNA, DEBTOR.
RANDOLPH C. BUGNA, APPELLANT, v.
EDWARD E. McARTHUR, APPELLEE
No. 93-55238.
United States Court of Appeals, Ninth Circuit.
Submitted June 10, 1994
Decided August 16, 1994

Facts

Bugna and McArthur were business partners. Bugna, a licensed real estate broker, agreed to purchase for McArthur a 14.4 percent interest in a California partnership called Lakeview, Ltd. McArthur tendered a $90,000 earnest-money check, but Bugna promptly returned the uncashed check with the assurance that McArthur would be able to complete the purchase after certain technical problems were cleared away. Months later, McArthur learned that Bugna was snapping up the 14.4 percent interest for himself.

McArthur sued Bugna in California state court for fraud and breach of fiduciary duty. A jury award of $90,000 in compensatory and $300,000 in punitive damages was affirmed on appeal. Bugna then filed for bankruptcy and McArthur initiated proceedings to have the $390,000 declared nondischargeable under bankruptcy code section 523(a)(4), which denies the debtor a discharge "from any debt . . . for fraud or defalcation while acting in a fiduciary capacity." 11 U.S.C. 523(a)(4).

The bankruptcy court reviewed the state court record, found that collateral estoppel precluded Bugna from relitigating the issues of fraud and breach of fiduciary duty, and held the entire award nondischargeable. Bugna appeals the bankruptcy court's nondischargeability order, challenging both the bankruptcy court's collateral estoppel finding and its ruling that punitive damages are nondischargeable under section 523(a)(4).

Rule of Law

Section 523(a)(4) provides that a debtor cannot discharge any "debt . . . for fraud or defalcation while acting in a fiduciary capacity." 11 U.S.C. 523(a)(4). Thus, by its express terms, section 523(a)(4) precludes Bugna from discharging his entire liability to McArthur only if a state court judgment imposing punitive damages is a "debt" within the meaning of section 523(1). California law governs the collateral estoppel effect of the state court determination of fraud here. Under this law, collateral estoppel bars relitigation when "(1) the issue decided in the prior action is identical to the issue presented in the second action; (2) there was a final judgment on the merits; and (3) the party against whom estoppel is asserted was a party . . . to the prior adjudication." *Garrett v. City and county of San Francisco,* 818 F.2d 1515, 1520 (9th Cir. 1987).[33]

Discussion Issue No. 1

Are state court findings that the debtor committed fraud and breach of fiduciary duty binding on the debtor in dischargeability proceedings? Does collateral estoppel apply in this case?

Though we have apparently never decided this issue, the Supreme Court has held that collateral estoppel applies in dischargeability proceedings. *Grogan v. Garner*, 498 U.S. 279, 284 & n. 11, 111 S.Ct. 654, 658 & n. 11 (1991).[34] In Grogan, all the elements of collateral estoppel were satisfied. The bankruptcy court was therefore required to apply collateral estoppel once the creditor invoked it.

The bankruptcy court correctly found these criteria were met. 1. The issues of fraud and breach of fiduciary duty were actually litigated and formed the basis for the jury's fraud verdict. The state court of appeal affirmed the punitive damages award after finding that the "evidence of actual fraud was overwhelming." Bugna was a party to the state court adjudication, he had adequate opportunity and incentive to litigate, and the judgment against him is final.

Discussion Issue No. 2

Does the Bankruptcy Code section 523(a)(4) preclude discharge of punitive damages?

The second question is whether the issues faced by the bankruptcy court in the dischargeability proceeding were identical to those litigated and determined in state court. There are two issues under section 523(a)(4): whether the debtor incurred the debt by committing fraud or defalcation, and whether the fraud was in relation to the debtor's fiduciary responsibilities. The court correctly found that these issues were litigated and resolved against Bugna in the state court proceeding. Bugna had a full trial on the issue of fraud, and the verdict on breach of fiduciary duty subsumed a finding that Bugna owed McArthur a fiduciary duty as his partner and real estate broker.

Holding/Decision

The appellate court held that the bankruptcy court correctly concluded as a matter of collateral estoppel, that the compensatory and punitive damages Bugna owes McArthur are a debt "for fraud . . . while acting in a fiduciary capacity." (11 U.S.C. 523(a)(4)), and they are not dischargeable. The court also affirmed the state court's finding that the debtor committed fraud and breach of fiduciary duty.

Implications for Prosecution and Prevention of Fraud

1. This decision provides notice that fraud committed while there was a fiduciary relationship will ensue against the perpetrator of the fraud.

The perpetrator cannot turn to the court for new policies to discharge this debt or claim for punitive damages.

2. The "fresh start provision" of the bankruptcy code was intended for primarily "honest but unfortunate debtors" (see *Grogan v. Garner,* 498 U.S. 279, 286, 111 S. Ct. 654, 659, 112 L. Ed. 2d 755 (1991)). Bugna incurred liability of punitive damages through the commission of fraud while acting in a fiduciary capacity. Thus, this act of fraud is neither "honest nor unfortunate" and therefore, the defendant's acts do not warrant a "fresh start" of dischargeability.

3. A note for victims of fraud is that it is essential that the prosecution of fraud be swift, deliberate, and effective. Bearing in mind that judgement relating to fraud may not be escaped by merely filing of bankruptcy.

CREDIT UNION FRAUD
U.S.
v.
CHRISTIANSEN, 958 F.2d 285
UNITED STATES OF AMERICA, PLAINTIFF-APPELLEE
v.
CHRISTIANSEN, DEFENDANT-APPELLANT.
No. 91-30155.
United States Court of Appeals, Ninth Circuit.
Submitted December 4, 1991. Submission Deferred December 17, 1991.
Resubmitted February 21, 1992.
Decided March 3, 1992.

Facts

Christiansen embezzled over $96,000 from the credit union she managed, breaching the trust vested in her by her employer. She argues, however, that the district court erred when it enhanced her sentence for abuse of trust. The sentencing guidelines make clear that the enhancement may not be applied when the elements of the underlying offense include abuse of trust. Embezzlement appears to be just such an offense, for it involves a breach of trust. Yet because we discern a qualitative difference between a breach of trust and abuse of trust, we find that the abuse of trust enhancement may be applied to embezzlers such as Christiansen, whose position of trust contributed in a substantial manner to facilitating the crime.[35]

Christiansen worked as the branch office representative of the Alaska USA Federal Credit Union in Bethel, Alaska. Her duties included supervising employees and accounting for cash and negotiable instruments.

During her term as branch office representative, she failed to produce the required cash count reports. A surprise audit revealed that she had embezzled $96,795. She pleaded guilty to one count of embezzlement of credit union funds in violation of 18 U.S.C. 657.

As recommended in the presentence report, the district court imposed two-point enhancements for "more than minimal planning" and "abuse of a position of trust." The court sentenced Christiansen to 17 months and ordered her to pay partial restitution. It also imposed three years of supervised release contingent on her completing 600 hours of community service.

Rule of Law

The Sentencing Commission guidelines, U.S.S.G. 3B1.3, makes it clear that the "abuse of trust" enhancement may not be applied if abuse of trust is included in the elements of the specific offense. The intent of the Sentencing Commission was to prevent a defendant from being punished twice for the same conduct.

Discussion of Issue(s)

1. The sentencing guidelines make it clear that sentencing enhancement may not be applied if abuse of trust is included in the elements of the specific offense (U.S.S.G. 3.B1.3.). The defendant Christiansen argued that the finding of a breach of trust is essential for her conviction under 18 U.S.C. 657.

2. Courts have long focused on this element in considering embezzlement charges. In an early case, Supreme Court described embezzlement as "the fraudulent appropriation of property by a person to whom such property has been entrusted, or into whose hands it has lawfully come."[36] Later courts have retained this requirement. For example, the Fifth Circuit reversed an embezzlement conviction after finding that the stolen funds had not been entrusted to the defendant. The court held that "[t]he essence of embezzlement lies in breach of fiduciary relationship deriving from the entrustment of money." *United States v. Sayklay,* 542 F.2d 942, 944 (5th Cir. 1976).[37]

3. The critical exception is that the sentencing guidelines can apply the enhancement in instances in embezzlement where the defendant is someone in a significant position of trust (Findlaw, http//:www.caselaw. com/scripts/, 1994).[38]

Holding/Decision

The court acted appropriately and affirmed their decision. The appellate court justified its affirmation by stating "Christiansen's embezzlement scheme involved repeated thefts over two and a half years." The fraud was committed in her high position as branch representative, providing her with the ability to conceal her crime because of her position. The court therefore felt that the defendant contributed in some "substantial" way to facilitating the crime by exploiting the trust relationship to embezzle the monies. (933 F.2d at 1227).

Implications for Prosecution and Prevention of Fraud

1. The court will hold persons such as managers or anyone who has control and a fiduciary relationship over the assets to a higher standard of "breach of trust" in order to apply the enhancement provision in cases of embezzlement.

2. The conviction and sentence for embezzlement will involve a) jail term of a minimum of 12 months, b) a fine to cover court and investigation costs, c) full or partial restitution, and additionally sanctions, such as in this case, of three years of supervised release continuing on her completing 600 hours of community service.

3. A subtle message that this case sends to perpetrators is that the higher or more critical the level of fiduciary control and responsibility over the assets and embezzlement funds, the greater the chance that the court will enhance the punishment within the sentencing guidelines and discretion of the court.

Summary

As you reviewed the cases on fraud, the main question is why study cases? The author believes that the study of cases provides reality and a sense of concreteness regarding the types of fraudulent acts that wind up in the courts. The reader will understand the consequences when a perpetrator is caught and the decision is made to prosecute based on existing laws. These cases will also provide the reader with signals to the kinds of internal investigatory processes that could be followed to secure a conviction of fraud.

FINAL PERSPECTIVE ON FRAUD CASES

After reviewing the legal cases decided by courts in the United States of America, I found that utilizing the following guidelines that analyze and synthesize information found in cases works well.

Guidelines for Reviewing Cases

Court:	Appellate State or Federal Court Federal District Court or Circuit Court Circuit Court State or Federal
Year:	199__, 200__ (the year varies)
Parties:	Know the parties to the case, such as United States, Plaintiff/Appellee vs. Christiansen Defendant/Appellant
Facts:	Read the facts carefully to understand the charges, the issue, the positions and claims of the plaintiff and defendant, the prosecutor and defendant.
Rule of Law:	Each case presented is governed by rules of law. For example, cases could be based on the RICO state or federal statutes, the bankruptcy statutes, the statutes on embezzlement, fraud, mail fraud, or theft. Understanding the rule of law enables the reader to decipher the reasons for the court reaching a decision.
The Issue(s):	The issue(s) in each case are different. The court uses these issues to decide the case. It is these issues around which the prosecution and the defendant, the plaintiff and the defendant, argue their positions based on the facts and rule of the law.
Discussion:	The discussion in each is based on the facts and information including prior cases, interpretation of statutes and decisions by other courts. The information presented will provide the reader with a clearer understanding of the judges and court to reach the final decision.
Holding/ Decision:	This refers to the final judgement, position, and conclusion of the court. The holding or decision either affirms the agreement of the Plaintiff/Appellee or the Defendant/Appellant. The holding or decision includes the finding of guilt or innocence. If guilty, then "conviction will follow with

a sentence which could include a) a jail term b) a suspended jail term/probation c) a fine for court costs, and or costs of investigation d) an order for restitution of funds or property e) a series of sanctions which include hours of community service or months of probation after the jail term. Also, there could be an order to limit further involvement practice in particular profession or business enterprise.

Implications: This section provides the reader with points to further understand the significance of the court's decision on the issues of fraud.

Additionally, there are numerous suggestions that can be incorporated in the business entity's development of internal controls that will detect, prosecute, and prevent fraud.

Caveat: The authors of this text merely selected a sample of cases to be included in this section; these cases in no way represent all of the possible fraudulent conduct of individuals and entities. Readers are encouraged to continue their review of fraud cases in local/national newspapers, the internet, professional magazines, and the records of the court which document cases that were tried each day, week, and month in your jurisdiction.

Conviction Rates

The data reviewed on the cases presented in this text indicate that the conviction rate for fraud and criminal prosecution of health care fraud according to Justice Department 1999 statistics show an increase in the conviction rate of 14 percent from 73 percent in 1993 to 87 percent in 1997 (J.L. Albert, *USA Today,* February 23, 1999)[39]. A further review of the Justice Department statistics for the same period indicates that the conviction for fraud prosecution in other areas is about 87 percent in 1997. The message here is that of those cases that are not resolved before they go to trial, there is a high probability that the defendant will be convicted for the crime of fraud.

The Typical Sentences

The review of the cases that are presented in this text indicate that the courts tend to follow sentencing guidelines, especially at the federal courts, who are bound by the United States Sentencing Commission Guidelines and the statutorily required minimum sentence (See the *United States v. Sharp,* 883 F.2d 829 (9th Circuit, 1989)[40]. Each state in the United States has sentencing requirements for each offense and these guidelines guide the sentencing decision of the court. The general outline for a sentence for fraud could include all or a combination of the following items:

- Jail term: The court will impose a sentence of several months/years in prison for fraud.
- Fines: The court will impose fines, which include the costs for court expenses and/or the costs associated with the investigation of the fraudulent acts.
- Restitution: The court will require the convicted person to make full or partial restitution to the victims of the fraud. The amount of the restitution will influence the decision of the court with respect to sentencing. In the case of *Jones v. State of Florida* the court gave Jones one year in jail and 25 years' probation after release during which time Jones will be required to repay 100 percent of the embezzled funds of $90,000.
- Probation: Almost all of the sentences have a provision for probation for a number of months and years after the serving of the jail term in the case *United States v. Christiansen* (958 F.2d 285 (9th Circuit 1992)), the court in addition to 17 months in jail ordered three years probation contingent upon the completion of 600 hours of community service.
- Forfeiture: The court can order forfeiture of assets wherever they are found. The RICO Act at the federal and state levels is used to recover the assets that are gained from the illegal and fraudulent activity. The Federal Statute 18 U.S.C. 1961, 1962, 1963 provide for prison term up to 20 years and forfeiture of any assets and interests to property that the person has acquired or maintained in violation of federal or state laws and RICO sections 1961, 1962, 1963. The net result is that all property seized, the right and title reverts to the state or federal government. It should be noted that property transferred by the defendant to a third party is subject to such forfeiture. The innocent third party must file a show cause order to establish that the property was obtained in the normal course of business at market value and that the third party did not have any prior knowledge that the property was secured as result of an illegal act on the [part of the defendant].

Sanctions: The court can institute a number of sanctions against the convicted party. In the fraud cases presented in this text, upon finding the defendant guilty of fraud, the court ordered that for example the attorney or the agent preparing the financial statements, or the United States. These sanctions are followed up by referral to the local bar association as in the case of an attorney and in the case of health care fraud to the state licensing body to revoke the doctor's license. In the RICO cases in this chapter, the court will order the complete divestment of the defendant in the operation of the business entity. The same sanction in securities fraud will take place where there is a conviction of fraud. There can be a recommendation to cease and desist from being involved in any way in such business/profession.

A Caveat.   The above sentencing of the courts at the state and federal levels reflects the current state of prosecution for fraud. It will become necessary that each accountant and the legal staff in each entity continues to monitor the decisions rendered by the courts. The courts appear to handle fraud convictions very harshly with sentences that will always include jail term, restitution of funds, fines, forfeiture of assets, probation upon release, and other sanctions including being barred from practicing one profession as in the case of accountants, attorneys, and other professions.

WHERE DO WE GO FROM HERE: THE FRAUD PREVENTION STRATEGIES RECOMMENDED FOR ALL ENTITIES

This book attempted to present to the reader that fraud is alive in every type of business or entity in the private and public sectors. The challenge is how to detect, investigate, and prevent fraud with appropriate internal controls.

- Personnel policies should address the company's policies on fraud simply that it will be monitored, and if detected, the perpetrator will be prosecuted, suspended, and terminated, even if there is a full restitution of the gains from the fraudulent acts.
- The rights of the employee should be clearly stated in two areas. The whistle-blower/informant should feel free to come forward with the information of suspected fraud and this employee should be protected. RICO and the whistle-blower statutes protect the employee from retaliation of any kind. The second concern, which should be articulated, is that the suspected employee has constitutional rights to the Fifth amendment against self-incrimination. Thus, the investigative process

as we discussed in this text should be fair and objective and with the protections for employer and employee alike. Remember that the suspected employee has the right to retain private counsel during the investigation, if requested by the employee.

- The discussion about fraud should begin at the hiring process and continue as part of the staff education process of the entity.
- If the employer finds sufficient grounds for accusing employees of fraud and a decision is made after confirmation including a fraud audit, the employer should submit the matter for prosecution (even if this will result in adverse publicity). The chances for conviction are very good and could accompany restitution and recovery of the lost assets including money. The question is whether prosecution will serve as a deterrent to employees?
- The best policy is to institute the kinds of internal controls that were suggested throughout this text in order to reduce the opportunities for fraud and these include internal auditors, audit committees, whistle-blowers/informants, and deterrent measures once fraud is detected.

FINAL THOUGHT ON THE PROSECUTION OF FRAUD

Fraud is a very expensive disadvantage of doing business in every society. Other societies call it corruption while we call it fraud, embezzlement, and theft. The estimate of losses to fraud is about 200 billion dollars a year in the United States, based on documented fraud[41]. Over the years, individuals have given much publicity to welfare fraud and vigorous prosecution resulted in many convictions. For example, in the case of *Pennsylvania Public Welfare Department v. Davenport,* the court found the defendants guilty of welfare fraud (495 U.S. 552 1990). Most recently, the prosecution of Medicaid fraud against Colombia Hospital corporation for millions of dollars signals that fraud will be prosecuted not just against middle and lower level employees but against top executives including Chief Financial Officers in the company. The convictions of top executives sends a chilling message to all sectors of society (*U.S. v. Colombia Hospital respondents,* 1999). This text provides information on a wide range of fraudulent conduct including telemarketing, bankruptcy, securities, insurance, banking, church (Legions case), governmental, and other personal and business frauds. The challenge for our society is to get the message across that fraud will not pay, it will be prosecuted vigorously, it will destroy reputations of individuals and families, careers will be lost forever, forfeiture and restitution reaches all the assets secured through the fraudulent acts. The larger issue is how do you get people in "high places" to stop commiting fraud on victims and society.

Recently, the Federal Securities and Exchange Commission (SEC) charged Attorney Lewis Rivlin and consultant Edwin Earl Huling III and others with securities fraud in the sale of $6.2 million in sham securities under Prime Bank to groups of investors included an Ecuadorian Charity for underprivileged girls. The SEC also charged Alfred Husscar Velarde, a former law partner of Rivlin, with aiding the fraudulent investment scheme. Velarde agreed to a plea bargaining to settle the charges by paying a $20,000 fine and promising to refrain from violations of federal securities law. The other defendants' cases continue with no resolution in sight[42]. In case you wonder why this case is mentioned, Rivlin is the former husband of Federal Reserve Vice Chairman Alice Rivlin, who announced that she was leaving the central bank to devote more time to her second job as head of the District of Colombia financial control board. The Rivlins were divorced in 1977, some 22 years prior to this alleged securities fraud of her husband. Is this embarrassing to past and current families of the accused? The answer is that such fraudulent conduct reaches the reputation of everyone.

Another case of great concern to this author is the matter of *Arden M. Merckle v. State of Florida.* Merckle, Chief Circuit Court judge, was convicted for bribery, receiving unlawful compensation, and extortion resulting from conduct which included failure to disclose the receipt of these funds. The defendant appealed his sentence because the court went beyond the recommended guidelines. Merckle was sentenced to five years in jail.

The appellate court of Florida refused to reduce the sentencing arguing that no other public servants are subject to as stringent code of ethics as are judges (281 So.2d 21 (Fla. 1973)) (9336. So.2d. 584 (1976))[43] which require that a judge "should respect and comply with the law and should conduct oneself at all times in a manner that promotes public confidence in the integrity and impartiality of the judiciary." Howard T. Murphy's message in the Merckle case that judges, like any other perpetrator of fraudulent conduct, have a responsibility to enhance the confidence of the "American people who want desperately to respect judges." The existence of a judiciary as the keeper of justice in a free society "represents what the public needs to respect the justice system." (*Merckle vs. State of Florida* 529 So.2d 269, 1998)[44]. This case of erosion of public trust is further explained in the case of the Sheriff.

The Sheriff of Marion, Florida was accused of theft and fraud in diverting over $170,000 of County funds to his own personal use. The

Sheriff was convicted and sentenced to jail, plus restitution. The shame and embarrassment were severe and far-reaching. If the Newmans rule is applied, the Sheriff of Marion could be denied pension. In the Newmans case, the former Sheriff forfeited all rights and benefits under the state retirement system and was ordered to refund all retirement benefits paid to him. See Newmans, retired Sheriff Appellee, 701 So. 2d 573, 1997.[45]

In conclusion, I am led to these final words: "Prevention of fraud is far better than cure." No one wins when fraud is committed; the employer and individual or entity that is victimized will suffer. The perpetrator(s) and the families are penalized, but the costs for the prosecution of fraud is so great that if not reduced through prevention of fraud through internal controls, the cost of business will continue to rise, as well as the costs of investigation and prosecution, as the acts of fraud become more intricate and complicated. Internal controls, education, early detection, and vigorous prosecution will all help in controlling fraudulent acts in our society.

REFERENCES

[1] Michael Risinit, *The News Journal,* Daytona Beach, March 15, 1999.

[2] The F.B.I. Crime Statistics, Department of Justice, Washington, DC, 1997.

[3] *Lyons v. U.S.* (1999) in *Orlando Sentinel,* May 1999.

[4] Medical Fraud: Columbia Hospital Corporation, in *Orlando Sentinel,* May 1999.

[5] Peter Eisler and Barbara Pearson, "Health Care Fraud," *USA Today,* February 8, 1999.

[6] Peter Eisler and Barbara Pearson, "Health Care Fraud," *USA Today,* February 8, 1999.

[7] *State of Illinois v. Raymond J. Gornick,* (1992), 227 ILL. App. 3d 272, 169 Ill. Dec. 159.

[8] *People of the State of Illinois v. Collins,* (1985), 106 ILL. 2d 237, 87 Ill. Dec. 910, 478 N.E.2d. 267.

[9] *People v. Speed* (1982), 106 Ill. App. 3d. 890.62 Ill. 686, 436 N.E.2d. 712.

[10] *People v. Steidl* (1991), 142 Ill. 2d 204, 154 ILL Dec. 616, 568 N.W. 2d. 837.

[11] *People v. Scharlau* (1990), 141 ILL.2d 180, 199, 152 ILL. Dec. 401, 410, 565, N.E.2d. 1319, 1329.

[12] *U.S. v. Jeffrey Allen Fischer,* Nos. 96-3587, 97-2877 and 98-2091, United States Court of Appeals, Eleventh Circuit, March 4, 1999.

[13] *United States v. Copeland* (1998), 143 F.3d 1439.

[14] *United States v. Paradies* (1996), 98 F.3d. 1226-89.

[15] *Charles Esskuchen v. State of Florida,* by Bryan N. Purvetter, *The Orlando Sentinel,* April 27, 1999.

[16] *Martin Donohue v. State of Florida,* No. 88-1069, District Court of Appeal of Florida, Fifth District, August 24, 1999.

[17] *Fresneda v. State of Florida* (1987), 347 So. 2d. 1021.

[18] *Balance v. State of Florida* (Fla. 1st DCA, 1984), 447 So. 2d. 974.

[19] *Fletcher v. State of Florida* (Fla. 1st DCA. 1981), 405 So. 2d. 748.

[20] United States Trustees Program, Department of Justice http://www.USD OJ.gov/ust/bf. 98 ht.m. (August 1998).

[21] United States Trustees Program, Department of Justice, http://www.US OJ.gov/ust/bf 2nd/98.ht.m and 3rd.ht.m. (August 1998).

[22] *Ibid.*

[23] San Sentinel, Associated Press, "Fraud in IRS Centers," Washington, D.C., Sentinel Newspaper, November 7, 1999.

[24] *Bates v. United States* (1997), 96 F.3d 964.

[25] *U.S. v. Berlier* (1991), 948 F.2d 1093, in Find Law http://Caselaw. Find law.com (9th. Circuit, 1999).

[26] *The Orlando Sentinel*, Associated Press, "Fraud Study Report," New York, New York, March 27, 1999.

[27] *Ibid.*

[28] Rene Stutzman, "Embezzlement Case," *The Orlando Sentinel,* July 7, 1999.

[29] *Kidder v. Brandt* (1997) U.S. Court of Appeals, No. 97-2123, (11th Circuit, Court of Appeals).

[30] Find law http://laws. Find law.com., 9th/2/958/ht.m. (April 1999).

[31] *State of Florida v. Sun Oil Co.* (1988), 522 So.2d. 474.

[32] In re: *Bugna v. McArthur* (1994), 33 F.3d. 1054.

[33] *Garrett v. City and County of San Francisco* (1987), 878 F.2d 1515, 1520.

[34] *Grogan v. Garner* (1991), 498 U.S. 279, 284; 111 S.Ct. 654, 658 8n.11.

[35] *U.S. v. Christiansen* (1992), 958 F.2d 285.

[36] *Moore v. United States,* (1995), 160 U.S. 268, 16 St.C. 294, 295, 40 L.Ed. 422.

[37] *United States v. Say Klay,* (1976), 542 F.2d. 942, 944.

[38] Find law, *http://caselaw.com.* Cum/scripts, 1994.

[39] J.L. Albert, "Embezzlement," *USA Today,* February 23, 1999.

[40] *United States v. Sharp* (1989), 883 F.2d 829.

[41] Davia, Coggins, Wideman, Kastantin, *Fraud Discovery and Control,* New York: John Wiley & Sons, 1992.

[42] Marcy Gordon, "Fraud," Associated Press in *Palm Beach Post,* West Palm Beach, June 9, 1999.

[43] *Merckle v. the State of Florida* (1998), 281 So.2d, 21, 1973, 9336 So.2d.

[44] *Merckle v. State of Florida* (1998), 529 So.2d 573.

[45] *Newmans v. State of Florida* (1997), 701 So.2d. 573.

Chapter 15

Ethical Conduct and Fraud Prevention

This chapter discusses the perspective that ultimately the greatest prevention of fraud in any organization is when each employee or person associated with the entity makes a conscious decision to ensure that the entity is not defrauded in any way by its conduct or the conduct of any individual in the organization. Thus, the information in this chapter provides a definition, examples of ethical behavior which might be questionable, ethical implications of gifts, ethics within the organization, the ethics of the whistle-blower/informant and ethical standards for employees.

DEFINITION AND PERSPECTIVE OF ETHICAL AND MORAL CONDUCT

Any discussion of fraud would be incomplete without discussing what constitutes acceptable behavior on the part of an organization's employees. Among other things, employees are generally expected to be ethical and moral. However, the terms *ethical* and *moral* have different meanings to different people. What is ethical and moral to one person may be unethical and immoral to another. Accordingly, it is essential that top management of every organization carefully consider—and publicize for all employees to know—the standards of conduct for their organization. This recommendation was also made by the Treadway Commission on Fraudulent Financial Report.

What are Standards of Conduct? This is our quick definition: Standards of Conduct are those criteria which an organization adopts as constituting acceptable and unacceptable behavior on the part of its employees, and which may be used as the basis for disciplinary action.

The key to this definition are the terms *criteria* and *basis for disciplinary action.*

What a Standards of Conduct Statement does for an organization, no matter how small, is to advise employees—all employees, management included—what employees may do, and what they may not do as employees in their relationships with others, particularly those others with whom their employer does business.

EXAMPLES

Let's consider a few examples of what can happen. Assume that you are a purchasing officer for a company and that your employer has no Standards of Conduct Statement. A salesperson for a major supplier visits your office one morning.

1. You talk for a while and when you feel like smoking, you find that you are out of cigarettes. He or she offers you a cigarette. Do you take it? Why? Why not?

2. You accept the cigarette offered and thank the salesperson. It is a new package of cigarettes that he/she hands you. It is your favorite brand. He or she says, "Keep the pack! I've got a whole carton in my sample case." Do you? Why? Why not?

3. You keep the pack, thanking him. You feel its $1.50 cost is insignificant. You go to light the cigarette and find that you have no matches. He takes out an attractive cigarette lighter and hands it to you. You light your cigarette and attempt to hand it back. He or she says, "Keep it! I have more." Do you? Why? Why not?

4. You estimate the lighter's value at about $25 and figure that it's part of the supplier's normal promotional expense. You decide to keep it and thank him or her. You talk for an hour and notice that it is twelve noon. He or she does too. He or she suggests that you go to lunch and continue your conversation. You agree. You have a fine lunch and two martinis. He or she insists on picking up the check for about $40. Do you allow him or her to pay? Why? Why not?

5. After lunch, back at your office, the salesman is showing you his company's catalog. You like a product that his or her company sells and which your company needs to buy. The price appears competitive. You tell him or her that you wish to place an order for $10,000. He or she suggests that you may wish to increase the order to $15,000. He or she states that for a $15,000 order, customers get an all-expense-paid trip for two to Acapulco. You increase the order to $15,000. It's an extra three months supply, but your company can use it. Your wife

always wanted to go to Acapulco, and now you can go together—
for free!

6. Acapulco is great. After your return, with your suntan still with you,
your salesperson friend visits you again. This time he or she asks you
if you would like to go to Europe, all expenses paid. All you need to
do is order $50,000 worth of Product X, of which your company uses
a great amount. The price is a bit higher than the competition's, but
you decide to buy it anyway. You tell him or her you would like to
visit Italy.

Sound familiar? It happens every day in just about every industry.
Regardless of how you may have responded to the questions of propriety
in each of the six instances described above, there are no standards of
propriety to guide your organization. It is not our intention here to suggest
standards to you. What we do strongly recommend is that your organization
carefully consider the likelihood for employee gratuities and draw a line
between what is acceptable and what is not. These Standards of Conduct
for employees should be required periodic reading for all employees.

The consequence of not issuing a Standards of Conduct is that someday
a business will find itself in a situation where an employee in a key position
has caused the organization significant financial harm, and no disciplinary
action will be possible.

The following quotation was taken from a speech given 23 years ago.
It is no less relevant today than it was when it was delivered by John C.
Biegler, senior partner of Price Waterhouse & Company, before the Harvard
Club and the Harvard Business School Club of Philadelphia on
January 12, 1977:

> Uncertainty is the enemy of ethics. Many corporate employees have behaved
> improperly in the misguided belief that the front office wanted them to. If
> standards are not formulated systematically at the top, they will be formulated
> haphazardly and impulsively in the field. . . . While the independent
> auditor's external review is an indispensable supplement to a corporate
> system of internal controls, it is not a substitute for it. Management must
> take the major responsibility for implementing and improving them.

There is an adage that says something like this, "You don't get something
for nothing." It is worth remembering. For every gratuity you take,
there is a *quid pro quo* (Latin: something for something, or this for that).
Some organizations have adopted very rigid standards of conduct that
allow employees to accept no gratuities. Others tend to allow gratuities

that fall below a set monetary amount, such as $10 or $20, for example. Some allow an employee who is offered a free lunch to accept it without being embarrassed, provided it falls within certain parameters.

Perhaps the most important thing accomplished by limiting the gratuities an employee can accept is that it tends to sensitize the employee to the *quid pro quo* theory. Consider for example, the following scenario, which actually happened. Only the details have been changed, for obvious reasons.

Assume that you live in New York and are employed by a large national general construction contractor. You are a senior project manager for your company, with the authority to make major contractual adjustments. You find it necessary to visit Mr. Jones, a major subcontractor in the Los Angeles area.

At the close of the day, he says, "Let's go out and have dinner." You agree to go if you can pay. He accepts. At dinner an extremely attractive young woman, Marsha, who seems to know Mr. Jones, comes over to your table. It appears that they are good friends, and she has dinner with you and Jones. Foregoing dessert, Jones remembers a late business appointment and rushes off, but suggests that you and Marsha have dessert and an after-dinner drink on him.

Marsha is very charming. You and she dance, and end up going to her home where you become intimate with her. Later that evening, you return to your hotel. The next day, you cannot get her off your mind and that evening you decide to return to her home. She answers the door and is surprised to see you. You suggest that she invite you in, and she replies, "Who is paying for tonight?" What do you do? (If you wish, you may change she to he and Marsha to Mark.) As mentioned, this story is not fiction. Only the names have been changed. In the real case, the incident hit the newspapers in the man's home city before he arrived. He was married. Enough said.

Obviously, the big question in the acceptance of gratuities of any kind is in the *quid pro quo* that is expected from the gift recipient in return. Logically, if the gratuity is worth something, the giver must recover its cost in the products he or she sells. Accordingly, might we then consider the gratuity in the same category as a kickback? Why not?

Consider this situation: You are a new internal auditor for the Bluebird

Corporation, only recently graduated from college. One day, you find yourself reviewing invoices for the purchase of various housekeeping supplies used by the corporation. It is a low-priority audit, but has been scheduled as a part of your familiarization training. You pick up an invoice for XYZ Corporation for a large order of detergents, priced at $10,325, to be used for general plant cleaning and maintenance purposes. Bored, you notice the usual things one would expect to find on an invoice of this sort: 12 50-gallon drums of detergent XXX, 20 5-gallon containers of industrial floor wax, and so forth. You are about to put the invoice back into the file when a notation in the "Remarks" section of the invoice catches your eye. It says, "Deliver television set to Harry Kari residence at 624 Market Street." You determine that Harry Kari is the Bluebird purchasing agent who made the purchase.

Checking further, you find that XYZ Corporation is a new vendor to Bluebird, and you also notice that the unit prices paid to other vendors for identical items purchased in the recent past were about 10 percent lower. You check with your audit supervisor and tell him what you have found.

After pondering the situation, put yourself in the position of the audit supervisor and respond to the auditor who has just presented you with this observation.

Every month Marty, a general traffic agent for a major railroad, would visit the traffic department of a major manufacturer that shipped a significant amount of freight over the rail lines of Marty's company. Every month, Marty was expected to take the entire traffic department out to a long, expensive lunch, complete with cocktails. To facilitate the monthly party, it was necessary to take these employees out in two shifts, so that all could attend. Marty claimed that if he were to miss a month, freight tonnage shipped on his railroad would decline substantially. In effect, the railroad that employed Marty was kicking back a substantial sum each month to obtain the business of the major manufacturer.

The Federal General Services Administration, rocked by widespread fraud in the late 1970s, found itself in a situation in which many key contracting personnel had been accepting significant gratuities—many could easily be called kickbacks. They soon found that without clearly defined standards of conduct with regard to the acceptance of gratuities, no administrative action could be taken against the individuals involved, even when the gratuities were quite large. In one instance, a GSA contracting representative, influential in approving significant contract changes for a major government contractor was found to have received many gratuities. The GSA employee had been entertained in grand fashion every time the contractor's representative visited Washington, or when he visited the contractor's plant. The GSA subsequently reacted by declaring that no gratuities would be tolerated and that there would be no exceptions. This posed more than one problem when employees were the recipients of small token gifts, such as desk calendars, all of which had to be returned.

Greed has been part of the human race as long as it has existed. The objects of greed that could formerly be confined to what we could see in our immediate neighbors and neighborhood have now been expanded to include the whole world and will no doubt go further as technology permits. Marketing has increased the velocity of new product introductions; with each new product comes an added opportunity for greed.

ETHICAL IMPLICATIONS OF GIFTS

While not everything is fraud, there are business practices involving gifts. In the case of the *U.S. Government vs. Mike Espy,* (1999),[1] the U.S. Supreme Court ruled that gifts given by a business entity to a governmental official are "a crime only if prosecutors prove they are directly linked or in some way influences an official act."

"Without the Supreme Court decision, it would be a crime even for a championship sports team to give a jersey to the president when they visited the White House," the Justices said in a unanimous decision.

The decision was a defeat for Independent Counselor Donald Smaltz in a case that stemmed from his corruption investigation of former Agricultural Secretary Mike Espy. Smaltz had asked the high court to reinstate the conviction of a California Agricultural Cooperative for illegally giving gifts to Espy. Espy was acquitted in a jury trial in December 1998 of all 30 corruption charges involving gifts from Sun-Diamond Growers, a raisin and nut cooperative in California and other companies. Sun-Diamond had been convicted of giving $5,900 in illegal gratuities to Espy including tennis rackets, luggage, meals, and other gifts. The Federal Appeals Court threw out the conviction against Sun-Diamond. The court held that "there can be no conviction of the business cooperative unless there is direct evidence that the gifts to Espy were linked to his official actions."

The Espy, California Agricultural Cooperative and Sun-Diamond Grower's cases raise a strange ethical issue for the fraud auditor. When there is evidence of questionable gifts on the books, as these are uncovered during an audit, should this be noted in the report? The answer is yes.

What is clear is that through self-reporting, the auditor will not be able to determine whether the gifts were intended to "influence an official act."

However, it is unethical for the recipient or the corporate giver to hide or conceal these gifts. There are accounting reporting requirements and tax consequences for such non-disclosure. One possibility for the parties is prosecution for income tax evasion.

These cases point out the fact that the giving of gifts continue to be a normal activity of business entities. However, an *Espy Caveat* should include organizational policies that say:

1. All gifts to workers, governmental officials, and entities outside of the organization will follow procedures/policies established by the organization. These policies will include:
   — full disclosure of the gift in organizational records.
   — disclosure to the internal and external auditors.
   — if a business deduction is claimed, the record should be clear as to the purpose these gifts.
2. The Audit Committee of the company should periodically review the corporate gifts to ensure that corporate policies are being followed.

ETHICS WITHIN THE ORGANIZATION

Ethics, in the context discussed here, refers to the behavior and conduct practiced within an entity or organization. Even though we generally think of ethics as being good, within this context, ethics are neither good nor bad. Ethics refers only to present behavior or conduct within an entity or organization. If an entity's ethics are questionable or bad, *per se,* then it means that the behavior or the conduct of the constituents of the entity is not in the best interest of the community as a whole and may not even be in the best interest of the entity itself. We believe that the entity is not directly capable of illegal behavior or conduct. Only individuals are directly capable of illegal behavior or conduct, but the entity will be held responsible for the conduct of individuals.

The entity has but one line of defense in a society in which the behavior or conduct of individuals is in question because of personal value systems resulting in questionable ethics: it must establish standards of conduct for its constituents. Standards of conduct are a clear statement by the entity as to what behavior or conduct is permissible and what is not. Presumably, if the standards of conduct are violated by a constituent, the constituent must accept the consequences for such violations of the corporate policies.

THE ETHICS OF WHISTLE-BLOWERS/INFORMANTS

The importance of clear standards of ethical conduct will result in more effective internal controls which will reduce the number of fraudulent incidents conducted by employees.

While private and community based organizations are not bound by the federal and state's whistle-blower's statutes, it is instructive that many of the federal and governmental contractors have had cases brought against them for fraud because of a whistle-blower. Helmsley had her fraudulent behavior disclosed by her accountant, and of course she was prosecuted for income tax fraud, convicted, and sent to jail. The recent cases against the Columbia Health Care System was brought by employees who had blown the whistle using the False Claim Act which protects whistle-blowers. Since the detection of fraud comes by accident or by a whistle-blower, there should be corporate rules that protect the whistle-blower from undue backlash because of the disclosures of fraudulent conduct. The case discussed in this text indicate that witnesses who testify to the fraudulent conduct helped in securing convictions of the Columbia Health Care executives. Thus there is some anticipation of continued protection from the employer. An informant/whistle-blower's protection policies should be instituted. One caveat is that the policies should ensure that employees who make spiteful, frivolous claims against another could be subjected to employer sanctions. A sound ethical system.

The discussion which follows indicates some broad implications from the False Claims Act of 1863 as amended in 1986 which provides notice that "the government of the United States will prosecute anyone or businesses/entities which knowingly, recklessly, and with intent to defraud, execute such schemes and actions which result in fraud against the government."[2] Many states do have similar False Claims Acts modeled after that requirement in the federal statutes.

THE WHISTLE-BLOWER STATUTE IN THE UNITED STATES OF AMERICA

This law was designed to encourage private citizens (including employees) to help the government fight fraud. "It is estimated that almost 10 percent of the United States annual budget is paid to companies or persons who are defrauding the government in Ashcraft and Gerel (1999)."[3] These acts include overcharging for products sold to the government, submission of vouchers for services that were never rendered. Between the 1980s and

1996, there were over a billion dollars recorded in several hundred claims prosecuted in behalf of the U.S. government. It should be noted that whistle-blowers received more than $100 million from the funds that were recovered. Ashcraft and Gerel (1999),[3] reported that $752 million was recovered in 1996 and 1997.

False Claims Act of 1863

Abraham Lincoln was responsible for the passage of this law which was to protect the government from fraudulent suppliers. This act of 1863 was amended in 1943 and recently in 1986. The amended False Claim Act provides:

Federal whistle-blower False Claims Act, general provisions to False Claims Act	Related policies private businesses should have in place for detecting fraud
1. Preparing a false record in order to get a fraudulent claim paid by the government	Preparing a false voucher to get a fraudulent payment from the industry/entity
2. Submitting a claim with deliberate ignorance or reckless disregard for the truth of the statements in the claim	Submitting a voucher/claim without verifying accuracy of the data in the voucher/claim
3. Conspiring with any person to have a false claim paid by the government	Conspiring with another employee or person to secure payment based on a false claim made to the employer/entity
4. Causing someone else to submit a false or fraudulent claim	Knowingly encouraging someone else to submit a false or fraudulent claim
5. Holding property of government with sole intent to conceal and defraud said property	Holding property of the entity/industry with intent to defraud and conceal said property (computers, etc.)
6. Fraudulently buying property of the government from someone who is not authorized to sell said property on behalf of the government.	Fraudulently buying property of the industry/entity from channels or a person not authorized to sell property for the industry/entity

7. Delivering or creating a false statement/receipt to the government for its funds or property	Delivering or creating a false receipt to the industry/entity for its funds or services/products.

These are some of the key elements of the False Claims Act, but other key provisions include:

- Proof ("Preponderance of the Evidence"). This is the same burden of proof in civil cases for damages rather than the criminal law test of proof beyond a reasonable doubt.
- Attorney's Fees. The act requires the party who defrauded the government to pay the attorney's fees of the whistle-blower.
- Retaliatory Actions. The act protects the whistle-blower from retaliatory actions by his employer.
- The Process of Filing the Claim. The act permits the whistle-blower to file the claim in court. This filing will be secret and under seal. After the case is filed, the U.S. attorney will investigate the merits and make a decision in 60 days from the filing of the claim. If the U.S. attorney believes the case is meritorious, the U.S. government takes over the claim and prosecutes the wrongdoer. The government generally intervenes in 25–33 percent of the cases according to Ashcraft and Gerel (1999) and Justice Department Statistics (1998).[4]
- The Whistle-blower's Monetary Gains/Incentives. Even though the U.S. Attorney prosecutes the claim the whistle-blower initially brings, it is essential to know the following about the monetary benefits which is ensured to the whistle-blower:

    He or she retains full rights to a portion of the proceeds in a successfully prosecuted case where recovery of funds result.

    If the whistle-blower prosecutes the case alone and successfully proves fraud, the law requires the wrong-doer to pay up to three times the defrauded amount stolen from the government.

    Mandatory civil penalties of $500 and $10,000 per false claim will be imposed.

    The whistle-blower generally receives from 10 percent to 30 percent of the recovered moneys from such law suit and prosecution.

Filing such a claim and being a whistle-blower is risky business. The employee should always consult an attorney to ensure that the facts are properly investigated and documented before such public claim of wrong-doings is made against the employer or entity. Libel and slander and other civil damages may result from a false claim brought by the employee. The injured party has rights which shall be protected.

ETHICAL IMPLICATIONS FOR BUSINESS AND OTHER ENTITIES

The recent findings of fraud against the Columbia Health Group signals that chief executive officers are not insulated from criminal and civil prosecution for fraudulent acts against the government. While restitution and recovery of these ill-gotten funds soothes the anger, the bottom line is whether the adherence to high ethical standards linked to internal controls against fraud will in fact serve as deterrence and a process of internal identification and correction prior to the devastasting prosecution of such frauds. A final thought on the ethics is in the form of a question, "Are the risks of commission of fraud worth it?"

ETHICAL STANDARDS FOR EMPLOYEES

The ethical behaviors of employees within an entity is influenced by two factors:

1. Understanding of the policies of the organization with respect to fraud
2. Willingness to control their own behavior which will preclude personal involvement in fraudulent conduct

The Understanding of the Policies on Fraud

This understanding begins at the hiring and orientation process each employee undergoes. It is during this early stage that the understanding about expectations of fraudulent detection and reporting is communicated and hopefully inculcated in the employees' behavior.

Employees' Willingness to Control Their Own Fraudulent Behavior

The data will support that almost all employees make a conscious decision to protect the assets of the entity by not getting involved in any fraudulent conduct. This willingness could be taken to tangible extremes by the employee who informs on the fraudulent conduct and wrong-doing of another employee and is willing to testify in a criminal proceeding against the accused employee.

To ensure ongoing support for employee's compliance with corporate policies on fraud control/detection and reporting, it is necessary that standards of conduct conform to:

- Clearly written language with no ambiguities as to intent and expectations of conduct with respect to identifying and reporting suspected fraud.
- Clearly written consequences for detection and prosecution of fraudulent behavior.
- Equitable treatment regardless of level or status. Justice will require that all acts of fraud should be prosecuted without special treatment for the individual's status. For example, the manager versus mail room assistant. Only with fairness will the message be clear that when it comes to fraudulent behavior there is no preferential treatment.
- An ongoing and systematic staff training regarding the policies of fraudulent behavior and its consequences.

This final note on ethics cannot be overstated. The positive results from policies that emanate through the ethical behavior of employees come through modeling by everyone, but in particular top management, middle management, and persons who hold fiduciary positions in all departments. Even when things are quiet and no one has been detected as a perpetrator of fraud, this does not mean that all is well, that there are no incidences of fraud going on in the organization. Diligence, education, sound internal controls, detection, and prosecution will all help in enhancing the ethical behavior of all employees.

REFERENCES

[1] *United States Government v. Mike Espy*, 1999.
[2] False Claim Act of 1863 as Amended in 1988.
[3] Ashcraft and Gerel (1999) Prairie Law Journal, http// *www.Prairie*Law.com
[4] United States Justice Department (1998) Fraud in the Health Care, Washington, D.C.

Bibliography

American Institute of Certified Public Accountants, *Audit and Accounting Manual*. New York: American Institute of Certified Public Accountants, 1990.

Aylesworth, George N. and Marianne Swan. "Telecommunications Fraud Devices," *FBI Law Enforcement Bulletin* (March 1986): 1–4.

Bar Bri. *Evidence*. New York: Harcourt Brace Jovanovich Legal and Professional Publications, 1984.

Beekman, Mary Ellen. "Automobile Insurance Fraud Pays and Pays Well," *FBI Law Enforcement Bulletin* (March 1986): 17–21.

Chimel vs. California, 395 US 752 (1968).

Cookingham, Vincent P. "Organized Crime: The Corporation as Victim." *Security Management* (July 1985): 28–31.

Dee, Joseph M. "White-Collar Crime: A Tie That Binds," *Security Management* (January 1985): 18–22.

Denes, Richard F. "Commercial Bribery: The White-Collar Crime of the '80's," *Security Management* (April 1985): 56–62.

Hurley, John E. "Cargo Documentation Fraud," *Security Management* (February 1983): 39–40.

Inbau, Fred E., John E. Reid, and Joseph F. Buckley. *Criminal Interrogation and Confessions*. Baltimore: Williams & Wilkins, 1986.

Jensen, D. Lowell. "Who Pays the Price of White Collar Crime?" *Security Management*. Part I (September 1986): 141–148; Part 2 (October 1986): 87–92.

Katz vs. US., 389 US 347 (1967).

Kleberg, John R. and C. Allen Shaffer. "Evidence Exhibits in White Collar Crime Cases," *FBI Law Enforcement Bulletin* (July 1981): 1–6.

Legal Lines. *Criminal Law*. 4th ed. Gardena, California: Law Distributors, 1976.

Legal Lines. *Criminal Procedure*. 6th and 8th eds. Gardena, California: Law Distributors, 1972, 1980.

McChesney, Kathleen L. "Operation Defcon: A Multiagency Approach to Defense Fraud Investigations," *FBI Law Enforcement Bulletin* (March 1988): 16–19.

North vs. U.S., USSC (1989). 264 US appellate 265 (1989) 829 Fed 2d50 (1987).

Orsagh, Thomas. "White Collar Informers: Getting Your Money's Worth," *Security Management* (October 1986): 39–43.

Osborn vs. U.S., USSC (1966). 395 US 752 (1968).

Pizzo, Stephen, Mary Fricker, and Paul Muolo, *Inside Job: The Looting of America's Savings and Loans*. New York: McGraw-Hill Publishing Company, 1989.

Raffel, Robert T. "Airline Ticket Fraud," *FBI Law Enforcement Bulletin* (December 1985): 1–4.

Seger, Karl A., and David J. Icove. "Power Theft: The Silent Crime," *FBI Law Enforcement Bulletin* (March 1988): 20–25.

Seleno, Jim. "Check Print," *FBI Law Enforcement Bulletin* (February 1989): 14–17.

Thornburgh, Richard L. "Characteristics of White Collar Crime," *Illinois Police Officer* (Summer 1977): 29–33.

U.S. Department of the Army. *Intelligence Interrogations.* Washington, DC: Field Manual 30-15. March, 1969.

U.S. Department of Justice. *Prevention and Detection of Fraud, Waste and Abuse of Public Funds.* Special National Workshop. Washington, DC: Law Enforcement Assistance Administration, November 1979.

U.S. Department of Labor, Office of Inspector General, *Semiannual Report,* October 1, 1988–March 31, 1989, U.S. Government Printing Office.

U.S. Department of Labor, Office of Inspector General, *Semiannual Report,* April 1, 1989–September 30, 1989, U.S. Government Printing Office.

U.S. Department of Labor, Office of Inspector General, *Semiannual Report,* April 1, 1990–September 30, 1990, U.S. Government Printing Office.

U.S. Department of Labor, Office of Inspector General, *Semiannual Report,* October 1, 1989–March 31, 1990, U.S. Government Printing Office.

U.S. Department of Labor, Office of Inspector General, *Semiannual Report,* October 1, 1990–March 31, 1991, U.S. Government Printing Office.

U.S. Department of Treasury, *Interviewing.* [Text 361. Glynco, Georgia: Federal Law Enforcement Training Center, October 1978.]

U.S. Department of the Treasury. *Interviewing Part II (Note-taking/Statement-taking).* [Text 361. Glynco, Ga.: Federal Law Enforcement Training Center, March 1979.]

Villano, Clair E. *Complaint and Referral Handling.* Operational Guide to White-Collar Crime Enforcement. Washington, D.C.: U.S. Department of Justice/Law Enforcement Assistance Administration, May 1980. (One of several guides on white-collar crime matters published in 1979–1980 by LEAA pursuant to Grant Number 77-TA-99-0008 granted to Batelle Memorial Institute Law and Justice Study Center. All guides are valuable.)

Wolf, Marshall L. and John Bree. "Blue Monday at the Bank," *Security Management* (May 1986): 49–52.

Index